Ethnography and Language

in Educational Settings

edited by
JUDITH L. GREEN
University of Delaware

CYNTHIA WALLAT
National Institute of Education

Volume V in the Series
ADVANCES IN DISCOURSE PROCESSES
Roy O. Freedle, *Editor*

ABLEX Publishing Corporation
Norwood, New Jersey 07648

Printed in the United States of America

ISBN 0-89391-035-X   ISSN   0164-0224
ISBN- 089391-078-3 (paperback)

ABLEX Publishing Corporation
355 Chestnut Street
Norwood, New Jersey 07648

Contents

Preface to the Series

Roy Freedle
Series Editor

This series of volumes provides a forum for the cross-fertilization of ideas from a diverse number of disciplines, all of which share a common interest in discourse—be it prose comprehension and recall, dialogue analysis, text grammar construction, computer simulation of natural language, cross-cultural comparisons of communicative competence, or other related topics. The problems posed by multisentence contexts and the methods required to investigate them, while not always unique to discourse, are still sufficiently distinct as to benefit from the organized mode of scientific interaction made possible by this series.

Scholars working in the discourse area from the perspective of socio-linguistics, psycholinguistics, ethnomethodology and the sociology of language, educational psychology (e.g., teacher–student interaction), the philosophy of language, computational linguistics, and related subareas are invited to submit manuscripts of monograph or book length to the series editor. Edited collections of original papers resulting from conferences will also be considered.

Preface to Volume V

The unifying theme of this book is the presentation of new approaches to ethnographic analysis of social interaction in educational settings. The presentation of these methodologies is accompanied by discussion: What is ethnography? What is ethnographic method? Why "do" ethnography or use ethnographic methods? What types of questions can ethnographic methods be used to address? How can ethnographic methods be used in the study of social, communicative, educational, and cognitive processes in educational settings?

The authors represent an interdisciplinary group that attended an invitational conference, Face-to-Face: Analysis of Social Interaction, held at Kent State University in November 1977. This group was composed of researchers from sociolinguistics, psycholinguistics, anthropology, sociology, ethnography of communication, sociology of teaching, educational psychology, educational policy, developmental psychology, and curriculum and instruction. The chapters resulted from the dialogue begun at this conference and focus on the themes just cited. These themes, although of concern to each participant and author, are not equally treated in each paper in this volume; hence the essays are grouped according to primary focus articles.

The articles in Section I provide a general framework for the study of language as a social process in educational settings of home and school, a general definition of ethnography and ethnographic methods, and a discussion of issues related to the study of face-to-face interaction in educational settings, with a special emphasis on ethnographic methods, their value and potential problems.

The articles in Section II describe specific methodologies for capturing, identifying, and analyzing social organization of groups, conversational contexts, and conversational organization. Among the participant perspectives considered are those of the observer-researcher, the student, and the teacher.

The articles in Section III provide specific examples of how ethnographic and quantitative methodologies can be used to complement each other and therefore strengthen our understanding of the nature of the outcomes of social interaction processes, e.g., cognitive processes, group participation, and instructional models.

Section IV is a transcription of the conference roundtable discussion on "Needed Directions and Issues in Analysis of Social Interactions in Educational Settings," with two invited postscripts. The discussion summarizes the theses of this book and invites the reader to join this interdisciplinary dialogue by acting on the needed directions identified. The two postscripts show how the perspectives presented throughout the conference and in this book can be applied to the study of complex social and cognitive issues that exist in educational settings. The postscripts, therefore, identify some places to begin further research.

Judith L. Green
Cynthia Wallat

Introduction

This book is concerned with a number of conceptual issues and methodological questions related to the application of ethnography and ethnographic methods to the study of face-to-face interaction in educational settings. In addition to issues in ethnography, the articles in this book also address theoretical and conceptual issues related to communicative and educational processes in school and out-of-school settings. The information, therefore, is of interest to researchers in many areas—communicative and social development, the study of teaching, and discourse processes, as well as researchers from other disciplines concerned with studying human behavior in natural settings.

THE EYE OF THE STORM

In order to understand better the value of the theoretical constructs and methodologies presented here and to make decisions about potential use or modification of the methods in future research, the reader needs to be aware of some problems associated with the application of ethnography to education. Distinctions between micro- and macro-ethnography and definitions of ethnographic method are elaborated by Gumperz, Lutz, and Sevigny (Section I); the brief discussion which follows is intended as a general introduction to the concept of ethnography.

Applying ethnography and ethnographic methods to the study of communicative and/or educational processes is problematic. Ethnography is traditionally applied to the anthropological process of studying a "whole" culture. The product of an ethnography is a definition of what the culture under study is, what being a member of that culture means, and how the culture under study differs from other cultures. In carrying out an ethnography, the anthropologist generally spends an extended period of time in the field in order to develop a description of the whole culture under study. As Lutz indicates in Chapter 3, an ethnography centers on the researcher's observations of the complete cycle of events that regularly occur as the society under study interacts with its environment.

The problem, or rather the controversy, surrounding ethnography applied to educational settings can be defined as a problem both of definition and of focus. Traditionally, the anthropological ideal has been to describe the whole culture; educational institutions (e.g., home, school) would be only one aspect of building an ethnography. As Lutz suggests, one can focus on less than the ideal and thus produce micro-ethnographies through attention to analysis of face-to-face social interactions. This would involve following an event or series of events through a complete cycle.

Micro-ethnographies produce descriptions of what it means to participate in various social situations that occur within the whole culture. Rather than knowledge of what the whole culture is, the micro-ethnography builds our knowledge of what is required to participate in a lesson or other social situations. Like macro-ethnography, micro-ethnography also observes cycles of events that regularly occur across time. By observing patterns for participation and membership within and across contexts, the micro-ethnographer can describe rules for construction of context, rules of group membership, as well as the goals of specific social interactions and the products of these social interactions (e.g., cognitive knowledge, social rule learning).

Given that the micro-ethnographer does not study the whole culture, what this researcher must do is carefully lay out the parameters of what is to be studied; that is, define the unit of analysis which is being considered the *whole*. Erickson (1977) contends that less than the social, historical, and political perspectives of a culture can be considered as a whole. He argues that because the study of face-to-face interaction in social settings involves consideration of relations between parts and the whole, such work involves systems thinking:

> It is in this sense that ethnographic work is "holistic," not because of the size of the social unit, but because the units of analysis are considered analytically as wholes, whether that whole be a community, a school system...or the beginning of one lesson in a single classroom (p. 59).

What Erickson provides is a way of defining analytic wholes. Methodologies for identifying and describing various types of analytic wholes are further elaborated by Corsaro, Erickson and Shultz, and Green and Wallat in Section II.

The controversy does not center solely on the question of what is holistic ethnography. Included in the controversy are such questions as: How do ethnographic studies differ from observational studies? How are ethnographic studies systematic? Does doing ethnography preclude using statistical procedures? Can ethnographic methods (e.g., participant observation, informant interviews, case histories, case studies, mapping and charting) be used without carrying out an ethnography?

Ethnographic and Observational Studies: Some Distinctions.   The distinction between ethnographic studies and observational studies can be seen in the procedures and decisions of the researcher, both in planning the study and in carrying it out. The ethnographer engages in a systematic, multistep data collection and analysis process which includes the use of a variety of ethnographic methods—participant observation, informant interviews, mapping and charting patterns recorded in field notes, case histories, and/or case studies. Although not all these methods are used in every ethnography, an ethnography will include more than one method. The methods are the tools of the ethnographer, the heuristic devices to obtain typologies of behaviors, institutions, events, etc., that occur as the society engages in interactions with its environment.

An ethnography does not end, however, with the construction of a typology by the researcher. The ethnographer takes this typology to the participants for validation from the participants' perspectives. The validation procedure is necessary given that the purpose of an ethnography is the description of a culture and the definition of membership and participation in the culture. Once the typology has been validated, it serves as a framework for later observations and for further description of social, political, and economic processes that occur in the culture.

When applied to the classroom or other educational settings, *ethnography* means that the researcher wants to understand what is occurring in the education setting, how it is occurring, what definitions of the event the participants hold about these occurrences, and what it takes to participate as a member of the various groups within and across these occurrences (e.g., peer groups, friendship groups, instructional groups, adult-child groups). The ethnographer does not judge what occurs as good or bad, as effective or ineffective; rather, the ethnographer describes what is occurring and after considering the recurring patterns of behavior in the environment, defines rules and processes for participation and membership.

Observational studies, on the other hand, tend to be directed toward a specific research goal (e.g., identification of effective teaching strategies or effective parenting behavior). The researcher generally uses the goal to select or to construct an observation instrument that will lead to attainment of the goal of the study. These instruments are frequently designed to include variables derived from previous work or the researcher's commitment-based or experience-based beliefs about effective teaching or parenting (Dunkin and Biddle, 1974). These variables form a limited set of categories (e.g., warmth, question asking, criticism) into which all observations are assumed to fit. The categories are considered to be reflective of broader constructs (e.g., indirect vs. direct teaching, authoritarian vs. democratic classroom environments). The results of these studies are general statements about teacher or parent effectiveness, or the identification of strategies that correlate with some type of external measure of effectiveness (e.g., a sociogram, a standardized test).

This approach can be described as a *top-down* approach; that is, an approach which begins with a definition of general variables and then filters the event through these variables. Little or no attempt is made to observe patterns in the environment and construct new variables or modify existing variables to reflect what is occurring in the specific situation. The ethnographic approach, in contrast, can be described as a *bottom-up* approach. The typology of variables that results from such a study is derived from observation of the patterns that recur; that is, the bits of data (e.g., the videotaped interaction, the field notes) are searched systematically for recurring patterns of behavior. The ethnographer's purpose is to describe what is occurring, to develop a typology or model that reflects the occurrences, and then to test the validity of this model in other similar situations.

The difference between these two methods can be described as a difference in both intent and approach/method. The researcher engaged in observational studies generally assumes knowledge of the process to be studied (e.g., effective teaching) and therefore looks for behaviors reflective of the process (e.g., warmth, criticism). The ethnographer, on the other hand, does not assume prior knowledge of what a process will look like in a specific context; rather, the ethnographer tries to describe what the process is (e.g., teaching) in each situation and to identify the factors that occurred from the perspective of the participants in the process. The ethnographer is concerned with a description of the event as it occurs not in judgments of effective-ineffective. Although the ethnographer does not ignore previous work on the identification of strategies, s/he does not assume that the strategies identified previously generalize to the present context; rather, the ethnographer assumes that meaning is context-bound. The ethnographer's goal is to find the patterns in the data that exist within and across the various contexts under study.

Qualitative and Quantitative Procedures: Some Considerations.
Whether doing ethnography precludes using statistical procedures is still

unresolved: Lutz argues that, traditionally, ethnography has not been statistical. Statistical procedures, however, are not precluded from ethnographic studies by definition. In micro-ethnographies in educational settings, statistical procedures may be useful in answering some of the researcher's questions. Since ethnographically derived variables have greater face validity than do most clinically or experimentally derived variables, at issue is not *do* we quantify, but rather, *what* do we quantify.

Nor does the issue reduce to experimental ethnographic methods. Ethnographies and/or micro-ethnographies can be used to identify "what" should be studied experimentally. In turn, what we have found from past experimental work can be used to frame future micro-ethnographic studies. Experimental methods enable us to look in detail at processes, to manipulate them, to explore them. Ethnographic methods enable us to explore how the experimentally identified processes and components of processes actually exist in natural environments. As Sevigny suggests, there is strength in combining qualitative and quantitative procedures. Chapters 9 (Hall and Gutherie), 10 (Garnica), and 11 (Cherry Wilkinson) demonstrate the value and complementarity of qualitative and quantitative methods.

OVERVIEW OF THE VOLUME

Section I: Theoretical Considerations and Directions

The articles in this section frame the two themes of the conference: the nature and study of social interaction in educational settings; and the use of ethnographic methods for the study of social interaction in educational settings. Chapters 1 (Gumperz) and 2 (Cook-Gumperz) discuss new directions for understanding the nature of social interaction in educational settings as well as past approaches to the study of this topic. The articles by Lutz (Chapter 3) and Sevigny (Chapter 4) deal with ethnographic perspectives for the study of face-to-face social interaction. The final paper in Section I (Wallat, Green, Conlin, and Haramis) discusses issues in doing micro-ethnography and/or action research in formal educational settings.

Chapter 1 provides a broad historical perspective to classroom interaction analysis and the definition of the classroom as a sociolinguistic environment. In addition, Professor Gumperz discusses the characteristics of instructional discourse and shares a methodology for studying discourse in the formal educational setting of the classroom.

Jenny Cook-Gumperz (Chapter 2) surveys the contributions of empiricist and nativist models to the study of child language and then proposes a contextualist model for the study of children's acquisition of language as a resource. This chapter also includes a discussion of sociolinguistic theory and communicative development in exploring how talk rather than action can be used to accomplish the goals of changing another person's plans.

Lutz (Chapter 3) and Sevigny (Chapter 4) then focus specifically on definition, various ethnographic methods, and issues in applying ethnography to the study of social interaction in educational settings. In addition, Sevigny presents a systematic, triagulated method for the study of social interaction in educational settings. In addition, Sevigny presents a formal educational situation from the perspective of the researcher as participant and as participant-observer.

In Chapter 5, Wallat, Green, Conlin, and Haramis provide an historical survey of calls for action research and teacher as researcher and also propose a set of criteria to guide both researcher and practitioner interested in doing classroom research. This article argues that the perspective of teachers and school personnel can be gained not only through the researcher's asking specific questions but also through providing time and support for teachers to develop questions for current and future projects.

Section II: Systematic Approaches to the Study of Social Interaction

The articles in this section include a model of micro-ethnography of a preschool educational environment (Corsaro), a methodology for identification of naturally occurring contexts (Erickson & Shultz), and a methodology for sociolinguistic ethnography and the identification of instructional contexts (Green and Wallat). Each paper details a systematic methodology for studying different aspects of face-to-face interaction in educational settings.

In Chapter 6, Corsaro describes a multiple-step, systematic procedure for gaining access to a research setting and for identifying and validating variables involved in the formation of freindship groups among preschool-age children. Corsaro describes in detail his field methodology that included a variety of methods—multiple types of field notes, audio and video tapes of events, and informant interviews.

Erickson and Shultz (Chapter 7) describe a systematic methodology for identifying participation structures (contexts) based on observation of contextualization cues and roles and relationships among participants. In addition, they introduce the concept of type-case analysis and describe methodologies which permit the researcher to build a model of one context and then test the model in and across other similar wholes or contexts.

Green and Wallat's article (Chapter 8) on mapping instructional conversations provides a systematic, multiple-step procedure for capturing, describing, and mapping the unfolding conversational structure of lessons and for validating conversational, pedagogical, and social variables. In addition, the paper presents the underlying sociolinguistic premises for the system.

Section III: Combining Ethnographic and Experimental Methods—A Beginning

The three papers in this section share one characteristic. Each uses ethnographic methods in conjunction with experimental methods and constructs.

Hall and Guthrie (Chapter 9) offer a description of a longitudinal study of language and cognition that utilizes observation of language as it occurs in a variety of natural settings and the relationship of this language to formal measures, such as intelligence tests. They offer a sample of an in-depth interview technique for obtaining demographic information and historical information from parents about language use and factors which may influence the acquisition of language and cognition by children. The authors demonstrate the value of qualitative/quantitative interface.

Garnica (Chapter 10) also demonstrates the value of combining qualitative and quantitative methodology. She describes how participant observation can be used to identify social variables (e.g., rejection from group, gaining access to group) which can then be quantified. In addition, she demonstrates how experimental methodologies (i.e., sociograms) can be used to identify the focal unit of analysis (e.g., a particular group of students or an individual student).

The final chapter in Section III (Cherry Wilkinson) builds a systematic case for the value of ethnography and/or ethnographic methods for testing our assumptions about teaching and learning. Cherry Wilkinson describes how, as a result of using sociolinguistic and ethnographic methodology, she concluded that the teacher-expectation model which was derived from traditional teacher-child interaction studies was not valid in its present form.

Section IV: Postscripts

Section IV is both a concluding section and a beginning. Chapter 12, the transcription of the roundtable dialogue by prominent researchers and educators who were invited to the face-to-face conference to discuss "Needed Directions in the Analysis of Social Interaction in Educational Settings", sums up the issues presented in the volume and discussed throughout the conference. Chapters 13 and 14 are papers invited to provide some suggestions for future research.

Chapter 13 (Bernier) discusses the transactional nature of the teaching-learning process and suggests how the analysis of face-to-face interaction contributes to our knowledge of the ideological systems reflected in this process. Bernier suggests intense study of how school teachers and students negotiate cultural and ideological diversity. This chapter, therefore, can be a starting point for those interested in the study of how culture and ideologies are transmitted during teaching-learning transactions.

In the final chapter, Frederiksen discusses how conversational analysis can contribute to the study of cognitive processes and how, in turn, research on cognitive processes can contribute to our understanding of conversational processes. He proposes how these two areas complement each other and suggests a model to be used in future studies. This paper, therefore, serves as a beginning point for those interested in conversational analysis and cognitive development.

I THEORETICAL CONSIDERATIONS AND DIRECTIONS

1 Conversational Inference and Classroom Learning

John J. Gumperz
University of California at Berkeley

CLASSROOM ENVIRONMENT AND URBAN SCHOOL FAILURE

In the recurrent controversy over the failure of urban education, what about the school and classroom environments leads some children to learn and others to fall behind remains a major unsolved problem. That factors other than mere differences in language or cultural background are at issue has been demonstrated by the research of the 1960s and early 1970s. Hypotheses derived from cultural deprivation, and from linguistic deficit and differences models have been tested extensively and found to be incapable of explaining the failure of minority children to achieve in urban schools (Baratz and Baratz, 1970; Labov, 1969; Melmed, 1971; Simons, 1974, 1976; Simons and Johnson, 1974). Perhaps the most suggestive evidence for the role of classroom environments comes from statistics on school performance which show that the gap in average achievement level between middle-class children and poor or minority children increases as a function of grade level. (Gibson, 1965; Harlem Youth Opportunities Unlimited, 1975; Katz, 1964).

There is little doubt that what the child learns in school is determined by a combination of forces. Ogbu's (1977) recent work, for example, has convincingly shown that the goals, policies, and practices of the society at

I am grateful to Sarah Michaels, Janice Shafer, and Herbert Simons who collaborated on earlier drafts which form the basis for this paper and supplied several examples. The ideas expressed here were in large part developed in collaboration with Jenny Cook-Gumperz.

large—the opportunities and role models that society provides for individuals of minority background—significantly affect motivation to learn.

Clearly, schooling as such is not the sole cause of educational failure. Society has its own powerful selection mechanisms which may override the effect of educational reform. Yet it is also true that if we look beyond the macro-statistical trends to individual careers, many minority students do quite well, under conditions that lead others to fail. After all, children spend a large part of their formative years in school and what happens there can either change or reinforce preexisting values and attitudes. To understand modern educational problems we need to know how and by what mechanisms cultural, political, and economic factors interact with teaching strategies to affect the acquisition of knowledge and skill.

Interesting initial insights into what takes place in the classroom come from the early autobiographically oriented writings of teachers themselves, such as Holt (1964), Kohl (1967), and Kozol (1967). These point to the contrast between the official descriptions of curricula and program goals and what actually takes place in the classroom. They argue that (a) curricula fail to capture what really motivates children to learn; (b) the school environment fails to give the teacher scope for using his/her own individuality in solving the problems of the classroom; (c) emphasis on middle-class values and on setting uniform standards of behavior in the face of overcrowded classrooms and other administrative pressures, often encourages dysfunctional strategies, such as focused answer-guessing, that do not lead to learning.

Autobiographical accounts are valuable because they focus attention on problems that experienced teachers know exist but that have not been examined systematically. Classroom experience, whatever its effects, clearly involves complex and subtle processes and many more factors than can be handled by traditional formal behavioral measures which concentrate on a limited set of predetermined variables. Systematic measurement will ultimately be necessary, but before such measures can be devised, we need to begin with ethnographic work in order to isolate the processes that are demonstrably meaningful in terms of the particiants' perceptions. In this paper we survey some recent directions in the micro-ethnographic study of classroom interaction and then go on to suggest ways in which conversational analysis can contribute to this perspective.

THE CLASSROOM AS A SOCIAL ENVIRONMENT: THE ETHNOGRAPHIC EVIDENCE

Some of the most revealing recent classroom ethnographies concentrate on the contrast between home and classroom learning experiences. In one of the first and most influential of these, Philips (1972) compared patterns of classroom participation among reservation-reared Indian children and among non-Indian children. She found that the Indian children participated more enthusiastically and performed more effectively in classroom contexts which minimized both the obligation of the students to perform publicly as individuals and the need for teachers to control performance styles and correct errors. Preferences for these contexts reflected the kinds of relationships that the children were accustomed to on the reservation, where lateral networks of children in groups were much more important than hierarchical role-differentiated networks of adults and children. Philips attributes the generally poor school performance of Indian children to the far greater frequency in conventional classrooms of conditions which, for them, create unfamiliar and threatening frameworks of participation. She proposed the notion of "participant structure" to characterize the constellation of norms, mutual rights, and obligations that shape social relationships, determine participants' perceptions about what goes on, and influence learning. Philips's findings are supported by a number of other ethnographic investigations where learning or failure to learn have been attributed to discontinuities between the participant structures of the home and community and those of the school: Native Americans (Cazden & John, 1971; Dumont, 1972), Afro-Americans (Heath, 1977; Kochman, 1972, Labov, 1972), Hawaiians (Boggs, 1972), rural Appalachian whites (Heath, 1977), and working-class British (Bernstein, 1974).

This work highlights the point that children's responses to school tasks are directly influenced by values and presuppositions learned in the home. It demonstrated, moreover, that classroom equipment, spatial arrangements, or social grouping of teachers and students are not the primary determinants of learning. What is important is what is *communicated* in the classroom as a result of complex processes of interaction among educational goals, background knowledge, and what various participants perceive over time as taking place.

Measuring Communication: Frequency Distribution Approach. How can we measure or study this communication process? Most of the evaluational measures of classroom performance that have been used over the last few decades in such systems as the Flanders System of Interaction Analysis (1967) build on the tradition of small-group studies developed by Bales (1951) and others.

Such evaluational studies typically begin by listing those qualities that the investigator considers to be indicative of good or poor teaching. These qualities are translated into behavioral categories which observers take into the classrooms as a basis for coding a given stretch of interaction. Observers' counts are then tallied to provide quantifiable measures of teaching style.

Methods such as these have been valuable in pointing to important differences between suburban and inner city classrooms. Leacock (1969) who used them in connection with her ethnographic work, found teachers in inner city environments to be more controlling, more critical, and less accepting of natural learning errors than their suburban colleagues. Where Ogbu (1977) studied the effect of macro-social factors on students' life chances, Leacock's work argues that classrooms are part of schools and teachers operate within a system of educational knowledge and ideology. This ideology influences teachers' strategies so that in suburban schools we find an underlyling assumption of cultural similarity and a tolerance for errors and transgressions which does not exist in ethnically diverse urban schools. Given Rist's (1970) impressive evidence for the importance of teacher expectations in evaluations of ability and in ultimately determining individual progress we can begin to see how outside factors can enter into the learning process.

But useful as these quantitative measures are in demonstrating that cultural differences do create problems in the classroom, they have been unable to account for the cognitive effects of classroom environments. One difficulty is that the basis for analysis is the coder's interpretation of behavior rather than the behavior itself. When interpretations of behavior differ as they do in most ethnically mixed classrooms, there is no way to safeguard against cultural bias in evaluating performance and to distinguish between differences in cultural style and differences in ability. Without reference to the actual process of interaction, nothing can be said about how participants react to and make sense out of particular tasks.

Micro-Ethnographic Approaches to Classroom Communication.   Some initial qualitative insights into everyday processes of classroom interaction come from the microethnographic analyses of Erickson and his students (Florio, 1978). Among other things, this work has shown that it cannot be assumed, as earlier small-group analysts had assumed, that the classroom constitutes an undifferentiated structure where teacher and child interact as individuals. At work within each setting are interaction processes that lead to subgroup formation and determine the contexts which guide and channel behavior.

Micro-ethnographic studies build on the considerable methodological advances made in the study of nonverbal behavior by such pioneers as Birdwhistell (1970), Condon (1969), Hall (1959), Scheflen (1974), and others. These methods are valuable in that they provide replicable ways of discovering automatic types of behavior that are not ordinarily commented on, but which nevertheless guide interaction and reveal the unstated conventions that may influence teacher evaluations of student performance. Erickson and his students' study of primary schools (Florio, 1978), for example, shows that during a typical class session the children move sequentially through different types of participant structures. Some have established names, such as "show and tell," "storytelling"; others do not. But each involves different modes of cooperation and learning, as well as rules for the evaluation of behavior and for the interpretation of what goes on. Children must learn what these structures are; they must know how transitions between structures are signaled and what behavioral strategies are required to gain the teacher's attention or to obtain entry into a place of study and secure cooperation of the peer group. Knowledge of strategies appropriate to these structures is a precondition for obtaining access to learning.

McDermott (1978) applied similar techniques of nonverbal analysis to an investigation of the process of getting turns at reading in an urban elementary school. Like many urban classrooms, the room he studied is organized into high and low reading groups. He was able to show that because of the organization of the students into separate subgroups and because of the teacher's definition of the lower group as requiring more explicit and consistent direction, much of the teacher's time with that group is spent in looking around the room to ward off possible interruptions and similar kinds of control behavior. As a result, children in the low group on the whole receive less actual reading instruction and tend to do less substantive work when in contact with the teacher than children in the high group. They are, in fact, deprived of the intensive exposure to reading that they require in order to learn to read.

McDermott's findings recall those of an earlier informal ethnographic account carried out in Berkeley (Lewis, 1970), which describes a reading lesson in which children seated in an informal group arrangement are successively called on to read sentences in a story. When a Black child fails to make a phonetic distinction between the vowels in *pin* and *pen,* the teacher, who had recently been to a lecture on Black dialect and had learned that (a) failure to make this distinction is a feature of the dialect of many low-reading Black children, (b) "proper pronunciation" is a precondition to reading, writes the two words on the board and asks the child to pronounce the two words in isolation. When the child still does not make the distinction, she removes him from the group and asks him to join another low reader in the corner of the room, telling him to practice his letters. In the minutes that followed this incident, the two children who had been singled out took a reading game and started to work with it enthusiastically, making considerable noise, whereupon the teachers said: "Stop playing and start working."

In interrupting what went on here, one should note that the linguistic fact at issue, the failure to distinguish between *pin* and *pen,* is characteristic of approximately 80 percent of the Black children and 40 percent of the Anglo children in California. In that very group, in fact, there was an Anglo child who also did not distinguish the two vowels, but perhaps because of the association of ethnicity with the phonetic feature involved, the teacher who had recently attended a linguistic lecture on Black English failed to notice this. In any case, it seems doubtful that the child who was asked to leave the reading group understood the reason for his being singled out, other than as simply discriminatory. The effect of this incident was to remove the child from situations that he might have enjoyed and learned from.

Additional information on small-group processes is provided by Cook-Gumperz and Corsaro (1976), who view the nursery school classroom as an ecological space and show how, over time, certain verbal and nonverbal conventionalized activities and participant structures become associated with spatial subdivisions. That is, certain locations within the classroom space come to be regularly used for formal games; other kinds of environments allow for freer play. The social conventions thus created directly affect the nature of talk and the interpretation of what is said in these locations. These same conventions furthermore lead to the adoption and frequent use of formulaic utterances which are understood only by those who have experience in the classroom. For example, Cook-Gumperz and Corsaro note a child saying "We're teachers," and show that, given the classroom experience, this must not be interpreted literally as saying "We *are* teachers" but rather as, "We're doing important work, we don't want to be disturbed."

In another case children standing near the entrance to a playhouse repeatedly call out "Nobody can come in." This is an instance of the frequent children's practice, in which an utterance from the game is used to announce that the game is in progress. Repeated observations of what children do in these cases suggest that they interpret such utterances as something like "You can join the game if you follow the rules." Such data, which are supported by findings from conversational analysis in a variety of settings, suggest that we cannot assume that procedures for interpreting communicative intent are shared. Children, teacher, and outside observers may reach different understandings depending on their social presuppositions and their knowledge of relevant signaling conventions.

Although the last two examples involve speech whereas Erikson and McDermott's studies deal with nonverbal signs, the effect is the same. In each, something is being conveyed through words, or movements, or gestures which, when interpreted by participants in relation to their background knowledge, serves to channel interaction and affect opportunity and ultimately perhaps motivation to learn.

LANGUAGE IN THE CLASSROOM

Micro-ethnographic studies of nonverbal behavior have been and will continue to be highly successful in revealing previously unnoticed features and unspoken norms of subgroup formation and social presuppositions which affect classroom learning. But work with nonverbal signs requires great technical expertise. Equipment is expensive and often obtrusive. Analysis is time consuming and can deal with only small bits of interaction at a time. Work carried out in Berkeley during the last few years has begun to develop methods for analyzing verbal strategies and to isolate features of the verbal message which are rhythmically coordinated with nonverbal behavior and which also reflect the operation of participant structures (Bennett, Erickson, Gumperz, 1976; Gumperz, 1977; Gumperz & Herasimchuk, 1973). When applied to classroom interaction, these linguistic measures of verbal behavior can serve not only to simplify analytical techniques but also enable us to establish a more direct relationship between socioecological factors and what goes on in the classroom. Before going into the theoretical assumptions that underlie this type of conversational analysis, it is necessary to review some current approaches to the study of classroom language.

Experimental Approaches.   Perhaps the best-known system for analyzing classroom language is that of Bellack (1966) which attempts to overcome the objections to the social psychologists' reliance on counts of isolated content categories, treating verbal interactions as interrelated sequences of acts. Bellack proposes that the structure of discourse in the classroom arises from sequential constraints on selection such that one type of act is likely to follow or be followed by others of specific types. That is, verbal interactions among teachers and students in a classroom are conceptualized as moves in a Wittgensteinian language game that follows implicit rules of behavior.
Bellack suggests that:

> If we can identify the various types of verbal moves teachers and students make in playing the game of teaching and the rules they implicitly follow, we would be able to investigate the functions these verbal actions serve in classroom discourse and hence the meanings that are communicated (p. 10).

A similar approach forms the basis for the more linguistically oriented analysis by Sinclair and Coulthard (1975), which attempts to specify the role of both grammatical forms and content in the functioning of classroom moves.
Though an important step forward from the simpler tally studies, both these analyses are limited by being based on data collected in experimental situations where teachers were instructed to teach predetermined lessons; what was examined were their actual lectures. Their social significance of classroom speech is evaluated in terms of statistical profiles of utterance functions. Yet since function is taken as a given, what is studied is the significance of teachers' and students' moves in relation to the stated lesson goal.

Linguistic Pragmatic Approaches. Other semantic analyses of adult-child conversation by psycholinguists and linguistic pragmaticists build on the speech acts theorists' distinction between propositional content and illocutionary force to focus on participants' interpretation of message intent. (Ervin-Tripp, 1977; Ervin-Tripp & Mitchell Kernan, 1977; Garvey 1975; Keenan & Schiefflin, 1976). The focus of the analysis here is on what Searle calls "utterers meaning" (Searle, 1975), i.e., what a speaker intends to achieve by an utterance, rather than on reference or dictionary interpretation. By taking account of the linguistic and extralinguistic settings in which a sentence occurs, it can be shown that speakers and listeners regularly build on context-dependent presuppositions to arrive at interpretations which are often quite different from their literal meanings. Given this approach, if a teacher is heard to make a statement, such as "I don't see any hands," when a question has been asked and several children begin to call out, this statement can be analyzed as a request for a show of hands and a directive to be quiet. Pragmatic analyses explain some highly significant aspects of conversational inference. But they assume that linguistic mechanisms involved in interpretation of intent can be analyzed entirely in terms of grammar and lexicon. They do not analyze indirect messages, such as "We are the teachers" (Cook-Gumperz and Corsaro, 1976), where interpretation rests on formulaic conventions which arise in particular classroom situations and not on lexical or grammatical rules available to all speakers of the language.

Linguistic pragmatics, moreover, takes the sentence as the starting point and tend to assume that the context can be determined on the basis of extralinguistic information. When, as in a classroom, setting and participants are constant, it is assumed that all conversationalists share one definition of the situation. There is no attempt to account for the changing nature of participant structures and for the role of verbal and nonverbal signs in signaling these changes. Furthermore, the major problem of urban education—the problem of differential learning, resulting from the varying effects that similar teaching strategies may have on students of different background—is not dealt with.

The recently completed year long study by Cazden and Mehan (Mehan, Cazden, Foles, Fisher, & Maroules, 1976) focuses directly on participant structures. Cazden taught for a year in an ethnically mixed urban classroom and in the course of her daily activities was able to build a number of interesting experiments into her teaching schedule. A main concern of this study was to show how small-group participant structures are reflected in conversational practices and to elucidate teachers' and students' discourse strategies. Among the important findings cited in preliminary reports are that, although children and adults have different ways of formulating what are functionally similar tasks, teachers as a whole rely more on lexical specificity and children rely more on context, but these differences do not result in differences in efficiency of communication or teaching efficiency (for similar findings, see Gumperz & Herasimchuck, 1973).

Cazden and Mehan take an interactive approach which concentrates on the mechanisms through which turns at speaking are assigned and verbal interaction is controlled. Their theory builds on the ethnomethodological studies of conversation (Garfinkel & Sacks, 1969; Sacks, Schegloff, & Jefferson, 1974). What is examined are constraints on sequencing of utterances as they appear in such naturally occurring instructional routines as teaching the content of a story, teaching problem-solving strategies, giving instructions, and the like.

Ethnomethodological studies of conversation have made a basic contribution to sociolinguistics by demonstrating that speaking is not simply a matter of individuals saying what they want, when they want to say it. Conversational cooperation is managed: to have their say, participants must be able to attract others' attention, generate what Goffman (1974) has called *conversational involvement,* and negotiate for space in an ongoing interaction. This negotiation process is affected both by extralinguistic constraints and by semantic ties which cut across utterances. Sacks and Schegloff (Sacks, Schegloff, and Jefferson, 1974) have pointed out that conversations of all kinds are characterized by what they call adjacency pairs, such as question-answer, greeting-greeting, request-acknowledgement, where the occurrence of either the first or second member is dependent on that of the other. Such intersentential ties constitute an important resource for conversational management. Following a similar line of reasoning, Cazden and Mehan (Mehan, Cazden, Coles, Fisher, and Maroules, 1976) demonstrate that instructional talk differs from casual conversation in that it is based on a tripartite structure of initiation-response-evaluation.

Findings such as these clearly show that participant structures are in large part created and sustained through discourse conventions. Like nonverbal signs, these discourse conventions are rarely overtly discussed and must be learned indirectly through active participation in the instructional process. We can assume that, to the extent that learning is a function of the ability to sustain interaction, the child's ability to control and utilize these conventions is an important determinant of educational success. But focus on the structural underpinnings of verbal interaction is not enough. We must go on to determine how this knowledge is acquired, what role differences in home and ethnic background play in the acquisition process, and how the acquisition process interacts with evaluation of educational progress and the child's motivation to learn.

Conversational Inference Approach.   One way of accomplishing this is to apply methods which builds on the linguistic pragmatists' distinction between *propositional content,* or literal meaning, and *illocutionary force,* or intended effect, to analyze conversational management in classroom activities. This is the goal of the research currently carried on in Berkeley. The theoretical notion on which our analysis rests is the concept of conversational inference: the situated process by which participants in a conversation assess other participants' intentions and on which they base their responses.

To understand the issues that underlie our use of this concept, we must begin by examining Paul Grice's (1973) notion of *conversational cooperation,* which underlies much of the work in modern pragmatics. This term is commonly understood to refer to the assumptions that conversationalists must make about each other's contributions and to the conversational principles or principles of rational action they rely on in judging intent. It is also evident, however, that cooperation implies joint action involving what students of nonverbal communication have called *speakership* and *listenership signals.* Thus whatever inferences are made, are made within the context of, and dependent on, this mutual exchange of signals.

The initial problem that any potential conversationalist faces is to create what Erving Goffman (1974) has called *conversational involvement:* to enlist others' attention and to induce and sustain their active participation in talk. To do so, participants must at least in very general terms—explicitly or implicitly—agree on what the interaction is about. That is, even though they may differ on specific details of what is meant at any one time, they must share at least some basic expectations as to knowing where the talk is going, or what is likely to follow. Without this sharedness, interactants are likely to lose interest, interactions tend to be brief or perfunctory, and productive exchanges are unlikely to result.

When participants are questioned or analysts are asked to describe a conversational sequence, they ae likely to resort to descriptive labels such as: A was telling a story about X, explaining why s/ he did X, teaching or showing B how to do X, giving a lecture about X, interrogating B about X, or chatting with B about X. Such descriptive statements are generalizable in terms of what ethnographers of communication have called *speech events* (Gumperz & Hymes, 1972) or psychologists and discourse analysts call *scripts, frames,* or *schemata* (Tannen, 1979; Schank & Abelson, 1977). One might be tempted therefore to argue that the study of conversation must begin by describing and listing these broader interactional units and then go on to state how and under what conditions they are used and what styles of speaking they require.

This type of description presents no serious problem in the case of the bounded event, such as ritual performances, formal lectures, courtroom scenes, or even staged experimental classroom lessons, such as have usually been studied. But everyday conversation never takes the form of such set routines. The very labels we use are often quite different from what we really intend to do. If I tell someone "let's have a chat," this does not mean I intend to engage in the activity of chatting. Nor is it possible to predict what activity is being enacted simply by specifying what is known beforehand of the extralinguistic setting and giving the social characteristics and personal goals of participants and the content of what is being said (Cook-Gumperz & Gumperz, 1976). Verbal interactions of all kinds, formal and informal, rarely take the form of set, sequentially specifiable routines. Most talk is characterized by frequent and often quite subtle shifts in focus and maintenance of conversational involvement and requires that participants be able to recognize and follow these shifts.

To the extent that we can talk about conversations' being governed and controlled by shared expectations, we must assume that these expectations are signaled and sharedness is created by negotiation as part of the interaction itself. One common way this is done initially is through what Garfinkel and Sacks (1969) have called *formulating utterances,* such as "let me tell you what happened the other day"; "Let me explain . . ."; or "Mr. Speaker, Ladies and Gentlemen." Other ways of formulating include shifts in style from colloquial to formal or rapid delivery to slow, careful and contoured speech, or in the case of bi- or multilingual societies, dialect or language switching (Gumperz, 1977).

These formulating signals do not accurately predict what will occur; they do, however, generate some predictions as to what is *most likely* to follow. If a speaker signals that s/he is about to tell a story, we look for an introduction and a set of descriptions and allow the speaker time to produce these before attempting to change the subject. An explanation implies producing a set of logically connected reasons. Chatting leaves us free to change topics at will; discussing implies jointly working out the implication of one or a limited set of topics.

Note however that unilateral signaling of activities by a single speaker is not enough. All participants must be able to fit individual contributions into some broader theme roughly similar to the activities we have just described. They must recognize and explicitly or implicitly agree to formulating utterances and/or at least acknowledge shifts in focus by building on them in making their own contributions.

One common way in which conversational cooperation is signaled and monitored by participants is through what Yngve (1970) calls *back channel* signals: interjections, such as "OK," "right," "aha," or nods or other body movements. Other signs of cooperation are implied indirectly in the way speakers express responses, that is, in whether they follow shifts in style, agree in distinguishing new from old or primary from secondary information, in judging the quality of interpersonal relationships implied in a message, know how to fill in what is implied but left unsaid or what to emphasize or deemphasize. The term *conversational inference* refers to the cognitive process which reflects such judgments.

Consider the following brief exchange:

1. A: What are you doing tonight?
2. B: Nothing.
3. A: OK, let's go to the movie.
4. B: All right.

Note that the surface propositional content of speaker A's initial utterance hardly justifies B's response. We never do just "nothing." What he is most likely to mean is "nothing that can't be changed." B's "OK" suggests that that's how he interprets A's reply. In other words, B responds, as conversationalists everywhere do, to what he decodes as the communicative intent of the message. A's subsequent remarks and B's acknowledgment confirm or at least do not contradict this interpretation.

Brief and commonplace as this example may seem, it illustrates that conversational inference is, for the most part, indirect. Linguistic signaling of communicative intent involves signs which go beyond what is usually included in the linguists' analyses of grammar and lexicon. To participate in exchanges such as these, speakers must be able to recognize the first utterance as a possible invitation and must know enough about turn-taking to identify what follows as an acknowledgement. I shall use the term *contextualization convention* to refer to some of the nonlexical and nongrammatical, yet nevertheless linguistic, cues involved in conversational inference.

One way in which these conventions function is as guideposts or measuring sticks against which to apply what Grice (1973) calls *principles of conversational implicature*. We use our knowledge of grammar, lexicon, contextualization conventions, as well as whatever background information we have about settings and participants, to decide on what activity is being signaled or to establish likely communicative goals and outcome. We then build on these predictions to identify the communicative intent which underlies particular utterances. Note that judgments involved here are fundamentally different from the grammaticality or appropriateness judgment on which linguists build their analysis. Grammaticality judgments are all-or-none judgments. A sentence is either acceptable or not. If it isn't, the assumption is that linguistics is not concerned with its meaning.

Contextualization conventions channel interpretations in one direction or another. The basic assumption is that *something* is being communicated. What is at issue is *how* it is to be interpreted. The judgments involved are contingent judgments; they are either confirmed or disproved by what happens subsequently. If they are confirmed, our expectations are reinforced; if they are disconformed, we try to recode what we have heard and change our expectations of goals, outcomes, and speakers' intent.

One other characteristic of contextualization conventions is that they are not automatically learned along with grammar and phonology as a natural consequence of learning what the linguist would call *a language.* Speakers may show little or no difference when we examine their perceptions of grammaticality or appropriateness, but they may differ greatly in the way they contextualize talk. Contextualization conventions are acquired as a result of a speaker's actual interactive experience, that is, as a result of an individual's participation in particular networks of relationship (Gumperz, 1976). Where these networks differ, as they do in ethnically mixed settings, or in interaction between children and adults, varying conventions arise. Contextualization conventions are thus subculturally specific; they have the characteristics of what Morgan (1978) calls "conventions about language use" rather than conventions about language.

The following example from one of our earlier classroom studies will illustrate these points. A second grader has been asked to tutor a first grader in reading and is encountering some initial resistance. The interaction begins with the first grader's question:

1. First grader: Page thirty-three, where's thirty-three?
2. Tutor: Thirty-three.
3. FG: Thirty-three, is this thirty-three?
4. T: Thirty-three.
5. FG: Kay. Well, I was, I was over here.
6. FG: Come...
7. T: The...
8. FG: Ba... The? The? The...
9. T: Morning...
10. FG: Morning... is... coming?
11. T: Over.
12. FG: Over! The morning I....

An adult listening to the initial exchanges here might very well think that the children are just engaging in word play and might be tempted to comment "Stop playing and start reading," as the teacher in one earlier example did. But if we look at this example within the context of our total record of children's talk, a record which includes a large number of ethnographic observations made over a period of time, we note that the children here use their own contextualization conventions relying on stress, rhythm, and intonation to convey information that in adult talk is commonly put into words.

Based on an analysis of these conventions, we can begin to put into words or fill in what is implied but was left unsaid. Thus, in line 2 and line 4, the tutor uses a low-fall intonation to imply: "That's right, you know where it is." In line 6, the first grader uses a sustained, nonfalling intonation contour reflective of reading style to suggest: "I'm reading: come ..." In line 7, the tutor copies his style as if to say "the word is: the ...: In line 8, the first grader first uses questioning intonation twice as if to say: "Did you really say: the?" and then goes on reading: "the." The tutor then confirms by using reading style to give the next word: "morning." An adult here might have acknowledged with "that's right." In line 10, the first grader goes on to read: "morning is coming." The last word given in questioning intonation indicates lack of certainty and the tutor in line 11 uses a high-fall intonation to correct. In line 12, the first grader copies her intonation to acknowledge the correction and goes on reading.

Nothing about these contextualization practices is totally unfamiliar to American adults. We all recall using similar patterns on occasion. The point is that they are used with such frequency and carry such a high signaling load that adults are unlikely to understand their significance. When adults use such intonations they are likely to surround them with qualifying phrases, lexical acknowledgement, and the like. As we have pointed out, we are not referring to differences in appropriateness norms but to interpretive preferences. These preferences are partly governed by the linguistic cues we perceive, but they also depend on cultural presuppositions of what the activity is like and what we know about participants.

The next two expisodes come from a classroom where the teacher was frequently found to use an indirect strategy (repeating a child's answer with statement or question intonation) to signal that an answer is correct or incorrect. In examining what is communicated in the course of these episodes, we find that the children rely heavily on the teacher's intonational signals and often rely on these contextualization cues rather than lexical content.

Episode 1

1.	Teacher:	Um in the story it said something about he ran and he ran and he went back, uh down through the baseboard. What does that mean? Where would you find the baseboard?
2.	Tommy:	In the basement.
3.	Child:	In the basement.
4.	Teacher:	In the basement. Any place else?
5.	Andy:	Or the garage.
6.	Tommy:	In the junkyard.
7.	Teacher:	In the junkyard would you find a baseboard?
8.	Andy:	Uh uh, in the ba..., in the uh...
9.	Paula:	In the garage.
10.	Andy:	Yeah, in the garage.
11.	Teacher:	A baseboard is a part of a what?
12.	Tommy:	House.
13.	Teacher:	What part of a house?
14.	Tommy:	A chimney.
15.	Teacher:	A chimney?
16.	Tommy:	Roof!
17.	Teacher:	Roof?

Episode 2

18.	Teacher:	... all right, who can tell us something else about Alexander?
19.	Child:	He lived...
20.	Tommy:	He...
21.	Teacher:	Where did he live, Georgette?
22.	Frank:	In the...
23.	Tommy:	In the house.
24.	Teacher:	*Georgette,* where did he live?
25.	Georgette:	In a cup.
26.	Teacher:	In a cup? Georgette nods "yes"
27.	Paula:	He lived in the mouse hole.
28.	Teacher:	He lived in the mouse hole. All right in a what? Did he live in a barn?
29.	Children:	No!
30.	Teacher:	Frank, what did he live in? Did he live in a barn?
31.	Frank:	No.
32.	Teacher:	Where did he live?
33.	Frank:	In a hole.
34.	Teacher:	He lived in a hole in a what?
35.	Frank:	In a house.
36.	Teacher:	In a house.

These examples are typical of others we have observed, in which the overall goals of these situations is for the teacher to ask the students narrow questions about a story, with one particular answer in mind, and the children are to come up with those answers. Although the teacher does not specifically state whether an answer is right or wrong, she employs indirect strategies, such as repeating the answer with falling intonation to signal that the answer is correct (line 4, line 36) and with rising intonation if it is incorrect (lines 7, 15, 17, 26). The children show evidence of having understood these signals by trying to produce another answer whenever the teacher indirectly signals that an answer is wrong. This suggests that there is an unstated communicative convention at work which the children have internalized.

There are times, however, when their reliance on such discourse strategies leads them astray. In lines 5 and 6 of Episode 1, two answers are given in succession. Line 7, which contains indirect cues to suggest that a wrong answer has been given, explicitly mentions only the second. Perhaps this is why, in lines 9 and 10, the incorrect answer of line 5 is once more offered as an answer. In this episode, because the teacher's indirect signals provide no indication of the kind of degree of error in the children's responses, they have only a yes/no signal to rely on, and resort to what looks like a series of relatively wild guesses.

In Episode 2, additional ambiguities arise. In line 21, the teacher asks Georgette, "Where did Alexander [a mouse] live?," but Tommy answers out of turn, giving the correct response. The teacher ignores his response and restates the question with contrastive stress on Georgette, as if to say, "I asked Georgette, not you, Tommy." Georgette's attention, however, seems tuned to signals of evaluation and she interprets the question as saying "That answer was incorrect," and offers another answer ("In a cup"). It then takes the teacher six more questions to elicit Tommy's original response, "In the house." One possible explanation for the other children's taking so long to come up with the obvious is that they, too, like Georgette,. assume that Tommy's answer had been evaluated as incorrect. This confusion may have been due to the teacher's inconsistency in invoking classroom rules. More often than not, when pupils talked out of turn, they were not sanctioned as long as they offered the right answer. In the light of this well-established pattern, the children were reasonable in assuming that Tommy's answer was incorrect. Examples such as this show how, for children perhaps more than adults, unspoken context-based rules of interpretation interact with content and with what is known about the history of past experience in this type of activity in the interpretation of intent.

At the beginning of this chapter, I asked "What is it about the school and classroom environments that leads some children to learn and others to fall behind?" I proceeded to discuss the findings that show that factors other than mere differences in language or cultural background are at issue. In our final example, I shall demonstrate how one of these "other factors," differences in interpretive processes, can lead to problems in ethnically mixed classrooms. In these classrooms, interpretive problems arising from developmental differences in contextualization conventions are compounded by ethnic differences. It has frequently been noted that in ethnically mixed urban schools, even first graders exhibit significant differences in their ability to perform such tasks as cutting out figures, doing drawings, or working with pencil and paper. This is frequently seen as evidence that middle-class children are exposed to books, paper, and writing instruments in the home, but minority group children do not have these advantages and therefore have more learning to do in the school.

Initial observations in our current classroom ethnography project at first seemed to confirm this. Even during the first day of school, middle-class children followed the teacher's instructions and settled down quietly to work with crayons or scissors. Lower-class Black children on the other hand seemed to show little interest in these tasks. They tended to walk away, make excuses to leave the room, or sometimes do something quite different from what was wanted. When asked to sit down, they tended to call the teacher or the aide to ask for help and even after an explanation they were often heard to comment "I can't do this" or "I don't know how to do this."

A little reflection and knowledge of the children's home environment, however, soon reveals that there is little evidence that the children in question had not been exposed to books or similar tasks at home. Many Black parents are, if anything, more than usually eager to have their children learn to read and to provide them with paper and educational toys. All children in the room moreover had gone through a kindergarten class where they had done a great deal of similar work. We began to hit upon a solution when we examined tape-recorded instances of children responding with sentences like

I don't know.
I can't read.
I don't want to do this.
I can't do this.

All such sentences were pronounced with similar intonational contours, characterized by high pitch register, sustained tone, and vowel elongation on the last syllable. We then played recorded samples to a group of Black judges and asked whether they thought the child in question really didn't know or didn't want to cooperate. The judges agreed in saying what the children really mean to say in these cases is "Help me; I don't like to work alone." They denied that such statements implied inability to perform, even though we told them that this is how white judges are likely to interpret them. Once we became aware of the special communicative import of the children's intonation contour, we began to see more and more evidence that the children really were asking for company rather than signaling lack of ability. One child who had asked for and received help from the aid actually said, when she started to leave again, "Don't go away, I'm going to need some more help in a minute."

A few months later, one of the Black children who had been most persistent in asking for help called the researcher over to show her that he had finally mastered some addition and subtraction tasks which he had been trying to understand for some time. She looked over his work and said: "Perfect." Whereupon he commented, "I could do them by myself now." "I am going to show it to Mrs. P. [the aide] also." When the researcher turned away, the head teacher, Mrs. J., walked by. The child looked at her and said, using the intonation contour previously referred to, "Mrs. J., I can't do this." The teacher stopped, turned to him, and once more went over the correct procedure with him, telling him, "you ought to be able to learn this." When the researcher, who had watched the scene with amazement, asked the child why he had called the teacher, the child answered with a smile and said, "I decided it was about time for a quick trick."

Interpretation here and in many similar situations presupposes knowledge of contextualization conventions. When we recognize a certain way of talking as potentially meaningful, we respond accordingly. But when, because of differences in ethnic background, we do not recognize this meaning potential, this is not attributed to our own lack of knowledge but is reflected in our interpretation of intent. Given the realities of interethnic contact, this may lead to cultural bias in evaluations of ability. We are thus beginning to show how verbal communciation can be analyzed to find interactional explanations for some of the questions of teacher expectation that Rist, Leacock, and others have identified.

The paper could logically end at this point, since I have achieved my goal of discussing conversational intent and classroom learning, but the reader could be left wondering what form a research study based on the directions I have suggested might take. Therefore, given the theme of this book, the presentation of ethnograhic approaches to face-to-face interaction, I would like to end instead with a discussion of our current classroom ethnography project as an answer to this question.

THE THEORY APPLIED

Our current classroom ethnography project combines conversational analysis with detailed participant observation. Two research assistants are spending the better part of the year in the classroom, working as aides under the supervision of the teacher and participating in instruction and in planning teaching strategies. Their goal is to acquire a member's knowledge of how the school day is organized and of what problems teachers and students face, in addition to compiling the usual background information on children's home background, peer networks,and the like. In the course of this ethnographic work, they are able to make lists of recurrent or typical events, such as "rug time," "reading lesson," "math lesson." Notes are made on participant structures and communicative goals involved in such events as well as of teacher's instructional procedures, control strategies, treatment of errors, as well as of children's turn-taking and participating strategies and their responses to the teaching situation. Wherever possible, case records are compiled, illustrating what, given our theory of communication, seem like significant incidents in the school experience. This ethnographic record serves as the sampling basis for regular tape and videotape recording to illustrate key aspects of the classroom experience.

Conversational analysis focuses on sequences selected from this record. The goal of this analysis is twofold: (a) thorough examination of functionally equivalent verbal activities to identify developmental and social differences in conversational strategies, (b) to show how these differences affect teachers' judgments and the child's classroom experience and motivation. Findings of this study are qualitative; their validity depends on the power of the analytical tools to isolate interpretative conventions general enough to be reflected in a variety of events, and on the ethnographic representativeness of illustrative episodes. A recent example of this type of analysis appears in Michaels and Cook-Gumperz (1979). Some features in our method of analysis are quantifiable, such as the notion of thematic tying. In a recently completed study, Green (1977) has devised a discourse coding system which accounts for thematic tying and the role of contextualization cues in the perception of content. She has demonstrated that such a coding system based on conversational structures has better interrater reliability and better predictive value on short-term criterion tests than a more traditional frequency distribution system, the Flanders system.

We expect that once our findings have been cross-checked and validated over a number of situations, the materials we come up with can be used in a variety of ways. To begin with, these individual case records can be used directly by teachers as self-training devices, to give teachers better insight into their own strategies and into the interpretive strategies of children. At a more general level, such episodes can be analyzed for systematic differences in interpretation among participants. We have preliminary evidence that children from certain kinds of ethnic or communicative backgrounds typically interpret certain indirect strategies in one way, whereas children of other backgrounds interpret these same structures differently. Similarly, we are beginning to accumulate evidence on how the natural differences between adult and children's strategies affect interpretation and how information that the teacher gets about the nature of intergroup differences in speech (*pin-pen* example), as well as pressures created by shifts in classroom size, can affect students' ability to learn.

REFERENCES

Bales, R. F. *Interaction process analysis.* Cambridge, Mass.: Addison-Wesley, 1951.

Baratz, S., & Baratz, J. Early childhood interaction: The social science base of institutional racism. *Harvard Educational Review,* 1970, *40,* 29–50.

Bellack, A., Kliebard, H., Hyman, R., & Smith, F., Jr. *The language of the classroom.* New York: Teachers College Press, 1966.

Bennett, A., Erickson, F., & Gumperz, J. J. Coordination of verbal and non-verbal cues in conversation. Ms. report on workshop held at the University of California, January 1976.

Bernstein, B. Elaborated and restricted codes: Their social origins and some consequences. In J. J. Gumperz, & D. Hymes (Eds.), The ethnography of communication. *American Anthropologist,* 1964, *66*(6), 2, 55–69.

Birdwhistell, R. *Kinesics and context: Essays on body motion communication.* Philadelphia: University of Pennsylvania, 1970.

Boggs, S. T. The meaning of questions and narrations to Hawaiian children. In C. B. Cazden, V. P. John, & D. Hymes (Eds.), *Functions of language in the classroom.* New York: Teachers College Press, 1972.

Cazden, C. B., & John, V. P. Learning in American Indian children. In M. Wax, M. S. Diamond, & F. Grering, (Eds.), *Anthropological perspectives on education.* New York: Basic, 1972.

Condon, W., & Ogsten, W. D. Speech and body motion. In P. Kjeldergaard, (Ed.), *Perception of language.* Colombus, Ohio: Charles Merrill, 1969.

Cook-Gumperz, J., & Corsaro, W. The socio-ecological constraints on children's communicative strategies. Context in children's speech. In J. Cook-Gumperz & J. J. Gumperz (Eds.) *Papers on language and context,* Working Paper #46. Berkeley, Calif.: Language Behavior Research Laboratory, 1976.

Dumont, R. V. Learning English and how to be silent: studies in Sioux and Cherokee classrooms. In C. B. Cazden, V. P. John, & D. Hymes (Eds.), *Functions of language in the classroom.* New York: Teachers College Press, 1972.

Erickson, F. Some approaches to inquiry in school-community ethnography. *Anthropology and Education Quarterly* May, 1977, VIII: (2), 58–69.

Ervin-Tripp, S. Is Sybil there? The structure of some American English directives. *Language in Society,* 1977, *5,* 25–66.

Ervin-Tripp, S., & Mitchell-Kernan, C. *Child discourse.* New York: Academic Press, 1977.

Flanders, N. Teacher influence in the classroom. In E. Amidon & J. Hough (Eds.), *Interaction analysis: theory, research, and application,* Reading, Mass.: Addison—Wesley, 1967.

Florio, S. *Learning how to go to school.* Unpublished Ph.D. dissertation, Harvard University, 1978.

Garfinkel, H., & Sacks, H. *Contributions to ethnomethodology.* Bloomington, Ind.: Indiana University Press, 1969.

Garvey, C. *Contingent queries.* Baltimore, Md.: Johns Hopkins University Press, 1975.

Goffman, E. *Frame analysis.* New York: Harper & Row, 1974.

Green, J. *Pedagogical style differences as related to comprehension performance, grades one through three.* Unpublished doctoral dissertation, University of California, Berkeley, 1977.

Grice, H. P. Logic and conversation. In P. Cole & J. Morgan (Eds.), *Syntax and Semantics* (Vol. 3). New York: Academic Press, 1973.

Gumperz, J. J. Social network and language shift. In J. Cook-Gumperz & J. J. Gumperz (Eds.), Papers on language and context, Working Paper #46. Berkeley, California: Language Behavior Research Laboratory, University of California, 1976.

Gumperz, J. J. Sociocultural knowledge in conversational inference. In Saville-Troike (Ed.), *28th Annual Round Table Monograph Series on Languages and Linguistics.* Washington, D.C.: Georgetown University Press, 1977.

Gumperz, J. J., & Herasimchuk, E. Conversational analysis of social meaning. In R. Shuy (Ed.), *Sociolinguistics: current trends and prospects.* Georgetown University Monographs in Language and Linguistics, Georgetown, Va.: Georgetown University Press, 1973.

Gumperz, J. J., & Hymes, D. (Eds.), *Directions in sociolinguistics.* New York: Holt, Rinehart, & Winston, 1972.

Hall, E. T. *The silent language.* New York: Doubleday, 1959.

Harlem Youth Opportunities Unlimited. *Youth in the ghetto.* New York: HARYOU, 1964.

Heath, S. B. Towards an ethnohistory of writing in education. In M. Whiteman (Ed.), *Writing: perspectives on written language.* Hillsdale, N. J.: Lawrence Erlbaum, in press.

Holt, J. C. *How children fail.* New York: Dell, 1964.

Keenan, E. O., & Schiefflin, B. Topic as a discourse notion: a study of topic and conversations of children and adults. In C. Li (Ed.), *Subject and topic.* New York: Academic Press, 1975.

Kochman, T. *Rippin and runnin.* Urban, Ill.: University of Illinois Press, 1972.

Kohl, H. *Thirty-six children.* New York: New American Library, 1967.

Kozol, J. *Death at an early age.* Boston: Houghton Mifflin, 1967.

Labov, W. The logic of non-standard English. In Alatis, J. (Ed.), *Georgetown monograph series on languages and linguistics, 22,* 1969. Sociolinguistic patterns. Philadelphia: University of Pennsylvania Press, 1972.

Leacock, E. B. *Teaching and learning in city schools.* New York: Basic, 1969.

Lewis, L. Culture and social interaction in the classroom: An ethnographic report. Working paper #38. Berkeley, Calif.: Language Behavior Research Laboratory, University of California, Berkeley, 1970.

McDermott, R. Relating and learning: an analysis of two classroom reading groups. In Shuy R. (Ed.), *Linguistics and Reading*. Rawley, Mass.: Newbury House, 1978.

Mehan, H., Cazden, C., Coles, L., Fisher, S., & Maroules, N. *The social organization of classroom lessons*. Center for Human Information Processing, University of San Diego La Jolla, California, December 1976.

Melmed, P. J. Black English phonology: the question of reading interference. *Monographs of the Language Behavior Research Laboratory*, No. 1. Berkeley, Calif.: University of California, Berkeley, 1971.

Michaels, S., & Cook-Gumperz, J. A study of sharing time with first grade students: Discourse narratives in the classroom. In *Proceedings of the Berkeley Linguistics Society* (Vol. 5), 1979.

Morgan, J. L. Two kinds of convention in indirect speech acts. In Cole, P. (Ed.), *Syntax and Semantics* (Vol. 9). New York: Academic Press, 1978.

Ogbu, J. U. *Racial stratification and education. IRCD Bulletin*, 1977, *XII*, 3.

Phillips, S. U. Participant structures and communicative competence: Warm Springs children in community and classroom. In C. B. Cazden, V. P. John, D. Hymes, *Functions of language in the classroom*. New York: Teachers College Press, 1972.

Rist, R. C. Student social class and teacher expectations. *Harvard Educational Review*, 1970, *39*, 411–415.

Sacks, H., Schegloff, E., & Jefferson, G. A simplest systematics for the organization of turntaking for conversation. *Language* 1974, *50*(4); Part 1), 696–735.

Schank, R., & Abelson, R. *Scripts, plans, goals, and understanding*. Hillsdale, N.J.: Lawrence Erlbaum Associates, 1977.

Scheflen, A. E. *How behavior means*. New York: Doubleday, 1974.

Schegloff, E., & Sacks, H. Opening up closings. In Turner, R. (Ed.), *Ethnomethodology*. London: Penguin, 1974.

Searl, J. Indirect speech acts. In P. Cole, & J. Morgan (Eds.), *Syntax and semantics* (Vol. 2). New York: Academic Press, 1975.

Simons, H. D., & Johnson, K. Black English syntax and reading inference. *Research in the teaching of English*, December 1974.

Simons, H. D. Black dialect and learning to read. In J. Johns, (Ed.), *Literacy for diverse learners*. Newark, Del.: International Reading Association, 1974.

Sinclair, J., & Coutlard, M. *Towards an analysis of discourses. the English used by teachers and pupils*. England: Oxford University Press, 1975.

Tannen, D. What's in a frame? Surface evidence for underlying expectations. In *Advances in discourse processing, Vol. 2, new directions*. Norwood, N.J.: Ablex, 1979.

Yngve, V. On getting a word in edgewise. In *Papers from the sixth regional meeting of the Chicago Linguistic Society* 1970.

2 Persuasive Talk—
The Social Organization
of Children's Talk

Jenny Cook-Gumperz
Institute of Human Learning, University of California, Berkeley

Some may see the theme of this paper as rather esoteric, as somewhat of a departure from current thinking on child language. I want to argue that, for children, language has primarily a rhetorical character; children begin their use of language aware of some of the communicative operations possible with language alone, that is, with an articulated verbal symbol system, after a long apprenticeship of communication without benefit of spoken language. In this way children are aware of the special influence, the additional purchase, that use of such a verbalized system can gain for them. Such a statement may make children seem rather too sophisticated practitioners of the communicative arts beyond their years, but in order to make the initial shift of perspective that enables us to take a child's-eye view of language as a phenomenon, we need to introduce this idea.

My title—persuasive talk—is meant in two ways: first, that talk, verbal language, is itself a powerfully persuasive tool, in the sense usually meant by rhetoricians and by classical grammarians who saw language as a persuasive force in its grammatically correct forms and, like Burke (1969), based their notion of language on the primarily rhetorical functions of human communication. Secondly, I shall explore some examples of children's talk (with children aged three plus and four years old) where they are using language to persuade; that is, using strategies dependent on *spoken speech alone* to alter the course of someone else's behavior, opinion, or actions.

Work on this paper was supported by NIHM grants 26063 and 26831. I am grateful to Susan Ervin-Tripp for her support. Many of the ideas expressed here are part of my continuing collaboration with John J. Gumperz. I thank Judith Green and Cynthia Wallat for their helpful editing and many substantive suggestions.

25

Several things can be meant by persuasion:

a. For ethnographers of speech events, persuasion has in many cultures a prescribed ritual form, such as different forms of oratory and occasions that are defined as needing different rhetorical styles (Block, 1976)
b. Persuasion in our culture can mean the production of reasoned arguments, the influential value of a reasoned series of statements
c. Persuasion can also mean the rhetorical force of ordinary langauge used in its appropriate stylistic forms. The stylistic form itself can be influential, the choices of metaphor and the various ways of selecting words and acts which are rhetorically powerful (Burke, 1969). It is in this third Burkian sense of persuasion that I shall refer to children's talk as *persuasive*.

LANGUAGE AS A RESOURCE: THE SOCIAL POWER OF LANGUAGE

In this paper I propose to look at children's uses of talk in situations which are persuasive; that is, where only talk, not action, is used to accomplish or try to accomplish the goals of changing another person's action or plan. Secondly, I want to present the proposition that talk itself, verbal language, exerts for children a persuasive force in their lives. I shall examine the second proposition first.

Language introduces into children's lives a powerful means of communication—a way of influencing the actions of others in relation to self—that makes it impossible for normal children not to use this means of expression. For most children, language is a natural extension of their social communicative experience. It is a useful resource for operating upon and within the social world they have entered at birth.

Evidence for this view: that children begin early in their lives to be aware of the social power of language can be shown in many ways, from the fact that language can be used to obtain goods and services to being able to extend the length, complexity, and satisfaction of contact between self and others (Richards, 1974). Some recent studies, for example, Halliday's (1975) "Learning how to mean" and Scollon's (1975) "Conversations with a one-year-old," show how a metalinguistic awareness develops in children and how the child centers his/ her attempts with language upon the need to make sense, to fit the "word" into the action pattern, which for the child carries a social communicative meaning.

Halliday (1976) has also described the child's early awareness of the social usefulness of language as the development of a *grammar of rhetoric*. By *rhetoric* he means that "language is doing things with words to achieve practical ends," and he contrasts this idea about language with what he calls the grammar of logic and logical categories, which is the formal or normative view of language, in the following ways:

> By the time a child is two years old, he knows quite a lot about the nature and functions of language. He is not only using language; he is also beginning to talk about it. He is constructing a folk linguistics, in which (a) saying, and (b) naming-meaning denote different aspects of the same symbolic act. And language functions for him both in reflection and in action: as a way of thinking about the world (including about himself), structuring his experience and expressing his own personality, and as a way of acting on the world, organizing the behavior of others and getting them to provide the goods and services he wants.
>
> Soon, however, the child will go to school; and once he is there, his ideas about language will be superseded by the folk linguistics of the classroom, with its categories and classes, its rules and regulations, its do's and, above all, its don'ts. Here a fundamental ideological change takes place in the child's image of language–and, through this, of his image of reality. Up till now, language has been seen as a resource, a potential for thinking and doing; he has talked about it in verbs, verbs like *call* and *mean, say* and *tell,* and by *rhyme.* From now on, language will be not a set of resources but a set of rules. And the rules are categorical—they operate on things; so he must talk about language in nouns, like *word* and *sentences,* and *noun* and *verb;* and *letter*...(p. 4).
>
> [He suggests that] we have enshrined in our folk linguistics these two views: one of *language as resource,* the other of *language as rule.* The two co-exist; but since one is a product of our primary socialization and belongs to the reality that is learned at our mother's knee, while the other is part of secondary reality and belongs to the realm of organized knowledge, they impinge on each other scarcely at all. But in our prevailing ideology, the dominant model is that of language as rule (our schools teach the formal grammar of logic, not the functional grammar of rhetoric) (p. 5).

This is a rather different view of language. Language is seen as a resource in the social world, a means of directing and controlling self and others, rather than as a scheme for representing the outside order or operating logically within it. So by *the persuasive force* of language I mean to suggest all that is implied by the idea of a rhetorical use of language to achieve effective communication. To quote Halliday again: "Rhetoric (as classically defined) was concerned with the nature of argumentation, and so with the structure of discourse; discourse seen as something that is arguable, something that can be denied, disputed, contradicted, doubted and urged" (p. 7).

That is, language is seen as existing within a complex pattern of social behavior to be used to achieve socially defined goals. Given this description of a rhetorical view of language, the question that most quickly comes to mind is how, if at all, does this view differ from linguistic pragmatics, the more socially sensitive approach to linguistics which has recently altered views of children's language acquisition (Ochs and Schiefflin, 1979).

Linguistic Pragmatics: A Historical Perspective

Pragmatics has had a wide influence on the studies of child language acquisition, partly perhaps because many of the questions raised by pragmatics were already concerns in the study of child language. Elizabeth Bates (1976) in a recent review of pragmatics has described the shift that has taken place in child language studies as a movement away from the *empiricist* model of language learning toward a model which sees children's language learning as a part of social context.

> In the empiricist approach language is determined entirely by environment, language is learned by imitation: in the late 50s and 60s, linguists and psychologists moved away from the empiricists' view to the *nativist model* which holds that the child is biologically equipped with certain clues about the nature of language and sets out actively searching his speech environment for structures that correspond to those clues. In this model although a rich or impoverished environment can affect the rate of development, the crucial aspects of language are not derived from speech input but imposed on it . . . the limitation of these models has led to the *contextualist* model in which context does not just cause language but is an integral part of the structure of language. Meanings are conveyed through a creative combination of utterances and social settings (p. 1).

Such a statement suggests many questions for study, such as how and in what forms the child acquires notions of social setting. But beyond our own sense as members of our culture and perhaps as mothers or child caretakers at some time or other, linguistic pragmatics suggests no way of knowing what the social experience of the child is, and how this social experience is to be taken as a part of the meaning beyond reference for the child's linguistic experience. In other words, theoretically, linguistic pragmatics has a theory of language-in-use but no accompanying social theory or theory of social learning to indicate in their own terms the salience of social phenomena. More than this, language itself is for the child a social phenomenon in its own right. Perhaps the question we should first consider in the study of child language is the place of language in the life space of the child.

The Place of Language in the Life Space of the Child.   The study of child language has, for the most part, focused upon the child's acquisition of language skills, since it assumes the usefulness of language to the child to be self-evident, the place of language in the life space of the child has not been a theoretical or practical consideration. Views drawn from developmental psychology and from some recent work on prelanguage learning have, however, stressed the integration of the child into the social world and of preverbal learning with subsequent development of language. Martin Richards (1974) has summarized the developmental perspective:

> She [the mother] and other people that surround the infant relate their actions to his and so provide him with a means of building connections with their world and an entry into their social culture. They also act as mediators for him of the wider social order and it is through them that the child begins to learn about his place in the world (p. 7).

Recent work on the prelanguage experience of the child (Bruner, 1975; Carter, 1975) has begun to document in detail how children's language use grows out of a rich nonverbal communicative system which mother and child develop together. For example, work by Carter has shown how a particular gestural schema becomes transformed in use into a verbal form—the expression "look at." Bruner's study has shown how the gesture of take and return becomes part of a verbal game where verbal routines of "thank you" and "here you are" are mapped into the game. Such studies show that for small children the *continuum of communication stretches not from silence to talk, but from nonverbal to verbal communication.* This is an emphasis somewhat different to that of adult communicative experience. Anecdotally, many parents and teachers must have noticed that with children a "silence" during a face-to-face encounter rarely seems to bother children, where for many, perhaps most, adults a silence is a "pause which must be filled in" in all but the most intimate adult situations. So for children talk, verbal communication, stands in a somewhat different relation with the total communicative context than it does for adults—for whom the verbal forms of communication are assumed to be of absolute priority.

In the next section of this paper, I want to show some of the details that can be gathered from others' empirical work on children's language for the role that language plays in the child's total communicative system and to develop some ideas about how children use language in ways that may be specific to their own development of sociolinguistic skills.

Language Learning as Part of a Continuing Dialogue.   Recent studies of early acquisition (Bloom, Lightblown & Hood, 1975; Cross, 1978; Lieven, 1976; Keenan & Schiefflin, 1976; Snow, 1977) show that language learning takes place as a part of a social dialogue between mother and child; and to a lesser extent between children themselves. In a recent study, Lieven (1976) shows that *three* children of initially similar developmental stages develop differentially, according to the degree of conversational encouragement received from their mothers. The mothers vary in the extent to which they build upon their children's conversational offerings and make them into conversational partners. A good example of a mother developing her child's contributions is the following:

Kate at 19 months and her mother:

K: Na-ah (crying and fussing)
M: I wonder what your problem is, is it that the sun is in your eyes?
K: Bye (rubbing eyes).
M: Yes, that's your eye. Is the sun shining in your eye? Would like to pull the curtain?
K: Dah.
M: Think it would be a good idea to pull the curtain?
K: Curtain.
M: Yes, pull the curtain and then the sun won't come in your eyes. You see the sun's gone now.
K: Na.
M: It's not here anymore.
K: More.
M: It's behind the curtain (Kate laughs) (p. 122).

Lieven comments that Kate's mother goes in for a long extended sequence of conversation about the problem before she attends to it and changes the subject only when the previous topic has been resolved. The framework within which the child will eventually be able to say *The sun is in my eyes* as a request to the mother to do something about it seems to be already foreshadowed for the child, in this conversation. Across time, Lieven found that how much mothers picked up on the child's conversational contribution and built it into an extended exchange contributed to a growing developmental deviation between children who initially had similar mean utterances length; that is, showed a similar degree of language competency in terms of the length of their utterances.

   This point was further borne out by Snow's (1977) work on a younger but more extensive sample, where she found that the mother's role in providing a conversational context for the child made a difference in the speed of language development. In addition, work on the prelinguistic stages by Bruner and associates (1978) shows that language learning takes place as part of a dialogue which grows out of the observable regularities of a shared life with the caretaker. The well-practiced activities of mothers in taking care of the needs and of playing with their children enable mothers and babies early in life to achieve a great deal of rhythmic synchrony and complementarity in their reactions to each other (Condon, 1974). Studies of crying responses also showed similar reciprocal learning.

   So, from the evidence of these studies, we can conclude that from the beginnings of life a child is experiencing satisfactory social communication which builds up from the earliest rhythmic and gestural beginnings into wider and more complex patterns, such as those studied by Bruner and associates. Lieven's (1978) and Snow's (1979) findings bear on observations of the earlier studies of children's syntax by Brown and Bellugi (1963) on *telegraphic utterances* that children learn from the mother's expansions of their utterances. The data remain much the same but the underlying model of language learning is changing to one where the child's role is not passive but *collaborative*. Lieven is suggesting that the child is as much an initiator as a responder in many communication situations, and in this way often structures his/her own opportunities for learning. Snow's study complements Lieven's, and shows how "even in the pre-speech period the changes that take place in mother's speech reflect their children's growing ability to operate as conversational partner" (p. 4).

Given the complexity of the adult communication system which must find its expression in as simple a daily occurrence as casual conversational encounters, how do children learn to use their developmentally scarcer linguistic resources in social interaction through talk? The finding that the rate of children's language development depends greatly on the place given to them by adults in conversational encounters, and that this place is determined in part by the child's own initiation of communicative exchanges with the mother, accounts for some of the developmental variation in language learning. It also makes the child an active participant in a situation where the child's own communicative needs are seen as necessary to the development of the adult-child relationship. But beyond the child's initial participation, the child has to learn the sociolinguistic skills necessary to maintaining and introducing topics, the skills of turn-taking and of entering conversations by establishing a turn.

All these studies begin to show that language learning takes place as a dialogue which grows out of the observable and experienced regularities of shared life—the conversation of mother and child, and of children themselves. Language once acquired will continue to grow, insofar as it is practiced, as it must be, as a part of a continuing language between self and others, and perhaps insofar as language use adds to the quality of effectiveness of this dialogue. Children, however, as Lieven's and Snow's studies show, experience widely differing roles as communicators. This raises the question of the imperfect character of much adult-child verbal interaction, since misunderstandings between child and adult are as likely to be caused by either partner.

The Imperfect Character of Much Adult-Child Verbal Interaction

Since successful communication depends on dialogic collaboration, it appears that once the child has acquired rudimentary control over language the child may be more disadvantaged than before acquiring language. The conversational work that mothers may be willing to do with very small children to make their contribution into a conversation changes; and the child, perhaps, takes on a new, more demanding role as a conversational partner. Once the child can put together a multi-word utterance, the child's entry into conversational competence is just beginning; entering and maintaining a conversation requires discourse skills which are developmentally very complex, and this may create problems. For example, the child must make assumptions about the knowledge of the audience—what is known, what is not known—and put this into a verbalized form.

In order for children to learn these and other discourse skills through dialogue they need to extend their role as collaborative partners. The following example from the work of Keenan and Schiefflin (1976) demonstrates much about the imperfect character of adult-child interaction as well as the complexity of the task facing children in becoming more sophisticated collaborative partners.

Toby and David, 33 months. Eating midday meal, facing caretaker, Jill. Jill has just asked if Toby and David would like a banana in jelly—British term for Jello.

22.1	Toby:	no no jelly/(tenkel)/
22.2	Jill:	You eat your dinner then.
22.3	Toby:	(tenkel)/
22.4	Jill:	What?
22.5	Toby:	(tenkel)/
22.6	Jill:	tinkle?
22.7	David:	yeah
22.8	Toby:	no tinkle/(tenkle) (repeats)/
22.9	Jill:	You're a prank (p. 358).

What this example shows is that the child at the multi-word stage is faced with a heavier demand in becoming a partner. In addition to heavier demands on the child, the foregoing episode is an example of how adult repairs on children's conversations may or may not work and the difficulty in overcoming adult-child miscommunication.

The reader is told that this example is a "natural episode"; but the reader cannot have enough information about what occurs prior to the beginning of the quotation and what occurs after to make a judgment about the whole interactional sequence. Our conclusion must be that Toby has failed to communicate his request, but he presumably did not wish to formulate it very strongly because options other than the acceptance of closure were open to him at the point of the misunderstood repair. For example, he could have shown Jill his request "tenkle" by taking her to the cupboard where "tenkle" (tins of jelly) may be kept. Toby chooses to give up the attempt in so far as he doesn't make a further issue out of being misunderstood; he remains a responder rather than taking the floor to lead an active search after his "meaning."

The reader will note that the word "presumably" was used in the preceding discussion of both the possible cause of adult-child miscommunication and the possible causes of the child's choosing to accept this miscommunication. In viewing the task for the child as predominantly a linguistic activity, we are not able to take into account that we know children have many other communicative strategies—often nonverbal ones—to achieve the purpose they really want.

Perhaps one of the critical questions that needs to be focused upon more often is to look at children's *communicative success* and ask how *does* the interaction continue? What are the possible verbal as well as nonverbal strategies used to induce others to continue to talk and to take control of the floor if this is necessary. We could also ask a second question: what *sociolinguistic strategies* does the child use; and in what ways do children differ from adults as communicators?

In the previous examples, we have considered adult-child communication. If we are to understand the strategies a child does use in communication, we must also consider what strategies a child uses in peer interactions. Several researchers have focused on one feature, linguistic topicalization; that is, how children introduce new information and syntactically mark what is already known to a conversational partner who is also a child. Keenan and Klein (1975) have suggested "that in producing socially appropriate responses, young children rely heavily on the form of one another's utterances" (p. 117). They give examples of how children closely follow on the form of the preceding utterance in order to mark both prior knowledge and new information that is in the conversation. So that what may look on first inspection like a repetition is not so.

For example:

Child 1: '/like 'that/
Child 2: yeah/like 'that/ (with rising intonation)
Child 1: going to 'scratch/ (with rising intonation)
Child 2: going to scratch/ (p. 376).

These repetitions show that in peer interaction, when children repeat utterances, they are, in fact, creating for themselves the thematic continuity or topic relevance that can later be achieved through different discourse conventions. That is, children use *different strategies* from adults to achieve the same *rhetorical purpose* of agreement or collaboration with other people. They use repetition with varying prosodic/intonational markers in place of a variety of adult speech acts and semantic forms to add information that is not coded lexically.

One last example will now be presented to illustrate the differences in sociolinguistic strategies children and adults use in maintaining conversations. Corsaro (1977) in working with adult-child conversations has focused on the role that repetition has for adults (rather than for children), where repetition operates as a request for clarification.

Corsaro suggests that clarification requests serve the function of clearing up misunderstandings in social interaction and usually take either the form of simple repetition or expansion, as in the following illustration:

Krister is telling a make-believe story to the adult:
    K-A: Have a—he (referring to a monster) has a knife and cut my window off and got in
    A-K: He had a knife and cut your window off?
    K-A: Yeah (p. 189).

He suggests that misunderstandings such as that between Krister and the adult conversationalist can arise for a number of reasons. Many of these misunderstandings "involve not only the child's misuse of linguistic constructions semantically, but also are due to differences in adult and child interpretive competencies" (p. 52).

Corsaro also suggests that requests for clarification serve the function of marking off or "filling in" one's turn or place in an interaction. I suggest that because of the limited and normatively variant nature of children's contributions, adults repeat the child's remark as if to keep some kind of recognizable continuity going in the conversation; additionally the adult's repetition may also be to provide the right kind of intonational contour for ending the utterance to which the adult can tie the next utterance. In the following example, the adult uses repetition to find his own *thematic ties* within the discourse and to gain control over the thematic development of the conversation, perhaps suggesting that adults have a different notion of the development of a conversation than children.

Buddy and father in Buddy's home
    B-F: I got this (shoebox)
    F-B: Oh, you want to buy some shoes, huh?
    B-F: Yeah
    F-B: OK (p. 189).

To summarize, for children, getting people to do what you want is a major communicative problem. Children are *more likely* to experience misunderstanding with adults when they are the initiators of the conversation than when they respond within a frame set by the adults themselves, and yet as we discussed in the previous section, their communicative development is increased by their own successful attempts at initiation. As adults, we take for granted that children's access to verbal techniques is more limited since their control of adult syntax-semantics is still developing. The question that as researchers we could do well to pose is what kind of role as communicators can children have at, say, three or four years of age. Although we as adults often ignore or fail to understand children's communicative wants, research on child-child peer conversation can show that children can be very successful and subtle communicators with each other.

Our question in this paper will be what kinds of strategies do children use with each other? Given the imperfect character of much adult-child conversation, this peer interaction must be considered as a very important area of communicative experience for children.

What do children do to achieve the social outcome that they want to achieve? As analysts we do not always know because the exclusively linguistic perspective for selecting many instances of children's language means that the episode often leaves off before the full outcome is achieved. In order to foreground the notion of what is a *social activity* we have to do two things: One, we must find out in what ways the participants themselves are able to recognize the speech as being a part of the process of social activity; and secondly, in what ways and how they code this event.

A New Direction: Focus on the Activity and Not the Act

In considering in what ways children use their *language as a resource to accomplish social actions* we shall need to look at the children's ability to begin to structure and complete a social project using language. As we have argued, the more usual approach in child language is to adopt a linguistic focus and to explore the separate speech acts used to do a task, such as requests made by different forms of direct or indirect request acts. In a recent analysis of request forms Garvey (1975) explains that the indirect acts can be analyzed by explicating the assumed implicit performatives; and by discovering the illocutionary force of an act as a request.

In this paper we take as our primary goal the discovery, not of acts, but of the social strategies that children use, and examine the use of acts in relation to the *apparent goals of the interaction.* Consider the following example cited by Garvey (1975):

(A approaches a large toy car that B has just been sitting on.)
A: Pretend this was my car.
B: No!
A: Pretend this was our car.
B: All right.
A: Can I drive our car?
B: Yes, OK. (Smiles and moves away.)
A: (Turns wheel, making driving noises) (p.42).

Garvey comments:

> The climax of this sequence is a permission-directive, which suggests, anticipating our later discussion of social meaning, that the child is able to use deferential alternatives appropriately. It is the shift to an inclusive pronoun that shows extraordinary deftness, however, because it suggests an imbedding set of moves as well and possibly a social allusion to solidarity and sharing (p. 42).

As Garvey suggests, if we look at the event as a complete activity episode, what is important is the social suggestion of sharing the car as a means to using it, which puts the linguistic form of an indirect request "Can I drive our car?" into a very different social perspective. The social effect of the act is to shift the perspective of the whole episode. The shift requires more than reliance on the indirect form for its effect. The social perspective of "our car" has a different effect than reiteration of an indirect form within the same context, as for example "Can I use your car; please may I drive your car" or "If you'll let me use your car, I'll be very careful." The switch of pronoun, in this example, implies a knowledge of social categorization which makes this a very different social project, one which shifts from requesting to persuading. So that if we look at this sequence from the point of view of the social activity being accomplished, it is much more complex in its underlying intent than are the other possibilities just cited which are linguistically just as complex. I suggest that the change of pronoun reveals a discourse strategy which involves what Sacks (1967) has called a "membership categorization device" showing that the child can recognize and manipulate knowledge of social relations in order to build up a strategy to let the speaker have use of the car across *a stretch comprising more than one turn;* that is to use a communicative buildup, a developed talk strategy composed of three different speech acts to reach the desired goal.

Mishler (1979) in his recent paper on children's "trading talk" showed that it is necessary to know the use of speech acts in context before being able to judge their meaning in use. Once the entire sequence is revealed any *simple speech act* may take on a different character.

He comments:

> For example, the initial announcement in the Suzy Q episode "I gott—I gotta Suzy Q." turns out, on analysis of the full sequence which follows, to be an indirect request but this cannot be determined on the basis of the immediate exchange which follows. It is only when we can see that this was one cycle, a failure to trade, within the full trading sequence that we can specify it as an indirect request.
>
> A similar problem of interpretation presents itself for other exchanges within the overall structure of the trade. For example, take the politeness exchange that concludes the Suzy Q sequence:

S5: What about some of these?
S1: I *do* want this fer a Suzy Q. Do you wanna Suzy Q?...
S5: Thank you Steven.
S1: You're welcome.

If this exchange were treated in isolation, it would appear that the first speaker's (S5) statement had the illocutionary force of an offer. In such a case, we would expect that the recipient of the offer would produce the first part of the politeness exchange which follows an offer, that is "Thank you." Instead, he restates the terms of the trade and makes the counteroffer. By accepting the trade, the first speaker (S5) has now been relocated so that it is now appropriate for him to begin the closing exchange and for the initial "trader" to terminate the sequence with "You're welcome" (p. 13).

For the reason that interpretation of a speech act is context bound and that interpretation is dependent on consideration of the total social situation, we are suggesting an alternate focus upon the social activity the child is performing. Garvey's example, getting use of the car, and Mishler's example, getting rid of the Suzy Q for something the child likes better, are both instances of *persuasion* in our terms. Through use of several *linked speech acts*, as a strategy, the child in each case was able to achieve the social project of altering the behavior of someone else through talk, and talk alone.

These two examples, perhaps, show that children seem quite able to switch their strategies. Yet, as I have just argued, children are considered to have difficulty with the development of extended themes; that is, as conversational partners they deviate from adult expectations. We can only find out in what ways children do differ from adults in their sociolinguistic conventions and uses, the relevance of these differences for their performances in context, by studying longer sequences of talk from the perspective of the social goals or projects that the children are accomplishing in using talk, that is, from the focus on the *activity* rather than on the act as such.

Related to such analysis, two notions need to be considered: indirectness and complexity. Our notion of *indirectness* rests not upon the speech act, but upon the social action of achieving control over another's actions without direct confrontation through the use of choices of verbal strategy. Our notion of *complexity* consists of being able to conduct a sequence of exchanges which build up to the desired goal—or achieve the goal through interchange that is a dialogue.

Our point is that defining the social significance of children's verbal resources requires us to evaluate the strategies without actual social contexts and consider them as means children use to achieve social projects. For instance, the child's role as communicator is very different in child-child peer play than it is when the child is part of an adult speech event or when the child is part of an adult-determined situation. To examine speech acts as separate entities often gives a false impression of the potential communicative achievements of children, in contexts that are both self- or other-determined.

Only those well versed in child development or in living with two-to-five-year-olds will be able to remind themselves of the different ranges of communicative abilities that small children have, and of the different misunderstandings that take place, even though, where speech acts are analyzed item for item, we can find some evidence of the child's fairly advanced pragmatic usage. The key question, however, is in what ways can children use language in social situations to obtain their objectives. This requires not single acts but a putting together of sequences of acts that can be an adequate or effective stimulus to action in their own right. Inspection of any corpus of transcribed child-child or child-adult talk will show that children more rarely use lengthy sequences of talk and achieve fewer topic-continuous interchanges than adults. For these reasons we suggest an alternate approach to the study of speech-in-action, of looking at the naturally occurring sequences of social activity using speech.

Our question in the remainder of this paper will be how children's own sociolinguistic conventions differ from those of adults and how these differences are related to their developmentally different perception of language itself.

The Multi-Modality of Speech in Action

I have argued that verbal, that is, lexicalized, language is only a part of the total communicative complex which children and adults use. We can begin this section, by considering how much of the message is carried through the verbal channel in any child language situation. For this reason, child language study requires us to give more consideration to the social context and goal of the interactive uses of language. The child's view of the social activity will determine the child's view of the place of verbal language in the total communicative situation and can lead adults who may have started with a different assumption about the social context to some wrong conclusions about appropriate and inappropriate responses. If we accept, as many researchers of early language learning are beginning to do, that the child is a *collaborative* learner in everyday contexts, then we cannot judge children's performance by solely adult criteria.

The first factor we must remind ourselves of is the *multi-modality of spoken language.* This factor was often neglected in the previous focus on the syntactic structure and logical qualities of language. But if we keep our initial distinction of *language as a resource,* we see that communication can occur along several channels: syntactically-semantically; paralinguistically and pro-sodically and/or kinesically (gesture, facial expression, body movement, etc.). These language resources form a multi-channel system of communication.

As suggested in a previous paper (Cook-Gumperz, 1975) the child's response to the multiplicity of communicative channels is to use alternate channels, rather than to rely solely on foregrounding, the lexico-semantic channel, as the main carrier of meaning and backgrounding the other channels. In that paper, the child's situated, or context-specific communication skills were defined as using *iconographic* interpretive procedures as distinct from the adult's *discursive* procedures that focus on the sequential presentation of syntactic-semantic information as primary. This hypothesized model of communication can be seen in the different surface quality of children's talk: the linking together of monologue, singing, and referential-specific information. This may be an indicator of less social constraint on children's talk, verbalized "inner speech" (Vygotsky, 1963) or it may be the result of a different coding of the social situation and a different sense of the appropriate and effective strategies for communication. As we have mentioned before, a different set of sociolinguistic conventions exists. We hope through study of the use of persuasion to find situations where words and words alone are used and can be effective in altering the outcome of the child's social projects: situations where we can see children work hard to get their meaning across and where they use their developmentally available strategies to the full.

Persuasion as Part of the Flow of Everyday Speech Activity

Within everyday life in our culture, persuasion does not have the character of a separate or ritual *speech event;* unless other specific contextual changes are present (such as political speeches, court of law, TV ads). As Mishler (1979) has also suggested in discussing children's trading talk:

> A related advantage of the types of speech events that occur during the ongoing flow of conversation in a natural social setting is that the language itself is the primary source of information and data. Sociolinguistic analyses of speech events, particularly those of ethnolinguistics and anthropologists, often refer to rituals and ceremonies where linguistic forms and sequences are provided by general cultural norms, which also specify the meaning and significance of the talk (for example, Frake, 1972). This allows the analyst to use his/her general understanding of the culture to understand what is being said, and how, but the language itself is frequently treated "merely" as illustrative of the more general cultural analysis. In the instances under examination here, we will not have the advantage of a formal and prescribed ritual to rely upon. We are thrown into the sea of talk and will have to find its structure from the inside (p. 4).

Along with displays of anger, instructions/ directions, and reminiscences, persuasion remains just such a part of the everyday repertoire of speech activities, influenced but not governed by other cultural contexts of language usage, spoken and written. There are no specific ritual speech constraints for children to learn in order to be said to be "doing persuading" except a greater than usual determination to affect (or resist) the course of others' *verbalized* wishes. *Persuasion* is not letting up when the intent of a single speech act is misunderstood or does not have its intended effect, and continuing verbally to attempt to influence the actions of another without resort to direct action or verbal imperatives.

Therefore, in situations of persuasion, children show their maximal range of language resources. Persuasion is almost a mind-demonstration of the full range of children's resources that can be used in ordinary situations. Most importantly, persuasion is an occasion where children rely upon their own belief in the *inherent power of words* to accomplish actions.

For the purposes of this paper, I describe persuasion as a verbal suggestion which is repeated more than once in an attempt to bring an alternation in the activity or belief of another person. One interesting feature of persuasion is the need to use *more than a single verbal strategy or utterance* in order to persuade, *verbal arguments* must be constructed, and utterances must be multiple and most probably varied. There is an underlying aspect of persuasion, the notion that the verbal suggestions must be seen to be satisfactory, so that the verbal action must have some kind of immediate closure.

We can expect that when children attempt to persuade someone, they have a definite social goal in mind and they attempt to reach that goal by verbal means alone. This view contrasts with those found in previous works on children's developmental use of speech in experimental contexts. Shatz and Gelman (1974), for example, have argued that children under four are likely to prefer an action strategy rather than a verbal strategy in response to some speech acts of indirect requests and commands.

The situations we have selected for analysis all occur as part of an ordinary day's activity in child-child play with or without some adult participation and as such are naturally occurring sequences. The sequences do not present an adult-determined (or loaded) interpretive context in which the child acts somewhat as a puppet, without his/her own definition of the context and social goals being taken fully into account.

Persuasion as an activity, is special in that the persuader must take the initiative and introduce a new topic and often continue talking without relying on what Keenan and Klein (1975) suggest is necessary for most child response: the form of the other's utterance to achieve coherence, since the other person may ignore the persuader's initial overtures. Such situations must last longer than a single interchange and so give us some useful indications of how children themselves see the ways of achieving topic continuity. Much of small children's talk references the immediate and visually available context. In persuasion, the speaker has often to address the more abstract qualities of the social context and the relationship itself. The following example of persuasion from two pairs of children, a pair of three-year-olds and one of four-year-olds, will be used to illustrate persuasion as defined above.

Some Examples of Children's Persuasive Strategies

I have chosen sequences of tape recordings of children at play in home and school environments. Consideration of the longer event in the full transcript suggests that these sequences are self-contained, naturally occurring episodes—that is, that all phases of the activity begin and end with the short sequence we have selected. We do realize in the analysis that the history of the interaction is of course much longer and the episode I analyze is embedded within a longer period of interaction.

Example 1[1]   takes place in a nursery school. The children, a boy (J) and girl (M) aged about 3½ years, often play together and have a close "school"-specific relationship.

J and M had been playing mother and father in the playhouse earlier in the morning. The game had finished and they had gone their separate ways to get their morning snack and do other things. When observed M was playing with some toy animals (horse, cows, a zebra, and sheep) on a rug. J goes over to M, and stands behind her while she is kneeling on the rug moving the animals around making them do various things. After standing for awhile, he says:

J: Let's go to bed honey let's go to bed. (This remark made in slightly high pitch, has a rising contour on each phrase and a slight lengthening on the two phrase-final words.)

M: (after a pause) No, I'm playing with these animals (another pause). The animals are going to bed. (This is said in a higher pitch, the last word is lengthened.)
Pause

J: Honey, it's nighttime let's go to bed (same intonational contour as the previous utterances).

M: Yes It's nighttime the animals are sleepy (pause). They're all going to bed. Horse is going to bed (M is moving the animals around and putting them on their sides to make them go to sleep).
J stands for some time watching M putting the animals to bed. Neither speaks; then J walks away (p. 17).

---

[1]This example is taken from "Context in Children's Talk" by Jenny Cook-Gumperz and John J. Gumperz, 1976.

Here, J clearly alluding to the previous game by adopting the rhythm and prosody of that game, and by implication asking M to resume the game. M either did not understand him or chose not to cooperate. Most likely the latter, since she uses the suggestion of J's remarks, but puts them to use in signaling a game of her own. In other words she is incorporating J's suggestions as a part of her own play. Since the game had stopped, the need to restart the game probably required certain statements of purpose. J here has failed to persuade M to change her game; he has presented his case by *contextualizing* his message, that is, using a change of voice tone to mark the change of context that he desires and that is necessary to his case. In a sense he "acts out" the character of daddy in his attempt to be persuasive. To an adult it might seem that his failing is in not announcing his context change in advance to M, thus providing her with the additional information it seems she would need to understand his utterance in its change of specific context away from that actually taking place. To an adult J's remarks, occurring when they do, seem "out of context" for the present event that M is engaged in; for an adult would most probably respond with a reproach. M, however, does not react as if J's request were at all odd; she merely does not seem to wish to comply with it. She uses the idea of "going to bed" as if it applied to the development of the plot of *her own* game.

One could, perhaps, suggest in this situation that the child depends on *prosody* to carry information which contextualizes a remark which otherwise would appear to be out of context. An adult mode of dealing with this need to change context for this request would be to begin with a lexicalized announcement, such as "M, remember our game this morning (or just now) how about playing some more?" In contrast, J repeats his request in his attempts to be more persuasive and elaborates the idea by saying "It's nighttime." When his second utterance is not successful, however, he does not seem to find an alternative strategy but finally lets the idea drop. J does not establish a further "argument" within his activity of persuasion other than to switch prosodically into the character of daddy/husband and to give some scene-setting justification which he lexicalizes as "it's nighttime."

Example 2.   Our *next example* involves two three-year-olds, L and S, who are regular playmates. Here there is definite attempt on the part of L to establish an "argument," in the technical rhetorical sense, for change of action she wants from S. She links together a chain of speech acts to build up a response situation, instead of using her full repertoire of speech communication.

An afternoon at home with L and S, while mother, D, has an adult visitor.

L and S have just finished a game and have been offered apple and ice cream; they take their bowls and sit at the breakfast table to eat. (adult talk in the background)

1.   S: you have three//
2.   L: 'want an other apple   yes   yes//say yes//
3. a. S: no
   b. no/thank you//
4. a. L: want another apple/that's you (singing)
   b. no I don't want it/you can have it/
   c. d'you want it/
   d. say yes/
   e. and I'll give it to you//
5.   S: no
6. a. L: no say yes
   b. what did I say
   c. yes/yes say yes (louder)
7. a. S: if I don't want to say yes I don't want to/
   b. cause my sister says if you don't want to say yes/
   c. you don't want to/
   d. my sister...(trails off)
8. a. L: no/
   b. you doo want to say yes/
   c. you don't don't say you don't *want* to/
   d. you say/
   e. I don't I don't...I don't need to talk like that/
9.   S: I don't need to talk like that// (said with her mouth full)(pause)
10. a. L: no/its too late/you can't say it again//
   b. too late
   c. and goodbye an that's for nothing//

In utterance 2, L offers S a piece of apple, that is, she attempts to get rid of her extra piece. Each word in her utterance is stressed equally in staccato rhythm. S responds with a polite refusal, with a tone of formality, a polite but firm "no." L repeats her offer with a slight rise in pitch on "apple." The final phrase is "sung" with a special vowel elongation of the "you ou." Perhaps L uses a "singing voice" for the utterance rather than choosing to lexicalize her meaning further, for example by saying, "I'm talking to you."

In 4c, L begins to construct her argument, by telling S that it's all right, she can have the apple as L herself doesn't need it. The two phrases have an intonational pattern that in British English we would interpret as one of "disavowal/disclaimer." This passage is spoken in normal adult intonational contour: quick and light with emphasis on "you" and "have" and with a very short pause between the two segments. The contrastive request has the stress on "want" with a high rise and is informally elided, as a rephrasing of the first two requests/offers. In the final segment of utterance, the conditional is implied (if you) say yes (then) I'll give it to you.

This insistence on saying yes—an act of politeness, as conditional on receiving extra apple—is a strategy that the children must often have experienced. Here L put this strategy to her own rhetorical use—to construct a stage in her "argument" to persuade S to relieve L of the apple she doesn't want in the first place. S replies in the negative and L repeats stages 4d and 4e, her argument; however, these are repeated by L in a tone of impatience. The "no" is high-pitched and the "what did I say" phrase is left with a long pause as an incomplete hanging fragment, a typical adult strategy for getting a child to answer. Finally, in the end, L answers her own incomplete question.

In utterance 7, S begins her long speech of refusal much louder than before. The intonational phrasing in this passage is very important for it suggests something of the child's process of thinking and of S's attempt to construct an "argument" through semantic contrast that misfires.

In the first phrase of 7, the stress is on the first "want to," while the second "want" is lower in tone; each word is said in a slightly staccato enunciation and the rhythm is slower, more than seems normal. This passage does not have an adult intonational phrasing.

In the second clause, the pitch increases on "cause my sister says" and then falls at the clause boundary to a mid-position that suggests there is more to come. The expected stylistic-semantic contrast from sister's pithy saying doesn't come off, possibly because for an adult the expected contrast would be an alternative semantic choice, "If you don't *want* to say yes/you don't *have* to," with the stress on the two contrasting verbs, providing a special marking to the new information which stylistically "tops" the argument. S's slightly staccato delivery and her longer pause at the second utterance boundary make it possible that she is groping for this contrastive semantic difference but is unable to find the word; she then trails off at a mid-fall without an ending.

L responds to S's long speech with a similar attempt at a stylistically contrastive argument. The exchange of apple has been forgotten. The issue has now become "saying Yes." L has difficulty in this speech; she comes in on the fading part of S's speech, contradicting her by saying no. She reiterates "want to say," with the strong emphasis on *do*. She then hesitates and falters. Due to her difficulty in encoding here, the staccato rhythm probably breaks up the idea; stress does not occur in the places expected in normal adult speech. What makes these utterances difficult to understand is that they sound very similar stylistically to S's speech, but they express a very different idea. The probable pattern for this speech as adult form would be the following:

"/you do want to say yes/you don't say "I don't want to" *you say* "I don't need to talk like that" (where *that* references the phrase "don't want to"). L manages to contrast stylistically, but in order to get the idea across in speech they need a different contrastive intonational contour. The third "you say" (italicized) needs to have marked rising intonation to act as a frame for what follows and to prepare the hearer for the denouncement. L's encoding difficulty, however, causes her to repeat "I don't" three times, and instead of rising on "you say," she swallowed this phrase and puts all the stress heavily and therefore in a seemingly marked way on "need." Even though this strategy is accidental, it may have worked because S repeats L's last phrase with her mouth full.

L's "finale" is performed in a separate stage. Such a semantically "marked" ending is very unusual in children at this age, although not so later. This clearly separates this activity of "verbal persuasion" from what came before and after, as a very definite form of verbal game—a game of disputation, a matching of wits.

Features of this event show that L and S seem to have learned one very important and basic principle—that discussion and rhetorical arguments are made by *stylistic contrast*. In the two long speeches, these contrasts did not quite work in what was actually said, either semantically or prosodically, but the two girls were groping toward these stylistic contrasts. The idea of contrast is a fundamental—a deep, linguistic notion on which the whole principle of understanding spoken speech rests. It may not seem too farfetched an idea to assume that the two children may extrapolate these principles to the forms of linguistic reasoning at the semantic/stylistic level. Both L's and S's long speeches are set up as rhetorical arguments with stylistic contrasts, and the whole sequence of L's interchanges builds up an argument as an act of persuasion which rests on a switch of semantic perspective both through choice of words and through the use of intonation for the acts of disavowal.

Example 3. S and C have been having a tea party with their stuffed animals. C then begins to play a game of marbles, running marbles down a chute; S helps but she really doesn't have much part in this game, she watches but wants to get S's attention back to the party game, so, as C plays, this episode takes place.

1.   C: No (speaking to self)
2. a. S: That's the party isn't it
   b. I think one wants a bit more sugar
3. a. C: No he doesn't (very loud)
   b. Want a bit more sugar no want a bit more sugar no
   c. want a... (C walks along questioning the animals as she says this)
4.   S: Teddy does you know (C stops, turns, looks at S who is standing a little behind her)
5.   C: wuf, wuf wuf he does doggy does
6.   S: Yes

7.   C: Only this is doggies that's enough
8.   S: and this is Teddy's
9.   C: and this
10.   S: and that
11.   C: MINE and that's Sarah's Not really going to drink it
12.   S: No
13.   C: It's only in here
14.   S: really...
      Adult enters
15.   A: do you want the other game down?

In example 3, two four-years-olds have been having a tea party with their animals; one of the girls, C, has begun a different game of marbles which doesn't involve S. S's task of persuasion is getting C to move back to the tea-party game. She has tried once before unsuccessfully. In this example S manipulates her partner by initiating a topic shift and a turn interruption as strategies.

The indirectness in this example involves not only the indirect speech act in 2b using the conditional and abstract pronoun "one" which may have been learned idiomatically and so not carrying its full semantic weight, but also the use of this speech act in conjunction with the topic shift. C responds to S's redirecting of interest by actively negating S's proposition in 2b by "questioning" the animals rhetorically. S breaks the "rule of turn-taking" by moving to assert that Teddy does want more sugar in utterance 4. This strategy of simple assertion in the context created by S leaves C no alternative but to join in S's strategy and "top" her assertion by speaking for doggy, "Doggy does" (utterance 5).

This instance of persuasion is an example of our notion of complexity where the initial indirect speech act strategy is embedded within a series of moves appearing to use the children's knowledge of conversational procedures and of the juxtaposition of assertion that cannot be easily negated, given the context as a strategy.

Example 4.   Typical winter afternoon at home. L and S are playing in the breakfast area, while the mother, D, is in the kitchen. They have modeling dough on the table and some toys and blocks on the floor. L, earlier, made a request for S to play Mummies and Daddies but S did not respond.

S is now modeling with play dough and singing to herself.
L is playing on the floor with pieces of cardboard and blocks.
1. L: pew—pew did you have a fright (*pew* is a gunfiring sound)
2. S: No
3. L: pew pew pew
4. S: we're not allowed to spit
5. L: pew pew I'm not spitting on S pew pew

6. S: here we go round the table (singing)
7. L: pew pew
8. S: don't holla holla dolla (singing)
9. L: S never plays Mummies and Daddies
10. D: doesn't she
11. L: no you never play Mummies and Daddies, S (as L says utterance 9, she is still playing with the blocks, etc.; she doesn't go toward her mother or make any other indication to draw her into the conversation; or change her activity).
12. D: (the mother) I'm sure she plays Mummies and Daddies with you. I often hear you playing Mummies and Daddies together don't I?
13. L: shall we play the S
14. S: Look what I got
15. D: that's nice
16. L: Sorry to throw a box on you S
17. D: no don't throw things around L
18. L: I'm saying sorry to S not to you
19. S: cause you didn't hit me and cause she's not little
20. L: no she's big.
21. S: look I'm carrying
22. L: ha ha (heavy heaving breathing sounds; both children leave area.)

In example 4, the children, again L and S, use both indirect speech acts (utterance 4, "We're not allowed to spit") as a way of saying "don't spit" and manipulation of conversational procedures to achieve their social project. In this case, L appears not to be successful, at first, in persuading S to finish her modeling and join L in a game. L uses the conversational device referred to by Sacks (1967) as "third-person listenership" in utterances 9 and 11 to achieve her goal; that is, she depends on the fact that although the conversation up to utterance 9 has involved only two people, there are three people present and therefore *potentially available* in the setting.

Statement 9 which is made as if addressed to any person present is a rhetorical device. Although by using the third person pronoun, it is by implication not addressed to S but to the "silent" conversational partner/listener-the mother. L's strategy assumes (a) that the mother would hear and respond, which she does; (b) that S hears also, since she is present at the scene and would possibly join in with a denial of such an extreme statement. In utterance 11, L leaves nothing to chance and does mention S by name, therefore directing her comment at her as well as her mother. Her response to the mother's denial, "doesn't she," is a very loud and emphatic "NO." In utterance 12 the mother continues to respond "on cue" with both a denial of L's extreme statement and a tag question probably to elicit a positive response from L. In utterance 13, L continues the three-way conversation by addressing S with a dietic "then" in her statement, presuming all the positive statements ("If you often play shall we play again"). L's strategy fails as S responds only by talking to the mother. L's more direct strategy works, however, as she turns the tables on her previous conversational partner, her mother, by this time joining with S in excluding the mother by third-person reference. This strategy succeeds in getting S to leave her modeling to play again with L as well as turning the conversational relationship around. The game between the two little girls begins as soon as utterance 20 ends and they leave together for the play area.

CONCLUSION

In this paper I have proposed a view of language that is child-centered, that focuses on language as intrinsically rhetorical, as speech-in action, in contrast to language considered mainly as a logical system of meanings and relationships. Our adult models for communication have always assumed that syntactic and semantic components of our communication are the most important, that lexicalized speech is the chief carrier of meaning, and that we as adults have backgrounded other communicative channels for the purposes of interpretation. But for the child the context plays a more important part in what s/he is communicating. As I have suggested previously, the situation and the total event are treated as a single interpretive unit by the child. This could be described as saying that children are more context-reliant than adults, but it is really more than that. It means that, for children, their interpretations of the meanings of others' utterances rely upon their *accumulated situational knowledge* as much as on their linguistic knowledge; on their social experience as much as on their growing linguistic ability.

I have suggested that language is viewed by the child as a *phenomenon* in its own right, one among several ways of communicating within social situations. The communication continuum for children should be seen not as stretching from silence to speech but rather as from nonverbal to verbal communication. When studying a child-centered view of language-in-use it is necessary to explore occasions of language use developed and initiated by children. Language has a different place in the life space of the child than in that of the adult. Too often, the language capabilities of children are judged from adult-organized occasions where the child as a communicator is operating within a situation not of her/his own choosing or organizing and by communicative conventions that differ from those developed by children for their own purposes.

For these two reasons we have sought out occasions to examine where children are using language for their own social purposes, as active collaborators or initiators in the communicative situation. We have used the term *persuasion* to cover such occasions where children formulate for themselves their social projects and where these can be achieved solely through the use of langauge/speech rather than through other forms of social action. Persuasion we take to be a situation where children rely on their own belief in the *inherent power of words to accomplish actions.* Persuasion can be described as a verbal suggestion which is repeated more than once in an attempt to bring about an alteration in another person's actions or beliefs.

In analyzing situations of persuasion, we have found that children rely much more equally upon all the modalities of speech to communicate. For example, for children, prosody carries a very significant part of the signaling load, as does rhythm. We have also found that (a) small children aged three to five have knowledge of the social operation of conversations; (b) that children have a basic notion of linguistic contrastiveness that extends from phonological through syntactic to semantic alternations. We have shown how children have used these two sociolinguistic principles of ordering of the social and specifically linguistic features of language for rhetorical-stylistic purposes in the social activity of speaking. We have attempted to demonstrate how children are able to see the need for linking together speech acts as strategies and to answer this need in specific occasions by constructing semantic arguments using all the linguistic features at their disposal. We have suggested that one particular value of studying what we have called *persuasion* is that in these self-defined and organized speech occasions from within the ordinary stream of daily talk, children have the opportunity in a naturally occurring context to demonstrate fully their capacities as communicators.

The main thrust of the argument of this paper has been that if we are to develop a child-centered model of language and discourse processing we must study children in occasions where they are not experimental puppets, responding to adult-defined and organized situations, but must see them operating naturally as social beings in the everyday activity of communicating. Only by beginning at this point of looking for the naturally occurring contexts of activity can we build up a socially realistic and appropriate model of children's capabilities. Otherwise, we always run the risk of imposing an adult-centered linguistic model upon the productions of children and so often misunderstand the specific range of capabilities that children themselves develop early in their use of language. We, too early, assume that children, as apprentices to adult skills, are themselves aware only of the adult model to which they should be approximating, rather than seeing them as *practitioners* of communication beginning with the activity of communication and moving on gradually to develop closer and closer to adult performance standards. After all, it takes all of childhood to grow up, and then maybe some!

REFERENCES

Bates, E. Pragmatics and sociolinguistics in child language. In A. Moorhead & D. Moorhead (Eds.), *Language deficiency in children*. Baltimore, Md.: University of Maryland Press, 1976.

Bloch, M. *Political language and oratory in traditional society*. London: Academic Press, 1976.

Bloom, L., Lightblown, P., & Hood, L. Structure and variation in child language. *SRCD Monograph* 160, 1975. .

Brown, R., & Bellugi, U. Three processes in child's development of syntax. *Harvard Educational Review*, 1964, *34*.

Bruner, J. The ontogenesis of speech acts. *Journal of Child Language*, 1975, *1*.

Burke, K. *Rhetoric of motives*. Berkeley, Calif.: University of California Press, 1969.

Carter, A. The transformation of sensori-motor morphemes into words: a case study of the devloepment of more and mine. *Journal of Child Language*, 1975, *1*.

Condon, W. A. Speech makes babies move *New Scientist*, 1974, *62*, (901).

Cook-Gumperz, J. Child as a practical reasoner. In M. Sanchas & B. Blount (Eds.), *Sociocultural dimensions of language use*. New York: Academic Press, 1976.

Cook-Gumperz, J., and Gumperz, J. J. (Eds.) *Papers on language and context*, Working Paper #46, Language Behavior Research Laboratory, University of California, Berkeley, 1976.

Corsaro, W. The clarification request as a feature of adult interactive styles with young children. *Language in Society*, 2, Vol. *7*, 1977.

Cross, T. Mothers' speech and its association with the rate of a linguistic development in young children. In N. Waterson & C. Snow (Eds.), *The development of communication*. London: Wiley, 1978.

Garvey, C. Requests and responses in children's speech. *Journal of Child Language*, 1975, *2*.

Gumperz, J. Report on interethnic communication, unpublished manuscript, Language Behavior Research Laboratory University of California, Berkeley, 1977.

Halliday, M. A. K. *Learning how to mean*. London: Edward Arnold, 1975.

Halliday, M. A. K. *Ideas about language*. Inaugural lecture at the University of Sydney, Australia, 1976.

Keenan, E. O., & Klein, E. Coherency in children's discourse. *Journal of Psycholinguistic Research*, 1975, *4*.

Keenan, E. O., & Schiefflin, B. Topic as a discourse notion. In C. Li (Ed.), *Subject and topic*. New York: Academic Press, 1976.

Keenan, E. O., & Schiefflin, B. *Developmental pragmatics*. New York: Academic Press, 1979.

Lieven, E. Conversations between mother and young children: individual differences and their possible implications for the study of language learning. In N. Waterson & C. Snow (Eds.), *Development of communication*. London: Wiley, 1978.

Mishler, E. Would you trade cookies for popcorn: talk of trade among six-year-old children. In O. Garnica & M. L. King (Eds.), *Language, children and society*. New York: Pergamon Press, 1979.

Ratner, N., & Bruner, J. Games as social exchange in the acquisition of language. *Journal of Child Language*, 1978, *5*.

Richards, M. I. *The integration of the child into the social world*. Cambridge and London: Cambridge University Press, 1974.

Sacks, H. Unpublished lecture notes. Irvine, Calif.: University of California, 1967.

Scollon, R. *Conversations with a one-year-old*. Honolulu: University of Hawaii Press, 1975.

Snow, C. The development of conversations between mothers and babies. *Journal of Child Language*, 1977, *4*.

Vygotsky. L. *Language and thought*. Cambridge, Mass.: MIT Press, 1963.

3 Ethnography— The Holistic Approach to Understanding Schooling

Frank W. Lutz
Eastern Illinois University

INTRODUCTION

This chapter sets forth a particular definition of ethnography and argues for its worth in educational research. In doing so, I may appear to be too hard on other research methods and educational researchers who utilize them. I apologize if the following conveys such an impression. I myself, have, utilized various research methods in pursuit of answers to research questions. I quarrel not with the methods of other researchers, but with the occasional contention that ethnography is not empirical. True, it is not statistical, but nothing could more empirical. Additionally, and more importantly for our purpose in this chapter, I believe that applying the term *ethnography* to a broad range of studies which utilize some number of ethnographic methods or techniques but do not conform to the rules of ethnography (either in data collection or analysis), and also do not result in an ethnography, is counterproductive to ethnography as a methodology and the educational research which ethnography could produce.

Ethnography and ethnographic methods have become increasingly in vogue among educational researchers during the last decade. That trend seems likely to continue into the next decade. In general, I believe this to be a promising situation for educational research. Yet one can note two commensurate and somewhat related and disturbing cross currents. As educators twist the tool to fit their data (rather than shape their understanding of the data with the tool), ethnography, in particular, and sometimes ethnographic methods are often modified and occasionally bastardized. As this happens, ethnographers in anthropology have a defensible platform from which to voice their disciplinary bias that none but anthropologists should engage in ethnography. The expression of that bias is merely the second disturbing crosscurrent detracting from the productive use of ethnography in education. The first is the production of poor research and ethnography by people in education who, untrained in ethnography, claim to engage in it.

Of course, there are degrees of quality in ethnographies which, as often as not, exist in the eyes of the reviewer. In addition, there are legitimate uses of ethnographic methods short of ethnography. It seems best to disregard the first question of honest differences of opinion about the quality of an honest-to-goodness ethnography. Although quality is always a matter of concern, the second question is the one of importance to the thesis presented here. This thesis involves the difference between ethnography and ethnographic methods. *Ethnography,* as will be expanded upon more fully later in this chapter, is, according to Geertz (1973), first and foremost a "thick description." As such, it involves many techniques or methods which can be described as ethnographic, including, but not limited to, participant observation, interview, mapping and charting, interaction analysis, study of historical records and current public documents, use of demographic data, etc. But ethnography centers on the participant observation of a society or culture through a complete cycle of events that regularly occur as that society interacts with its environment. The principle data document is the researcher-participant's diary. Ethnography is a holistic, thick description of the interactive processes involving the discovery of important and recurring variables in the society as they relate to one another, under specified conditions, and as they affect or produce certain results and outcomes in the society. It is not a case study, which narrowly focuses on a single issue, or a field survey that seeks previously specified data, or a brief encounter (for a few hours each day for a year, or 12 hours a day for a few months) with some group. Those types of research are ethnographic but *not ethnography!* They may be good research but, when they are passed off as ethnography, they are poor ethnography and poor research.

ETHNOGRAPHY VS. MICRO-ETHNOGRAPHY

Having rejected research using a *selected* and limited sample of ethnographic methods as ethnography—including those limited to various types of formats for scoring and recording the interaction of small groups—I shall turn to the question of scope of ethnography. Is the study of primary or small groups ethnography, particularly when those studies have severely limited boundaries for data collection which prohibit extrusion of data collection into the larger environment?

The notion of "Face-to-Face Analysis of Social Interaction" tends, in my view, to define the object of research as dyadic or at least small-group situation, and to relate the methods of data collection and conceptual analysis to the general purview of sociology and social psychology as distinct from anthropology. Even taken in its broadest sense, the phrase tends to limit the observations, data analysis, and theoretical framework to a type often termed *micro-ethnography,* as contrasted with the broader notion of ethnography as usually applied in the field of social or cultural anthropology. Such a tendency is, unfortunately, consistent with the type of ethnography or ethnographic work most often encountered in education. It applies to the study of small groups, often to a larger group, such as a whole class, and occasionally to single schools. This limitation tends to exclude studies of educational issues and questions in a broader and at least as important context—that of the school district-community, cultural perspective. I suggest that the narrow focus, while generating some important knowledge, fails to shed light on the more complex issues that account for much of what goes on (or doesn't go on) in schooling.

In an instructive and very insightful article, T. M. S. Evens (1977) speaks eloquently and analytically of the theoretical problems inherent in a single and narrow reliance on either transactionalism or structural functionalism. He does an excellent job of pointing out the methodological inconsistencies in each method. I recommend the entire article to the serious student of the methods suggested in this book. A brief quotation from his conclusion will serve our purpose; and I can then move on to some application of his conclusion to my own concerns about how anthropology and ethnography are applied to research in education. Evens concludes:

> Like the process whereby individuals interact in pursuit of their own separate concerns, the program whereby they mind and construct their collective interest is both heteronomous and autonomous. Barth (for example see Frederick Barth's "Analytic Dimensions in the Comparison of Social Organizations," *American Anthropologists: 74,* 207–220) is right; incorporation (the process of the individual acting in the interest of the group as opposed to his own single self-interest) is in a sense transactional; but in a sense it is not—it is metatransaction. It at once deviates from and transcends transaction (p. 593).

Thus, Evens suggests that there is *transaction,* the process of individuals in pursuit of their separate concerns; and *metatransaction,* the process of incorporation or people in pursuit of collective interest. As the two conditions overlap in time and space, specifying which process one is observing is a problem of focus.

The question of focus is always arbitrary—for the photographer, the biologist, or the social scientist. What brings one thing into clearly observable focus distorts another thing. To focus the camera lens on the butterfly on one's nose distorts the face; to focus on the face distorts the horizon in the background; to focus on the horizon distorts both the face and the butterfly. The same is as true in the social sciences as it is in photography. The social scientist has a right to be arbitrary. But one should not call the picture of a perfectly good butterfly a picture of a horizon.

To focus on transaction is to distort incorporation. To focus on face-to-face interaction is certainly not to do ethnography; in fact, it is likely to prohibit it. As Evens points out, transaction fails to account for a great deal of human behavior. That a great deal of important learning occurs beyond the one-to-one, face-to-face transactional process of teacher and student is at least one of the basic arguments for schooling, or learning in the group situation called *public schooling*. It can be argued that ethnography, as defined here, is the best research method to study such other and important schooling phenomena.

The narrower the focus of a study of schooling processes, the more likely important, perhaps necessary, variables are to be unseen and unaccounted for. Not only are statistical studies guilty of this narrow focus, but micro-ethnography also tends to be too limiting when taken as individual studies. How can the behaviors of the urban teacher (Smith & Geoffrey, 1968) be understood without reference to *The Man in the Principal's Office* (Wolcott, 1973)? Or the principal's behavior be understood except in the broader context of the central office, school board, and community described by Iannoccone and Lutz (1970)? Such understanding is certainly not likely to be developed by the observation of face-to-face interaction alone or understand through the application of transactional analysis alone. Such understanding requires a broader, holistic approach rooted in the cultural context in which school districts are constituted, school boards are elected, superintendents are hired and fired, schools are built and staffed, and in which teachers and pupils go about the business of schooling.

Ramsey (1978) has pointed to a situation that has tended to limit the focus of ethnography in education. She suggests that the experience and training of the anthropologists in education on the one hand, and the educator-anthropologists on the other, affect the values and norms and therefore the perceptions of the researcher. As one result, the classroom or the individual school is most likely to be the focus of anthropological research in education. Strangely, the anthropologist who chooses education as the society to be studied is often less familiar with, and less informed about, that society than his/her fellow anthropologist, studying an exotic culture, is about that culture. The anthropologist studying education is often unaware of the types of bureaucratic control exercised by federal agencies, state education departments, local boards and central office staff, as well as the influence of individual school administrators and teacher organizations. Far from being free of bias, however, such researchers enter the field with beliefs about public schooling developed through twelve years of personal participation and perhaps as many more years as parent and/or taxpayer, as a more or less disinterested (nonresearch) participant observer (Lortie, 1975). For such a person the research focus is most likely to be the classroom or a school where "everyone knows" education takes place.

Educator-anthropologists who may know better (often coming out of some educator role—most probably teacher) find the classroom and/or the school their natural focus and entry into that participant-observer role. Such a person has had the same exposure to "preprofessional" data as the anthropologist; in addition, these ethnographers are well steeped in the "perspectives" developed in teacher education institutions and the "best practice" ideologies of the working profession in the classroom. For both anthropologist in education and educator-anthropologist, the classroom and/or the single school is the most likely focus of research dictated by their biases and their ease of entry and data accessibility.

THE QUEST FOR MEANING

Whether one engages in micro-or macro-ethnography, one should be engaged in the search for meaning! The first step in this search is the development of as complete as possible a body of data that describes the phenomenon being studied. That is ethnography! According to Geertz (1973), ethnography is "thick description." From this thick description, the anthropologist attempts to build a model of the important and recurring variables and the relationships among these variables, that describes and accounts for the phenomenon. The anthropologist develops from the ethnography an operational model (from the data of events *observed* by the researcher) and a representational model (from the data gathered from "native" informants about the "native" *interpretation* and meaning of what happened). These models are combined by anthropologists, using general anthropological theory, into an explanatory model that conceptually explains and predicts behavior within the culture under specified conditions (Caws, 1974).

This, I believe, is the essence of theory building, an aspect of research frequently neglected in the usual psychostatistical research conducted in education. Too often we test meaningless or weak hypotheses with very powerful statistics, based on very large samples, almost always selected more on the basis of convenience than by a randomized procedure from the population which we intend to generalize. Important to my thesis here is that the more we limit our ethnographic focus, the more likely we are systematically to limit our ability to *discover* some extremely important variable affecting the phenomenon which originates outside our narrow focus. Thus, seriously to limit the focus of ethnography in education is to compound a problem of psychostatistical research in education—the very problem that such research should alleviate. Are there important and recurring conceptual variables that emanate outside the face-to-face, pupil-teacher transaction—or even the classroom or school interaction—that affect such often researched topics as classroom discipline, pupil achievement (learning), or curriculum structure? Can we ever understand, predict, affect, or control these educational processes unless we discover that these relationships exist?

THE HOLISTIC APPROACH

In order to counter the problems just suggested, educational research should engage in macro-ethnography. I refer to research that seeks explanation within a broad cultural content, regardless of where the focus begins, and couches that explanation in an even broader cross-cultural approach. Wolcott (1975) identifies what he considers to be appropriate criteria for making judgments about ethnographic research in schools. Although I take exception to certain aspects of his "criteria", the article is extremely helpful in guiding decisions about such research. I would like to identify four "ingredients" that I believe to be important if one is to pursue the holistic ethnography approach recommended here. These are:

(a) Use of a researcher trained to do ethnography (I do not necessarily mean an anthropologist as opposed to an educator-anthropologist)
(b) Entry into the educational system which permits the pursuit of data vertically as well as horizontally through the cultural system
(c) A crosscultural perspective of the research
(d) Ability of the ethnographers to develop "thick description" and bring anthropological models and theory to bear on that ethnography.

Rearding these four ingredients, some amplification may be helpful.

Trained Ethnographer. It should be unnecessary to point out that ethnography cannot be done by any bright person who happens to be a participant in a society. Too often (particularly in doctoral research or school district evaluation) we have allowed anyone who can see and hear and write a sentence to do "descriptive research," and some call that ethnography. Every person who can change a tire is not a mechanic; a person who can repair a faucet is not necessarily a plumber; anyone who can drive a nail is not a carpenter; all who can do a chi square are not statisticians; nor does it follow that everyone who can write a paragraph describing an encounter between a teacher and a parent is an ethnographer.

Who then is an ethnographer? It is easiest and most reliable to define an ethnographer as a person who *has published* one or more ethnographies— just as a novelist is a person who has published one or more novels. Based on such a definition, a person could be employed based on proven ability. The person's work and the criticism of that work can be reviewed and the decision can be made based on previous accomplishment. This is likely to be expensive if one seeks proven excellence.

Another method would seek persons whose education and background have been systematically designed so as to produce ethnographers. Such persons should be able to demonstrate in some fashion that they have been trained in ethnographic methods, particularly participant-observer field methods. They should possess in-depth knowledge and understanding of anthropological theory and models. They should be able to supply some unpublished examples of the application of these theories and models and some type of ethnographic work in which they have engaged. Examples of these may be unpublished papers, master's and/or doctoral theses. Although the run-of-the-mill anthropologist may be more likely to be a good ethnographer than the run-of-the-mill teacher, the risk of getting a poor ethnographer based on a degree alone still exists. I would not bet on a horse unless I saw its record of past performances under track conditions similar to those of the race day. As noted earlier, some anthropologists will hold certain biases about educational cultures that will distort their data and make their conclusions as useless or harmful as the nonanthropologically trained educator's.

Entry and Access. Lots of things are descriptive. A whole class of statistics is "descriptive;" an essay can be "descriptive;" a map or picture is "descriptive;" a case study is "descriptive;" and ethnography, in its particularly holistic "thick" sense, is "descriptive." Because of this situation, I have come to despair of the use of the term *descriptive research,* for it masks so many kinds and so wide a quality of research. Ethnography is a very special kind of description—a thick description—requiring special skills and a well-defined method.

Essential to "thick description" is that the data that may be collected by the researcher not be limited by personal bias, theoretical framework, or the setting. I have already spoken about some of the limitations that can be due to the personal bias of the researcher. Some discussion of the limitation that may be set by an a priori, firmly believed, and rigid theoretical framework will be discussed later. Here I would like to discuss the nature of the research setting and entry into the field as that can restrict data collection and the quality of the ethnography and the research.

It is undoubtedly necessary for every ethnographer to establish some type of "contract" with the society to be studied. Such a "contract" may include: specifications about what records may and may not be examined; where the ethnographer may or may not go, when, and under what circumstances; which meetings may be attended and which are closed; how long the researcher will stay in the field; who (if anyone) has access to the field notes, and even who has the right to review and/or approve the ethnography and its analysis prior to publication, or under what circumstances they may or may not be published at all.

Although some agreement about the research conditions and their possible effect on the society being studied is, of course, necessary, a good general rule of thumb is that the more restrictions placed on the researcher, the more likely they are to adversely affect the research and its usefulness. For me the bottom line is this: I would never engage in ethnography (or other types of research) if I were required to amend my findings or their analysis to suit *anyone else.* I might take the risk of not being allowed to publish but never of being forced to publish (under my name or not) findings that I felt were incorrect or misleading—this includes the exclusion of important relationships because they were embarrassing to the society being studied.

Here is the crux of the matter. An ethnographer studies real, living and dynamic people and societies. What is found can help or hurt certain people and relationships. These people will recognize this fact before, during, and after the field research, and they will try to influence the researcher to "understand" their position, behavior, and point of view. In fact this propensity of the "natives" to want the researcher to understand their position is always an effective key to the researcher's ability to obtain certain data. Of course, the ethnographer wants to know and therefore seeks the "native" interpretation of events and meaning of events—this is called the *representational* model of the society. But the researcher must be free also to seek the *operational* model (the view of events and meaning as seen by the "unbiased" researcher) and then to combine this with the representational model into a final explanatory model based on the anthropologist's understanding of the representational and empirical models. Anything that restricts the ethnographer's liberty to complete access to data seriously restricts the research and its usefulness.

There is absolutely no use in instituting a research project to discover if, in the final analysis, one is prohibited from discovering.

Depending on the situation, there are techniques for safeguarding individuals and/or organizations from harm without prohibiting the development of good ethnography and its findings. If the research is more nearly *pure* research—that is, concerned only with conceptual relationships and not initiated in order to effect any change at the specific organization level—the following can be recommended: All names and places can be coded. Only the type of organization or society and its characteristics survive such coding. No one should be able to identify the specific organization or society or any of its individuals under these circumstances. My own ethnogrpahy of the Robertsdale School District (Iannoccone & Lutz, 1970) is such an ethnography. I think it is impossible for anyone to identify the school district or the individuals concerned. Yet, I have had dozens of people tell me that the events and situations described in Robertsdale are just like those in their own district. We were interested in relevant and conceptual variables that could help explain governance in local school districts and we were apparently somewhat successful in that effort *without* identifying the specific persons or place.

But what if that research had been commissioned and subsidized by the Robertsdale School Board? What if the major purpose of the research had been an evaluation? I think there are two answers that can be lived with. For me the more acceptable is to develop a "contract" providing for two products. The first is the evaluation for the school district. It is produced through the free and open access necessary to all ethnography. It may well produce some findings that the client did not wish to discover—but there they are. The school district is free to accept and use these findings or to reject them as "untrue" and protect its status quo. The second part of this same contract would allow the ethnographer to develop the coded type of ethnography from the same data and after some specified time (usually one to three years) to publish a Robertsdale type of ethnography which leaves the particular person and place unnamed, unharmed, and unchanged.

Another type of contract is possible which would prohibit *any* publication (other than "in-house") unless approved by designated persons within the society. I would not be pleased with this type of "contract," but I could accept it, under certain circumstances, as long as I was free to seek data and include it and its analysis in the in-house report. Under no circumstances can I imagine myself permitting in-house "editing" of the data and interpretations except as that editing and interpretation were considered data for the final report. When the researcher is not free to seek data and write the final report, the research-evaluation is best called *whitewash* and not evaluation-research.

Cross-cultural perspective of the research.   In the preceding section, I mentioned that the search for important and recurring variables in an ethnography must go beyond the narrow focus of a classroom or school. This expansion beyond the culture of a single classroom or school I shall refer to here as *cross-cultural perspective.*

Three types of cross-cultural perspective may be identified. The first deals with the perspective of the researcher and will be dealt with under "anthropological theory." Of the two types of cross-cultural perspectives related to the research, the first concerns a single educational phenomenon as it is observed, described, and explained in *more than one* culture. This is important research but not exactly what I have in mind here. For the present, I am concerned with research limited to a single national culture. The second type involves the notion that a classroom may be observed as a cultural system, the school observed as a cultural system, and the school district and the larger society may each be observed as cultural systems-all within a single national culture. As we move from each subcultural system to the broader system, the actors in each system often hold alternative roles across the arbitrary cultural boundaries requiring separate behaviors, and such roles may be governed by different, often conflicting sets of expectations, norms, and values. Any specific observed behavior or representational meaning may be affected by or be affecting any other. Behavior is a classroom cannot be understood apart from the influences of smaller peer groups, the larger school, and the total school district-community. It is this particular cross-cultural perspective that I wish to examine here.

One can see how conditions that restrict data collection, mentioned in the previous section, must affect the researcher's ability to bring a holistic cross-cultural perspective to the ethnography. When viewed as a separate entity, the potlatch of the Kwakiutl Indians of the northwestern United States seemed to many anthropologists irrational and destructive to the culture. Later, more holistic ethnographies viewed the potlatch as a rational, integral, and necessary part of Kwakiutl culture.

The foregoing may serve to "illustrate" the cross-cultural approach I have in mind. If the potlatch is viewed as a cultural phenomenon, separate and by itself, its meaning and rationality is lost. If one views the classrooom as a culture, separate and by itself, it is likely that much of the meaning and rationality of the behavior observed will be lost. The more the researcher is limited in opportunities for data collection, the thinner the description; the thinner the description, the poorer the ethnography—all things being equal. Therefore, it is argued that the narrower ethnographic approach to the study of education is less satisfactory to the holistic cross-cultural approach.

Anthropological theory. A third meaning of the term *cross-cultural approach* is sometimes used. This refers to the perspective the researcher brings to the research rather than the perspective of the research itself. In this reference, we refer to an understanding of the ethnographic literature describing other cultures. To this I would add a broad knowledge of anthropological models, concepts, and theory. This combination, which I refer to as *anthropological theory,* is the fourth ingredient required to do good ethnography in education.

Some have argued for purely descriptive ethnography, without the use of theory to guide data collection or to provide meaning or understanding of the data collected. I acknowledge the fear of allowing preconceived "theoretical" notions to bias and distort the ethnography (the data), but I am at least as concerned about the random collection of data (unguided by any concept), the covert or unspoken bias that any social scientist must bring to his/ her observations, and the dangerous discovery of something left unexplained.

It seems to me to be a terrible wast of time merely to wander around collecting things without any concepts to guide what one collects and, of necessity, avoids collecting. Imagine someone, totally without concepts, wandering about empirically attempting to understand the world by collecting, in some fashion, everything he comes upon and not knowing any system to classify those specimens. The notion boggles the mind. Everyone—layman and social scientist alike—must have, or must invent, some system to categorize the data observed.

This necessity leads directly to the second concern. If we must operate with some conceptual notions, the failure to be explicit about them is as self-deceiving and at least as likely to distort the ethnography as is the explicit statement of that conceptual framework.

Finally, disregarding the first two problems of attempting ethnography totally without concepts or without specifying them, the problem of discovery of something without at least an attempt to understand its meaning and relationship to other existing knowledge is at best not very useful and, at worst, very dangerous. Imagine someone empirically experimenting with the elements carbon, hydrogen, oxygen, and nitrogen without understanding the theoretical properties of $C_3H_5(NO_3)$, nitroglycerin. The same potential exists in the social sciences. At one level we may foment revolution; at another we merely replicate Columbus's error when he failed to understand that he had discovered a "new world." At the very least, knowledge alone is a lower-order activity, in the cognitive domain, than is understanding and synthesis.

Often models developed from less complex societies can provide useful, fresh, and creative views of our more complex organizations. Wolcott, (1977), used Hoebel's (1972) definition of moiety to examine the adopting (or lack of adoption) of an innovative practice in school districts. His ability to use this model makes the research more generalizable. This ability to draw from a broader range of anthropological models and theories, in order to make sense of the data and to understand them, I refer to as the *fourth ingredient.*

In its narrow sense, and as defined up to this point, ethnography is thick description alone. But I would suggest that, if limited to this narrow definition, ethnography falls short of its research potential. As description alone it is knowledge alone, a body of data without analysis. It is the cognitive domain of knowledge without understanding or synthesis. It cannot be generalized beyond the specific case. It is a useful picture of some culture or society, at some moment in time. It preserves something that may otherwise be lost. In that sense it is useful and may even be fascinating and interesting. But it is useless in helping others explain or predict complex human behavior in organizations.

Geertz (1973) has said, "Any chronic failure of one's explanatory apparatus ... tends to lead to a deep disquiet ... " (p. 100). Further he states, "Cultural analysis is (or should be) guessing at the meanings, assessing the guesses, and drawing explanatory conclusions from the better guesses—not discovering the continent of meaning and mapping out its bodyless landscape" (p. 20). Finally and concisely he says, "... it is not worth it, as Thoreau said, 'to go round the world to count the cats in Zanzibar" (p. 16).

Thus, ethnography is thick description, but that thick description is not sufficient for what is proposed here, for it leaves us without prediction or explanation. Through research, meaning and understanding can (or should) be brought to human experience in complex organizations. As Harris (1975) points out:

> The manifest inability of our overspecialized scientific establishment to say anything coherent about the causes of life styles does not arise from any intrinsic lawlessness of life-style phenomena. Rather, I think it is the result of bestowing premium rewards on specialists who never threaten a fact with a theory (p. viii).

It is this threatening of facts with a theory, that is the fourth essential element of good ethnography. If a fact cannot be accounted for by a theory, then either it is not a fact, or if you are sure it is a fact, the theory is insufficient and must be modified. Confronted with this dilemma, the ethnographer returns to the field for additional observations, informant data, to consult some written record, or recheck a diagram. If additional observations as well as informant information and other data sources consistently reaffirm the fact, the ethnographer carefully gathers data about the conditions and related variables surrounding the fact. This information is then used to modify or restate the theory, making it a better theory. Through this process Columbus would have understood that he had discovered a "new world," and not a westward route to the East. This is the process of good ethnography and through that process, I believe, what presently passes for educational theory can be improved.

SUMMARY

I have tried to demonstrate that there is a critical need in educational research to broaden our perspectives not only beyond the usual psychostatistical research but also beyond the narrow focus of face-to-face interaction and micro-ethnography. In doing so, ethnography in schools must go beyond the usual scope of the classroom or the individual school, explaining educational processes in the broader context of the school district and the culture. Further, the concepts of face-to-face interaction and transaction are not sufficient to accomplish this goal. Four essentials in accomplishing this research goal have been suggested: (a) a trained ethnographer as researcher; (b) thick description as ethnography, used as the data base; (c) a cross-cultural approach to data collection; (d) the use of anthropological theory in analysis. By engaging in such research we are very likely to develop more meaningful hypotheses about educational processes and more humanistic educational theory.

REFERENCES

Caws, P. Operational, representational and explanatory models. *American Anthropologist,* 1974, *76-(1),* 1–10.

Evens, T. M. S. The predication of the individual in anthropological interactionism. *American Anthropologist,* 1977, *79-(3),* 579–597.

Geertz, C. *The interpretation of cultures.* New York: Random, 1973.

Harris, M. Cows, pigs, wars and witches. New York: Random, 1974.

Hoebel, E. A. *Anthropology: the study of man* (4th ed.). New York: McGraw-Hill, 1972.

Iannoccone, L., & Lutz, F. W. *Politics, power and policy: the governing of local school districts.* Columbus, Ohio: Charles E. Merrill, 1970.

Lex, B. Voodoo death: new thoughts on an old explanation. *American Anthropologist,* 1974, *76-(4),* 818–823.

Lortie, D. C. *School teacher.* Chicago: University of Chicago Press, 1975.

Lutz, F. W., & Ramsey, M. A. The Voodoo killer in modern society. *Personnel,* May–June 1976, 30–38.

Ramsey, M. A. Cultures and conflict in local school districts. In F. W. Lutz & L. Iannaconne (Eds.), *Public participation in local school districts.* Lexington, Mass.: Lexington Books, 1978.

Smith, L. M., & Geoffrey, W. *The complexities of the urban classroom.* New York: Holt, Rinehart & Winston, 1968.

Wolcott, H. F. *The man in the princpal's office.* New York: Holt, Rinehart & Winston, 1973.

Wolcott, H. F. Criteria for an ethnographic approach to research in schools. Human Organizations, Summer, 1975, *34-(2),* 111–127.

Wolcott, H. F. *Teachers vs. technocrats.* Eugene, Ore: Center for Educational Policy and Management, 1977.

4 Triangulated Inquiry—A Methodology for the Analysis of Classroom Interaction

Maurice J. Sevigny
The School of Art
Bowling Green State University

INTRODUCTION

The history of science is replete with examples of conflicting systems of knowledge that emerge within particular disciplines. During times of conflict, basic theoretical assumptions and presuppositions of the taken-for-granted research models, or paradigms, are questioned. Kuhn (1970, p. 6) labeled such conflicts *scientific revolutions.* He built upon the notion that scientific revolutions are a natural factor in scientific advancement and demonstrated that science possesses built-in mechanisms that insure the relaxation of the restrictions that bind research, whenever the paradigm from which they derive ceases to function effectively. Led by paradigm change, scientists often adopt new instruments and look in new places; more importantly, during scientific revolutions, scientists often see new and different things when looking with familiar instruments in places they have looked before.

When a new paradigm is evoked, scientists will be reluctant to embrace it unless convinced that two all-important conditions are being met. First, the new candidate must seem to resolve some of the outstanding and generally recognized limitations of the existing paradigm. Second, the new paradigm must promise to preserve a relatively large part of the concrete problem-solving ability that has accrued to science through its predecessors. As a result, new paradigms often preserve, modify, or build upon the concrete parts of past methods, while permitting additional concrete problem-solutions.

We find evidence for scientific revolution in the proliferation of philosophical debate over fundamental issues. Within the discipline of educational research we find a growing discontent with the experimental methods adopted from psychology and the taken-for-granted paradigms derived from physical science. This critical attitude has produced a climate for scientific revolution for paradigm change.

The major assumption underlying this paper is that it is both *feasible* and *necessary* to develop alternative orientations toward data collection strategies which might further research on those questions which are less amenable to experimental design or pure statistical treatment. We need to develop methods to collect data related to discovering how the process of schooling interacts with the student's predispositions, purposes, assumptions, values, expectations, and attitudes—what I refer to as *the participant perspective*. My own research (Sevigny, 1977) has focused upon the study of classroom interaction in the university studio art classroom. To move toward a holistic understanding of studio classroom events, I have developed a multiple methodology which I call *triangulated inquiry*. Triangulated inquiry represents an attempt to alter the traditional approaches to classroom investigation.

In this paper, I offer a rationale for adopting such changes. Secondly, I shall explicate the features of some alternative practices adopted from the social sciences. Finally, I shall present the specific features of *triangulated inquiry*.

THE LIMITATIONS OF TRADITIONAL OBSERVATION MODELS

In their review of the research on teaching, Dunkin and Biddle (1974) concluded that most findings on achievement variables have minor significance; in many cases, there is contradictory or "muddy" evidence. At best, those few positive findings can only be classified as tentative. We know much more about the nature of instruction than we knew, largely because of researchers' use of classroom observational instruments. Yet, we know far less than many would have hoped about the relationship between student achivement and teacher/student interaction. Perhaps Rosenshine and Furst (1973) have a point when they suggest that we have spent too much effort in instrument development when our efforts would have been better directed toward testing the utility of those instruments for studying the social events which accompany instruction.

Researchers of student achievement have generally employed what has been called "a black box approach"; that is, operationally defining and crudely measuring an assumed linear relation between input and output variables. Their efforts have been *quantitative;* that is, rooted primarily in statistical theory and analysis. This may be due to their having been trained to ask the kinds of questions which lend themselves to experimental testing and variable measurement.

Research training, at the graduate level, has been grounded in statistical theory and quantitative strategies. Many social scientists have criticized observational systems for their failure to provide qualitative data related to how the members of the classroom society construct interaction into mutually organized social activity. For example, Speier (1973) argued that, because systematic observers generally ignore such data, they have designed narrow classification schemes, based on informed learning theories. These theories in turn become the rationale for studying the classroom environment and provide the researcher with theoretical purpose and the means for generating hypotheses out of those purposes. Of the Flanders system (Flanders, 1970), he wrote

> What is treated as a relevant problem of study are the types of teacher influence used in the classroom—is solved by quantitative inspection of the amount a teacher talks, a student talks, or the amount of silence of both. But what is amount of talk? The number of words per minute? The number of sentences? Is the teacher's silence equivalent to the students' silence? What is silence? Is it merely the measured interval of time between two uttered sounds? Or might it be something far more subtle, such as unwillingness to speak when called upon to do so, or a pause in the middle of one's remark that clearly belongs to that person and to that remark? (p. 23).

Speier underscores questions of a *qualitative* rather than *quantitative* nature—questions which should be answered if a complete (or *holistic*) understanding of social interaction is to be attained. My own position would assert that neither approach used alone could be as effective as an approach which combines the two. The same belief was voiced by Margaret Mead (1976) when she wrote:

> We must come to realize that the extension into the human world of the methods of the physical sciences can be stultifying and dangerous. It is only when we realize that there are two distinct and complementary—rather than antagonistic—sources of knowledge that we can fully develop methods appropriate to each other and consider how such methods can serve to support and reinforce each other. Many researchers take the position that human understanding is arrived at through a capacity for inter-subjective inference and human empathy (p. 905).

The observer's capacity for subjective interpretation of human action is generally ignored in the methods systematic observers use to go about their recognition of specifically coded behaviors in the first place. The result has often been that coded systems use such overly generalized categories as "teacher asks question' and "student responds," which lend themselves primarily to frequency measurement and say nothing of the unique and qualitative dimensions of classroom interaction. Recognizing the importance of the subjective view is long overdue in educational research.

The shortcoming of traditional observation systems is that they quantify, through the screen of the observer, and they do not qualify, through the screens of the participants. Systematic observers have chose to ignore the *internal* states of the participants of the classroom setting. Educational research needs a change in research methodology which would enable classroom investigators to collect *subjective* data.

In summary of the state of the art, I have found that the search for single variables to explain learning outcomes has to be less fruitful than a search for related, or clustered, variables. Past research has failed to carefully map out the complexity of classroom learning. It has proceeded to data processing before understanding the contexts against which the variables are considered. Past efforts have relied too heavily on available and popular instruments because they were convenient, not because they were most appropriate to the real questions that were being asked. Though past efforts may have considered qualitative questions, they have not attempted to find ways that such data could be made more amenable to analysis. Finally, they have failed to interface the quantitative and qualitative data, since they had little regard for the contributions each can make to the other. They have failed to perceive the strength that could be found in the their combined capacity for rich description. Until educational research tries to deal with such deficiencies, any attempts to find causal explanations for schooling outcomes will remain primitive. I do not contend that quantitative methods are necessarily wrong, but used alone they are inadequate. The potential strength of a multiple approach will now be examined.

QUALITATIVE RESEARCH

Ethnography: Participant Observation and Informant Interviews

The task of the qualitative methodologist is to capture what people *say* and *do* as a product of how they interpret the complexity of their world. In order to grasp the meaning of a person's behavior, the qualitative researcher seeks to understand social events from the person's point of view—to gain understanding through the participant's perspective. Anthropologists often employ the drama metaphor: the researcher, rather than appearing in the audience watching the drama unfold on stage, is himself on the stage, acting a role in the production and interacting with the other actors. Research which examines phenomena from the actor's perspective is commonly referred to as *participant observation.*

It is misleading to regard participant observation as a single method. Rather, in common parlance, it refers to a characteristic blend or combination of data-collection techniques that are employed to study social phenomena in natural settings. That is, participant observation combines several methods toward a particular research end. That end is *analytic description* in the form of written accounts called *ethnographies.* An ethnographic description employs concepts, constructs, propositions, and empirical evidence through thorough and systematic data collection, classification, and reporting. What is reported are the unique variations of social phenomena as they have been observed or experienced in the actions and the language of the participating members.

Although the term *participant observer* is widely used in the social science literature, few attempts have been made to separate differences in the participant observation research stances available to scientific observers. The kinds of data researchers gather will depend in part upon how they participate in the setting. There are four possible research stances for the participant observer: the complete participant, the participant-as-observer, the observer-as-participant, and the complete observer. My research (Sevigny, 1977) makes use of a multiple comparative case study design which enabled me to study similar instructional events from the varying vantage points afforded by each of these four stances. It seems fair to say that in those few studies which have employed participant observation in classroom settings, researchers have generally assumed a stance of the observer-as-participant, or the complete observer. In most cases, it has not been feasible for the investigator to assume the role of a student participant.

There are at least three reasons for supplementing direct observation with student participant report:

1. The organization is typically being manifested in several locales simultaneously.
2. The organization has typically been in existence for some time before the scientist undertook his study.
3. Many of its features or determinants (i.e., motives, intentions, interests and perceptions of its members) are only imperfectly inferable by direct observation.

The first two reasons show a need to supplement the researcher's own observation with indirect observation reports, which can be obtained only from perceptive persons who were on the scene in the scientist's absence. These persons are called *informants* and they must be carefully questioned for the researcher to piece together the facts and the validity of the informant's account. This particular field strategy is known as *informant interviewing*. It is a regular feature of the participant observation methodology.

The need for subjective data emphasizes yet another reason for interviewing the members or participants concerning their motives, their intentions, and their interpretation of the events in question. The investigator can thus obtain a critical check on the validity of some of the inferences he makes about the subjective side of events. By assuming an active part in the relevant activities of the group, the participant observer is receiving the same localization as ordinary members; he acquires a perspective which allows for his successful participation, and consequently he encounters similar events and experiences. In this way, the researcher acquires some sense of the subjective side of the events which he could less readily infer if he observed without taking part. Having become a part of the phenomena, the researcher has attained personal knowledge and the question of validity is not tested against the corpus of scientific knowledge but against the everyday experience of a community of people.

Although the active participant observer can acquire some sense of the subjective side of experience, this sense still remains his own and it cannot be assumed to represent that of others. Informal interviewing of the feeling states of other participant members of the same setting is necessary to supplement, or to validate, the generalizations which the members hold. The research function of the empirical observer's participation is bringing to awareness the subjective issues which can be probed through informal interview of the other *responders* in the setting. This particular research technique is known as *respondent interviewing*. Both informant and respondent interview data are central to a triangulated methodology.

The qualitative observer may also collect a variety of other data for use in his final analysis and ethnographic account. These data may include personal documents, diaries, photographs, video or audio recordings, institutional records, sample products, or anything which may be potentially useful to holistic assessment. Each of these may prove to be particularly important in obtaining a particular type of information in gaining a richer understanding of complex social events (Webb, 1966).

Those committed to preserving the integrity of the situation maintain that any face-to-face situation is of importance in and of itself in determining the meaning of what goes on in that situation. Concrete human events are always to some degree dependent upon the situational context in which they occur and can be explained only through the perceptions shared in the situational context in which they have taken place.

Ethnomethodology

A holistic account demands a multiple methodology, which can provide a variety of interrelated data as well as produce multiple perspectives. A particularly strong holistic orientation is found in the approach taken by a branch of social research known as *ethnomethodology*.

The term ethnomethodology was first coined by Garfinkel (1967) to refer to the shift in attention toward investigations of the production practices—or the "doings"—which constitute the "social order" of particular social encounters. The research interests of ethnomethodologists are the regularities and changes in selected features of behavior that are meaningful to the individual members of a social setting. In social settings, actions do not occur as isolated events but, rather, are linked to each other as one member responds to, and anticipates the actions of, others. Any particular action, then, is embedded in a process of interaction involving several participants responding to each other's actions. Ethnomethodology permits description of social situations so that the researcher may gain understanding of how the members of a setting go about *constructing* and maintaining social reality. They examine, then, a multiple interpretation of a social event.

As a basis for interaction research, ethnomethodology offers educators an alternative paradigm for investigating the classroom setting. Ethnomethodological data collection incorporates a variety of qualitative methodologies, including those of participant observation. A difference, however, is found in its underlying assumptions and the basic theoretic stance it takes toward social interaction.

The philosophical features of an ethnomethological stance are derived from the work of Alfred Schutz (1966) who translated Husserlian phenomenology from epistemological to sociological concerns. The central features of Schutz's writings form the basis of the theoretical structure of all phenomenological sociology and of ethnomethodology in particular. Schutz focuses on the "actor's" devising of conduct through what is called *intentionality*. Intentionality takes on meaning according to the actor's system of relevance and the purpose at hand. Therefore it is subjective and unique to the individual's biographical situation. In order to understand social interaction, the actor must be able to "typify" the actions of those with whom he interacts. Schutz (1953, p. 18) labeled this phenomenon the "reciprocity of motives." The assumption made is that motives of another are typically the same as one's own would be in similar circumstances. This human capacity for typification allows us to anticipate the actions of others and to give meaning to everyday encounters. Schutz's conception of the typification process asserts that all knowledge of the world involves interpretive constructs sets of abstractions, generalizations, formulizations—

each specific to a retrospective level of thought. All thoughts originate from schemes of reference and are interpreted as "facts."

The ethnomethodologist is not concerned with the discovery of facts, but rather with the question of how people account for facts within particular settings. Their basic assumption is that individuals have meaning structures which allow them to operate on a social level. Furthermore, those meanings are believed to be contextually related to the events in which action occurs. A research question which investigates the interpretation and meaning that participants give to a social interaction is clearly an ethnomethodological problem.

Returning to Garfinkel's development of the ethnomethodological stance, we find a second major premise extensively expressed throughout his writing—the "documentary method of interpretation." Documentary methods of interpretations are the member's way of giving structure and order to a social reality. Ethnomethodologists seek to describe the documentary method by participating in the daily life of, and focusing their attention on what is normally taken for granted by, the participants. They refrain from judging the adequacy or predicting the consequences of a member's account.

Of fundamental concern here is the question of how order and meaning can be produced. The answer to these questions has been said to be found within "rules," "norms," and "definitions." Ethnomethdologists are concerned with these topics, but they distinguish between the "basic rules of everyday life" and the "normative rules of conduct." In the classroom, for example, the "normative rules" would be the sanctioned standards of the teacher or the group, and the "basic rules" would be the underlying and informal structure which allows individual members to make action choices toward or against the normative structures. Garfinkel (1963; p. 190) labeled these "constructive expectancies"; that is, the underlying expectancies which allow for the construction of social interaction.

Social order in the classroom exists as an emergent phenomenon, having no existence apart from the member's accounting and describing practices. Ethnomethodology views expectancies as a *general scheme of interpretations*—rules as not altogether normative but as quite problematic for the participant who must employ everyday logic or knowledge to determine whether the rule is appropriate to the situation. This, then, is the dynamic process by which norms become constructed and situationally interpreted, evaluated, and applied to social events.

One should emphasize that ethnomethodology is not an alternative sociology aimed at a more efficient solution to traditionally formulated social problems. Its very existence was stimulated by a new set of research questions and a new set of theoretical assumptions. As such, ethnomethodology must be viewed as a scientific enterprise which is separate from, yet a part of, the larger discipline of sociology.

In summary of the essential features of an ethnomethodological stance, one can say that:

1. Reality is interpreted rather than discovered; that is, reality is socially constructed, negotiated and maintained.
2. Human behavior is rational and rule-guided.
3. Human behavior is typified according to its contextual level.
4. Taken-for-granted rules (background expectancies) form the structural property of social acts.
5. Background expectancies are the basis of values and moral order, and although interpretation of this moral order is problematic, individuals are motivated toward compliance with their definitions for legitimating that order.
6. Social settings are self-organizing; individuals work to eliminate inconsistencies and discrepancies that arise in the setting.

TRIANGULATED INQUIRY

The notion of triangulated research is not entirely novel. Beittel (1974) referred to a method he called the "Roshomon Effect;" Lewis (1961) developed the stance he called "The Multi-faceted Panoramic View"; Cicourel (1974) promoted the concept of "Indefinite Triangulation." These proposed methodologies call for multiple comparisons of a single phenomenon, group, or unit at two or more points in time or they purport to use multiple perspectives to measure a single phenomenon at a single point in time. I propose *the comparison of several groups using varied perspectives and multiple procedures at two or more points in time.*

This conceptualization is rooted in an ethnomethodological orientation toward interpersonal events. It assumes that when a singular method or perspective is used as the absolute measurement, the researcher, in effect, has isolated his case study to an absolutism that limits its generalizability to its own content. Triangulated inquiry offers stronger potential for generalization through built-in mechanisms which rule out rival hypotheses. Through cross-validation strategies, researchers can design strategies for internal replication. The triangulated approach asks whether other plausible interpretations are allowed from differing participant perspectives, while allowing for cross-validation measurement.

In contrast to experimental methodologies, a research design using triangulated methods encourages flexibility in its initial implementation. Practitioners enter natural settings without predetermined hypotheses or preconceptions (or perhaps misconceptions) on the phenomenon or the setting. Consequently, data-collecting strategies change as field experiences progress. These designs are temporally developing and their strength lies in an increased potential for the heuristic discovery of variables and relationships among them, as they occur naturally and holistically in the setting.

Research design, data collection, and data analysis are interrelated components of this research approach. The progressive refinement of the observation focus is highly dependent upon such ongoing analysis.

A Multi Case-Study Design

My research is triangulated through a temporally developing multiple case-study design which expands the traditional concept of participant observation through incorporating *four* of the potential research stances available to participant observers. These are (1) the complete participant; (2) the participant as concealed observer; (3) the observer as participant; (4) the complete observer.

Participant Observation: The Concealed Observer. The participant as concealed observer is the most difficult stance to maintain (and in many situations impossible); its advantage is that the investigator protects the data from the invalidity of observer effect. Even though this stance can protect data against the effects of being observed, the strategy has limitations. The concealed observer has given up some investigative mobility and loses the option to question his host in ways natural to an interview. Hidden identity constrains the researcher to identify primarily with the subgroup of which he has become an active part and therefore delimits the nature of the data he has access to. Another danger is that in "going native" one can easily lose sight of observation goals.

In assuming a hidden identity as an art student in a university setting I was able to gain access to important data related to students. But I was not able to gain complete access to the teacher's perspective. Had this one field experience been the sole data-collection strategy, the resulting account would be less than holistic. A follow-up study, using the same instructor in a similar context, allowed for a change in the participant-observation stance. Hence, the multiple comparative case-study design was selected as a method of compensating for the limited range of data possible from any singular participant observation stance. A more complete notion of triangulated inquiry combines multiple observation perspectives with multiple data-collecting strategies, multiple data processing, and multiple data analyses. The comparative case study design stimulates constant reflexive comparisons, which quickly draw attention to similarities and differences, enabling speedy generation of plausible hypotheses.

My temporally developing design involved a four-year period of research which began with the full participant stance. Initially, little attempt was made formally to record or collect data. My goal was exploratory, to develop sensitive awareness to student-teacher interaction. In time, the research focus narrowed to student and teacher behaviors related to aesthetic judging and performance appraisal.

Five exploratory full participant field investigations served to bring to a conscious level the perspectives of (a) the artist, (b) the art student, (c) the studio teacher. As a full participant, I become my own research subject. Informal self-reflective analyses and historical reconstructions were used to draw attention to the appraisal dynamics from these three perspectives. To gain sensitivity to the perspective of the beginning student, I assumed the complete role of beginning music student for one semester. As a comparative technique, I followed this experience with full participation as a beginning acting student, then by a semester's participation as beginning student in a studio area in which I had no prior training. In the fifth exploratory study, I assumed a participant observer role as studio instructor. Following this exploratory phase, participant observation techniques were assessed and two additional case studies were designed for formal data collection.

Interwoven throughout these observation studies was a conscious attempt to attend to what Harris (1968) referred to as the "emic/etic analytic." The *etic* perspective has come to mean an approach coming from *outside* the system being studied. An etic approach to research derives its constructs from scientific theories *external* to the phenomena and previous to their investigation. Phenomenal distinctions and subclassifications are those already accepted by the scientific community. Systematic observation which employs standardized category classification falls squarely within an etic approach of scientific investigation.

Contrastingly, an *emic* approach is concerned with the study of behavior from the perspective of the participants—from *inside* a single, culturally significant unit. In an emic description, criteria are used that are drawn from contrasts made from within the system itself and are relevant in terms of the *internal* functions, interpretations, and meanings for the participants themselves. Participant observers employ the emic approach in that they focus upon the purpose, goals, motivation, attitudes, and interpretations of the participants of social phenomena. Qualitative research methods assume given a choice between the participant and the observer, it is the participant who has better access to his own inner state. It is further assumed that knowledge of that inner state is an essential factor for holistic understanding of interpersonal events.

Although the real-world distinction between the emic and etic perspective is not always as clear as the simplified construction just presented, the distinction can provide a practical framework for structuring participant observation research. In my own research, it provided yet another device for triangulating the observation data. The etic perspective served as the entry framework which allowed me to begin the task of organizing my observation perceptions into classes of behavior. As I became more aware of the internal orderings (the emic perspective) I could alter, modify, or build upon the initial classification scheme, thus refining the classification and description of social phenomena into a blend of the emic and etic perspectives. Separating each field investigation, and interwoven throughout them, was a conscious effort for formal study of the etic perspectives offered in areas, such as cultural anthropology, motivational psychology, linguistic analysis, social interaction, systematic instructional observation, symbolic interactionism, cognitive psychology, creative development, and learning theory.

In the formal data-collection phase, I assumed the research stance of the concealed observer, by adopting group membership as art student. Certain conditions were predetermined to insure that other participants in the setting would be unaware of my research intention and therefore treat me no differently than they would any other student. I performed all the studio activities expected of regular students, including all outside assignments. To protect my identity, I found it necessary to abandon my artistic ego and to adopt a less proficient style of drawing. Initial observations centered on student working process. This enabled me to mimic drawing styles and a compositional approach most like the average beginner. By so doing, I did not draw special attention to myself as student. I was careful to rotate my positioning and proximity to a variety of class members to provide a wide range of social and informant relationships, protecting the data from overbiased representation. Ethnographic notation was accomplished in the 3-hour time block that immediately followed each classroom experience.

I used several devices to assist my recall. Index cards were concealed among my art supplies, enabling me to make undetected shorthand notations of significant events or utterances. My art work served as a visual record for recalling my own participation. Two other recall strategies proved useful. The abandoned studio was photographed from many views. This series of location details was displayed above my typing station and a quick glance at a specific location usually triggered a whole chain of event recollections. The categorical classifications developed from the review of my field notes were also posted and provided additional stimulus for recalling episodes of the day.

The participant observer does not record every event observed; encyclopedic recording is neither possible nor particularly useful. What was included or left out depended upon the particular focus I was pursuing, and upon the particular relevance to the questions or major concern at the time. Typically, notation entries included accounts of student/teacher behavior, sample dialogue descriptions of nonverbal behavior, reconstructed histories, summaries of student responses, introspective analyses, behavioral frequency counts, attendance patterns, social interaction accounts, and methodological notations. At the end of each notation session, new questions emerged and general observation focal points were established for the subsequent session.

To facilitate analysis, the field notes were typed on ditto reproduction masters, with a 2-inch margin. Entries were subcategorized as observation notes (ON), methodological notes (MN), and theoretical notes (TN). Categorical labels and supportive information were periodically entered in the margin space, upon periodic review of the field notes (see Appendix A for sample). In the post-field analysis, the field notes were run off in duplicate sets and then indexed and cross filed. As evidence for a particular theoretical notation increased, it was elaborated upon in a longer essay and kept in a separate journal of "Theoretical Asides." Key propositions for further study were extracted from this volume. Though most of the descriptive propositions emerged during the ongoing analysis of field operations, many of them did not reach full maturity until the post-field analysis.

Informant/Respondent Interviews as Concealed Observer. Informal interviewing was the second major strategy used to collect data. The specific strategy followed the data-reliability criteria established by Wolcott (1975). The studio laboratory provided excellent opportunities for informal interviewing, as well as the chance to eavesdrop on peer dialogs related to class events. Respondent interviews were obtained during the regular interchanges that occurred during the breaks, before class initiations, and after class sessions. Frequent exchanges took place in the snack bar and many other informal occasions that brought students together outside the classroom setting. Initially these encounters were purely social. They served to establish relationships and provide the necessary atmosphere for the personal disclosures which came later. Respondent interviews functioned as a cross-validation technique for comparing personal responses to those of others in the setting. A conscious attempt was made to collect responses from a wide range of classroom participants.

Additional sources of data included transcriptions from group lectures and classroom critiques, photographs of student work selected for exhibition throughout the term, slides of the development of my own work, posted grades, summative interviews, and interviews with former students and colleagues of the subject.

Upon the completion of the field experience, my true intentions and observation activities were disclosed to the instructor and several of the key informants. The instructor/subject consented to a follow-up study, which would allow me to assume a more direct observation stance. This procedure permitted triangulating the observation perspectives. It also provided additional opportunity to collect verbatim dialogue and to expand interview data related to the teacher and student perspectives, while adding the additional perspective of the trained ethnographer and systematic encoder. By this time, the investigative focus has evolved to the examination of the behavioral patterns of student achievement types. That is, I was questioning the representativeness of data collected from my perspective and participation as a high-achieving student. I concluded that a holistic account should compare and contrast the interpretive perspectives, interactive patterns, behavioral responses, and production strategies of representative student types assessed as "advanced," "average," and "below average."

Participant Observation: The Complete Observer/Observer-as-Participant. The final field study was designed to compensate for the data-collection limitations of the full participant and concealed observer stance. Though the student population was new, the same instructor served as subject. This time, however, my research role was that of complete observer, moving gradually toward the observer-as-participant. In the initial five weeks of the course, my activity was limited to listening, watching, and recording; I did not interact with participant members. By mid-term the recording and observer effects became minimal and I became increasingly interactive, utilizing both informal and formal interview techniques to collect responses from both the teacher and students. To achieve a triangulated perspective, observations were conducted using three observational approaches: (a) field observation notation, (b) informant ethnographic observation, (c) systematic encoding.

The three observation approaches enabled studio instruction to be synthesized from three different, yet highly related, perspectives: the beginning art student perspective, the studio teacher perspective, and the perspectives of the trained observer viewing the interaction of the participant perspectives. To stabilize the record of the instructional process so that events could be carefully transcribed and analyzed at a convenient pace, collection of data was accomplished in three stages: (a) event recording, (b) event encoding, (c) event analysis. This procedure employed a reel-to-reel tape recorder with a dual track stereo recording option.

From the beginning, the teacher/subject wore a wireless transmitter allowing for sensitive sound pickup of all teacher/subject interactions. The stereo feature allowed for a recorded overlap of ethnographic data. Unobtrusive positioning of a whisper-sensitive mike and an amplifier made it possible to describe the nonverbal dimensions of the transactions without being detected by the participant members (see Appendix B for sample). The dual-track option allowed for simultaneous playback, as well as isolated listening for transcription purposes. These ethnographic overlaps proved invaluable in the post-field analysis and qualitative interpretation of classroom events. Observation notation sessions again followed each class period.

The dialogues were systematically transcribed with conversational structuring encoding (see Appendix C for samples). Field notations were examined to produce keener categorial classifications, amenable to systematic encoding practice and quantification. One hundred and fourteen qualitiative variations were developed into the *Sevigny Subscript Coding System* for use with Kelly Duncan and John Hough's (1975) OSIA (*The Observation System for Instructional Analysis).* These emic discriminators were extracted from classifications which emerged from the ongoing analysis and categorization of the field notations.

In the post-field phase, multiple analyses were performed upon the data and encoded interactions. These included (a) interaction event analysis, (b) standard variable analysis, (c) subscript variable analysis, (d) Pearson product-moment correlation, (e) conversational structuring analysis, (f) ethnographic notation analysis, (g) ethnomethodological analysis, (h) nonverbal behavioral analysis. This practice enabled the descriptive report to include a blend of qualitiatve and quantitative evidence. Triangulation was used to expand systematic encoding so that it produced a more discriminatory display of instructional events. Without a qualitative sense of the scene, before encoding, a systematic observer might easily misperceive the meaning of situational events and indexical language, since he is unlikely to "see" those events in the same way as the participants. A triangulated approach corrects for this limitation and allows the researcher to extrapolate and organize the essential features of phenomena into a descriptive account that includes the multiple perceptions of participant members. This synthesis of perspectives allows for a holistic grasp of classroom phenomena that would not be possible from any singular observation perspective or through any singular data-collecting strategy.

To be sure, a research design of this complexity demands much time and multiple research skills. As a novel approach, it is not free from flaw nor without limitation. Holistic assessment takes as its problem the nature of the total system, rather than a particular process or variable within the system. Such research produces in a mass of data and demands awesome amounts of time for its processing and analysis. Triangulated inquiry employs multiple operations each of which is, in effect, a small study with a research design of its own, but each of which is important and holistically related to others. It is difficult to present any one of these substudies in isolation from the others to which they are intricately connected. The reliance upon triangulated interpretation confronts the investigator with unusual problems of bulkiness in his reporting. Tabular summaries did facilitate the reporting by effectively consolidating classroom behavior. A new problem, however, becomes apparent. The flow of descriptive reporting is easily broken when tables are introduced. The writer is faced with a task of artfully weaving the tabular displays and the very telling and discrete qualitative incidents into a large and coherent pattern that communicates persuasively.

A temporally developing design, by definition, demands a longer investigation period. My study evolved over four years of intensive field operations and analysis. Such temporal factors must be considered by those contemplating selection of this type of design. In addition, triangulated inquiry demands a wider range of investigative skills. Furthermore, its potential for problem solving is dependent upon the creative imagination of its implementer. Discovery rests with perceptiveness and ability to make key linkages among isolated observation variables. Hence, the methodology is not suggested for every researcher but rather for those who have confidence in their capacity for creative problem solving.

My study provides classroom researchers in general, art educators in particular, with an illustrative model of the temporally developing and triangulated research design. I have found that the methodology offers a fruitful strategy for descriptive research. My study demonstrated, for example that ethnographic methods allow for descriptive discriminators which produce a keener analysis of the variables which operate in a given setting. Triangulation was used to expand systematic encoding so that it might produce a discriminatory display of instructional events. I also found that without a knowledge of the scene, prior to coding operations, the systematic observer may easily misperceive the meaning of indexical language and situational events—since he is unlikely to "see" those events in the way participants do. By connecting the spread and depth of the triangulated perspective, I was able to determine, and therefore grasp, an awareness that was much more extensive than that provided by any singular perspective or methodology.

This conceptualization of triangulated inquiry is not offered as the ultimate methodology, but rather as one alternative for creative investigators to explore and expand. It is presented, not as a solution, but as a stimulant for methodological challenge. One thing seems certain: until classroom investigators possess more solid and reliable descriptive information related to the orderings of social process in learning settings, the study of achievement will continue to shed but scattered light on the learning and schooling process itself.

REFERENCES

Beittel, K. R. *Alternatives for art education research: Inquiry into the marking of art.* Dubuque, Iowa: William C. Brown Co., 1973.

Cicourel, A. *Cognitive sociology: Language and meaning in social interaction.* New York: Free Press, 1974.

Duncan, J. K., & Hough, J. B. *The observational system for instructional analysis: General classes of instructional behavior and events.* Ohio State University, Department of Curriculum and Foundations. Columbus, Ohio, 1975.

Dunkin, M J., & Biddle, B. J. *The study of teaching.* New York: Holt, Rinehart & Winston, 1974.

Flanders N. A. *Analyzing teacher behavior.* Reading, Mass.: Addison-Wesley, 1970.

Garfinkel, H. A conception of, and experiments with, trust as a condition of stable actions. In O. J. Harvey (Ed.), *Motivation and social interaction.* New York: Ronald Press, 1963.

Garfinkel, H. *Studies in ethnomethodology.* Englewood Cliffs, N.J.: Prentice-Hall, 1967.

Glasser, B., & Strauss, A. Discovery of subsantive theory: A basic strategy underlying qualitative research, in *American Behavioral Scientist,* February 1965, *8*(6), 5–11.

Harris, M. *The rise of anthropological theory.* New York: Crowell, 1968.

Kuhn, T. S. *The structure of scientific revolution* (2nd ed.). Chicago: University of Chicago Press, 1970.

Lewis, O. *The children of Sanchez.* New York: Random, 1961.

Mead, M. Toward a human science. *Science,* March 1976, *191,* 4230; 903–908.

Rosenshine, B., & Furst, N. The use of direct observation to study teaching. In R. M. Travers (Ed.), *The second handbook of research on teaching.* Chicago: Rand MacNally, 1973.

Shutz, A. Common sense and scientific interpretations of human actions. *Philosophy and Phenomenology Research,* September 1953, *14,* 1–37.

Shutz, A. *Collected papers III: studies in phenomenological philosophy.* The Hague: Martinus Nijhoff, 1966.

Sevigny, M. J. *A descriptive study of instructional interaction and performance appraisal in a university studio art setting: a multiple perspective.* Unpublished doctoral dissertation, Ohio State University, 1977.

Speier, M. *How to observe face-to-face communication: a sociological introduction.* Pacific Palisades, Calif.: Goodyear Publishing Co., 1973.

Webb, E. (Ed.), *Unobtrusive measures: nonreactive research in the social sciences.* Chicago: Rand McNally, 1966.

Wolcott, H. Criteria for an ethnographic approach to research in the schools. *Human organization,* Summer 1975, *34*(2), 111–127.

Appendix A

Sample Field Notation with Margin Inserts

ON
eavesdropping
behavior

Today the portfolio critiques began. The procedure was for four students to go to the hallway and to hang their work (the 20 selected pieces) on the exhibition space and to wait for their turn. The model was late and so nine additional students bought coffee and sat around to eavesdrop on the appraisals.

ON
evaluative
event

breached
reality

ON
conflict in
interpretation
on scenic cues

The teacher strategy was similar to the class group critiques. In most cases he would ask the student to identify his preferences. Then he would begin to agree or disagree with the choices, offering the criteria for disagreement. In one case observed, the student had matted two. The student's selection was based upon the naturalism of the drawings. Mr. A did not like those two and suggested she mat two different ones. After the critique the student told me, "I just threw those damn things in at the last minute, I really think they're shitty!"

ON
continuum
ranking
behavior

While the critiques were in progress I noted several students reexamine their selections and make changes. On two occasions I saw students take pieces down from the wall while waiting their turn and replace them with "types" more like those being selected as "better."

ON
peer judgment
cue sharing
breaching

After observing four critiques the model came and we went into the studio. As we got there, one student said to me, "Please help me select my portfolio." I asked why. She said "'cause I think you will know what he wants and after watching the first few, I am sure what I like he won't."

TN
knowledge of
"other"
consensus

This seemed to indicate that she was not successful at cue search or cue match and that she had some sense of who was. At this point about six students gathered around, and one asked, "We'd like to see what you selected." "Why?" I asked. The consensus was that I was one of the better ones so that they wanted to see how they compared. "if we see what yours looks like, then we'll know better how we stand."

ON
visual
eavesdropping

The studio session was way out of pattern. Students were more interested in the evaluated activity and kept taking breaks or finding reasons for prolonged stays in the hall area. During the actual break, about seven of us were sitting on a bench in the critique vicinity. Mr. A decided to go for coffee. He tossed his keys and grade book on the chair beside us and left. We all looked at each other and the same thought impishly flashed across our minds. Giggling, one female

student said, "Don't you think we have a right to see our grade?" This
followed by "I dare you to look," "You dare me, huh?" in unison,
"*Yeah.*" She grabbed the book and fumbled through the pages, "Oh,
shit, the bastard gave me a fuckin' C." "Let's see..." We all shared a
glance with an eye glued to the end of the hall. I saw that the grades so
far were all between C- and B-. We all noted that they were lower than
we had anticipated. "I had no idea from the critique that I would get that
low a grade. Did you?" Another replied no. The consensus was that his
appraisals were ambiguous.

Critical comments do not seem to have meaning until the student can
interpret them through the grade symbol assigned to them
summatively. Students then begin by complaining about the
instruction. Insult led to insult. "He never says anything to help you,
just goes around giving verdicts like 'this is wrong that is wrong,' but
never 'Here's how to fix it!'" I felt this was a bit misperceptive. I thought
that the directions could be easily inferred from the comments and for
him to tell me explicitly would "rub me the wrong way." Obviously
different perceptions are operating in the setting.

One important feature of art learning appears to be the ability to
translate linguistic terms into task performance actions. To do so one
needs to be aware of the sensuous qualities of media and technique. One
needs to know the options. My wider experience range offers more
knowledge of options from the course history. Experimentation with
media and technical emphasis in fundamental courses develops a "tacit"
knowledge of options. Words somehow become referents for that
knowledge and when the word is heard, the aesthetic sense triggers
potential options.

---

cue match
by consensus
feedback need

TN
methods of
interpretation
TN
ON

TN
This could be
that I am at a
different level
of learning. I
can interpret
the comment into
action. Others
hear only the
comment. TN
cue translation

learning and
comprehension
tacit knowing

linguistic
knowing.

Appendix B

Sample Transcript from Dual-Track Recording of Nonverbal
(sample page)

The student comes to the table and proceeds to take her work out of the portfolio—the teacher stands back from the work and the student placing his hands on her hips. The student shrugs her shoulders, the teacher points to part of picture and begins waving hand across certain area—teacher points, squints. Student points to work, teacher steps in and takes sip of his coffee—teacher nods but continues focusing on work and then makes a flash eye contact with the student. Teacher scratches his nose and looks back to work. Teacher nods and then flips to a new painting, acknowledging the production response but reserving criticism. Squints at new painting and makes a comparative by placing next to another squinting again at them both. His voice tone carries little expression. Rather direct and bland in tonality no enthusiasm present in his delivery rather businesslike with coffee sipping offering him thought time. As he makes a negative comment, his head makes a shaking gesture. He is demonstrating a concept through symbolizing it on the blackboard trying to show how shape can be defined by color area rather than by linear outline. The student is pointing to a part of the picture which is illustrative of what he wants her to do. Teacher clarifies by pointing to another area in the work and then adding to the blackboard sketch. He is pointing to the part of the work in question and shaking head. When he makes a negative comment, his hands move in a jerking gesture—a choppy kind of movement across the specific area under criticism. This contrasts to a more flowing, dancing gesture that accompanies positive and holistic comments that relate to the unification and "the way it works together." With this student, the teacher has taken a position which is more behind the student than with the previous student whom he showed more positive affect toward (the A student). Hands are inserted in his pockets and now moves closer to the work. Glances quickly at student who remains rather stiff in her stance and neutral in her response. This student seems to accept the teacher authoritative role more than the previous who seemed to interact on a more equal and personal level. —The teacher uses hands to tie together related or unrelated parts. Hand gestures are necessary and important to direct attention focus to the isolate in question.

Appendix C

Sample Conversational Analysis

Observation 33:   students who are judged favorably are allowed to interrupt the teacher talk and to steal the speaker turn, whereas the poorer student is expected to assume a listener role.

For example, note how this A-level student gains control of the verbal interaction. ("cut-offs" are indicated by //).

    Brad: (pointing to one) this is the one that I just took the yellow and flowed it all in through there (gesturing)—then began to just change the yellows very slightly.

    Mr. A: mm hmm. It looks good, ah//

    Brad: and *this* (pointing to another)
is the one where she had us paint any shapes we wanted then paint over them with the still life. And this first one is in shades of green, except for that red dot that got on it in my portfolio.

    Mr. A: After you did the shapes you referred to the still life?

    Brad: Yeah, right.

In contrast, note Mr. Allen's interaction with the D-level student:

    Arlene: ...All of my pictures are like//

    Mr. A.: *Do* you feel that you do better on them when you have more time?

    Arlene: ah I//

    Mr. A: Okay. (turns away from this student and picks up another work)

5 Issues Related to Action Research in the Classroom— The Teacher and Researcher as a Team

Cynthia Wallat
National Institute of Education
Judith L. Green
University of Delaware
Susan Marx Conlin
Kent State University
and
Marjean Haramis
Hudson City Schools

One result of the increasing recognition of diversity in social goals in America is that teachers are faced with increasing demands to engage in professional and institutional analysis (Lynch, 1973; McCarthy, 1973; Wallat, 1977). These demands come from two sectors. The professional sector includes calls by the leaders of teacher organizations, such as the American Federation of Teachers, to build mechanisms for teacher input into research directions. The research sector supports this direction because of the need for teacher input into research which captures and describes various aspects of the natural setting of the classroom. Both of these statements of needed direction converge on a single issue: the need for the teacher to be an active participant in research and development teams.

Before proceeding, however, one problem must be acknowledged. Although both sectors have called for more teacher involvement in action research, the mechanisms for achieving this involvement and the value of this involvement have not been legitimitized. The present state of the art is a series teacher "shoulds," e.g., the teacher should be involved in research, and the teacher should extend his/her professional role to include teacher-as-researcher. These "shoulds" have generally been generated by educators and researchers without direct involvement of the teachers.

One of the central problems with regard to teacher involvement centers on the question: "What is the purpose of action research? Is action research something done *to* the teacher to obtain a label of good or bad teaching? Is it something done *by* the teacher alone for her own purposes? Or, is it something done *with* the teacher to gain an understanding of the teaching process? If it is something done *to* the teacher, then all that is required of the teacher is cooperation for the study. The purpose of research is thus limited to the researcher's view, and the participant's perspective of the classroom and the research is lost. If action research is something done *by* the teacher alone, access to the findings may be difficult as well as unvalidated. The limitations of both of the foregoing purposes will continue unless mechanisms to insure mutual validation become part of the dialogue of research. We argue that if action research is something done *with* the teacher, then the teacher becomes part of the research team and the potential exists for (a) mutual validation of the outcomes of the study, (b) generation of questions based on field practice, (c) refinement of the teacher's and researcher's perceptions of classroom processes, (d) extension of both the teacher's and researcher's roles.

In the sections that follow, issues related to action research and the enactment of the research role of teachers will be discussed. Section I is a select review of calls for redefining the teacher's role as researcher. Section II briefly discusses the potential conflict between the teacher's and the researcher's goals. Section III describes a series of steps used by the authors, two teachers and two researchers, in their move toward developing a collaborative action research team and toward resolving potential role conflict. Section IV provides a discussion of implications for development of action research.

SECTION I: THE CALLS FOR TEACHER INVOLVEMENT IN ACTION RESEARCH— A SELECT REVIEW

Calls for teacher involvement in action research can be placed in two groups; the first equates the role of the teacher as researcher with that of the teacher as diagnostician in his/her own classroom; the second views the role of teacher as researcher as that of the teacher working collaboratively with educational researchers to generate research questions and to carry out action research. Each of these views is discussed in the following section.

Teacher as Researcher/Teacher as Diagnostician

In 1963, James Conant presented a severe critique of *The Education of American Teachers.* He suggested that teachers needed to develop a research perspective in order to improve their classroom performance. The purpose of this perspective was professional development within the field. Conant felt that past training of teachers was not adequate and that teachers needed control over educational processes if they were to improve student achievement and to control their own professional lives.

Conant's criticism of campus-based pedagogical courses centered around his doubts that these courses offered student teachers the opportunity to study the processes of how social behavior emerges in the classroom. The general approaches to teacher training that Conant criticized were those that did not provide field experiences that allow student teachers opportunity to explore and perfect competencies based on how a teacher actually performs in public school classrooms. Conant also suggested that preservice should provide an experimental research frame of reference for teacher. The action research framework should center around student teachers' ability to evaluate the effect of their classroom organization techniques on student learning. Among the techniques for analysis Conant suggested were "If I do this, such and such will happen." "If a pupil behaves in this way in situation X, he will probably behave in this way in situation Y."

Conant's definition of the role of teacher as researcher seems to equate with the teacher as diagnostician and predictor of consequences of behavior within his/her own classroom. Action research defined this way is a vehicle for the teacher to implement a formative evaluation of the daily program.

Combs (1965) held a similar view to that of Conant, but he extended Conant's description of developing diagnostic research skills for teachers. His call for commitment of developing competencies that lead to analysis of classroom variables was presented in his definition of a "perceptual basis of social behavior" (p. 12). In his thesis on *The Professional Education of Teachers,* Combs outlined his theoretical rationale for this approach to action research by teachers as follows:

> The basic concept of perceptual behavior analysis is that all behavior of a person is a direct result of his fields of perception at the moment of his behaving: (a) how he sees himself, (b) how he sees the situation in which he is involved, and (c) the interrelations of the two. (p. 12).

Like Conant, Combs views the action research role of the teacher as equating with the role of the teacher as diagnostician. The major point of Conant's and Comb's calls centers around the need for individual teachers to monitor their own and their children's perception of classroom contexts. The need for teachers to have an increased awareness of teaching processes stems from their need to provide input into schoolwide evaluations and decision making, that is to have more control of their professional lives. Action research serves as a basis for evaluation in this call.

Combs and Conant did not directly address the broader action research role of the teacher, i.e., the teacher as collaborator with educational researchers, but they did lay the foundation for this role. Before teachers can have control of the teaching process they use to achieve their goals, however, they must become more aware of the processes they use to achieve their goals. Participation in collaborative research concerned with defining, describing, and analyzing their accomplishments of day-by-day classroom goals provides one major key to achieving increased awareness.

Teacher as a Member of the Action Research Team

A broader research role for the teacher has been urged for more than a decade (Lieberman, 1956; Haberman, 1970). More recently the American Federation of Teachers has spoken out (*Phi Delta Kappan,* 1978) and asked the National Institute of Education to address itself to the basic problem of building strategies to insure that research priorities emanate from teachers and classroom experiences so that the profession may begin "building a body of knowledge on what teachers know but may never have shared" (pp. 504–505).

The American Federation of Teachers advocates involvement of teachers in action research, but like Conant and Combs, it did not specify the mechanisms nor provide guidelines for accomplishing this task or determining the nature of the involvement. Section III will present one conceptualization of the value of this involvement and of how it is to be obtained. Before presenting guidelines for the teacher-researcher collaboration, however, we shall explore potential points of conflict between teacher and researcher.

SECTION II: TEACHER GOALS/RESEARCHER GOALS—POTENTIAL FOR CONFLICT

Recent reviews of the state of the art in evaluation have pointed to potential areas of conflict between the researcher's and the practitioner's views of the nature of action research (Bennett & Lumsdaine, 1975; Guttentag & Struening, 1975). Conflict can result when teacher and researcher do not agree about the conceptualization of the teacher's role in the teaching process and when their respective career goals and objectives clash.

Lieberman (1956) suggests that the role of the teacher has been defined in terms of the duties teachers perform as they manage learning—e.g., discipline and organizational structures. This conceptualization and other similar ones, such as those based on a researcher's commitment-based belief about the categories that reflect effective teaching—e.g., indirect behaviors vs. directive teaching behaviors (Dunkin & Biddle, 1974), have contributed to the lack of conclusive evidence on the nature of the teaching process as suggested by Conant and Combs. We must be concerned with the nature of the conceptualization with which we are working. Without a clear definition of the underlying conceptualization of teaching and of assumptions about the nature of the teaching process, researchers will have difficulty gaining access to classrooms and/or articulating the purpose and goals of their studies. To avoid conflict that can occur when teachers and researchers do not hold the same view of the process and the teacher's role, we must try to open and maintain dialogue between teachers, administrative staff members, and researchers. This dialogue will provide the key for ascertaining that the assumptions of all parties to be involved in the research will not lead to conflict and/or miscommunication.

Unless time is spent on clarifying the nature of the process being studied, methodology will not make sense to all the people directly and indirectly involved in the research project. A lack of communication can lead to anxiety about what the consequences of the outcomes will be on the classroom and school districts as a whole. The remainder of this section, will present an example of a completed reserch project in order to illustrate the nature of conflict that can arise and the effect of the conflict in conceptualization and articulation. This example was extracted from the on-going dialogue of the authors of this chapter about the nature of action research and potential problems and consequences of such research.

The following example was shared with the senior author by a teacher not directly related to the research project but one with whom this author has had considerable professional contact. The teacher in this example, teaches third-grade in a local public school in Ohio. She was asked to audiotape her discussion with the entire class for 10 minutes every day over the course of the week. The time of taping was left to the teacher's discretion. She was promised an analysis of her questioning style at the end of the project.

Since the teacher was familiar with Bloom's (1956) taxonomy of levels of thinking, she thought she would gain insight into her use of questioning strategies, but the feedback that arrived provided no such information. Six months after the project, the teacher received a copy of a letter sent to her principal thanking him for making the school available. The letter also mentioned that the analysis showed that the teacher's questioning style was "opinionated" or "directive."

The teacher in this example has gained considerable parental and professional recognition from her school district for her creation of multiple learning centers within an open classroom structure and for the quality of her program. The 10-minute tape segments on which the negative picture was based were recorded during the time the teacher set aside each day to discuss the procedures to be used by the students before they move to math centers. This segment was selected to meet the researcher's criterion of a segment in which the teacher interacted with the entire class. Since the teacher runs a center-based program, there are only limited times during the program day that she meets with the entire class; therefore, the time sampled cannot be considered representative of all teacher talk. The researcher, however, did not know this since he had spent no time in the classroom beyond the initial interview to obtain the teacher's permission and cooperation for the study.

Had the researcher taken the time to observe the class in order to gain background knowledge of the classroom structure, he might have been able to observe that being "opinionated" or "directive" at the particular time sampled fulfilled the teacher's objectives and instructional responsibilities. Had the researcher been in the classroom over time, he would also have had the opportunity to observe the outcome of this question/answer time and could have observed whether the children knew what was expected of them.

Given that the researcher did not open the dialogue with the teacher in order to clarify his goals and did not directly observe the classroom structure, the validity of the methodology and the outcomes must be questioned. In addition, this example demonstrates the potential negative effect that misuse or lack of clear articulation of findings can have on the professional life of teachers. Had the teacher not been perceived positively by administrators and parents in the district, had she not spent considerable time and effort in articulating her goals, and had she not been able to articulate the problems in time-sampling procedures used in the study, the consequences might have been greater. Although this teacher was able to offset the negative aspects of this research project, other teachers may not have the awareness of the teaching process that she has and, therefore, may not be able to offset such negative effects.

The foregoing incident is an example of action research "done to" teachers. The example supports Haberman's (1970) concern voiced in *The Art of Schoolmanship* that teachers are an "exploited minority" among professional educators. The teacher entered into this study with the hope that she would gain what Haberman and others call for, i.e., knowledge about the processes of teaching. Her hope was never realized. True, if teaching remains unreflective it remains unevaluated and, therefore, resistant to change, but lack of reflection must be attributed both to research strategies, such as those just presented, and to the lack of mechanisms to give teachers the opportunity to share what they know. Collaboration between groups of researchers and teachers can provide the bridge to solving the problem and to identifying the nature of the teaching process.

In addition to the problems already discussed, Haberman and other researchers concerned with the development of action research in the classroom have warned that at least two other problems face researchers in maintaining a dialogue and in gaining access to classrooms. The first has to do with perceived conflict between the researcher's and practitioner's roles. The second relates to the possible resistance of administrators to research that can be seen as a threat to the stability of the organizational and institutional arrangements of the school. The latter problem can be eliminated by a clear statement of the goals of the project, the construction of lines of on-going communication, and the establishment of mechanisms for sharing and disseminating the findings.

The first issue, potential conflict in objectives and career goals, can be minimized by frank acknowledgment of differences between the concerns of researchers and practitioners and by the establishment of collaboration and articulation mechanisms. This discussion may also serve as a catalyst for determining how both the researcher and practitioner can gain from the project. Acknowledging that the career goals and objectives of the researcher and the practitioner differ might lead to developing strategies of collaboration that can overcome role conflicts, such as the following outlines by Twain (1975):

1. The researcher's profession rewards publications that challenge existing values and assumptions of program practice.
2. The practitioner's professional rewards are based more on refining and less on challenging existing techniques.

Bennett and Lumsdaine (1975) go beyond pointing to potential conflict. These educators offer a specific suggestion for resolving potential conflict between the research and service roles of individuals in assessing educational programs. That suggestion is to build time for the researcher to serve as a "middleman" (p. 541). As a middleman, the researcher observes, feeds back information about the observation, and with the teacher, generates questions of interest to study.

To summarize, potential exists for conflict in action research, but professional educators suggest that a clear program of articulation and collaboration can reduce this threat. The next section presents the effort of one team, the authors of this chapter, to build an articulation framework and a collaborative study.

SECTION III: TOWARD ESTABLISHING A COLLABORATIVE TEAM FOR ACTION RESEARCH

The articulation framework for our research project was used to guide a team formation. This framework served to guide decision making and discussions between various groupings of the team members, the two researchers and two classroom teachers who are the authors of this paper. Although the catalyst for this article was a group meeting held six months into the project, numerous other meetings had taken place since the project's planning stage in the Spring of 1977. Two types of data form the basis of this section: a direct transcript segment from the six-month meeting and a summarization of the steps toward group formation. We hope that in sharing this team's collaborative efforts, we will provide both a mear s of dealing with criticisms discussed in the previous sections and a framework for others interested in establishing a collaborative research project.

Before presenting an overview of the project anJ the framework, we believe it is necessary to discuss what we mean by collaborative research. One area that role-conflict studies have not addressed is the area of differentiated roles of team members. Collaborative research means involvement of researchers, teachers, parents, administrators, and students, where possible; it does not mean that each has an equal role in decision making or input during all phases of the study. Role shifts occur depending on the needs of the situation. Continuity is provided by the researchers through the communication and collaboration network they establish with those involved in the study. For example, clarification of observation and findings requires intense teacher input. The teacher and the researcher have equal input at this point. When the researcher seeks to gain access, collaboration and communication is between researchers, administrators, and teachers. Parents and students, at this point, do not play a major role. On the other hand, when the teacher is conducting parent communication meetings about the project, the teacher will take the major role and the researchers a secondary or support role. Given this general definition of collaborative research and role definition within this type of effort, we now proceed to present the articulation framework that has enabled us to establish a collaborative team for an action research study in two kindergarten classrooms.

Steps for Developing a Collaborative Action Research Study: Articulating the Project

Eight steps of articulation have been used to date. Their purpose is establishing and maintaining a collaborative context, one in which those involved have the same frame of reference for what is occurring. This frame has been built slowly and systematically. The eight steps that form the articulation framework are:

Step 1: discussion of avenues of access for the study.
Step 2: discussion of needs that support initiation of action research projects.
Step 3: discussion of types of methodology and procedures available for helping to answer the questions of both the teacher and the researcher.
Step 4: discussion of how the use of new methodologies can be shared with students, administrative personnel, and parents.

Step 5: discussion of possible outcomes of each type of methodology used, i.e., long-range and short-range analysis; anticipated outcomes and unanticipated outcomes.

Step 6: discussion of responsibilities in terms of data collection.

Step 7: discussion of disseminiation logistics, such as obtaining legal clearance for dissemination and arranging for communication of research results to parents, colleges, and professional organizations.

Step 8: discussion of time management based on Steps 1–7.

Although presented as discrete categories for the purpose of discussion, in reality those eight steps are overlapping and interrelated. For example, discussions with teachers and administrators for gaining access covered all of these points.

Gaining Access/Articulating the Project.   Although actual permission was obtained from the administrators of the two schools in August 1977, steps toward gaining access had begun nearly two years earlier. In that two-year period, both researchers had had opportunity to meet with the kindergarten teachers in their role as supervisor for student teachers. During this time, the researchers and teachers were able to discuss the nature of observation techniques currently available, types of classroom research needed, research questions teachers might have, possible methodologies for capturing these questions, discussions of the contribution this type of research would make to our understanding of the nature of teaching, and ways we could share classroom research with others. As a result of these discussions, the teachers became very interested in participating in an action research study in which they would be active members of the research team. Their interest is reflected in the transcript segment presented later in this section.

With the teachers' permission, the research team spoke with their direct administrator, the principal, about the possibility of carrying out a naturalistic study of kindergarten teaching in their school. Both administrators were very supportive of the project. Since one teacher was in a university laboratory school setting, permission of her principal was all that was needed. The other teacher was in a public school and permission of the superintendent was also required. The public school administrator made the contact with the superintendent for the research team, attended the meeting, and helped articulate the project. The superintendent was delighted with the clarity of the study's design and saw the potential of using samples from tapes in both parent education and preservice education.

Procedures for Data Collection.   During discussions with the administrators and teachers, the responsibilities for each member of the research team with regard to data collection and analysis were presented.

<table>
<tr><td colspan="2" align="center">Chart 1
Design of the Study</td></tr>
</table>

Setting:	Two kindergarten classrooms in suburban Ohio. Kindergarten 1 (TM) is located in a university laboratory school.
	Kindergarten 2 (TH) is located in a suburban public school.
Sample:	Two kindergarten teachers and their respective students.
	(TM = 25 and TH = 24)

Data Collection

		September through May
Step 1	Videotape collection	*first + 2 consecutive days each school month week*
Step 2	Teacher's Audiotape Goals of each lesson	*first + 2 consecutive days each school month week*

Analysis of Data

Step 1:	Transcribe videotapes of classroom situations and audiotapes of teachers' goals and teacher perceptions.
Step 2:	Describe interactions according to the sociolinguistic ethnographic system.
Step 3:	Create maps based on conversational units obtained in Step 2.
Step 4:	Describe the social rules through analysis of the communicative and interpretive patterns on the maps.
Step 5:	Analyze teacher goals from teacher's audiotape transcripts.
Step 6:	Team meets with the teacher to
	a. Review tapes and maps
	b. Clarify goals
	c. Check validity of findings and descriptions.

Chart 1, the design of the study, presents a visual outline of the steps of the project.

As indicated in Chart 1, the setting of the study was two kindergarten classrooms in suburban Ohio. Kindergarten 1 was located in a university laboratory school which had access to videotape cameras and equipment. Kindergarten 2 was in a public school which also had access to a videotape camera owned by the school district. Permission to use the equipment was handled through the AV (audio-visual) services in each school. We presented the list of the year's taping dates to the respective AV services a few weeks before school began. The list also served as one of the articulation points of discussion with administrators.

Human Subjects Review Procedures.   In order to fulfill our responsibility to the community, administrators, the teachers, and the university, all had to be aware of any possible effects of the project on the classroom environment and possible effects on individual children. To meet this obligation, we prepared a presentation on the nature of the study and the effects of taping. The presentation to those involved was based on previous knowledge of researchers in the field. For example, we reviewed Fuller and Muller's (1973) summary of 13 years of studies using video-tapes and used the results of their analysis of 316 studies as background information concerning the position that videotaping has been effective in capturing the teacher's natural teaching style.

Since our major objective was to capture teacher/child interactions during different lessons, we were careful to describe the goals of the project in the same terminology to all concerned. A draft of a letter to parents was reviewed and modified by the teachers and administrators before parents were asked to give their permission for their child's participation. A copy of the letter to the parents and classroom visitors is included in Appendix A. This letter, along with the compete description of the design of the study, was submitted to both administrators of the school systems and to the Human Subjects Research Review Council at Kent State University.

Based on the presentation and the documents, the project was determined to be of no risk to students, teachers, and schools.

Time Sample.   The first hour of the school day was chosen for taping in order to permit possible exploration of the students' transition from home to school. Given this goal, the actual taping time started 10 minutes before the formal starting time of the school day and continued uninterrupted for 1 hour. No attempt was made to control what occurred. All teacher-student interactions were recorded systematically throughout the school year.

Teacher Goals and Objectives.   Unlike free conversation, the goals of each instructional context are usually set beforehand in the teacher's plan for the day. Since, in the reality of the classroom, goals often have to be changed or modified depending upon new situations that arise, we did not ask the teachers to dictate their goals for the lessons taped until after the children had gone home for the day. The purpose of asking the teacher to outline her goals was providing us with a method of correlating process-to-process variables. Chart 2 gives the guide questions for the teacher's self-interview.

Validating the Findings.   Since the sociolinguistic ethnographic system we were using had already been validated in an earlier study on process product outcomes (Green, 1977), our concern was to conduct an exploratory analysis of process outcomes in terms of social rules. Part of the analysis process included teacher validation of our findings. Researchers (Hymes, 1974; Scriven, 1972; Kaplan, 1972) have called for such construct validation. They support the need to capture the meaning of events or situations held by participants. In the study, to validate our findings, we asked both teachers to

---

Chart 2
Teacher's Self-interview

(a) Say day, month, date and year (e.g., Tuesday, September 14, 1977)
(b) Preschool session, i.e., 10 minutes before school
      Any specific goals?
      Anything that you remember that was special that you would like to comment on?
      Any specific organization? (After first day-any changes in organization?)
(c) First 50 minutes of school
    Nature of each lesson(s)
    Specific objectives for each lesson
    Any comments about anything special that you remember?
    Any visitors in the room? (not me)
    Why were they there?
    Any interruptions?
    Any changes in routine?
    Any change in objectives?
    Was there a student product? Please explain here if you have not already described the product in questions before this.
    Did you notice anything with the research today that should be considered for possible change in the future?
    Were there any reactions of the children to the taping today?
    Any complaints?

---

meet with us to review the goals extracted from their self-interview tapes and those identified in the analysis of the videotapes.

Steps For Developing a Collaborative Action Research Study: Establishing the Team

At the beginning of the project, each researcher was teamed with a single teacher (the one for whom she had advised student teachers). The first reason for this arrangement was that the researchers felt that it was essential to maintain rapport. To introduce a second person not familiar with that teacher's classroom environment might have produced unnecessary anxiety and interfered with data collection in the natural setting. We felt it essential that a close participant-informant relationship, one that went beyond the data collection period in the classroom, be maintained in order to bridge the potential gap that could have occurred between the two teams. To avoid a feeling of competition, each researcher took the responsibility of articulating what was occurring with the other research team, what kinds of questions we were beginning to explore, and what some of the similarities were between the two teachers. This type of sensitization process resulted in the discussions captured in the transcript segment presented later. As stated, this transcript segment reflects the first meeting of the entire research team six months into the project.

The second reason for the separation of the team and for the matching of a researcher with a particular teacher was logistical. Video-taping occurred simultaneously in the two classrooms, as did the interview and observation process. We felt that building two subteams was essential to efficient and reliable data collection. In addition, as stated in articles on criteria for ethnographically adequate description (e.g., Hymes, 1974), the researcher's knowledge of a culture plays a major part in the descriptive processes. We felt that by developing the two subteams, each researcher would develop a participant observer's understanding of the social situations being studied. The other, being naive to that situation, would then act as a check on the validity of the participant observer's perceptions of the analysis. This procedure, we believe, helps to bring more objectivity to the analysis process because the researcher who was in the setting takes on the role of participant informant for the researcher who is naive to the setting.

As indicated in Chart 1, the researcher's analyses of the videotape were systematically checked in meetings with the teachers. These meetings were held between the two researchers and the individual teacher. We did not bring the two teachers together to view the tapes since we are not attempting to compare the two teachers but are interested in describing each teacher's goals and how these are realized in the processes of teaching. Having given this brief description of the steps to access and project implementation, we now turn to the transcript segment from the first total group meeting mentioned previously. The reader will note that the teacher can use highly sophisticated terminology and are able to articulate the steps of the project as well as the issues involving action research. We feel that this reflects the efficacy of the approach we have used, since one criterion of ethnographic adequacy is agreement among participants of the conceptual scheme that gives meaning to the phenomena. As the reader will note, team members have a shared context and a shared set of concerns.

(The kindergarten teachers in the following segment of the audio tapes are Susan Conlin and Marjean Haramis. The researchers are Judith Green and Cynthia Wallat.)

> Susan: The teacher needs to be made aware that there is an
> acceptance and integrity for her role—that her role is OK. The
> first time I was taped I thought about such things as: Do I
> have enough "lesson?" Those thoughts very quickly went by
> the wayside, but it was only because the researcher's presence
> in the room flagged acceptance for everything I did and
> because of our discussions each day. I kept getting the
> nonverbal and verbal message that my role has integrity and
> that I am a member of the team. When Judith brings the
> equipment in, you forget it's there.

Marjean: Oh, you do! When I was talking with the children last time you were in, I was behind the jungle gym, and all of a sudden I saw Cynthia moving back and forth in the back of the room trying to get the children and me on camera. And I thought, Oh heavens! I forgot all about the camera.

Cynthia: That sounds like what happened in Susan's room. Before we had the wireless and we had to get as close as possible with the camera to pick up the interactions, Judith had all the equipment set up on a cart and was just getting ready to tape when Susan moved to another part of the room. Judith plaintively asked, "Are you moving" and Susan answered "Yes."

Susan: Do you know what happened? I think what changed for me was when I realized I wasn't a classroom teacher doing what was expected in a particular frame for research. I was the directed role and the research came from me or from what happened because of me. Once I realized that, I felt comfortable; and I felt, "Hey, this is very comfortable." It's nonthreatening and very comfortable. I'm learning, and I know you're learning.

Judith: Oh yes!

Susan: I know that I'm gaining. I know I have knowledge of the classroom that you haven't had a chance to experimentally tap. So, I learn from your terminology and your analysis. It's different because I don't have to think about how this research is going to turn out or how can I arrange to make something the researcher wants to happen. It happens and it comes from what I direct.

Judith: Right. The premise is that what is real in the classroom will happen again and again. If you don't get it the first time . . . well, if it's real, you'll get it again.

Susan: Real, that's it. You know, I think unfortunately that's what happened when you hear about most researchers coming in. For me, before this project, I thought a research team is coming in—Oh my God!

Marjean: I really did use to feel that way. The first year of the technology project [another project] I was suddenly confronted by researchers and people I didn't know and had no idea what their expectations were of teaching. No, if a researcher came to me and started talking about capturing the language of the classroom I would want to know whether they really wanted to ask a value question, such as, "Am I giving 'enough' discussion time?" or whether they had respect for my role and were going to respect my instructional roles and look at different behaviors at different times.

Judith: Right, we have to know when a child's speaking behavior occurs in relation to what. When we are doing the research, we have to know what is that behavior tied to. Sometimes it's tied to what happened three days before. Since we aren't in the classroom all the time we don't know what previous context a behavior might be tied to. We cannot make any valid judgments about whether the child's behavior is appropriate.

Cynthia: There are still a lot of things on those tapes that I could look at and not being in the room I don't know what you are doing. Then, how do I find out what you're doing? Do I sit back in my office and say, "Oh, she's doing this."

Susan: You know what's great? It's where your scheme of things fits in. I find the feedback sessions phenomenally helpful to me. With the multifactor frame you both have which I feel most comfortable with, you're touching on multiple faceted levels of research—visual, audio, tape by the teacher, your observations. You're hitting more than one level. If, for example, two researchers come in for a period of time with a piece of paper and attempt to document a particular phenomenon, such as social interaction with a scale, that to me is not enough documentation to tell what's going on in your room. I think multiple dimensional levels of research are important—what came before—what after—where they were in October—where they are going.

Judith: Marjean, what do you see as the value for you of the way we're dealing with the research project? I mean, we ask a lot of you. We come in and tape. We ask you to tape your goals and objectives or write them out. We take pictures of the children's work. Do you see those kinds of things as too time-consuming and obtrusive for you?

Marjean: They are time-consuming, but it makes me think about myself as a teacher. Am I really doing what I say I'm doing? Do I really follow through myself on what I think that I am doing? Am I giving the children direction verbally and nonverbally? Is their freedom within structure, or am I a "sit down," "do this"; "do that"! These labels—OK, we do have them. Am I showing warmth to the children, or am I so very strict? Just for me to see myself, am I really what I see myself as? I think the project has been of immense value to me. I'm interested in seeing more. Cynthia's always saying, "You're doing this. You're doing this." I want to see—am I really accomplishing what I want to do?

Susan: What's good for me is that articulating my goals at the end of the taping day forces me to face what do I want to do? Another thing is that I've become a better observer. I've become more aware of when I'm receiving cues from children and when I'm giving them.

Given that the reader now has a context for viewing the collaborative team, we turn to discuss implications of specific mechanisms introduced in the beginning of Section III to action research.

SECTION IV: IMPLICATIONS OF ACTION RESEARCH

Avenues of Access for Studies.   As demonstrated in the previous section, one important consideration of gaining access for classroom research centers around the nature of goals of the research project. Discussion of goals with teachers and administrators appears to be of uppermost significance since the value of the entire project depends upon the purpose to be achieved. Taking the time to set up meetings with teachers and administrators to clarify and articulate the overall purposes of the project leads naturally to consideration of other aspects of the research project, such as the role functions of each team member and under what aegis the research will take place.

If we pass too quickly through the stage of goal articulation, we may reinforce the view that classroom research is only another name for product evaluation or compilation of test scores and thus imply that collaboration is only superficially desired. Without attention to goals, we may also become entrenched in the view of the classroom research as something "done to" a program rather than a process which requires collaboration and shared support between researcher and practitioner. In addition, too brief a goal articulation period does not permit time for generation of hypotheses that are of interest to both parties.

To facilitate goal articulation between researchers, classroom teachers, and administrators, a list of points for discussion can be presented to the concerned parties at the same time requests for appointments are made. An agenda for the schedule appointment may also be given at this time. A sample list of questions for discussion is presented in Chart 3. These questions are a synthesis of the issues and concerns that the teachers involved in our

---

Chart 3
Discussion Question for Gaining Access/Articulating the Project

---

a. What are you looking for?
b. What is your procedure?
c. What form of documentation are you going to use?
d. How much time will the project take?
e. What are you going to do with the results?
f. How are you going to use this information?
g. How are you going to communicate with parents?
h. What do you expect of me as a teacher?
i. Depending on what you expect of me, to what degree is my input going to be recognized?
j. In what way does your research ability and my classroom ability work together?
k. How many days will you reserve to spend in the classroom before the project begins?
l. Will the pre-project observations be in isolated time slots or will you arrange for a full sampling of different lessons?
m. Who will conduct the observations during the proposed project?
n. How much time has each observer spent in the classroom?

---

collaborative research team believe can be used by other teachers to determine (a) the nature of the project, (b) the nature of teacher involvement, (c) the scope of the project (e.g., time requirements for teacher and students), (d) the value of the project to teacher and students, (e) the types of data analysis feedback, (f) the issue of what happens after the project is completed. These advance organizers are useful for assuring teachers and administrators that their input will be welcome. These guide questions can also be used by teachers as a basis for making initial judgments as to whether they wish to participate and whether their role will have integrity in the proposed project.

Discussion of Needs that Support Initiation of Action Research Projects.   In addition to articulating the goals of the project, why the project is needed must be articulated. In the present study, both researchers had had opportunities to meet with kindergarten teachers before the initiation of the planning stage for this research project. As discussed in Section III, the researchers had met both teachers separately in connection with professional meetings held every year at the college of education. Additionally, they had worked with the teachers in connection with their responsibilities as univesity supervisors of student teachers. Research needs for the profession as a whole had been an item discussed at various times in the formal and informal meetings between researchers and the teachers.

We realize that not all researchers will have direct access to schools because of their professional responsibilities. We have found that meetings, informal and formal, are invaluable for generating questions for classrooom research, as well as for establishing potential long-range research sites. Researchers concerned with various aspects of processes of schooling might wish to consider developing plans for scheduling meetings with teachers both at public school sites and on campus sites at regular intervals. The focus of the meetings may be dissemination of new research findings in terms of implications for classroom teachers or the exploration of areas of needed research. Recent policy statements by organizations, such as the American Federation of Teachers (discussed in Section I), offer support for efforts of educational researchers to plan and hold meetings with teachers to discuss needed projects at regular intervals. Guide questions, such as those presented in Chart 3, can be used as a framework for such talks.

In the present study, discussions of needs that supported the authors' initiation of action research centered around the lack of conclusive results in areas relating to teacher effectiveness. During the formal and informal meetings we had held, a recurring point was the cumulative negative effects on the teaching profession as a whole using labels such as "warm," "laissez-faire," and "opinionated." Each member of the team was committed to finding alternative means of measuring effective teaching.

The impetus for the research project described in Chapter 8 was general dissatisfaction with typologies that have been created to describe teaching processes and the lack of knowledge about what teaching means for a single teacher over time. The typologies have contributed to education's bad press through dissemination of such descriptors as "warmth" and "opinionated" or even "authoritarian." They do not permit description of whether the goals of the classroom have been reached. In addition, the relevance of typologies, such as those used in past research for capturing patterns of interpersonal relationships in classroom group structure, has not been demonstrated. Use of typologies has not helped teachers reflect on the relationship between group processes and achievement of their instructional objectives.

All members of the team accepted the limitation of the typologies as a vehicle for research on teaching. The team's need for an alternative methodology led them to agree to investigate teacher/child interactions through the sociolinguistic ethnographic system described in Chapter 8. This methodology permits description of evolving teaching processes on a message-by-message basis as teacher and students engage in the teaching-learning process rather than judgment and categorization of a behavior as "warm" or "directive."

To summarize, goal articulation and discussions of research needs provide the key:

1. To gain access to the schools,
2. To obtaining teacher collaboration,

3. To establishing a shared frame of reference between teacher, school personnel, parents, and researcher,
4. To generating research hypotheses based on field practices,
5. To building communciation and cooperation on a long-term basis between the public schools and the universities,
6. To selecting appropriate methodology.

The first two steps discussed lay the foundation for, and pave the way to, development of collaborative teams.

Discussion of Types of Methodology and Procedures Available for Helping to Answer the Questions of Both Teacher and Researcher

The issue of scheduling observation before decisions on methodologies and procedures are made is important. As shown in the examples of a negative research project in Section II, if the researcher does not take the time to determine whether the sampling segment procedure is representative, then the methdology or procedures selected may be inappropriate. The central problem facing the research team is the selection of a methodology appropriate to answer the question of the study and reflective of the process being studied. For example, categorizing individual behaviors and tallying their frequency does not provide a description of when the behavior occurred, in relation to what, and with what effect. In other words, categorizing individual behaviors does not describe teaching as an evolving process of engagement between teacher and students.

Given the detailed presentation of the methodology used in this study in Chapter 8, this section will focus on factors that contribute to problems in methodology such as those presented in Section II of this chapter.

Problems in methodology may result from

1. Assumptions about the classroom that the researcher brings to the study.
2. Mismatch in goals of the project and the goals of the classroom teacher.
3. Insufficient or too limited time sampling on which to base the analysis.
4. Lack of knowledge about the culture of the classroom and the teacher's goals and objectives.

The foregoing areas of potential problems are basically concerned with methodology for data collection and analysis, but problems can also occur in the data-sharing stage.

Problems in articulation of findings may result from

1. Lack of inclusion of validation procedures in which the teacher and/or students react to or explore their perceptions of the processes being researched.
2. Lack of consideration of mechanisms for sharing the data with the research field, local schools, and the teacher.

If the methodology is to serve as the means toward better understanding of classrooms, the method must provide a means toward capturing the teacher's goals and teacher-student engagement. Moreover, procedures must include a means of gaining information that the researcher and teacher see as valuable.

Erickson (1978) recently related an instance of the importance of continued verification of findings with the teacher. He told an audience of researchers concerned with the reality of the classroom that after he had completed his analysis of classroom tapes, he shared his findings with the teacher only to learn that his view of the situation did not concur with the teacher's view. Based on this recognition, Professor Erickson told the audience that his intended report would have to await further analysis and verification.

In addition to long-term outcomes, one short-term outcome is to provide the opportunity for the classroom teacher to meet other teachers working in the project. The project teachers can also be invited to share their perceptions and interpretations of the findings at professional meetings. One way to insure continued collaboration both during and after the project is to establish a system for receiving the teacher's permission for every public presentation of the tapes and, perhaps, to arrange for her presence. Since researchers from different frames of reference, such as sociology, psychology, speech and communication, and linguistics, will view the tapes from a different perspective than one gained from teacher education and classroom experience, we need to insure that teachers have the opportunity to share their view of what is going on in the classroom.

Discussion of Outcomes.   The outcomes of an action research study are varied. The specific outcomes of the study will depend to a great extent on (a) the goals of the study, (b) the needs of the participants as defined through multi-discipline discussions, of the type described previously. The most obvious outcome is that we can share parts of the tapes and the findings with colleagues, other researchers, and teacher education students. But the audience for the study is greater than this group. One can also arrange to give the parents and children from the classroom the opportunity to view samples of the year's work. If the team is to maintain a shared perspective for all directly and indirectly involved, mechanisms for sharing short-term outcomes are needed.

The specific purpose of sharing the outcome, i.e., the actual tapes, depends upon the teacher's or the researcher's objectives at the time of sharing. Parents and children will no doubt be interested in viewing a sample of kindergarten activities during the year. The teacher may want to keep the parents apprised of the project's development. The same tape can be used for these purposes. In addition, the tapes can be used for such other purposes as kindergarten orientation sessions with new children and their families and reinforcing home/school/community interaction within the district.

During the first 18 months of the study described in Chapter 8, the tapes were used:

1. To analyze two 13-minute segments in each kindergarten classroom.
2. To articulate one teacher's program at a conference on each teaching.
3. To share one teacher's program and the research project with parents.
4. To present the methodology and findings of this analysis at a variety of research conferences.

The link between these outcomes is that each provides for dissemination of information about the nature of teaching.

Dissemination of Research Results.   In the section on outcome, we discussed mechanisms for sharing the research with researchers from other fields, colleagues, parents, and children. Records should be kept of all these meetings to include dates, audience, and purpose of the meeting. In this way teachers will have the data they need for end-of-the-year evaluation of professional activities and service. The same type of records will serve as a check point for possible additions of clearance releases from parents and, of course, from the teachers involved in the study.

Although guidelines for research on human subjects are available and specify that researchers must obtain participatory permission from the children themselves if they are over seven years of age, the question of the use of classroom tapes in which children are identified by name has yet to be resolved. If records, such as those described in this paper, are kept on a wide scale by classroom researchers, we might offset criticism or legal problems because we took the initiative in specifying criteria for the use of classroom video data.

Discussion of Time Requirements.   The question of time management cannot be separated from the discussion of goals. Each team member brings to the project a set of time constraints based on her/his professional commitments. The focus of this discussion should be how to fit the purpose of the project into each member's existing schedule. Identification of the work of each member and functions will help in this aspect of the project. The following chart is one mechanism that might be useful for time requirement discussions.

Chart 4 Congruent Between Project Objectives and Work Schedule	
Classroom Teacher Responsibilities	*Responsibilities as a Research Team Member*
Lesson planning time	Audiotape of objectives for days taped.
Parent meetings and/or parent visits	Feedback on statement of the project prepared by educational/researcher.
Professional meetings within the school system	Use of segments of the videotape (possibility of using copies made without audio).
Professional organization meetings	Awareness of approximate dates of annual meetings from previous years can help in decisions about submitting proposals for presentations.
Orientation meetings with preschool children and parents	Arranging for copies of parts of tapes to serve as sampling of kindergarten activities.

Summary.   Although potential for conflict exists in expectations of each directly or indirectly involved partner in action research, these potential discrepancies in perceptions can be handled if a clear program of collaboration and articulation is available. Rather than an individual's becoming the target of criticism, the team can decide what modification or additions should be made in the collaboration and articulation program. The suggestions and mechanisms discussed in this section, though not all-inclusive, are derived from a successful collaborative strategy and articulation experiences and theroetical considerations proposed in Section I and II.

SECTION V: IMPLICATIONS AND FUTURE DIRECTIONS: THE CHALLENGE

In the introduction to this chapter, we added another "should" to the multiple volumes of information on conducting research. We suggested that research project reports "should" clarify for readers whether the theoretical constructs guiding the study mean that the project is (a) something done *to* the teacher or (b) something done *with* the teacher. We also suggested that we are still in the formative phase of demonstrating the value of collaborative research efforts to members of the educational community. That we are still in the formative stage of legitimizing the roles of practitioners in action research projects has been a concern of education for some time. Educational researchers, such as Patricia Carini (1976); John Elliott (1976); Susan Florio (1976); Edward

Chittenden (1978); Vito Perrone (1976); and Frederick Erickson (1978), have demonstrated through their collaborative work with practitioners that the responsibility of researchers to the field of education means that we cannot end our research project timetable at the point of writing the final data analysis report. The efforts and commitment of researchers, such as those cited, center around their acceptance of responsibility for demonstrating the value of alternative action research methodologies to other members of the educational community.

One example of how formidable is the challenge of articualting the value of action research can be seen in the educational research community's lack of agreement on the very meaning of action research. Isaac and Michaels (1975) have captured the extent of differentiation in perceptions of action research in their synthesis of major textbook definitions of research and evaluation. The characteristics of action research reviewed in their handbook include (a) action research as practical and directly related to an actual situation in the working world, (b) action research as flexible and adaptive, (c) action research as a methodoloy which can provide an orderly framework for problem solving and new developments that is superior to fragmentary approaches that otherwise typify developments in education, (d) action research as lacking scientific rigor. The last three words in the list of definitions of action research capture the crux of the challenge in solving issues related to action research in the classroom. The phrase "lacks scientific rigor" lies at the heart of a controversy which has even reached the level of comparing research paradigms on moral and ethical grounds. The assumption that action research is "better" because of an ideological framework can be seen in the following definition. In Elliott's (1976) review of the dilemmas facing research, he suggests that action research:

> ... aims to contribute both to the practical concerns of people in an immediate problematic situation and to the goals of social science by joint collaboration within a mutually acceptable ethical framework (p. 4).

The choice of words such as "superior" and "ethical" does not help to solve the problem of lack of congruence on the meaning and value of action research. Several of the researchers referred to in this section have made this point and it was referred to again at a recent organizational meeting of the American Anthropology Association's Council on Anthropology and Education (Annual Meeting, Toronto, March, 1978). The president of the council, Dell Hymes, reiterated the dilemmas of action research and discussed two major challenges for those concerned with (a) articulating the view that meaning is context-dependent, (b)implementing the research goal of increasing our understanding of human experience in context. The first challenge mirrors the first step of the articulation framework presented in Section II, i.e., taking the time to set up meetings to clarify the overall purpose of action research. The second challenge outlined by Hymes is particularly relevant to this book, i.e., taking the time to build awareness of how ethnographic studies can be implemented. Following Hymes's remarks, the members of the Council on Anthropology and Education began a dialogue on one of the major articulation problems facing research; i.e., how to cope with the proliferation of new terms that always accompanies a formative stage. The need for continuing this dialogue is apparent when one considers the existence of such terms as *ethnographic psychology, ethnomethodology, micro-ethnography, macro-ethnography, ideational systems, sociolinguistic systems, social network systems, constructivist research, thematic research, constitutive ethnography.*

If we take the time to continue the dialogue toward consensus and articulation which Hymes began, we will have taken another positive step toward developing a collaborative climate for dealing with issues in classroom research. The continuing surface of educational problems requires an atmosphere in which sharing on how to build collaborative strategies is considered as valuable as dissemination of research results.

REFERENCES

Bennett, C. A., & Lumsdaine, A. A. *Evaluation and experiment: some critical issues in assessing social programs.* New York: Academic Press, 1975.

Bloom, B. (Ed.), *The taxonomy of educational objectives: Handbook I cognitive domain.* New York: David McKay, 1956.

Carini, P. F. *Observation and description: an alternative methodology for the investigation of human phenomena.* Grand Forks, D.: North Dakota Study Group, 1976.

Chittenden, E. A. The development of collaborative relationships between researchers and teachers. Paper presented at the American Educational Research Association, Toronto, March 1978.

Combs, A. W. *The professional education of teachers.* Boston: Allyn & Bacon, 1965.

Conant, J. B. *The education of American teachers.* New York: McGraw-Hill, 1963.

Dunkin, M. J., & Biddle, B. J. *The study of teaching.* New York: Holt, Rinehart & Winston, 1974.

Elliott, J. *Developing hypotheses about classrooms from teachers' practical constructs.* Grand Forks, N. D.: North Dakota Study Group, 1976.

Erickson, F. Standards of predictive validity in studies of classroom activity. Paper presented at the American Educational Research Association, Toronto, March 1978.

Florio, S., & Walsh, M. The teacher as colleague in classroom research. Paper presented at the American Educational Research Association, San Francisco, April 1976.

Fuller, F. F., & Muller, R. A. Self confrontation reviewed: a conceptualization for video playback in teacher education, *Review of Educational Research,* 1973, *43,* 469–528.

Green, J. L. Pedagogical style differences as related to comprehension performance: grades one through three. Unpublished doctoral dissertation, University of California, Berkeley, 1977.

Green, J. L., & Wallat, C. What is an instructional context? An exploratory analysis of conversational shifts across time. In O. K. Garnica & M. King (Eds.), *Children, language and society.* New York: Pergamon, 1979.

Guttentag, M., & Struening, E. L. *Handbook of evaluation research* (Vol. II.). Beverly Hills, Calif.: Sage Publications, 1975.

Haberman, M. *The art of schoolmanship.* St. Louis, Mo.: W. H. Green, Inc., 1970.

Hymes, D. *Foundations in sociolinguistics.* Philadelphia: University of Pennsylvania Press, 1974.

Isaac, S., & Michael, W. B. *Handbook in research and evaluation.* San Diego, Calif.: Edits Publishers, 1975. ˙

Kaplan, A. *The conduct of inquiry.* Scranton, Pa.: Chandler, 1964.

Lieberman, M. *Education as a profession.* Englewood Cliffs, N.J.: Prentice-Hall, 1956.

Lynch, J., & Plunkett, H. D. *Teacher education and cultural change.* London Allen & Unwin, 1973.

McCarthy, D. J., *et al. New perspectives on teacher education.* San Francisco: Jossey Bass, 1973.

Perrone, V. Alternative research approaches to learning and teaching. Paper presented at the American Educational Research Association, Toronto, March 1978.

Scriven, M. Objectivity and subjectivity in educational research. In L. G. Thomas, (Ed.), *Philosophical redirection of educational research.* Chicago: National Society for the Study of Education, 1972.

Twain, D. Developing and implementing a research strategy. In E. L. Struening M. Guttentag (Eds.), *Handbook of evaluation research* (Vol. I). Beverly Hills, Calif.: Sage Publications, 1975.

Wallat, C. Professional directions; the social technologist role. *International Journal of Instructional Media,* 1976, *4,* 15–21.

APPENDIX A

DEPARTMENT OF
EARLY CHILDHOOD
EDUCATION
(216) 672-2656

Dear Parents,

Mrs. Haramis and Cynthia Wallat from Kent State are working on a project that includes video taping of various activities of the kindergarten children while they arrive at school and while they are having various lessons. The taping, if you give your permission for your child to participate, will be scheduled for one hour on the first two days of every school month.

The purpose of the taping is:

1. To have a record of kindergarten activities and teacher/child interactions over the school year.

The usefulness of this record of the kindergarten year includes:

1. A sample of kindergarten activities to share with parents in Hudson.
2. A record of kindergarten activities that can be used in teacher education.
3. A data bank that can be used for reserach on child development during the kindergarten year.

_____

_____

We would appreciate your permission to have your child participate in this project.

_____

_____

Child's Name _____

Parent's Permission _____

Parent's Signature _____

Date _____

APPENDIX B

KENT STATE
UNIVERSITY
KENT OHIO 44242

DEPARTMENT OF
EARLY CHILDHOOD
EDUCATION
(216) 672-2658

GENERAL PERMISSION FORM

TO: Student Teachers and Classroom Visitors
FROM: Dr. Judith Green and Dr. Cynthia Wallat

The classroom teacher is working on a project with us that includes video taping of various activities of the kindergarten children while they arrive at school and while they are having various lessons. Since we are taping continuously in the classroom for one hour, there will be times that you may be captured on the video tape. For this reason, we need your release to permit use of the segment in which you are recorded.

The purpose of taping:

1. To have a record of kindergarten activities and teacher/child interactions over the school year.

The usefulness of this record of the kindergarten year includes:

1. A sample of kindergarten activities to share with parents.
2. A record of kindergarten activities that can be used in teacher education.
3. A data bank that can be used for research on child development and communication during the kindergarten year.

_____

WE APPRECIATE YOUR COOPERATION IN OUR EFFORTS

_____

Your Name: _____ DATE(S) _____
Your Signature: _____
Purpose of visit (e.g., talk with teacher, observation, student teaching)

_____

_____

Kent State University Supports Equal Opportunity in Education and Employment

II SYSTEMATIC APPROACHES TO THE STUDY OF SOCIAL INTERACTION

6
Entering
The Child's World—
Research Strategies
for Field Entry
and Data Collection
in a Preschool Setting

William A. Corsaro
Indiana University, Bloomington

Two four-year-old girls (Betty and Jenny) and adult researcher (Bill) in a nursery school:

Betty: You can't play with us!
  Bill: Why?
Betty: Cause you're too big.
  Bill: I'll sit down. (sits down)
Jenny: You're still too big.
Betty: Yeah, you're "Big Bill"!
  Bill: Can I just watch?
Jenny: OK, but don't touch nuthin!
Betty: You just watch, OK?
  Bill: OK.
Jenny: OK, Big Bill?
  Bill: OK
        (Later Big Bill got to play.)

Doing ethnographic research in a preschool peer setting is not easy. Even after months of careful field entry and daily participant observation, the researcher still can not completely overcome some obstacles of intrusion. However, as the above dialogue (wherein I received a lasting nickname) indicates, certain of these obstacles can become less difficult with time, patience, and determination.

*This research was supported by grants from the National Institute of Mental Health (Grant No. 1 F22 MH01141-01 and No. 1 R03 MH 2895-01).

This paper is a methodological report of field entry and participant observation in a nursery school. My aim is to provide the reader with a "natural history" (Becker, 1958) of the data-collection and initial-analysis phases of the research process. I shall trace the process by which I became a participant in childhood culture and describe and evaluate some of the patterns in the ethnographic data.

Although there is a growing interest in peer interaction and play among preschool children (Bruner, Jolly, & Silva, 1976; Garvey, 1977; Lewis & Rosenblum, 1975; Schwartzman, 1976), there have been few detailed ethnographies of preschool peer environments (see Schwartzman, 1978, for a recent exception). I believe there are two reasons for the relative sparsity of such research. This first is theoretical. Major theoretical approaches to human learning and development view socialization as the process by which the child becomes an adult. As Speier has so aptly put it, "the traditional perspectives have overemphasized the task of describing the child's developmental process of growing into an adult at the expense of the direct consideration of what the events of everyday life look like in childhood" (1973, p. 141). It is the growing concern with childhood culture and children's peer activities as topics of study in their own right which has prompted a need for ethnographic studies of peer environments.

A second reason for the sparsity of ethnographic research on young children is methodological. Recently, there has been a growing number of observational studies of peer interaction in both laboratory (Bronson, 1975; Garvey & Hogan, 1973; Garvey, 1977) and natural settings (see Blurton-Jones, 1973; Hutt, 1971 for naturalistic research by ethologists; Barker, 1966; and Herron & Sutton-Smith, 1973, for ecological studies; and Keenan, 1974, 1977; Meullar, 1972; and Schatz & Gelman, 1973 for naturalistic studies of language development). A major shortcoming of many of these studies is the tendency of the researchers to remove themselves from the social contexts of the peer activities. As a result the data are interpreted from the adult's perspective, and there is a failure to capture background information on the children's perceptions of their activities and social-ecological environments.

Detailed ethnography, including participant observation, is difficult in peer settings for several reasons. First, there is the general problem of obtrusion. This problem is compounded by the necessity of negotiation with adult caretakers (parents and teachers) before field entry into peer activities can proceed. Once successful negotiation with caretakers is complete, the researcher faces the problems of physical size and perceived power (i.e., adults are much bigger than children and are perceived as being socially more powerful) in his initial contacts with children. The latter problem can be reduced substantially with gradual and, what I term, *reactive* field entry strategies; the problem of physical size can never be completely overcome, but it can diminish in importance over an extended period of participant observation.

A second problem in ethnographic work with young children has to do with adult conceptions of children's activities and abilities. As adults, we often explain away what we do not understand about children's behavior as unimportant (i.e., silly), or we restructure what is problematic to bring it in line with an adult view of the world. Thus, there is a tendency to view children's play as practice at being an adult (anticipatory socialization). Such interpretations are not always incorrect nor are analyses of peer activities from this perspective without merit, yet these adult interpretations and assumptions about children's behavior are themselves topics for inquiry (Schwartzman, 1978). One of the central aims of ethnographies of childhood culture is the suspension of such interpretations. The researcher must attempt to free himself from adult conceptions of children's activities and enter the child's world as both *observer* and *participant.* In the following sections of this report I describe several specific methodological strategies I employed in an attempt to enter the child's world.

ETHNOGRAPHIC CONTEXT AND POPULATION

This report is based on a year long ethnographic study of peer interaction in a nursery school. The school is part of a child study center staffed and operated by a state university for both education and research. The teaching methods, curriculum, and schedule employed in the school allowed for a substantial period of self-selection of activities by the children. As a result I was able to sample a broad range of peer interactive episodes. Figure 1 depicts the physical layout of the center; Figure 2 shows the school with major social-ecological areas labeled.

There were two groups of children at the school, attending morning and afternoon sessions. Each group was staffed by one head teacher and three full-time teaching assistants (TAs). In the morning group, there were 24 children (11 boys and 13 girls) ranging in age from 2.11 to 3.11 years. There were 26 children (15 boys and 11 girls) in the afternoon group who ranged from 3.9 to 4.10 years of age. All but two of the children in the afternoon group had attended morning sessions at the school the year before the research. The occupational and educational backgrounds of the children's parents ranged from blue-collar workers to professionals, with the majority of the children coming from middle- and upper-class families.

Field Entry and Data Collection

Phase One: Gatekeepers.   My research in the child study center was based on what Schatzman and Strauss have called "mutually voluntary and negotiated entrée"; my hosts (adult caretakers including the director, teachers, and parents) held "options not only to prevent entrée but to

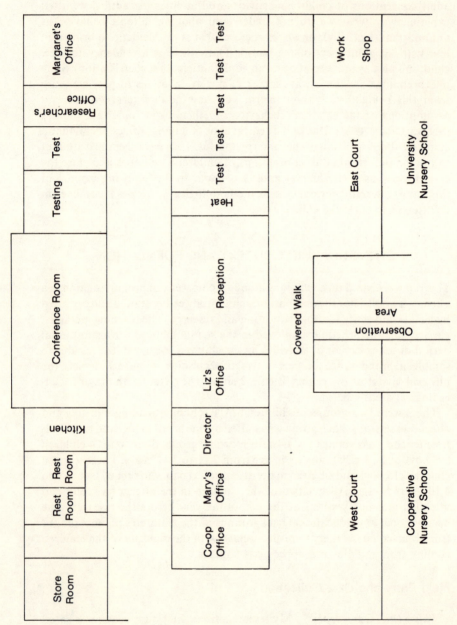

Figure 1. Child Study Center

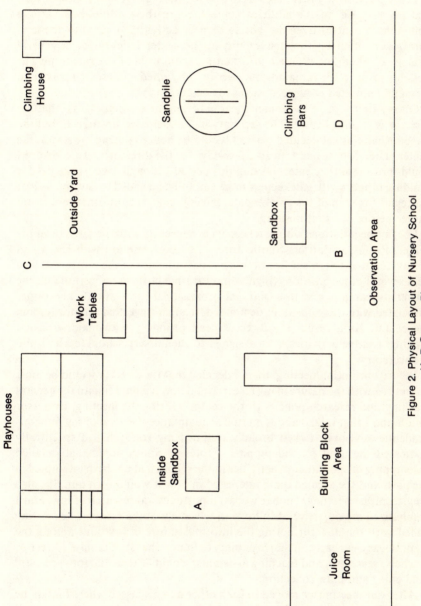

Figure 2. Physical Layout of Nursery School
(A–D Camera Placements)

121

terminate relations with the researcher at almost any stage thereafter" (1973, p. 22). Therefore, my first task was to develop strategies for presenting myself and my research to the adult caretakers. Since these adults had varying amounts of control over my access to peer activities, I refer to them as *gatekeepers.* During the first month at the center I developed a general strategy of obtaining as much information about each of the gatekeepers as possible prior to the initial meeting where I presented my research plans and formally requested their permission for access.

On my first visit to the center I learned from the secretary (Liz)[1] that the director was out of town. The secretary had anticipated my arrival, but the director had not yet decided where I would be housed during my stay at the center. Therefore, I had to wait a few days for the director's return before I could move into the center. During this period I thought over strategies for building rapport with gatekeepers more carefully. I decided to develop a set of strategies for each of the gatekeepers, relying on all the information I could gather before our first meeting.

I began negotiations with gatekeepers in a meeting with the director of the center, Professor Patricia Smith. In my first conversation with Liz, I had discovered that Professor Smith was not only director of the center, but also held several other positions (high administrative posts in an institute on the university campus and in a national professional association). The duties associated with these positions demanded frequent travel and time away from the center. As a result, the director dealt primarily with major decision making; routine activities were assigned to the nursery school teachers and the secretary.

Before our initial meeting, then, I decided that the director would be most concerned with the nature of my research and how it would fit into the general teaching and research policies of the center. During the meeting, Professor Smith and I first talked about mutual acquaintances (several of my previous academic advisors). I then broadly outlined my research and specifically addressed the need for videotaping. Professor Smith noted that detailed videotaping of spontaneous activities in the school had not been attempted in the past, and she seemed quite interested in how it would turn out. She also seemed pleased to have (in her words) a postdoctoral research fellow, and I emphasized my objective of fulltime involvement at the center. The meeting ended with the director noting the informal nature of relations among the staff. It was clear early on that my ability to fit into the "staff family" (director, teachers, secretary, and teaching assistants) would be essential for successful field entry and data collection.

After our meeting we moved to Liz's office and discussed where I might be housed. During my first visit Liz seemed anxious about the possibility of the

---

[1]Throughout this report, cover names are used to identify participants in the research study.

director's moving me into a large observational room presently occupied by one of the teachers (Margaret). During this discussion I suggested the possibility of occupying a smaller room next to Margaret. The director quickly agreed, and I moved into the center that afternoon. This was a fortunate decision because it put me in close contact with Margaret and prevented her from moving back into an overcrowded office she had previously shared with the other teacher, Mary (see Figure 1).

On my third day at the center I had my first of many long conversations with Liz. Liz had been working there since its inception and had more information (both in her head and at her fingertips) about the center than anyone else. In this first conversation with Liz I made an important discovery about the history of relations between researchers and the staff. The teachers were generally unhappy with much of the research at the center. The main problem was the researchers' attitudes and procedures for working with the teachers and children. From my discussion with Liz I learned that the teachers were often used to entice the children from the school to the experimental rooms and were seldom informed about the nature of the research or the eventual results.

This dissatisfaction with much of the previous and on-going research was also evident in later conversations I had with the teachers and TAs. As a result I attempted to create just the opposite impression for my research. I frequently asked the teachers, TAs, and the secretary for advice and response to my plans for field entry and data collection. Later in the study I often asked the staff, parents, and the children to help with data analysis and interpretation. I also frequently volunteered to help out in the school and the main office, and I soon became part of the "staff family" at the center.

My aim in this approach to field entry was not simply "to come off better" than the other researchers, but rather to build an impression of not being *just another researcher*. The people under study in field research should not view the researcher's presence as simply a means to some more important end (i.e., a dissertation, research report, or a monograph). As Becker (1970) has observed, to foster an impression of being important or doing important research can constitute a threat to the people one observes. Throughout the research process I worked hard to play down my status as a researcher and to emphasize my aim of fulltime involvement in the daily activities of the school.

I continued daily conversations with Liz throughout my first month at the center. Although the actual conversations covered a wide range of topics (my research, academic training, our families, and leisure activities and interests), they were primarily about the nursery school. I used the majority of the time I spent in my office writing up my recollections of parts of these conversations which seemed most relevant to the later field work. Overall, the information I obtained in conversations with Liz helped me estabish working expectations of most of the participants in the research settting before initial contacts. This method of collecting background data through informal interviewing is beneficial for building rapport and for obtaining information in an unobtrusive manner. In addition, the procedure allows respondents to volunteer information the researcher may have failed to elicit in more structured interviews.

During the first part of this month before the start of school the head teachers were away from the center most of each day. This time was spent in home visits designed to make the children's transition from home to school as smooth as possible. Near the end of the month the teachers were at the center more often and had several organizational meetings with their assistants. At this time I met the TAs and sat in on several staff meetings. It was also during this period that I had my first extended conversations with the head teachers.

About a week before school began I met with one of the head teachers (Margaret). Initially we discussed the current literature in the area of language acquisition and I suggested several recent sources she might find interesting. As the conversation progressed we moved from my office to hers where Margaret showed me several articles and books on language and early childhood education. The topic then shifted to my research plans, and I outlined my general interests in peer communication and childhood socialization. I also described my methodological plans and stressed the necessity for participant observation and videotaping. Like the director, Margaret noted the novelty of this type of research at the center. I asked for her help in field entry and stressed the value of the teacher's interpretations for later data analysis. Margaret seemed both surprised and pleased and said she would be glad to help. She went on to discuss her feelings of being "left out" of many of the research projects and noted that the researchers often failed to inform the teachers about the results of their studies.

I then moved to a description of plans for field entry, participant observation, and videotaping and asked Margaret for her reactions. She agreed with my plan to delay videotaping to later in the school year. She suggested I not attempt to move into the school to begin participant observation too quickly. Margaret said the first few weeks were usually somewhat traumatic for the younger children, and parents and TAs were also a bit tense during this period. She suggested I could learn a great deal about the children and the routine activities in the school by watching from behind the one-way screen in the observation area (see Figure 2).

As it turned out, this was one of many long conversations I had with Margaret. Her observations were always helpful both for data-collection strategies and for later data analysis and interpretation. As the study progressed Margaret developed a keen interest in the research and thought many of the patterns in the data had implications for early childhood education.

A few days after my meeting with Margaret I had my first extended discussion with the other head teacher (Mary). I had briefly talked with Mary in the past, but had hesitated in setting up a formal meeting. Mary seemed extremely busy. I learned from Liz that Mary often gave talks and seminars on curriculum development in early childhood education and that she was also working on her dissertation, which she planned to finish in the early spring. One day, as Mary was leaving Liz's office as I was about to enter, we had a brief conversation about my research plans and her interests in curriculum development. I asked Mary for copies of her papers on curriculum and also set up a meeting for the next day to discuss my plans for observing peer interaction in the school.

In the meeting I outlined my research plans and asked for reactions and suggestions. Mary was most interested in the plans for videotaping, and she suggested camera and microphone placements in the school. She also predicted that my main problem in videotaping would be with sound due to the large amount of background noise in the school. I asked about the possibility of her helping with data analysis later in the year. She agreed and seemed pleased with the request. Near the end of the meeting I showed her the human subjects forms for videotaping and asked how I might go about obtaining parental permissions. Mary looked over the forms and suggested I add a brief introductory paragraph describing myself and the project. She also suggested I place the forms in the students' lockers during the first week of classes since parents often neglected to respond to forms brought home later in the school year.

Shortly after my meeting with Mary I revised the permission forms and asked Liz to run off copies. With this task completed, I reviewed my field notes and reflected on my first month of observations and informal interviews. Schatzman and Strauss have argued that field entry "is a *continuous* process of establishing and developing relationships, not only with a chief host but with a variety of less powerful persons" (1973, p. 22). At this point in the research I seemed well into this process. I had established important ties with several of the gatekeepers in the setting and had obtained a great deal of information about the center. I made up a list of all the information I had acquired in conversations with Liz, Margaret, and Mary as well as from documents (student rosters and descriptions of the goals of the center) provided by Liz. As I reviewed this material it became clear that information acquired at one point in the process can be extremely useful at later stages of the research (i.e., information from conversations with Liz for building rapport with the teachers, information from conversations with the teachers for initial contact with parents and later entry into the school, etc.). In the next phase of the research, concealed observation, I was to continue this process as I began to acquire background information on the activities in the school and the children themselves. This information would prove to be essential for later entry into the school and participant observation in peer interaction.

Phase Two: Concealed Observation

Observation Routine.   The first day of school I arrived at the center early and sat with Liz in the main office. Liz's office adjoins a walkway which leads into the school, and the children and their parents pass a large window in the office as they enter the school. As the children and parents filed by, Liz waved to them and identified each child for me as I jotted down physical descriptions next to their names on the morning group roster. With several repetitions of this procedure and my first week of observations I was able to associate all the children with their names.

After all the children had arrived I moved into the observation booth (see Figure 2). On this first day I primarily watched the activity and attempted to hear both teacher-child and peer conversations. I was surprised by the number, range, and complexity of the interactive events. At this point I had no idea of what to write in field notes. As it turned out I recorded only a few observations relating to how long parents remain in the school with their children.

For the afternoon session, I repeated the same procedure of watching the children pass Liz's office. Later as I watched the activities for the afternoon group I felt that things seemed more structured and defined. The children in this group had been at the school the year before and were familiar with the setting and each other. As a result several sustained peer activities occurred on the first day. I followed a few of these as best I could and attempted to record some of the verbal exchanges in field notes. This was difficult, however, because I did not know the children well and I had trouble hearing and understanding many of their utterances. I dropped this strategy after the first day, but then readopted it in a modified form near the end of this period of concealed observation.

During the first month of school I followed a fairly routine schedule. I observed from behind the one-way screen from the beginning until near the end of each session. I concentrated mainly on peer activities and moved to and from various locations in the observation booth to monitor behavior in all areas of the school. In field notes I recorded the topic or nature of peer activities, names of the children involved, and the location, duration, and a running summary of peer episodes.

Near the end of each session I would leave the observation area, enter the school and stand near the children's lockers (see Figure 2). I waited until parents began to arrive and then I helped the children gather things from their lockers as they prepared to leave. Occasionally I talked with the parents and children, but I did not identify myself as a researcher. As I discovered later in conversations with parents, many of them believed I was either a teaching assistant or a father of one of the children at this point in the research. The children seemed to take little notice beyond an occasional "thank you" for my help.

After the children had departed I helped the teacher and TAs clean up, and when the school was back in order I sat in on the teacher-staff meeting. During the meeting each TA reported on how s/he felt the day went and discussed any specific problems encountered. The teacher responded to these observations and made specific recommendations on how to handle similar problems in the future. The teacher then ended the meeting after discussing problems she felt merited special attention.

After the meeting I would return to my office and quickly jot down notes on what had transpired. I then looked over these notes and compared them to notes I had recorded earlier in the day. I was careful to mark both overlaps and differences in interpretations of the same and similar events.

Field Notes and Unit of Analysis.   As I mentioned previously, field notes recorded during concealed observation contained information on the participants, setting, and the nature and duration of interactive episode as the basic unit of analysis. The definition of *interactive episode* I worked with throughout the study was based on a review and analysis of notes collected during the first two weeks of concealed observation. My conception of the interactive episode is similar to Goffman's (1963) notion of "face engagement" with slight modifications to capture characteristics of peer interaction in this setting.

In the nursery school, interactive episodes are those sequences of behavior which begin with the acknowledged presence of two or more interactants in an ecological area and the overt attempt(s) to arrive at a shared meaning of on-going or emerging activity. Episodes end with physical movement of interactants from the area which results in the *termination* of the *originally initiated activity*.[2] For all the data (field notes and videotaped behavior) the interactive episode served as the sampling unit. One edited example of an interactive episode drawn from field notes collected during the period of concealed observation follows.

Example 1
Date: October 22   Scene: Playhouse (upstairs)
Afternoon episode #8   Participants: Laura (L) (4.1), Sue (S) (3.11),
                                             Theresa (Th) (4.9),
                                             Antoinette (A) (4.1),
                                             Allen (Allen) (3,9), and
                                             Teaching Assistant (T.A.)

[2]See Cook-Gumperz and Corsaro (1977) for a discussion of the implications of this definition for interaction in various settings in the school.

FN Field Note   MN Methodological Note
PN Personal Note   TN Theoretical Note

FN: Laura (L) is playing alone in upstairs playho ise. She is sitting on the bed near phone, dressing a doll. After about 5 mintues of solitary play she is addressed from below by Sue (S). Sue is near phone in downstairs playhouse.

S-L: I'll talk to you on the phone, OK? Ok, L?

S-L: (inaudible)

L-S: Yes

S-L: (In phone) I'm coming over, will you (inaudible)?

L-S: I might and I might not.

Both children hang up phones. S moves upstairs while L moves to head of stairs to meet her.

L-S: Well, hello.

S-L: Hi.

S and L now sit at table and talk (about 6 exchanges). S then gets up and begins walking down stairs and without looking back says:

S-L: Goodbye.

L-S: Goodbye.

(Later in same episode) S and L work together (upstairs) preparing a pretend meal. Antoinette (A) now moves upstairs and L goes to the head of the stairs and blocks A's entry.

S-L: She can come in

A is allowed to enter and she begins helping with meal. Now Theresa (Th) comes up the stairs.

Th: Can I play?

L-Th: No!

Th-A: A, A, can I play?

A-Th: OK. (Th enters and stands near table)

L-Th: This is only for girls!

L-Th: Can I be a little baby?

A-Th: Yeah, you can be a little baby.

L-Th: No you can't!

L: We can only have one baby.

Th now plays with A near table while L talks to S. Then L walks near where Th and A are sitting.

L-Th/A: Now what are you guys messing around for?

At this point a boy, Allen, enters playhouse.

L: We're having so many people!

L-Allen: Get out of my house! Get out of my house!

Allen-L: No, it's my house!

T.A. now moves near house and from below tells children to clean up the play house and then come down for meeting time.

PN: I was somewhat frustrated in an earlier attempt to record everything that was said. As a result I often rely on summaries here. It seemed L was getting upset from the time Antoinette arrived, even though A was allowed to stay.

MN: I am still trying to write too much verbatim conversation. Once I begin participant observation I will want to get very close to or *in* the playhouses. This may be difficult given that they are scaled to the size of the children and the teachers do not enter the playhouses.

TN: The children do not always verbally mark their comings and goings even in this type of family role play. Again I see what seems to be a defense of territory. Here it is related to both sex of the participants and the number of children involved by L. The number of children does seem to have an effect on the *stability* of the ongoing episode. L seemed to anticipate this problem in advance.

The recording conventions employed in Example 1 were first suggested in Strauss (1964) and are quite similar to those presented in Schatzman and Strauss (1973, pp. 99–100). The chief advantage of the convention is that it allows the researcher to separate out different types of information in the data (FN, PN, MN, TN) while insuring that varying types of data are tied to the specific interactive context in which they occurred. As the study proceeds, the researcher can search for patterns in field notes over time and across and within interactive episodes.

During the period of concealed observation I reviewed my notes twice a week, searching for early patterns in the data. As Greer (1967) has noted one can draw few conclusions from patterns in early field notes, but they may have far reaching effects on the rest of the study. Many of the patterns I isolated in notes during the period of concealed observation were discovered by focusing on theoretical notes and were the basis of later sampling decisions as well as the eventual generation of substantive hypotheses regarding peer activities in the school.

Although I do not have space to discuss each of the early patterns in the data here,[3] in the last action of this report, I present an analysis of a videotaped episode and a discussion of two interrelated hypotheses regarding the children's conceptions of "friendship" and their protection of interactive space. These hypotheses originated in patterns discovered in field notes obtained during concealed observation and are suggested by the data presented in the previous example.

---

[3]See Cook-Gumperz and Corsaro (1977) for an analysis of the effects of the social-ecological areas of the school in the children's communicative strategies, and Corsaro (1979a) for an analysis of the children's role play in peer interaction.

Advantages of Concealed Observation. Overall, the period of concealed observation was useful for several reasons. First, since teachers, parents, and children were all somewhat tense at the beginning of the year my presence as an observer in the school would have been quite obtrusive. From the concealed observation area I was able to learn a great deal about the children, the routine of the two sessions, and the features of peer interaction *before* actual field entry and participant observation. Second, if I had attempted field entry at the start of the school year the children may have defined me as a teacher as they did the other strange adults (i.e., TAs). Third, concealed observation allowed me to follow activities in all areas of the school without difficulty or disruption.

Cicourel (1964) suggests any knowledge of the research setting, independent of that which might be obtained in the actual field work, should be secured before field entry. All the advantages just cited tie into this central aim in field research. The knowledge I gained in my first month at the center and during concealed observation was of major importance for later entry into peer activities, participant observation, sampling decisions, and eventual data analysis and interpretation.

Phase Three: Participant Observation

Entry Into the Nursery School. At the start of the second month of the school year I moved into the school itself. My goal was to become an active participant in the children's peer activities. Participant observation was necessary for several reasons. First, it was essential the children perceive me as different from the teachers and other adults in the setting so that they would not suppress certain behaviors for fear of negative reactions. Secondly, once videotaping began I felt the children would find the equipment less obtrusive if they had become accustomed to my presence in their daily activities. Finally, becoming a participant in the children's activities was necessary for gaining insight into what *mattered most to them* in their everyday interaction in the school. This knowledge was of central importance for isolating patterns in field notes, analyses of videotaped episodes, and the generation of hypotheses.

In preparation for entry into the school I reviewed the methodological notes collected during concealed observation. In these notes I had continually reminded myself *not to act* like other adults when I moved into the school. During concealed observation, I discovered adults primarily initiated contacts with the children; that is, they were primarily *active* rather than reactive. The teachers directed and monitored the children's play, helped in times of trouble, or told the children what they could or could not do. Other adults (parents and researchers) mainly watched the children, often while standing over and peering down at them. The adults would frequently move from one group of children to another and initiate conversations without any real intention of engaging in extended interaction. Adult contacts with children were restricted to specific areas of the school. Adults seldom entered the playhouses, outside sandpile, climbing bars, or climbing house (see Figure 2).

Given this knowledge of typical adult-child interaction I adopted a simple, what I term *reactive,* entry strategy. For the first week in the school I continually made myself available in peer-dominant areas and waited for the children to react to me. For the first few days the results were not encouraging. I would enter the school shortly after the children arrived and sit down in a peer area. A number of peer interactive episodes developed and progressed as I sat nearby. I observed seven episodes in each session over a three-day period without any overt response from the children beyond several smiles and a few puzzled stares. Of all the many hours observing in this setting these were the most difficult for me. I wanted to say something ("anything") to the children, but I stuck with the strategy and remained silent.

On my fourth afternoon in the school I stationed myself in the outside sandpile directly behind a group of five children who were digging in the sand with shovels. They had defined their activity as "construction work" with two "bosses" and three "workers" (four boys and one girl). I watched for over 40 minutes, and first, two of the children and then the remaining three dropped their shovels and ran inside with no verbal marking. I suspect the construction project was completed or abandoned but was not sure since termination had not been marked explicitly.

I was feeling ill at ease and debating my next move when I saw Sue watching me from a distance. She was standing alone near the sandpile about 20 feet from where I was sitting. I smiled and she smiled back, but then to my dismay she ran over near the sandbox and stood watching a group of three other girls. My attention was then diverted by a minor disturbance near the climbing bars. Peter had (or so Daniel shouted) stolen Daniel's truck and a teacher had just arrived to settle the dispute. When I looked back to the sandbox, Sue was gone.

I then decided to move inside, but as I started to stand up I heard someone say "What'ya doing?" Sue had approached me from behind and was now standing next to me in the sandpile. I said, "Just watching." "What for?" she asked, and I answered, "Cause I like to." Then she asked my name. I said—and this turned out to be an important reply—"I'm Bill and you're Sue."

She took two steps back and demanded, "How did you know my name?" Remembering my methodological notes I now did something I noticed adults do not often do in conversations with young children—I told the truth with no attempt to simplify. "I heard Laura and some other kids call you Sue," I said. "But how do *you* know my name?" was Sue's response. I again pointed out that I had heard other children call her by name. Sue then turned and ran inside.

I had just decided that I had blown it when Sue re-emerged from the school accompanied by Jonathan. When they reached me Jonathan asked, "What's my name?" I told Jonathan his name, and then he, like Sue, asked how I knew. Again I was truthful, "I heard Peter [one of Jonathan's most frequent playmates] and some other kids call you Jonathan."

"See I told you he knows magic," said Sue. "Wait a minute," cautioned Jonathan, and then pointing to Larry and Frank, he asked, "Who are those kids?" I was able to identify both Larry and Frank as well as several other children Jonathan pointed out.

After my performance Jonathan turned to Sue and said, "I can't figure this guy out." He then ran off and joined Peter, Daniel, and Graham who were playing in the climbing bars. I noticed he turned and pointed to me after he reached the other three boys.

Sue then handed me a shovel, "You wanna dig?" "Sure," I said, and we shoveled sand into buckets. Later we were joined by Christopher and Antionette. This activity ended when one of the T.A.s announced "clean-up time," whereupon we put away our shovels and went inside for meeting time.

For the next several days children in both sessions began to react to my presence (ask who I was) and invite me to play. Although I was able to observe and in many cases participate in peer activities, the process was a gradual one. For nearly the first month the children were curious about me and why I was around every day. Table 1 summarizes the frequency of several "types" of questions which the children asked in attempts to identify my role in the school during the first three months of participant observation.

Table 1 indicates a gradual process of identification. There is a movement from general questions centering around adult characteristics to the last question about siblings, which is a question most typically asked of another child.

TABLE 1

Children's Questions regarding Researcher's Identity during Participant Observation

Question	N	# of Children	Temporal Range
Who are you?	48	32	Nov. 7–22
Are you a teacher?	40	28	Nov. 7–Dec. 1
Are you gonna play a game with me (us)?*	21	20	Nov. 15–Dec. 17
Are you a daddy?	13	10	Nov. 7–Jan. 28
Do you have any brothers or sisters?	10	5	Nov. 20–March 4

*Other researchers at the center often asked children, "Do you want to play a game with me?" as a device to encourage children to participate in an experimental study.

Children's questions provide data on attempts at identification. They do not, however, directly support the contention that the children had accepted me into peer activities. The reference, or nickname, "Big Bill," which surfaced near the end of the first month of participant observation, indicates a marking of the size difference between me and the children but also differentiates me from other adults.

In addition to the questions and the nickname, three other types of data demonstrate my acceptance as a peer. First, I was allowed to enter ongoing peer activities with little or no disruption. In most instances the children simply acknowledged my entry by addressing me in the course of unfolding events. In only a few cases were activities stopped and my presence questioned.

A second cue to the children's perceptions was my lack of authority. Given the nature of the research, attempts to control behavior were few and produced only when I felt there was a chance a certain activity might lead to physical injury. On these occasions my "Be careful's" were always countered with "You're not a teacher," or "You can't tell us what to do."

A third type of data is more indirect but occurred with a great deal of consistency. Throughout the school year, the children insisted that I be a part of the more formal peer activities. At birthday parties, for example, the children demanded I sit with them (in a circle) rather than on the periphery with the teachers and parents. Also several of the children demanded their mothers write my name, along with the names of the other children, on cookies, cupcakes, and valentines which were brought to school on special days.

Observational Routine.   Participant observation followed a fairly routine schedule. I would enter the school every morning and afternoon shortly after the children arrived, watch as episodes emerged, and then place myself in the area where an episode was underway. Practice and my reviews of personal and methodological notes improved my ability to enter into peer activities as the study progressed. My participation in peer activities can be best described as *peripheral.* I placed myself in the ecological area, moved when necessary, responded when addressed, and occasionally offered contributions when appropriate. My activity was peripheral in that I never attempted (1) to initiate or terminate an episode; (2) to repair disrupted activity; (3) to settle disputes; (4) to coordinate or direct activity. What I did was to try to play, to become a part of the activity without affecting the nature or flow of peer episodes.

Sampling was based on field notes collected during the period of concealed observation. My aim was to gain additional data to develop emerging patterns in field notes. Normally I would enter short summaries of events into a small notebook shortly after the end of each day. Every weekend I would review my notes searching for both negative cases and/or additional support for earlier patterns as well as indications of new patterns in the data.

Fulltime participant observation continued for three months (November through January). I began videotaping in late January, two days a week; participant observation continued on the other three days until the end of the school year in May. During this period, 633 episodes were recorded in field notes. I now present one edited example from field notes which bears on children's conception of "friends" and friendship.

Example 2
Date: December 3   Scene: Inside building block area
Morning Episode #3   Participants: Barbara (3.0), Susan (3.1)
                                           Linda (3.8), Adult Researcher
                                           (Bill), and T.A.
FN: I entered the block area after I watched Barbara (B) and Susan (S) leave the juice room together and move to this area where they began to gather blocks and toy animals. As I sat on the floor a short distance from them B said to me (R = Researcher):

B-R: Look Bill we're making a zoo.
R-B: That's nice. You have lots of animals.
S-RB: Yea, we're zookeepers, right B?
B-S: Right.

The two girls played for about 10 minutes, building small enclosures with the blocks and then placing the animals inside. There were a number of verbal exchanges. At one point S set some animals and blocks near me and said they were for me. I also built a small house and placed some animals inside. I then noticed that Linda (L) was watching us from a distance. After a few minutes L entered the block area and sat next to B and picked up some animals.

B-L: You can't play!
L-B: Yes I can. I can have some animals too.
B-L: No, you can't. We don't like you today.
S-L: You're not our friend.
L-BS: I can play here too.
B-S: No her can't—her can't play, right S?
S-B: Right.
L-R: Can I have some animals, Bill?
R-L: You can have some of these. (I offer L some of my animals)
B-R: She can't play, Bill, cause she's not our friend.
R-B: Why not? You guys played with her yesterday.
S-R: Well, we hate her today.
L-All: Well, I'll tell teacher. (L now leaves but then returns with a TA)
TA-BS: Girls, can L play with you?

B-TA: No! She's not our friend.

TA-B: Why can't you *all* be friends?

B-TA: No!

S-B: Let's go outside B.

B-S: OK

B and S now move outside and L begins playing with the animals they left behind. T.A. looks at me and grimaces, then moves into the juice room. I then stood up and saw that S and B had run to the swings and were now swinging together and talking.

TN: This episode is related to earlier patterns of protecting interactive space. Also as in some of the other instances friendship is used as a justification for exclusion. The temporal and numeral features of the discussion about friendship are interesting (i.e., "We hate her today," and the notion of one friend at a time).

Example 2 is representative of many other instances in the data involving attempts to protect interactive space. It was also one of several occasions where friendship was specifically discussed in this context. In the final section of this report I present an analysis of an example of videotaped data which further demonstrates the relationship between protection of interactive space and children's conception of friendship.

Phase Four: Videotape Recording.   Although there have been several studies involving the audio-video recording of adult-child and peer interaction (Cicourel, 1974; Lewis & Rosenblum, 1975; Garvey, 1974, 1977; Keenan, 1974, 1975, 1977), except for Keenan's work with her own children, these studies have not been grounded in extensive ethnographies of the settings and participants involved. In the present research, audio-video recording was based on initial patterns isolated in the prior field work.

In early January I reviewed my notes and drew up a list of the types of peer activities I planned to capture on videotape. The activities on this list, as well as those selected for recording in later reviews of notes as participant observation progressed, were directly related to emerging patterns in the field notes. In this sense, patterns in the ethnographic data were the basis for the theoretical sampling (Glaser & Strauss, 1967) of videotaped interactive episodes. Theoretical sampling led to the collection of a data set which was *representative* of everyday peer activities in the school and highly *conducive to theory generation* regarding peer interaction and childhood culture.

During the evening hours in mid-January I began initial testing of the audio-video equipment. I set up the camera and determined the video range and quality of several possible placements. I discovered I could capture activities in all areas of the school with four camera placements (Figure 2, A–D).

Audio recording, however, was a much more difficult problem. During participant observation I placed an audio recorder in several areas of the school. The playback of these tapes was not encouraging, and it was apparent that high-quality audio recording would be difficult to get in this setting. I tested microphone locations in all areas of the school and eventually placed microphones in the playhouses and over the building-block area, inside sandbox and work tables. In the remaining areas inside the school and in the outside yard I stored microphones in unobtrusive places (inside cupboards, on top of bookcases, and on posts of the wall which encloses the outside yard). When videotaping began I would move to these areas, pick up the microphones, and join ongoing peer events.

During the testing period I completed training my research assistant. The assistant (Jane) was a graduate student in linguistics who had prior experience in the collection and transcription of audio-video data. A research assistant was necessary for two reasons. First, I had become a participant in the school and it would be highly obtrusive for me to withdraw from peer activities and move behind the camera when videotaping began. Secondly, owing the audio problems made it imperative that I enter certain areas with a microphone and get as close as possible to the ongoing interaction.

I spent several sessions with Jane going over my general research aims, demonstrating the operation of the camera, VTR unit, and microphone mixer, and working out a hand-signal communication system. When videotaping began I used this system to relay instructions to Jane regarding when to begin and end recordings and when and how long to record children's departures from interactive episodes. The system became more complex as the study progressed and by the last month of the study Jane was excellent in her ability to anticipate my directions.

During the last week of January Jane and I set up the equipment in the school. On the first two days Jane stayed near the camera and I engaged in participant observation as usual. During the next three days we did some audio and video recording for testing purposes. I was pleased with the video quality of these recordings, but it was obvious that audio was to be a persistent problem.

I also used the first week to estimate the obtrusiveness of the equipment. Jane and I answered any questions the children had about the equipment. On the whole they showed little interest in the camera and seemed more concerned with Jane. Several of the children asked if she was my sister, wife, or girl friend. I explained to the children that Jane was my friend and was in the school to help me take some pictures. A few of the children posed when Jane stood behind the camera and later asked if we got any good pictures. Since the camera was stationary and Jane only occasionally stood behind it, the children soon accepted this new addition to their environment and went back to their everyday activities.[4]

The children also paid little attention to microphones hanging above several areas of the school. They did however, want to talk into the microphones I held during participant observation. Since background noise in the school often necessitated my using microphones in this fashion, I had to devise strategies to minimize obtrusiveness. Here again I relied on information gained earlier in the research as the basis for my strategy. When the children asked about the microphone I did not act surprised or upset, but simply told them I wanted to hear and record what they were saying. When the children wanted to talk, I simply let them talk. When I handed them the microphone they usually laughed, sang, shouted "hello," or became shy and said nothing at all. After each child had a turn they then went back to what they were doing before they noticed the microphone.

After the break-in period we videotaped twice a week and I continued participant observation on other days until the end of the school year. After each day's taping I reviewed and summarized the data. In the summaries I specified the number of episodes, where and when they occurred, the nature of the activity, the participants, and the duration in minutes and revolutions on the VTR counter.

Although I transcribed several episodes before the termination of data collection in May, the bulk of transcription and data analysis occurred over the summer months. I collected 27 hours of videotaped data which contained a total of 146 interactive episodes.

Data Analysis

Stage One: Patterns and Working Hypotheses.   Analysis like field entry and data collection, moved through a series of phases. The initial phase involved three processes: (a) identification of consistent patterns in field notes; (b) generation, initial testing, and refinement of working hypotheses; (c) theoretical sampling of additional field observations and videotaped episodes.

A review of theoretical notes led to the discovery of several patterns in the data and was followed by analyses of the field notes (raw data) from which the patterns were derived. At this point I identified the typicality of the patterns and their distribution across participants and interactive settings (cf. Becker, 1958).

---

[4]When videotaping, the camera was set up in one of the four locations in the school (Figure 2, A–D) and was not moved during a taping session. The camera was equipped with a zoom lens which made it possible to record interaction occurring at some distance from the camera.

Returning to the example of friendship, the theoretical notes contained numerous references to the children's discussion of friendship and their defense of play areas during peer interaction. When I examined field notes, I found references to friendship often preceded or accompanied defense of play areas. Also this relation between friendship and defense of play area appeared consistently over time and across participants, activities, and ecological areas of the school.

The next step in analysis was the formation and initial testing of working hypotheses. I hypothesized the children were primarily concerned with control over play areas and used friendship as a device to gain control and exclude others. An initial test of the hypothesis involved a sociometric analysis of field notes. If the hypothesis were correct, we would expect to find two patterns in the data: (a) peer episodes would most often be initiated and maintained by children who frequently played together (i.e., "were friends"), (b) acceptance into, or exclusion from, an ongoing episode would most often be based on frequency of prior contact.

A sociometric analysis of field notes *did not* support the hypothesis. First, there were no core groups or cliques in the school, but rather a pattern in which each child consistently interacted with a fairly large number of playmates (usually 8 or more in a group of 24). Second, I found no clear relation between frequency of contact and acceptance into (or exclusion from) play groups. In most instances the initial reaction to access attempts was negative regardless of interactive history.

Although children did restrict entry into ongoing episodes, the analysis of field notes suggested they were more concerned with "maintaining the stability" of the interaction than with control of territory of play materials. The data also indicated the children were aware of the relation between group size and stability and attempted to keep the number of interactants to a minimum (Example 1). The children were, however, more likely to base the exclusion of others on friendship rather than group size. But their conception of friendship was not related to frequency of past interaction. For the children, friendship was tied to the immediate interactive situation (i.e., temporally and contextually bound). In short, children playing together were friends while *for the duration of the interactive episode,* all others were not. As a result children attempting to gain access often found themselves excluded because they were not a part of the original activity.

Therefore, a revised hypothesis maintained that the children were aware of the fragility of peer interaction and attempted to minimize breakdowns by resisting access attempts. Justifications for exclusion, however, were not linked directly to the recognition of instability, but were tied to the children's developing conception of friendship.

This hypothesis, grounded in the initial pattern of protection of play areas and references to friendship, was one of several which served as a basis for theoretical sampling decisions in later participant observation and videorecording. In this sense theoretical sampling was employed as a search for negative cases to test and refine emerging hypotheses.

Stage Two: Transcription and Micro-Sociolinguistic Analysis. The initial phase of analysis and data collection continued until the end of the school year. At that point I began transcription and micro-sociolinguistic analysis of the videotapes. Transcription involves continual decision making on the part of the researcher in his reconstruction of the data form visual-auditory signals to a written description of specific interactive events. The transcription method I employed involved the literal recording of all verbalization and running description of paralinguistic and nonverbal features (body movements, gesture, gaze direction, proxemic distance and shifts, and object manipulation) of the interaction (Example 3).

Decisions regarding both verbal transcription and the running description were checked on the spot with research assistants. In the actual transcription process an assistant operated the videorecorder while I wrote out the verbal transcription and running description. With each entry in an unfolding episode I stopped to check my interpretations with those of the co-worker. Wherever there were alternative interpretations we would review the sequence as many times as necessary to arrive at mutual agreement. On some occasions teachers and parents were asked to listen to especially difficult sequences to arrive at accurate transcriptions.

I use the term *micro-sociolinguistic analysis* to refer to the analysis of communicative processes in face-to-face interaction. In line with Kendon (1975), I see the primary aim of micro-sociolinguistics to be the description and understanding of how occasions of interaction are organized and maintained.

In this project micro-sociolinguistic analysis involved the identification of contextualization cues the children routinely employed in attempts to communicate about the social activity they were engaged in achieving (Gumperz, 1976; Cook-Gumperz & Gumperz, 1976). *Contextualization cues* refer to specific communicative elements (linguistic, paralinguistic, and extralinguistic) which the children employed in the interactive process. Examples of contextualization cues referred to in Example 3 include linguistic communicative functions containing phonemic, syntactic, and semantic elements; paralinguistic features (intonation, stress, and pitch); gesture and proxemic features; and the manipulation of physical objects in the ecological setting.

Although this phase of analysis cannot be pursued at length here, I should point out that the identification of contextualization cues is seen as a methodological strategy for determining how children link linguistic information with propositional content on the one hand and extralinguistic cues and background expectations on the other. Cook-Gumperz and Gumperz have referred to this articulation of various elements of communicative events as a *process* of contextualization "in which contextual information is both coded as semantic information and signalled as part of the interaction. The signalling of context makes the context available to the participants as a potentially shareable *cognitive construct* which frames the range of possible interpretations both in terms of the relevance of presuppositions and as guides to further action" (Cook-Gumperz & Gumperz, 1976, p. 12).

Following the identification of contextualization cues, the analysis moved to examine the children's production and use of cues across social activities and situations. In this phase there was a search for patterns in the children's articulation of contextualization cues with both the accustomed expectations of various social-ecologial areas of the school and with conventionalized expectations based on sociological or cultural knowledge.

In Example 3 the micro-sociolinguistic analysis uncovers the children's use of contextualization cues in attempts to (a) gain access into an ongoing event; (b) protect interactive space by preventing the entry of additional participants; (c) arrive at a shared agreement which allowed for both the entry of new interactants into the play and the maintenance of the original interactive episode. (see Corsaro, 1979b).

Example 3
Date: March 3   Scene: Outside Climbing Bars
Afternoon Episode #4   Activity: Role play (police)
Time 30' 5"   Participants: Jonathan (4.9), Steven (4.10),
                                                            Graham (3.11), Tommy (4.3),
                                                            Antoinette (4.1), TA,
                                                            Researcher (Bill)

Steven (S) and Jonathan (J) are in climbing bars and Graham (G) approaches bars and attempts to enter. Steven and Jonathan had been playing "police" for some time before Graham's access attempt.

Transcription	*Description*
(1) S-G: No, you can't get in! You can't get in! You can't get in! You can't get in!	S is in bars and moves near where G is trying to enter and shouts down. Volume increases with each repetition.
(2) G-S: Yes we can!	G begins climing up board which is slanted against bars. Plural "we" seems inappropriate since G is alone.
(3) S-G: It's only for police! It's only for policemen!	
(4) S-JG: He's gonna have it, policeman. He's gonna have it.	S climbs down bars toward G. S is referring to J with the title "policemen."

Transcription	Description
(5) J-G: You're gonna have it dum-dum!	S is now standing on ground next to G. As he says "dum-dum," J jumps to ground and pushes G down. G is unhurt; the push was just hard enough to knock G off his feet.
(6) G-J: You are!	G gets back to his feet and moves toward J who backs off. S then moves in front of G and they exchange threatening karate chops, but there is no physical contact. Tommy (T) now enters area and stands near G.
(7) G-T: T, get them! Grab them! Grab them T.	G moves behind T, pushing him forward toward J and S.
(8) T-G: Kick 'em?	
(9) G-T: No, grab them, Grab them quick!	T moves toward J and S who are now climbing back into the bars.
(10) G-T: Quick T. Get in there!	T attempts to enter and S blocks his path.
(11) J-T: I'm gonna take care of you today!	J and T exchange threatening karate chops, but again no actual contact.
(12) G-T: Grab them T! Grab them! Grab 'em!	G moves next to T and near J. J lunges toward G.
(13) J-G: I'll *really* . . .	J places heavy stress on "really" as he reaches for G.
(14) G-J: You're gonna *really* get it though.	G also stresses "really" and completes utterance as he moves out of J's grasp.
(15) T-J: Oh yeah!	"Yeah" stretched out with heavy stress, and is definitely directed to J.
(16) G-T: Yeah, they *really* are.	G seems to assume T's utterance (15) was addressed to him. "Really" is again stressed.
(17) T-G: Come on let's go.	T turns and moves away from bars.
(18) G-T: Yeah	G follows T away from bars.
(19) J-S: Good! We got the run of our policehouse.	J moves higher in bars near S. "Our" is stressed.

S's first utterance to G (1) is a direct warning for him to stay out. The use of the second-person pronoun, repetition, heavy stress, and increasing volume makes this utterance a clear defense of the play area. In line 3, S offers a justification for G's exclusion ("It's only for police"). Of course, there is no way G can be a policeman since he could be a policeman only *if* he had been playing from the start of the episode. The justification for exclusion is similar to the one used in Example 2 ("You're not our friend") in that the children attempting to gain access are denied entry because they are not part of the originally initiated activity. References to friendship or play roles (policemen) are linguistic devices for conveying this fact of social organization and group solidarity in peer interaction.

S's utterance at 4 is a strategy *to involve* J in the protection of interactive space and also *to symbolize* or mark solidarity in the dyad. Instead of calling J by name (or assuming J will hear his threats to G), S *threatens* G through speech directed to J using the title "policeman." As a result S's one utterance performs multiple functions in this context. J takes up on his threat to G (5) and jumps down from the bars to push G to the ground. At this point G enlists help from T and the dispute continues until T recommends leaving and G agrees (18). The use of (and heavy stress on) the word "really" (13, 14, 16) is interesting in that it is preceded by a great deal of threatening behavior. It appears "really" (produced with heavy stress) implies the threats may turn into real fighting (i.e., the children now mean what they say).

The dispute did not end at 19, because G returned shortly thereafter and enlisted aid from a girl (Antoinette) and then from a T.A. With the aid of the T.A., G and A were able to move into the bars. At that point J decided to let them play and tells them his decision by whispering to them. He then attempts to persuade S to agree to the arrangement.

(195) J-S: We want to talk about it, so ..ah..let..let..S why don't we cooperate and why don't you agree to be a nice policeman?
    J is standing in bars next to S. G and A are also in bars.

(196) S-J: O..O..OK.
    S stretches out "OK" and seems unhappy but resigned to the arrangement.

(197) J-S: Here, shake hands.
    J reaches over bar and extends his hand to S. S and J shake hands while A and G watch from other end of bars.

(198) J-S: Hey! I shook it from over this bar.

(199) S-J: We have to get those robbers.
    S points to A and G.

(200) A-G: Come on. We..come on, let's go G.
    G and A climb higher in bars while S moves toward them.

(201) S-J: We have to get the robbers who stole the jewels.

(202) A-G: Come on G.

At this point in the episode the dispute over interactive space has ended and S and J have agreed to accept G and A into the bars. Most interesting, J and S arrive at and seal (the handshake) this agreement with each other rather than G and A. With the agreement G and A are allowed to play and are immediately assigned role in the interaction (robbers, line 201). I consistently observed (in field notes and other videotaped episodes) that acceptance of others into ongoing episodes followed this pattern of (a) agreement among defenders of an area to let others enter and (b) the assignment of positions (policeman, mother, baby, or "friend") to the new members. This pattern is in line with the working hypothesis that the children sense the instability of interactive episodes. Therefore, they initially resist intrusion, which increases intragroup solidarity, and only accept others into play after intragroup negotiation.

Stage 3: Indefinite Triangulation. Contextualization cues can take a number of forms depending on the communicative styles of participants.

Although all cues carrying meaning, *the meanings are conveyed in the course of interactive events*. The meanings of contextualization cues, unlike words which cannot be discussed out of context, "are implicit and cannot directly be talked about. Their signalling value depends on the participants' tacit awareness of their meaningfulness" (Gumperz, 1976; p. 17).

Therefore, in isolating children's use of contextualization cues it is essential that the researcher be a part of the peer interactive episodes under analysis. In the present research I was not only a participant in the peer episodes, but also directed the audio-video recording of theoretically sampled episodes. In analysis I relied on my tacit knowledge as a participant and benefited from videotape recording and consequent ability to examine *repeatedly* the interactive data. But even with the advantages of prior ethnography, participant observation, and videotape recording, the researcher must still *estimate the* validity of his interpretations of the data by involving others in the analysis process.

Cicourel (1974) has referred to this procedure of involving others in the research process as *indefinite triangulation*. Indefinite triangulation is a procedure in which the researcher creates "circumstances whereby the same and different respondents react to information obtained on a previous occasion." With indefinite triangulation, "the role of attention and memory becomes paramount, as does the respondent's ability to utilize specific lexical items or vocabularies" (Cicourel, 1974, p. 97).

In the present research the validity of my interpretations of children's use of contextualization cues and my conclusions regarding the more general patterns in the data were checked by indefinite triangulation. I asked different respondents (research assistants, teachers, parents, and the children themselves) to offer both general interpretations and specific judgments of playbacks of videotaped sequences or entire episodes. In this procedure the respondents' reactions were audiotaped and later compared to my own interpretations which had been recorded prior to the indefinite triangulation process. Indefinite triangulation led to the generation of background data which confirmed or disputed my interpretations of specific events.

In those instances where interpretations varied I refined and/or expanded my original conclusions. For instance, I replayed the videotaped sequences in Example 3 for two of the participants (G and J) and asked the boys, "What were you doing?" Both boys found objects (paper clips and microphone cable) in my office more interesting than the taped sequences which they said "happened a long time ago" (this session was just a week after the original event). With some probing, however, they did point out that "sometimes" they did not want other kids to play and "mess things up."

Jonathan observed that "sometimes it's OK for other kids to come in but sometimes we really *don't want them to play.*" The last part of his phrase was stressed and each word spoken slowly and in a sort of marching cadence. Later when I reviewed the entire episode I found he said the same words (with "you" substituted for "them") to Graham in an attempt to dissuade entry. Jonathan also said: "Sometimes we really mean it too" (i.e., you can't play).

Although using this procedure with young children is difficult, the foregoing responses were generally in line with my interpretations of the sequences. The boys' responses support my general conclusion that exclusion is a means of protecting interactive space and insuring stability. Also Johathan's use of the adverb "really" is interesting since this same adverb with a similar stress pattern was used consistently in the videotaped sequence (see Example 3).

Indefinite triangulation is an important methodological technique for estimating the validity of interpretations of qualitative data. It is also an important tool for the initial testing and refinement of hypotheses and, in this sense, a vital part of theory generation.

SUMMARY AND CONCLUSIONS

Given Examples 1–3 and the data from indefinite triangulation, I can now offer a few brief conclusions regarding the relationship between friendship and defense of play areas. Children are, due to repeated experiences of breakdowns, aware of the fragility of peer interaction in this setting. The children learn to minimize disruptions by resisting the access attempts of others. Justifications for exclusion, however, are a seldom directly tied to the recognition of instability, but rather are linked to the children's developing conceptions of friendship and growing awareness of means for differentiation (i.e., you can't play because you're not our friend, not a policeman, not a girl, etc.—all variants of "you're not one of us" *at this point in time*). These findings imply that social organization of this peer environment is a fragile one and demands the constant production of socially ordered events on the part of the young children. In this process of reality production, the children are also developing sociological and cultural knowledge related to social positions and characteristics of social interactants.

In this report I have presented a natural history of the field entry, data collection, and analysis process. I pointed to the importance of using information gained at one phase in the research process for later phases of data collection and analysis. The major advantage of this micro-ethnographic approach is the rich, extensive data it generates regarding children's communicative processes and social worlds. In this respect, I believe the use of more recent audio-video techniques must be grounded in traditional ethnographic techniques to insure both the *representativeness* of the data set and the *validity* of the researcher's interpretations and conclusions.

REFERENCES

Barker, R., & Wright, H. *One boy's day*. Hamden, Conn.: Archon, 1966.

Becker, H. Problems of inference and proof in participant observation. *American Sociological Review*, 1958, *23*, 652–660.

Becker, H. *Sociological work*. Chicago: Aldine, 1970.

Blurton-Jones, N. (Ed.). *Ethological studies of child behavior*. Cambridge: Cambridge University Press, 1972.

Bronson, W. Developments in behavior with age-mates during the second year of life. In M. Lewis & L. Rosenblum (Eds.), *Friendship and peer relations*. New York: Wiley, 1975.

Bruner, J., Jolly, A., & Sylva, K. (Eds.), *Play: its role in development and evolution*. New York: Basic, 1976.

Cicourel, A. *Method and measurement in sociology*. New York: Free Press, 1964.

Cicourel, A. *Theory and method in a study of Argentine fertility*. New York: Wiley, 1974.

Cicourel, A., *et al. Language use and school performance*. New York: Academic Press, 1974.

Cook-Gumperz, J., & Corsaro, W. Social-ecological constraints on children's communicative strategies. *Sociology*, 1977, *11* (3) 411–434.

Cook-Gumperz, J., & Gumperz, J. Context in children's speech. In J. Cook-Gumperz & J. Gumperz (Eds.), *Papers on language and context*, Working Paper #46. Language Behavior Research Laboratory, University of California, Berkeley, 1976.

Corsaro, W. Young children's conception of status and role. *Sociology of Education*, 1979a, *52*, 46–59.

Corsaro, W. We're friends, right: Children's use of access rituals in a nursery school. *Language in Society*, 1979b, *8*, 315–336.

Garvey, C. *Play*. Cambridge, Mass.: Harvard University Press, 1977.

Garvey, C., & Hogan, R. Social speech and social interaction: egocentrism revisited, *Child Development*, 1973, *44*, 562–568.

Goffman, E. *Behavior in public places*. New York: Free Press, 1963.

Greer, B. First days in the field. In P. Hammond (Ed.), *Sociologists at work*. New York: Doubleday, 1967.

Gumperz, J. Language, communication and public negotiation. In P. Sanday (Ed.), *Anthropology and the public interest: Fieldwork and theory*. New York: Academic Press, 1976.

Herron, R., & Sutton-Smith, B. (Eds.). *Child's play*. New York: Wiley, 1971.

Hutt, C. Exploration and play in children. In R. Herron & B. Sutton-Smith (Eds.), *Child's play*. New York: Wiley, 1971.

Keenan, E. Conversational competence in children, *Journal of Child Language*, 1974, *1*, 163–183.

Keenan, E. Making it last: repetition in children's discourse. In S. Ervin-Tripp & C. Mitchell-Kernan (Eds.), *Child discourse*, 1977. New York: Academic Press.

Kendon, A., Harris, R., & Key, M. (Eds.). Organization of behavior in face-to-face interaction. The Hague: Mouton, 1975.

Lewis, M., & Rosenblum, L. *Friendship and peer relations*. New York: Wiley, 1975.

Mueller, E. The maintenance of verbal exchanges between young children, *Child Development*, 1972, *43* (3) 930–938.

Schatz, M., & Gelman, R. The development of communication skills: modification in the speech of young children as a function of the listener, *SRCD Monographs*, 1973, *5*, 38.

Schatzman, L., & Strauss, A. *Field research: strategies for a natural sociology*. Englewood Cliffs, N.J.: Prentice-Hall, 1973.

Schwartzman, H. The anthropological study of children's play, *Annual Review of Anthropology,* 1976, *5,* 289–328.

Speier, M. *How to observe face-to-face communication: a sociological introduction.* Pacific Palisades, Calif.: Goodyear, 1973.

Strauss, A. *Psychiatric ideologies and institutions.*New York: Free Press, 1964.

7 When Is a Context?
Some Issues and Methods
in the Analysis
of Social Competence

Frederick Erickson
Michigan State University
Jeffrey Shultz
University of Cincinnati

(Scene: Wedding in an apartment living room. The couple being married and the priest stand facing one another. Witnesses and friends stand in concentric semi-circles behind the couple. Lennart Erickson, age six months, lies on a sofa in the opposite corner of the room. The priest speaks the last line in the wedding ceremony.)

> Priest: In the Name of the Father, and of the Son, and of the Holy Spirit.
> People: Amen.
> Lennart Erikson (happily, in the moment before anyone moves): Aaah!

Children and adults, in order to know whatever they need to know in order to operate in a manner acceptable to others in society (Goodenough 1957), need to know what forms of verbal and nonverbal behavior are appropriate in what social contexts. As Hymes (1974) notes, this involves much more than *linguistic competence,* Chomsky's term for a speaker's capacity to employ (a) surface structural rules of phonology and syntax, (b) deep structural interpretive procedures (Chomsky, 1965). For Hymes, *linguistic competence* must necessarily entail *social competence,* since acceptable speaking requires the ability to produce utterances that are not only grammatically appropriate, but situationally appropriate as well. The production of appropriate social behavior from moment to moment requires knowing what context one is in and when contexts change as well as knowing what behavior is considered appropriate in each of those contexts. We think that the capacity for monitoring contexts must be an essential feature of social competence; the capacity to assess when a context is as well as what it is. In this paper, we detail some theoretical and methodological issues in our ways of studying how people are able to decide "when" a context is as well as "what" it is.

How do persons assess what context they are in? What features of context do they seem to be attending to? Contexts can be thought of as not simply *given* in the physical setting—kitchen, living room, sidewalk in front of drug store—nor in combinations of persons (two brothers, husband and wife, firemen). Rather, contexts are constituted by what people are doing and where and when they are doing it. As McDermott (1976a) puts it succinctly, people in interaction become environments for each other. Ultimately, social contexts consist of mutually shared and ratified definitions of situation *and* in the social actions persons take on the basis of these definitions (Mehan, *et al.,* 1976).

These interactionally constituted environments are embedded in time and can change from moment to moment. With each context change, the role relationships among participants are redistributed to produce differing configurations of concerted action, e.g., two brothers can play together one moment and fight the next; firemen can play cards one moment and jump on the fire truck the next (Blom & Gumperz, 1972). Mutual rights and obligations of interactants are continually amenable to subtle readjustment (Cicourel, 1972) and redistribution into differing configurations of concerted action that can be called *participant structures* (cf. Philips, 1972, 1974), or coherently cooccurring sets (cf. Ervin-Tripp, 1972). These structures include ways of speaking, listening, getting the floor and holding it, and leading and following.

Differing participant structures may not only be juxtaposed back to back across time in getting from one social occasion to the next, e.g., from playing cards to riding the fire truck, but differing participant structures can also alternate within a single occasion; e.g., a card game may contain the primary constituent "slots"/getting ready/, /playing/, and /winding up/ (Mathiot, 1976; Pike, 1967; Goffman, 1974). Each slot can be expected to be marked by different distributions of speech events and speech functions across these primary slots within occasions.

Here the recent work of sociolinguists articulates with that of Scheflen, whose pioneering "context analysis" of group psychotherapy interviews (1973a, 1974) stands to date as the most comprehensive treatement of the sequential juxtaposition of differing participation structures within a single interactional occasion. Scheflen identified differences in interactional activity from one principal part of the therapy session to the next and identified the major junctures between primary parts. He found, as did Kendon and Ferber (1973), McDermott (1976a, 1976b), Shultz (1979), and Bremme (1976), that during junctures between principal parts of occasions major reorientation of postural configurations (*positions*) occurs among participants, and that across the duration of a principal part, these positions are sustained collectively. We have reported a related finding for changes in interpersonal distance (*proxemic shifts*) between speakers (Erickson, 1976b).

Postural and proxemic configurations are instances of a general class of culturally conventional signals termed *contextualization cues* (Gumperz, 1976). Such cues signal how messages are to be interpreted from moment to moment. Some cues usually apply as diacritical marks to behavior slots of relatively short duration, such as words, phrases, or asides (cf. Jefferson, 1972, on *sides sequences*). Other cues, such as postural shifts, mark boundaries of slots that are longer in duration. Apparently postural positions function to mark these longer, principal parts of occasions, but it would be premature to conclude that postural markers were necessarily the primary markers of major slots, or the only ones that participants attend to at major junctures. At any rate, what one sees and hears at the junctures between principal slots is a *redundancy of contextualization cues* (Fitzgerald, 1975). The multimodal nature of communication produces great modality redundancy across the verbal and nonverbal channels (Cook-Gumperz & Gumperz, 1976). Many dimensions of difference in performance form, in addition to the postural and the proxemic, can have contrastive relevance as *contextualization cues*—changes in voice tone, pitch, and other features of speech prosody; changes in linguistic code, style, and topic; changes in the tempo and rhythmic organization of speech and body motion; changes in gaze direction and facial expression; changes in the number of speakers and listeners (cf. Hymes, 1974; Birdwhistell, 1970).

In addition to modality redundancy, participants can also rely on the sequential relationships among different behaviors to inform them of their context. Only in sequential context can shifts in performance form, such as rate of speech, have potential for contrastive relevance; a shift to "faster" speech is only a shift in terms of the rate of speech immediately before the faster rate.

The contexting of *series position* makes possible yet another kind of cue redundancy, *temporal redundancy*. This redundancy may not be so important a factor in highly stylized formal activities, such as military rifle drill, in which the drill sergeant's command is instantly responded to by the soldiers with a simultaneous postural position shift. Yet there is temporal redundancy in even so temporally compressed a series of cues as: / present/ /(pause)/ /arms!/ /soldiers move position of rifles/. And, in more informally organized occasions, the multidimensional configurations of contextualization cues may be dispersed over longer strips of time, building up great temporal redundancy even though there is relatively little modality redundancy at any particular point in time across the series.

There is often a "ripple effect" of temporally redundant contextualization cues at the junctures between primary parts of the occasions; a behavioral raggedness Pike (1967) referred to as a structural *indeterminancy of segment boundaries.* This combination of modality redundancy and temporal redundancy in contextualization cues at junctures results in an interactional structure in which the junctures between major constituent segments are themselves durations across time—times of transition analogous to transition passages in music, by which a composer manipulates the expectancy of the listener that something new is about to happen (Meyer, 1956). (For a prolonged example of boundary indeterminacy, see the sixteen measures preceding the last movement of the Beethoven Sixth Symphony, together with the eight measures directly following the beginning of the movement.)

The combination of temporal and modality redundancy in contextualization cueing seems to function as an interactional fail/safe mechanism. It insures that, despite individual differences in interactional competence, whether due to difference in culture, to personality, or to level of acquisition of competence (cf. Cook-Gumperz & Corsaro, 1976), and despite differences in individual variation in focus of attention at any given moment, members of the interacting group are likely collectively and individually to "get" the socially important message that something new is happening.

Despite the redundancy of cues, it is usually not possible to determine (in informal occasions from the United States at least) an exact moment when the definition of situation has changed. Only after the cues for a change in context have occurred is it possible to determine that something has indeed changed. Thus it would seem that it is by retrospective evaluation, summing up the ongoing stream of interaction as a gestalt across time, that persons determine that the context has changed. While the change is happening, persons may perceive that something new is happening and that a change in their behavior may be called for. They may infer expectations of what will happen next. Then subsequent events may help progressively to make the definition of situation unambiguous; their expectations will be progressively confirmed or disconfirmed (Bremme, 1976). This is what ethnomethodologists refer to as "prospective-retrospective interpretive procedures" (Mehan & Wood, 1975).

The six-month-child in the wedding example cited earlier waited until a change in context had occurred before making his vocalization. He may have perceived the change in context as cued by the silence following the collective "Amen" in response to the priest's verbal closing formula, or he may have attended to the alternation from single speaker to multiple speakers. There was no large postural position change before the child's vocalization. Whatever part of the constellation of closing cues he attended to, that he had remained quiet throughout the preceding parts of the ritual and chose the moment following the "Amen" to make his vocalization suggests that he may have been attending to contexts and to the junctures between them during which something new was happening.

The previous example involved a shift between two occasions. Within a single occasion, the most socially important something new are its principal constituent parts: Scheflen calls the sequence of principal parts the *program* of the occasion, a notion similar to Miller, Galanter, and Pribram's *plan* (1960). One reason that moments of transition between one primary part of the plan and the next may be so redundantly marked is that these moments are choice points—new alternatives from among a range of options for participant structure are presenting themselves then for collective selection and definition. There are limits to the range of options (the paradigmatic set, cf. Ervin-Tripp, 1972) for what can appropriately happen next. Once the selection is made and the content changes, what follows may be entailed in—overdetermined by—the selection itself.

There is considerable, accumulating evidence suggesting that not only is social behavior hierarchically organized from large slots down to small embedded slots of microsecond duration (cf. Birdwhistell, 1970; Condon & Ogston, 1967), but that processes of interactional inference or social cognition are similarly organized. As experienced in social performance, hierarchically organized activity can be apprehended only as relationships of succession across time. The relatively undifferentiated complexity of the myriad "slots" of activity of short duration that are strung together in interactions like beads in succession across time is reduced by a *plan* into a simpler order; into *slots* of proportionally long duration and high social salience within the whole occasion.

In the inferential work of interactional competence, it is as if the string of constituent events, although continuous in time, were made by social salience (and the contrastive relevance of alternation in behavioral form) discontinuous in "mass" and "texture" across time. Interactional inference could be compared with fingering one's way along a rosary, which has beads of differing sizes as well as spaces between the beads, rather than fingering one's way along a string of perfectly matched pearls.

But, because interaction is not an object but a social accomplishment, interactional performance cannot be compared with the rosary itself. Rather, it is as if all participants in interaction collectively create and sustain the rosary in their feeling along it with their fingers—by what ethno-methodologists call *reflexivity*—mutually constitutive interplay between expectation and action (Mehan & Wood, 1975); *the participants became the rosary*—their collaborative doings constitute the social organization of the event.

From an analysis of the structure of their doings, by identifying differences in the texture of their activity across time and by specifying the alternative choices that are culturally appropriate at the points of change in texture, the analyst can describe the inferences which participants make in producing the social occasion. Empirically derived models of the organization of interactional performance with emphasis on the principal parts of occasions and the junctures between them are thus the first step toward developing models of the social competence of interactional participants. It is appropriate, then, to work analytically from the molar level of the plan on down, rather than from the molecular level of the word, gesture, sentence—or even the speech act—on up.

Recent attempts at such modeling can be seen in Sacks, Schegloff, and Jefferson's (1974) analysis of turn-taking in conversations, in McDermott's (1976a, 1976b) analysis of the organization of classroom reading lessons, in Mehan's (1976, 1979) studies of teaching sequences, and in Erickson's (1979) analysis of the social and cultural organization of *paying attention* and *explaining* in counseling interviews. Argyle and his associates at Oxford (1976) have been working on the theoretical and empirical problems of identifying primary constituent parts of whole interactional occasions. Other related work is that of Gumperz and Herasimchuk (1975) and Cook-Gumperz and Corsaro (1976).

A research group at the Harvard Graduate School of Education has also worked in this area, studying the social organization of such classroom activities as playing a board game (Shultz, 1979), talking with the teacher in the "circle" at the beginning of the school day (Bremme, 1976), and being interrupted during classroom events by visitors (Florio, 1978). (For additional work in this area, see Bremme & Erickson, 1977; Van Ness, 1977; Florio & Shultz, 1979; Schultz and Florio, 1979; Au, 1980; Erickson & Shultz, in press; Wilson & Erickson, in press.)

Recently, we have been interested in identifying shifts in participation structure within such occasions and within lessons, shifts from *less formal and instrumental* activity to *more formal and instrumental,* and back again. We find these shifts occurring between principal parts within occasions that both observers and participants in the classroom label *emically* (cf. Pike, 1967) as undifferentiated wholes when they give an initial answer to the question "What/time/is it now?"—/lesson time/, /snack time/, /first circle time/. Within the occasion, e.g., /lesson/, we find constituent "times" of differing participant structure, with differing rules of appropriateness for paying attention, getting the floor, maintaining topical relevance, fidgeting. When children "miss" such situational shifts within an occasion—especially the shifts from less instrumental to more instrumental activity that can be glossed as "getting down to business," they are sanctioned for situationally inappropriate behavior by the teacher and other children.

Essentially, our procedure for discovering the constituent structure of occasions consists of making judgments of *same/different* and *next* across real time. We work from audiovisual behavior records—sound film or videotape that is shot continuously, with the camera moving as little as possible, keeping all the participants in the occasion within the visual frame. Usually we begin our recording at least five minutes before the occasions we are studying begin (before /school/ begins in the morning, before a particular

/lesson/ begins). We continue recording until after those events of interest end (the children leave the classroom to go home for /lunch/, they are well into their /snack/ after having had a /lesson/).

If we are using videotape, the behavior records collected at a site arrive back at the laboratory as hour or half-hour reels of tape. We then begin a six-stage process of viewing the tapes analytically.

Stage 1. This stage of viewing follows the pattern by which the material was shot in the first place. We view each reel throughout, stopping it only very occasionally, taking most notes as the tape is running continuously. These intentionally sparse notes become an index of all the major occasions on the tape, showing (by tape deck counter numbers) the approximate location of occasions and of the transitions between occasions. At this stage we may index a number of reels before moving on the next stage.

Stage 2. After a *corpus* of tapes is indexed it is searched for analogous occasions of theoretical interest, e.g., all /lessons/, all /snacks/, or whatever. We choose one instance of a kind of occasions for more detailed analysis. Criteria for choice include the intrinsic interest the instance has for us (this judgment is arrived at through our intuitions about its completeness, the presence within it of phenomena of theoretical salience, and perhaps its salience for participants, if we have a sense of this from participant observation at the research site), and the quality of picture and sound on the tape.

Once the instance has been chosen, it is recorded on a copy tape. Again as with the original procedure for shooting on site we begin the copy recording at a point a few minutes before the occasion begins and continue copying a few minutes past the end of the occasion into the next one. In making the duplicate we use a time-date generator to print electronically on the duplicate videotape digital clock numbers that appear in playback superimposed on the screen. (The numbers indicate the elapsing of time in the following units: day, hour, minute, second, and tenth of second.) In much of our recent work a stopwatch can be used to identify real time, but the availability of superimposed time numbers during playback makes the analysis of timing far more accurate and much less laborious.

In viewing the tape during the second stage of analysis our procedures again follow those by which the material was recorded in the first place. We view the occasion as a whole, from before it to after it, focusing on what all participants are doing together, not on what individuals are doing separately. We note the approximate location in time of the beginning and ending of the occasion and the approximate location of what seem to be junctures between principal constituent parts of the whole. (In a whole occasion of roughly 10–20 minutes there are usually three or four main parts.) This process of establishing the approximate temporal location of junctures and principal parts requires two or three viewings. We attend at this stage mainly to the junctures between parts rather than to the parts themselves, both because the junctures have theoretical salience for us and because the pileup of temporal and modality redundancy at junctures make these moments discontinuous in interactional texture from those preceding and following them in time—during the juncture one sees the most intuitively obvious shifts in communication behavior form, nonverbally and verbally, including changes in postural configuration.

In each successive viewing of the whole occasion we take notes describing what is happening, verbally and nonverbally, during what seem to be the major junctures between parts, and we take notes describing what is happening just before and just after the junctures. Then we locate the descriptive information on a chart with a continuous horizontal time line, indicating on the chart the approximate temporal location of junctures between principal parts and characterizing the parts themselves in terms of very general features of participation structure and topic or main activity. This chart provides a synoptic "wide-angle" picture of the structure of the whole occasion.

At this point of analysis we may interview participants in the occasion in a *viewing session,* asking them to stop the tape as often as they can while viewing it with us; as often as they sense something new is happening. As they stop the tape, we elicit their characterizations of what is happening and what could reasonably be expected to happen, and *not to happen,* next. By this procedure we get a sense of participants' emic construction of the occasion—their point of view as members—before we proceed too far with our etic analysis of the formal properties of behavioral organization in the occasion, from the researcher's relatively distanced point of view.

Stage 3.   Here we locate precisely the junctures or transition sections between primary parts of the occasion and identify specifically the differences in participant structure across the junctures. In viewing the tape we proceed first by going to the approximate location of a juncture between two primary parts (the temporal location arrived at in Stage 2 analysis). Then we view this juncture repeatedly, from before it to after it, noting the changes in postural position, speech prosody, and any other features of speech style and topic that are occurring before, during, and after the juncture. Here, too, we often diagram the postural positions and distance relationships among the participants, the direction of gaze and shifts in gaze, and transcribe along a time line the speech of all participants. We note the temporal location of all phenomena we decide to describe in detail, using the time reference code printed on the videotape.

In these repeated viewings across a single juncture we decompose the behavioral gestalts in the material by trying to attend mainly to one aspect of communication behavior at a time, e.g., looking mainly at postural position shifts across the juncture and not listening to the words, then transcribing (over the same portion of videotape) the participants' speech without looking particularly at the nonverbal behavior accompanying the speech, then listening to intonation contour "tunes" and charting them without attending to the syntax of the speech. Whatever the communication channel or mode being attended to, the analytic viewing and listening procedure consists of playing the tape across a juncture, then rewinding back ahead of the juncture to the same starting point as before and replaying the tape. By this means one establishes the sequential order of communication events, locates changes in those events precisely in time, and collects descriptive information on the behavioral form of events.

Information from this analytic decomposition of the behavioral gestalt before, during, and after the juncture is reassembled in a synoptic chart of the interaction around the juncture. Such a chart—which may include the transcript of speech and organizes all phenomena accounted for analytically on a horizontal time line—is like an enlargement or close-up photograph of one portion of the "wide-angle" picture of the whole occasion that was provided by the synoptic chart prepared at Stage 2 of the analysis. At this stage of analysis we proceed analytically from juncture to juncture within the occasion, doing as much descriptive detail in charting each juncture and its immediate temporal *surround* as is necessary for our question of theoretical interest. We try to limit our description to those features of behavioral organization that are theoretically salient at the time; e.g., if we were interested in a shift from less instrumental to more instrumental activity within a lesson, we might look only in Stage 3 detail at that shift and do only a very general characterization of the whole occasion, moving then to identify and examine analogous instances of this shift in other instances of lessons (this is Stage 6 in the inquiry, and will be discussed later).

To reiterate a theoretical point made earlier, since interaction unfolds *in time,* distinctions between *same* and *different* can be made only in terms of the distinction *next.* Hence the researcher must rewind the tape and replay the same segment repeatedly. Such replaying allows an attention to sequence relationships in time that is analogous to, yet is a much more detailed and distanced mode of apprehending, than the participants' *retrospective-prospective* interpretive procedures for making sense from moment to moment as the occasion originally unfolded in time. This analytic principle applies to all the stages of inquiry we are describing.

Stage 4. Here we attend primarily to the participation structures ahead of the junctures we have focused on in detail in Stage 3. We go to each principal juncture of interest and rewind the tape back to the next previous principal juncture. Replaying the whole segment between the two junctures, we characterize the participation structure between them in fairly broad strokes relative to the level of detail with which the subsequent juncture and its immediate surround was described, i.e., for the whole participation structure between principal junctures we may not transcribe all the speech nor chart all the gestures of all participants. Rather we try to attend to the intuitively "biggest" things that are happening—what postural positions are sustained; what the topics of talk are; who does most of the talking and listening; what general interactional strategies are occurring across the whole segment that can be glossed in ordinary language, e.g., / getting ready to start/, / dealing with the main issue/, /taking time out/. As with Stage 3, the level of descriptive detail in Stage 4 varies greatly according to our research question at the time. We do not attempt exhaustive description, but analytic description for the purpose of model construction.

Stage 5.   At this point we attempt an initial test of the validity of our model of interaction structure. In the previous stages we have been constructing a model derived from analysis of a single case—a *type-case analysis,* in the terminology of Gumperz (personal communication). In the type-case model we propose to show principles of social organization underlying the surface form of communication behavior in interaction. In particular, we are interested in demonstrating the contrastive relevance to participants of contextualization cues at principal junctures within an occasion.

There are four types of evidence from which inferences can be drawn as to the social significance manifested in particular configuration of performance form. These are the requisite testing points for a single case-derived model of interaction:

1. During those moments the model designates as moments of transition there are descriptively specifiable shifts in interactional performance for occurring.
2. After a moment of transition, specific forms and functions of communication behavior—ways of listening, ways of speaking, kinds of topics, speech acts, postural positions, etc.—are differently distributed in contrast to their frequency of presence or absence and their sequential position of occurrence during the time prior to the moment designated by the model as a moment of transition.
3. After the moment of transition, kinds of interactional behavior which before the juncture were sanctioned if present (or absent) are no longer sanctioned by participants if these behaviors are present (or absent), and kinds of behavior previously not sanctioned are now sanctioned; i.e., participants behave as if rules of appropriateness differ from before the juncture to after it. (cf. Mehan & Wood, 1975; McDermott, 1976b, for elaboration of rules of evidence of this type.)

4. If in a viewing session the participants themselves or other informants are shown the juncture and its immediate surround, their accounts of what is socially appropriate before and after the juncture will agree with analytically descriptive evidence of types 2 and 3 above.

Stage 6.   This final stage involves establishing the generalizability of the single-case analysis conducted in the previous five stages. Here we search our indexed *corpus* of tapes for analogous instances of whatever kind of occasion we were investigating. We view all the occasions and locate all instances of whatever phenomena we are investigating, e.g., all shifts from less instrumental to more instrumental activity within a lesson. Then we examine all instances in the *corpus* (or a systematically selected sample of them), noting the distribution of communication forms and functions before, during, and after the juncture, as in Stage 3, but now limiting our attention to only those communication forms and functions that had structural salience in the model derived from the single case. If in the analysis of multiple instances the same types of evidence obtained as those discussed in Stage 5, then the generalizability of the analytic model has been initially demonstrated; i.e., we have shown that the single case is a typical case at least within the *corpus* investigated. If disconfirming evidence appears at the sixth stage of analysis, we reexamine the initial case and redesign the analytic model of it to account for the additional variation discovered by examining multiple instances. Or we may decide that another of the instances is more broadly representative of the organizing principles we have been discovering. Then, we restudy that case and construct from it the final type case model.

CONCLUSION

We have described a theoretical and procedural approach to the study of the social organization of interaction. This approach is by no means unique. It is generally similar to that used by Scheflen, Kendon, McDermott, and Mehan, among others. To our knowledge this approach has not yet been described in terms of specific procedural steps one takes while watching a videotape or film.

We have developed methods of working *from the top down.* We argue for the "psychological validity" of the results derived from such methods of analysis, which we think are congruent with the ways participants in interaction themselves must be construing interaction as it happens, attending first to longer segments as gestalts and then to shorter ones embedded within the larger frames. Type-case models of interaction structure point to what a collectivity of members need to know in order to produce the interaction.

The methods we have described can apply to a range of problems in the analysis of communication structure and interactional competence—from questions requiring more "macro" viewing strategies and notation systems to those requiring more "micro" strategies. The level of analysis varies with the research problem addressed, but the general approach applies accross levels. The particular level we have chosen to describe as a way of illustrating the general approach does not require slow-motion viewing equipment, which is one reason that level was chosen for discussion here.

The other reason for choosing it is theoretical. A theory of the interactional construction of social contexts is crucial to the understanding of how communication forms come to manifest social as well as referential meaning. One way of studying how contexts are socially generated and sustained in face-to-face interaction is to study the processes of organization by which contexts change for moment to moment and the processes of social cognition—interactional inference—by which participants monitor verbal and nonverbal indicators of such change.

In the comparative study of social competence one would expect considerable variation, due to culture, situation, and developmental level, of the following kinds: variation in how many participant structures can coexist as multiple frames within the same social occasion (cf. Goffman, 1974), in when and how often participant structure changes within the occasion, in the communicative means by which the changes are cued, in the cognitive processes of interactional inference, and in the content and range of options for performance that are conventionally available to participants at the choice points of major interactional junctures.

REFERENCES

Argyle, M., Clarke, D., & Collett, P. Project on the sequential structure of social behavior. Interim report to the Social Science Research Council, Oxford University Department of Experimental Psychology, 1976.

Au, Kathryn Hu-Pei, *A test of the social organizational hypothesis: relationships between participation structures and learning to read.* Urbana, Ill: Unpublished doctoral dissertation, University of Illinois, 1980.

Birdwhistell, R. L. *Kinesics and context.* Philadelphia: University of Pennsylvania Press, 1970.

Blom, J. P., & Gumperz, J. J. Social meaning in linguistic structures: Code switching in Norway, in J. Gumperz & D. Hymes (Eds.), *Directions in sociolinguistics.* New York: Holt, Rinehart & Winston, 1972.

Bremme, D. W. Accomplishing a classroom event: A microethnography of first circle. Working paper #3 Newton Classroom Interaction Project, Harvard Graduate School of Education, 1976.

Bremme, D., & Erickson, F. Behaving and making sense: Some relations among verbal and non-verbal ways of acting in a classroom. *Theory into Practice, xvi* (3), School of Education, Ohio State University, June 1977.

Chomsky, N. *Aspects of the theory of syntax.* Cambridge, Mass.: MIT Press, 1965.

Cicourel, A. Basic and normative rules in the negotiation of status and role. In D. Sudnow (Ed.), *Studies in social interaction.* New York: Free Press, 1972.

Condon, W., & Ogston, W. D. A segmentation of behavior. *Journal of Psychiatric Research,* 1967, *5,* 221-235.

Cook-Gumperz, J., & Corsaro, W. Social-ecological constraints on children's communicative strategies. In *Papers on language and context,* Working Paper #46, Language Behavior Research Laboratory, University of California, Berkeley, 1976.

Cook-Gumperz, J., & Gumperz, J. J. Context in children's speech. In J. Cook-Gumperz & J. J. Gumperz (Eds.), *Papers on language and context,* Working paper #46, Language Behavior Research Laboratory, University of California, Berkeley, 1976.

Duncan, S., Jr. Some signals and rules for taking speaking turns in conversations. *Journal of Personality and Social Psychology,* 1972, *23,* 283-292.

Erickson, F. Gatekeeping encounters: a social selection process. In P. R. Sanday (Ed.), *Anthropology and the public interest.* New York: Academic Press, 1976a.

Erickson, F. One function of proxemic shifts in face-to-face interaction. In A. Kendon, R. Harris, & M. S. Key (Eds.), *The organization of behavior in face-to-face interaction.* The Hague/Chicago: Mouton/Aldine, 1976b.

Erickson, F. Talking down: Some cultural sources of miscommunication in inter-racial interviews. In Aaron Wolfgang, (Ed.), *Nonverbal Communication* New York: Academic Press, 1979.

Erickson, F., & Mohatt, G. The cultural organization of participation structures in two classrooms of Indian students. In G. Spindler (Ed.), *The ethnography of schooling, educational anthropology in action.* New York: Holt, Rinehart & Winston, in press.

Erickson, F., & Shultz, J. *Talking to "The Man": social and cultural organization of communication in school counseling interviews.* New York: Academic Press, in press.

Ervin-Tripp, S. On sociolinguistic rules: alternation and co-occurrence. In J. Gumperz & D. Hymes (Eds.), *Directions in sociolinguistics: the ethnography of communication.* New York: Holt, Rinehart & Winston, 1972.

Fitzgerald, D. K. The language of ritual events among the *Ga* of Southern Ghana. In M. Sanches & B. Blount (Eds.), *Sociocultural dimensions of language use.* New York: Academic Press, 1975.

Florio, S. *Learning how to go to school: an ethnography of interaction in a kindergarten/first grade classroom.* Unpublished dissertation, 1978.

Florio, S., & Shultz, J. Social competence at home and at shool. *Theory into Practice, 18:*4 (Oct. 1979): 234-243 School of Education, Ohio State University.

Goffman, E. *Frame analysis.* New York: Harper Colophon Books, 1974.

Goodenough, W. Cultural anthropology and linguistics. In P. Garvin (Ed.), *Report of the seventh annual round table meeting on linguistics and language study.* Monograph series on Languages and Linguistics, Vol. 9. Washington, D.C.: Georgetown University Press, 1957.

Gumperz, J. J., & Herasimchuk, E. The conversational analysis of social meaning: a study of classroom interaction. In M. Sanches & B. Blount (Eds.), *Sociocultural dimensions of language use.* New York: Academic Press, 1975.

Gumperz, J. J. The conversational analysis of social meaning: a study of classroom interaction. In R. Shuy (Ed.), *Sociolinguistics: current trends and prospects.* 23rd Annual Round Table, Monograph Series on Languages and Linguistics. Washington, D.C.: Georgetown University Press, 1972.

Gumperz, J. J. Language, communication, and public negotiation. In P. R. Sanday (Ed.), *Anthropology and the public interest.* New York: Academic Press, 1976.

Hymes, D. *Foundations in sociolinguistics.* Philadelphia: University of Pennsylvania Press, 1974.

Jefferson, G. Sides sequences. In D. Sudnow (Ed.),*Studies in social interaction.* New York: Free Press, 1972.

Kendon, A., & Ferber, A. A description of some human greetings. In R. Michael & J. Crook (Eds.), *Comparative ecology and behavior of primates.* New York: Academic Press, 1973.

Mathiot, M. On building a frame of reference for the analysis of face-to-face interaction. Paper delivered at the Annual Meeting of the American Anthropological Association, Washington, D.C., Nov. 19, 1976.

McDermott, R. P. *Kids make sense: an ethnographic account of the interactional management of success and failure in one first-grade classroom.* Unpublished doctoral dissertation, Stanford University: 1976a.

McDermott, R. P. (with Gospodinoff, K.). Criteria for an ethnographically adequate description of activities and their contexts. Paper delivered at the Annual Meeting of the American Anthropological Association, Washington, D.C., Nov. 19, 1976.

Mehan, H., & Wood, H. *The reality of ethnomethodology.* New York: Wiley, 1975.

Mehan, H., Cazden, C., Fisher, S., & Maroules, N. The social organization of classroom lessons. A technical report submitted to the Ford Foundation, 1976.

Mehan, H. *Learning Lessons: Social organization in the classroom.* Cambridge: Harvard U. Press, 1979.

Meyer, L. *Emotion and meaning in music.* Chicago: University of Chicago Press, 1956.

Miller, G. A., Abianter, E., & Pribram, K. H. *Plans and the structure of behavior.* New York: Holt, 1960.

Philips, S. U. Participant structures and communicative competence: Warm Springs children in community and classroom. In C. Cazden, V. John, & D. Hymes (Eds.), *Functions of language in the classroom.* New York: Teachers College Press, 1972.

Philips, S. U. *The invisible culture: communication in classroom and community on the Warm Springs Reservations.* Unpublished doctoral dissertation, University of Pennsylvania, 1974.

Pike, K. *Language in relation to a unified theory of the structure of human behavior.* The Hague: Mouton, 1967.

Sacks, H., Jefferson, G., & Schegloff, E. A simplest systematics for the organization of turn-taking for conversation. *Language, 50* (4), 696–735.

Scheflen, A. *Communicational structure: analysis of a psychotherapy transaction.* Bloomington, Ind.: Indiana University Press, 1973.

Scheflen, A. *How behavior means.* New York: Anchor Books, 1974.

Shultz, J. It's not whether you win or lose, it's how you play the game. In O. Garnica & M. King (Eds.), *Language, children and society.* Oxford: Pergamon, 1979.

Shultz, J. & S. Florio. "Stop and freeze: the negotiation of social and physical space in a kindergarten—first grade classroom." *Anthropology and Education Quarterly 10,* 3 (Fall, 1979): 166–181.

Wilson, J., & Erickson, F. *Audiovisual Documentation of Everyday Life in Schools: A resource book on sources and uses of film and videotape:* E. Lansing, Mich.: Institute for Research on Teaching, in press.

Van Ness, W. *Social control and social organization in an Alaskan Athabaskan classroom: A microethnography of 'getting ready' for reading.* Cambridge, Mass.: Harvard Graduate School of Education Qualifying Paper, 1977.

8 Mapping Instructional Conversations— A Sociolinguistic Ethnography

Judith L. Green
University of Delaware
and
Cynthia Wallat
National Institute of Education

Instructional conversations are part of the everyday life of the classroom. More than content, however, is transmitted during instructional conversation. Social processes are also being constructed, modified, selected, checked, suspended, terminated, and recommended by the participants as they engage in instructional conversations (Blumer, 1976). These processes are constructed as a part of the unfolding instructional conversations and frequently co-occur with the presentation of content. In this paper, social action processes are viewed as actively constructed rather than static, preestablished structures or rules for functioning. In addition, in order to understand how language operates to produce the multiple outcomes of conversations, the context in which that processing takes place must be considered. Defined in this manner, knowledge of the classroom as a social system is analogous to knowledge of the classroom as an active communicative setting.

Many questions arise from this view of classrooms: What is the nature of teaching? How does socialization in classrooms occur? What is the culture of classrooms? The problem for those interested in exploring these questions is the same—how do we obtain an adequate description of the emerging structures of the classroom instructional conversations? Gumperz summarized the problem succinctly when he stated that "The question of how actors communicate information and influence and persuade others in actual

The authors would like to thank Dr. Margot Ely of New York University and Dr. Jerome Harste of Indiana University for their invaluable contributions to the editing of this paper. Work on this paper was supported by faculty grants from Kent State University, College of Education.

situations is far from being resolved" (1975, p. 1). The task facing the researcher interested in the emergence and negotiation of social processes in classrooms is one of capturing in detail the sequential development of conversational and social processes (Bossert, 1977; Parke, 1976; Stenhouse, 1975; Dunkin & Biddle, 1974).

How teachers and children construct both instructional and social contexts is the focus of a longitudinal study from which the data for this paper were taken. The remainder of this presentation will focus on a description of the methodology, a sociolinguistic ethnography that permits (a) mapping the evolving instructional conversations, (b) identification of contexts, (c) identification of social action rules. Analysis of the first 13 minutes of a naturally occurring class meeting in each of two kindergarten classrooms will be used to illustrate conversational mapping, context identification, and social rule identification.

MAPPING INSTRUCTIONAL CONVERSATIONS

The process of identifying context and rules begins with a multistep, microanalysis of the evolving instructional conversations. The product of this analysis is a series of structural maps that symbolizes the sequential evolution, message by message, of the instructional conversations as they are constructed by teacher and student interacting with, and acting on, each other's messages. The structural map level is the level at which the broad questions of social rule identification and context definition are possible. Examination of the structural map is based on the analysis of how participants within the instructional situation orient to the structural features of the situation during the course of their interactions. Mehan, Cazden, Coles, Fisher, and Maroules suggest that the participants "will make the researcher's phenomenon visible by their actions, especially in the absence of expected forms of interaction" (1976, p, 14).

In conversational analysis of the instructional conversation, both cohesive actions and/or breaches or potential divergences from the instructional goal highlight the rules that are being formed during the construction of the instructional conversation. Similarly, changes in focus of *when is group*, that is who the appropriate interactor is, the individual within the group or the group as a whole, also permits identification of context shift.

A more in-depth description of the process of identifying rules and context is presented in the section on specific social action rules and instructional contexts that were identified for the two 13-minute videotape segments. Before proceeding to the description of these aspects of the instructional conversation and classroom social system, the analytical system used to obtain the structural maps and the resulting descriptions will be presented. It is reasoned that knowledge of the system and its underlying theoretical framework is necessary in order to assess the adequacy of the description and the validity of the social action rules and instructional contexts that were identified.

THE DESCRIPTIVE ANALYSIS SYSTEM:
AN OVERVIEW

The descriptive system is based on theoretical constructs from the fields of sociolinguistics, conversational analysis, and the study of teaching. As outlined previously, the system is a multistep analysis system designed to describe the flow of the instructional conversation, to identify conversationally and thematically tied conversational-instructional units of varying length, to produce structural maps of the instructional conversation, and to provide insights from the basic units for the identification of social action rules and conversational contexts.

The descriptive analysis system is used as a heuristic device. In order to explore the broad questions of socialization and context definition, some form of microanalysis and structural representation is necessary. The descriptive coding system is used as a shorthand for representing the hierarchical units of the evolving instructional conversation and the creation of the structural maps. Although a coded representation is used, data reduction is kept to a minimum by requiring that decisions about meaning, function, and similarity of units be made only after consideration of the coded representation, the transcript included with the coded description, *and* the actual message, or unit, as it is transmitted on the videotape. The videotaped lesson, therefore, provides the context for, and final check of, description and interpretation. This procedure insures that decisions about message or conversational units are based on contextualization cues rather than on arbitrarily preset features of message and conversation, e.g., syntax, semantics, and/or turn.

THEORETICAL CONSTRUCTS UNDERLYING
THE SYSTEM

The theoretical constructs that form the basis for the components and structure of the system and the analysis procedures are presented to provide further clarification of the methodology described.

Teaching as a Conversational Process

Central to this approach is the conceptualization of teaching as a conversational process. Conceptualizing teaching thus means that the pedagogical strategies and goals must be considered, as well as the nature of conversation and the rules for conversational structure and participation.

Conversations are more than random strings of words whose purpose is the simple verbal exchange of ideas, opinions, observations, and sentiments. Conversations are complex social phenomena that include nonverbal and social properties of an interchange in addition to, or concurrent with, the verbal characteristics of the exchange (Markel, 1975). The complexity is reflected in the view of a message in a conversation as a tripartite entity that functions simultaneously as a "saying," a "making," and "doing" (McClellan, 1971). The *saying* part of a message is related to the form and semantic content of the utterance and the co-verbal and nonverbal cues to message realization. The *making* aspect is concerned with the relationships that exist between some messages and not others, that is, with the conversational obligation placed on either speaker to continue or another person to respond. The *doing* aspect of this description is concerned with the pedagogical social and conversational intent of a message.

By applying sociolinguistic constructs to the analysis of instructional conversations, the observer's interpretation of saying and making aspect is captured. Description of the doing aspect requires consideration of both pedagogical and sociolinguistic intent. To know whether this interpretation is ethnographically adequate requires confirmation by teachers and children. As Gumperz suggests (Chapter 12) explication of these constructs should be undertaken.

Conversational Creativity. Because conversations are created by participants as they interact with, and act on, their own message and the messages and behaviors of others, conversations are, in general, creative entities. They are creative in that it is not possible to predict what will occur at any point in the conversation. Unless a conversation is highly routinized and/or preset, an observer cannot predict what will be said, how it will be said or what form the message(s) will take.

In a conversation, therefore, a message can be defined only after it has occurred. That is, the end of a message can only be determined on a *post hoc* basis by observing the verbal, coverbal (prosodic), and nonverbal cues, and cues to contextualization (Gumperz & Herasimchuk, 1973) and the onset of a new message. Lack of predictability also occurs at the level of contextualization cues. Just which nonverbal and prosodic cues will be used by a speaker to help transmit the meaning of a given message cannot be predicted in advance. The following example will illustrate these concepts.

Line	Source	Message Text	Cues to Contextualization
095	Teacher:	We talked about the problem we have if five people talk at a time.	Emphasis on "we." Voice drops on "time." Slight pause after "time."
096	Teacher:	Is there a problem with listening if that?	Raise in pitch and stress on "is there."
097	Students:	uh huh	All students respond.
098	Teacher:	What happens if all of us talk at once?	T uses hands to include all students in question. Said in rising tone with no closure.
099	Students:	(Individual messages followed by multiple students talking at once.)	

In this segment, the teacher begins the sequence with the message "We talked about the problem if five people talk at a time" (designated line 095). By considering the contextualization cues (the drop in voice level on "time" and the pause after the word "time"), the message boundary could be determined; however, prediction of the next message was not possible. The teacher began this sequence by using a telling mode. From this, we might expect that the teacher would continue to give information about what she and the students had talked about previously or about the effects of speaking without taking turns. This teacher did not meet this expectation; rather, she changed conversational directions and moved from a telling mode to one of student involvement as indicated by the question "Is there a problem with listening if that?" (line 096). This question could not have been predicted in advance of its occurrence. In addition, the fact that this message would not be completely grammatical could not have been predicted.

The students, however, were not bothered by this lack of predictability since they were able to provide an appropriate response (line 097). The students had no trouble responding appropriately because the teacher's cues to message contextualization indicates that a response was necessary and the form of the question indicated a yes/no was acceptable. The student's response also completed the interaction unit with the teacher. Once again, what the teacher would do next could not be predicted. The teacher's next message "What happens if all of us talk at once?" (line 098) does not fit a predictable pattern. This message is uttered in such a way as to indicate that *all* children could respond rather than one child at a time as established previously. The children did respond simultaneously, thus illustrating her message.

In the remainder of this segment of the instructional conversation (Figure 1.1), the teacher continues to build on the message illustrated in line 098, "What

Transcript Lines	IU	Message Units / Transcript Text	Potentially Divergent Unit	Thematically Tied Instruction Units
098		WHAT HAPPENS IF ALL OF US TALK AT ONCE?		
099		All: I don't know. Can't hear		
100		WELL, IF ALL OF YOU TALK AT ONCE AND YOU CAN'T HEAR, IS THERE A WAY WE COULD DO IT SO WE CAN HEAR EACH PERSON?		
101		All: yea		
102		Peter: One at a time [said loudly]		
103		WHAT DID YOU SAY PETER?		
104		Peter: One at a time [said loudly]		
105		LET'S TRY YOUR IDEA.		
106		MAY WE TRY YOUR IDEA?		
107		Peter: [shakes head yes]		
			END OF	PHASE I

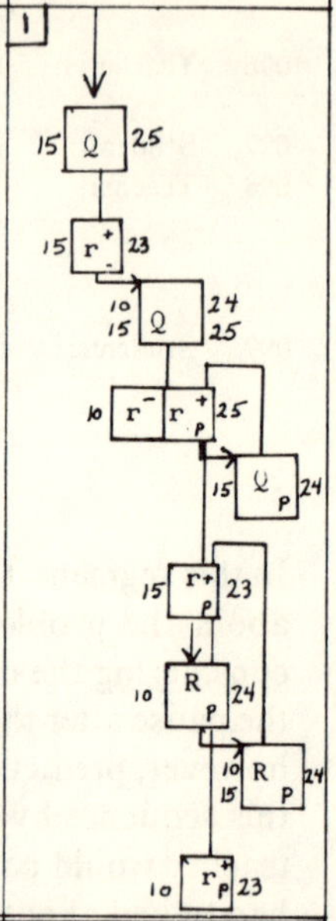

FIG. 1.1. Map of Instructional Conversation: Teacher M Phase I of the day's New Lesson (Review Participation Rules)

transcript Lines	IU	Message Units / Transcript Text	Potentially Divergent Unit	Thematically Tied Instruction Units
085		WE'RE GOING TO HAVE —		$\boxed{1}$
				8 16 ◇ R > 23
086		REMEMBER YESTERDAY WE TALKED ABOUT —		8 ◇ R > 25
087		Shauna: [off camera actions]	0 ($r^{\bullet}_{sh}$) 24	
088		SHAUNA		17 18 □ R_{6h} 24 25
089		NEWS AND VIEWS		18 □ R 25
090		AND IF EACH OF YOU WOULD LIKE TO HAVE A CHANCE TO SAY SOMETHING		8 □ R 25
091		AND WE TALKED ABOUT THE PROBLEM		8 □ R 25
092		James: You know what I'd like to—	8 (r^{o}_{j}) 24	
093		JAMES, EXCUSE ME	17 □ R J 24	
094		James: [ceases actions]	17 (r^{+}_{j}) 24	
095		WE TALKED ABOUT THE PROBLEM WE HAVE IF FIVE PEOPLE TALK AT A TIME		$\boxed{1}$ 18 □ R 25
096		IS THERE A PROBLEM WITH LISTENING IF THAT?		10 15 □ Q 25
097		St X: uh huh		10 (r^{+}_{x}) 25

FIG. 1.1. *(continued)*

happens if all of us talk at once?" She continues interacting with the children until she elicits the rule, "one at a time" (line 104). Her response to this suggestion, "Let's try this" (line 105) is followed by "May we try your idea?" (line 106). Once again, the teacher turns a direction message into a question and shifts from a telling mode to a student involvement mode. In this instance, the student who made the suggestion is asked for his approval which he indicates nonverbally by shaking his head (line 107). With this affirmation, Phase I, *Review of Participation Rules,* of the Day's News lesson is concluded.

This segment shows that conversations are creative; that is they do not occur in preset ways. It also shows that participants are able to participate in this creativity. The creativity aspect of conversational structure, therefore, has direct implications for the decision of a research methodology for the study of teaching as a communicative process. The previous discussion suggests that description and analysis of conversational units and structure must be undertaken on a *post hoc* basis. The procedure of *post hoc* identification of messages and other conversation units and structures was adopted as the principal approach to conversational segmentation and description for all levels of the analysis.

Specific Structural Characteristics of Messages. The previous section emphasized that messages are context-bound and that syntax and semantic units are not sufficient to determine message occurrence. Messages were shown to be observable and describable only on a *post hoc* basis by observing the onset of the next message and by observing the cues to contextualization. Given that a conversation unfolds on a message-by-message basis, consideration of message context and contextualization cues are critical aspects of conversational segmentation. Observation of the co-verbal/prosodic cues (pitch, stress, intonation, and tempo-timing-rhythm) and nonverbal cues (kinesic and proxemic) used by, and available to, the participants permits richer interpretation of message meaning, message boundary, and message ties (Gumperz & Herasimchuk, 1973; Harris & Rubenstein, 1975; Leiberman, 1975).

Once message boundary has been considered, description of the message is possible. Descriptively, a message such as the one line 096 (Figure 1.1) "Is there a problem with listening if that?" has a source (teacher), a form (question), a strategy or strategies (a request for confirmation and, simultaneously a request for clarification of the previous message), a level of comprehension desired (interpretive) and a tie (it is related to the previous message, line 095, as well as the one that follows). The complete set of possibilities for each of these characteristics of messages is presented in Table 1 (see Appendix A for definitions).

TABLE 1
Descriptive Analysis of Instructional Conversations

	Source		Form				Strategies												Level			Tie				Unit Resolution				
Transcript line	Teacher	Student	Question	Response +	Response 0	Response –	Focusing	Ignoring	Confirming+	Confirming–	Continuance	Extending	Raising	Clarifying	Editing	Controlling	Refocusing	Restating	Factual	Interpret	Applicative	Teacher	Student	Lesson		Resolved Interaction	Unresolved Interaction	Instruction Sequence	Phase	Lesson
1	2	3	4	5	6	7	8	9	10	11	12	13	14	15	16	17	18	19	20	21	22	23	24	25	26	30	31	50	60	70

In the descriptive system, each characteristic outlined in Table 1 is given a numerical equivalent to permit shorthand representation of the messages on the structural maps and to permit computer storage. The availability of the maps means that the research audience can retrace the steps used in the group in creating each context. In other words, the maps allow consideration of each message as it unfolds during the evolution of instructional conversations. Selection of each feature outlined in Table 1 and represented on the maps (e.g., Figure 1.1) was based on a synthesis of previous research on conversational structure, conversational analysis, and the study of teaching (Green, 1977).

Conversational cohesion. As suggested previously, conversations are not random strings of messages with no coherence. Conversations are social actions on the part of the participants who have little trouble creating a coherent or cohesive entity for the most part. As such, both cohesive actions and breaches in the cohesion being constructed highlight the structures and rules functioning to maintain the cohesion. In the previous example, the students had little difficulty knowing what actions were required. This action was mapped as cohesive by observing the behaviors of both the students and the teacher.

Conversational cohesion occurs in instructional conversations in several ways (Halliday & Hasan, 1976). Cohesion occurs because people, in all social situations, talk to achieve certain goals, project outcomes, and social acts (Cook-Gumperz Gumperz, 1976; Green, 1977). The instructional conversation, by definition is to be goal directed; that is, instructional conversations are expected to have thematic cohesion (Cook-Gumperz & Gumperz, 1976; Forsyth, 1974). Consideration of thematic cohesion leads to the establishment of two types of general thematic structures on the maps, *thematically tied* (cohesive) *instructional units* and *potentially divergent instructional units.* Each message and conversational unit identified in the segmentation level of the analysis is considered with regard to the cohesion being created. Those units that do not directly follow the thread of the lesson are placed in the column *Potentially Divergent Units* on the instructional map form. (See Figure 1.1) How the teacher maintains cohesion provides the cues to rule determination.

Thematic cohesion, however, is but one type of cohesion. Linkages occur between and across varying types of conversational units. That is, cohesion can occur on several levels. It can occur between individual message units to form units of completed interaction, e.g., question-answer, question-answer-confirmation. This aspect relates to the making aspect of a message. Conversationally and socially some messages demand action either by the person speaking or by the other participants. Sequences of tied or cohesive message units in the present system are called *interaction units.* Message cohesion is determined by consideration of social, semantic, and contextual cues, not on a predetermined basis such as turn, question followed by response, or question and response, followed by evaluation. On the maps, cohesion between message units is indicated by single lines connecting messages and by a single line separating messages in the transcript text. As in the case of predicting a message, it is not possible to predict the structure of an interaction unit and the length of an interaction unit before their production. Noting the beginning of a new interaction sequence and analyzing contextualization cues determines the boundary of the prior unit. Interaction units, like message units, are determined, therefore, on a *post hoc* basis. The map segment, Figure 1.2, illustrates the conversational cohesion between individual messages (interaction units) and the larger cohesion, thematic cohesion.[1]

An analysis of this segment shows that the first interaction unit is composed of five message units, transcript lines 025, 026, 027, 028, 029. This unit was determined by considering message delivery cues to contextualization—the syntactic, semantic, non-verbal and prosodic aspects of the message. Changes in voice and delivery flagged that the unit, although containing only one teacher sentence, was delivered as four separate messages. In contrast, each of the remaining interaction units in this segment is two messages long with the exception of the last unit (lines 060–063). In addition, the majority of these units are composed of a greeting by the teacher followed by a response to that greeting by the student.

Consideration of thematic cohesion across the interaction units indicates that each interaction unit is part of a larger unit which is an instructional sequence defined as *greeting*. In the analytic system, sequences of thematically tied or cohesive interaction units are designed as *instructional sequence units*. Arrows between interaction units indicate that these units are thematically tied to each other. Instructional sequence units are also indicated by a double-barred line at the end of the sequence and by the number in the upper lefthand box in the thematically tied instructional units column on the maps. In Figure 1.2, all interaction units belong to instructional sequence unit, 3 with the exception of lines 056–057. Lines 056–057 presents the beginning of a new instructional sequence that was interrupted by interactions tied back to instructional sequence 3. Instructional sequence

---

[1]In all map segments, interaction units are indicated by the bracket and the line after the last message unit in the interaction unit. On the map part of this form, the interaction unit is indicated by the single line linking the messages indicated by the squares (large for teacher, small for students). The numbers in the squares on the map relate to the coding shorthand presented in Table 1. The capital letters in the squares indicate the form of the teacher's message and the lower case indicate the form of the student's message (Q/q for question; R/r for response). Subscripts indicate to whom the message is directed (subscripts of teacher's form) or who is speaking (subscripts of student's form).

Transcript Lines	IU	Message Units / Transcript Text	Potentially Divergent Unit	Thematically Tied Instruction Units
				3
025		MY VOICE IS GOING TO GET VERY SMALL AND		8 R 23
026		I'M GOING TO GREET ALL OF YOU THIS MORNING BECAUSE [said in almost a whisper]		8 R 23
027		I'D LIKE TO SAY [said louder]		8 R 23
028		HELLO JAMES		8 R 25 / 15 J
029		James: hi		8 r+ 25 / j
030		HELLO STEPHANIE		8 R 25 / st
031		Stephanie: hi		8 r+ 25 / st
032		HELLO NYLA		8 R 25 / ny
033		Nyla: hi		8 r+ 25 / ny
034		HELLO SHAUNA		8 R 25 / Sh
035		Shauna: hi		8 r+ 25 / sh
036		HELLO JOY		8 25 / Jo
037		Joy: hello		8 + 25 / jo
038		HELLO ERIN		8 R 25 / Er
039		Erin: hi		8 + 25 / Er

FIG. 1.2. Map of Instructional Conversation: Teacher M Phase II of the *Welcome Lesson* (Individual Greeting)

172

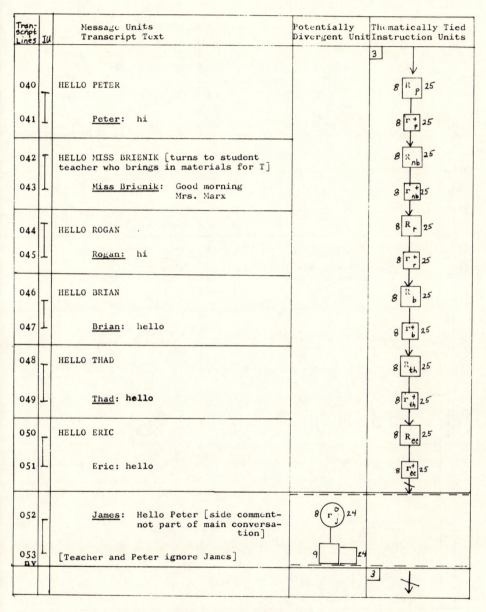

Transcript Lines	IU	Message Units / Transcript Text	Potentially Divergent Unit	Thematically Tied Instruction Units
				3
040	⊤	HELLO PETER		8 R_p 25
041	⊥	Peter: hi		8 r_p^+ 25
042	⊤	HELLO MISS BRIENIK [turns to student teacher who brings in materials for T]		8 R_{nb} 25
043	⊥	Miss Brienik: Good morning Mrs. Marx		3 r_{nb}^+ 25
044	⊤	HELLO ROGAN		8 R_r 25
045	⊥	Rogan: hi		8 r_r^+ 25
046	⊤	HELLO BRIAN		8 R_b 25
047	⊥	Brian: hello		8 r_b^+ 25
048	⊤	HELLO THAD		8 R_{th} 25
049	⊥	Thad: **hello**		8 r_{th}^+ 25
050		HELLO ERIC		8 R_{ec} 25
051		Eric: hello		8 r_{ec}^+ 25
052		James: Hello Peter [side comment- not part of main conversation]	8 r_j^0 24	
053 nv		[Teacher and Peter ignore James]	9 ☐ 24	
				3

FIG. 1.2. *(continued)*

Transcript Lines	IU	Message Units Transcript Text	Potentially Divergent Unit	Thematically Tied Instruction Units
054	⌐	AND HELLO NICHOLAOUS [rhythm changes-- said stressed and slower]		3 ┐ 8 R_nk 25
055	∟	Nicholaous: hi		8 r +_nk 25
056	⌐	ALL TOGETHER		4 ┐ 8 R 23
057	∟	AND CAN WE S ——		8 R 23
058	⌐	James: Peter, You didn't said Peter.	8 (r°_J) 24	
059	∟	I DID SAY PETER.		11 R_J 24 25
060	⌐	Peter: And hello yourself.	8 (r°_p) 23 25	
061		WELL THANK YOU. HA! HA! HA! HA!		10 R_p 24 25
062	∟	St. X: Well, well, well St. X: Well hello yourself.	19 (r_x° r°_x) 24 19	
			E N D OF	P H A S E II

FIG. 1.2. *(continued)*

174

units, like the other units presented so far, vary in length and as in the case of message and interaction units can be identified only through *post hoc* description and analysis.

Thematic cohesion or ties can also occur across sequences of instructional sequence units. Sequences of thematically tied instructional sequence units form the *phase unit* of the lesson, e.g., introduction, story presentation, greeting individual. The thematic consideration at this phase unit level focuses on the pedagogical purpose of the units. Lastly, sequences of tied phase units are designated as a *lesson*. Approached in this manner, a lesson is not a preset entity, but rather a product of the social-conversational-pedagogical actions of the participants as they interact with, and act upon, the messages and behaviors of others to reach the goal of instruction.

Summary of Structural Characteristics of Instructional Conversations. The following general characteristics of instructional conversations provide the framework and limits for the description of the unfolding conversation presented earlier. Instructional conversations are goal-directed and the teacher, by nature of his/her role, determines the general structure and the direction of the conversation. Students' messages are accepted, rejected, or ignored; students do not have the right of veto over topics. The teacher determines the topic even in the most "open" instructional situation; and finally, the teacher distributes turns. Topic and turn in instructional conversations, unlike those in free conversations, are not negotiated. In the instructional conversation, then, roles are specified and influence the nature of the participation.

Messages in an instructional conversation, however, are not all tied to the teacher's verbal messages and behaviors. The chain of instruction can take a variety of forms—e.g., verbal (v) to nonverbal (nv), nv to v, v to v, nv to nv + v. In addition, individual message units may be tied to or build on (a) the teacher's purpose, response, or behavior, (b) the student's purpose, response, or behavior, (c) the lesson or materials being used.

Description on a micro basis of the structure of the unfolding instructional conversations provides the material for the second level of analysis, the creation of the instructional maps. *Post hoc* analysis of thematic cohesion and breaches of this cohesion provides the material for the third level of analysis, the identification of context and the description of the social action rules being constructed. As suggested at the outset of this presentation, the participants "will make the researcher's phenomenon visible by their actions, especially in the absence of expected forms of interaction" (Mehan, Cazden, Coles, Fisher, and Maroules, 1976).

We now turn from a description of the analytic system to the description of the contexts identified and to the social rules defined.

ANALYSIS OF SOCIAL CONTEXTS
AND SOCIAL ACTION RULES

In the first part of this discussion, we presented a system for the description and analysis of unfolding instructional conversations. The product of this descriptive process is a series of structural maps that reflect the way the teacher and students built on their own messages and the messages of each other to reach the instructional goals of the teacher. In the rest of this paper, we discuss the contexts constructed and the social rules developed during the development of instructional conversations. The structural maps provide the vehicle for the exploration of such issues. As in the earlier discussion, the underlying theoretical constructs that permit the identification of both the contexts and the social action rules will be explicated so that the reader may evaluate the validity of the structures identified.

THE CONSTRUCTION OF THE
CLASSROOM SOCIAL CONTEXTS

Recent work on classrooms as communicative and social environments has shown that classrooms are neither undifferentiated communicative environments nor undifferentiated social environments (Phillips, 1974; Cook-Gumperz & Gumperz, 1976; Erickson & Shultz, 1977; Green & Wallat, 1979). Each classroom consists of differentiated forms of social organization each with particular demands for communication and specific definition of *when is group*. As we and others have argued, these organizations, defined as *contexts* in the present study, are socially active entities constructed by students and teachers as they engage in social interactions of the classroom to achieve specific instructional goals (Green & Wallat, 1979; Blumer, 1976; Cook-Gumperz & Gumperz, 1976; Erickson & Shultz, 1977). Context, defined in this manner, does not equate with lesson, e.g., if it is 9:15 a.m. Wednesday, it must be spelling pretest. Recent research has shown that contexts shift for the participants within as well as across the boundaries of lessons (Green, 1977; Green & Wallat, 1979).

The boundaries of contexts, like those of other conversational units, are determined by consideration of contextualization cues and the onset of the next context. Consider Figure 1.2 again (page 172). In this segment, the teacher begins the context by changing voice levels, moving from loud to soft to loud again. In addition to the prosodic cues, she also verbalizes what she is doing, "My voice is going to get very small and I'm going to greet all of you this morning because I'd like to say, hello James." As she transmits these messages, she moves from speaking to the whole group to speaking to one individual, James. This change is indicated by shifts in body position, use of hands, and the direction of eye gaze. The teacher continues in this segment to speak to each individual in the group moving from left to right around the circle. When she gets to the last individual in the circle, Nikolaous, she shifts the position of her upper body to face Nikolaous, slows her mode of message transmission and directly points to the individual. The message, "And Hello Nikolaous" is said slower than the others with pauses between "And," "Hello" and "Nikolaous." In addition, stress is given to the word "and."

Consideration of the next message shows that the context does not end with this message, however. The students reopen the conversation with a series of self-initiations (lines 058-063) which continue until one child, Peter, says "and hello yourself" to which the teacher responds, "Well, thank you. Ha! Ha! Ha! Ha!." Two additional students begin messages related to this exchange, but these messages are not completed. At this point, the teacher shifts body position, changes voice level, and begins a new context (Figure 1.3), a repeat with modification of Spanish words of the greeting song presented in the context prior to the one just discussed.

Application of the *post hoc* analysis procuedure helps to establish context boundary. Identification and definition of the nature of the context and the social action rules for functioning within the context are possible only when the nature of the social demands, the nature of the group processes, and the question of thematic and social cohesion are considered. Although sociolinguistic and pedagogical constructs provided the basis for the conversational segmentation and the construction of the structural maps, issues of social action rules and differentiation of instructional contexts find their roots in the work of social psychologists, such as Parsons (1959), Getzels and Thelen (1960), Waller (1965), Etzioni (1968), Grathoff (1970), and Argyle (1972). The work of these social scientists provides the theoretical constructs that form the basis for the next level of analysis, the definition of context and identification of social action rules from the analysis of the structural maps.

Theoretical Constructs for Social Action Analysis.   The work of social psychology provides the general constructs which offer insight into the relationship between features of social structure and the realization of social competence in the classroom. The fields of sociolinguistics and the study of teaching provide the means, the methodology, for analyzing how the social structure proposed by the social psychologist is realized as a part of the evolving instructional conversation.

The theoretical work of four social psychologists directly bears on the constructivist view presented in this paper: Etzioni (1968), Parke (1976), Dweck (1976), Yarrow, Rubenstein, and Pederson (1975). These researchers provide constructs most nearly consistent with the questions posed here and most compatible with the nature of communication in the classroom as projected in the first half of the paper. Each contributes to our understanding

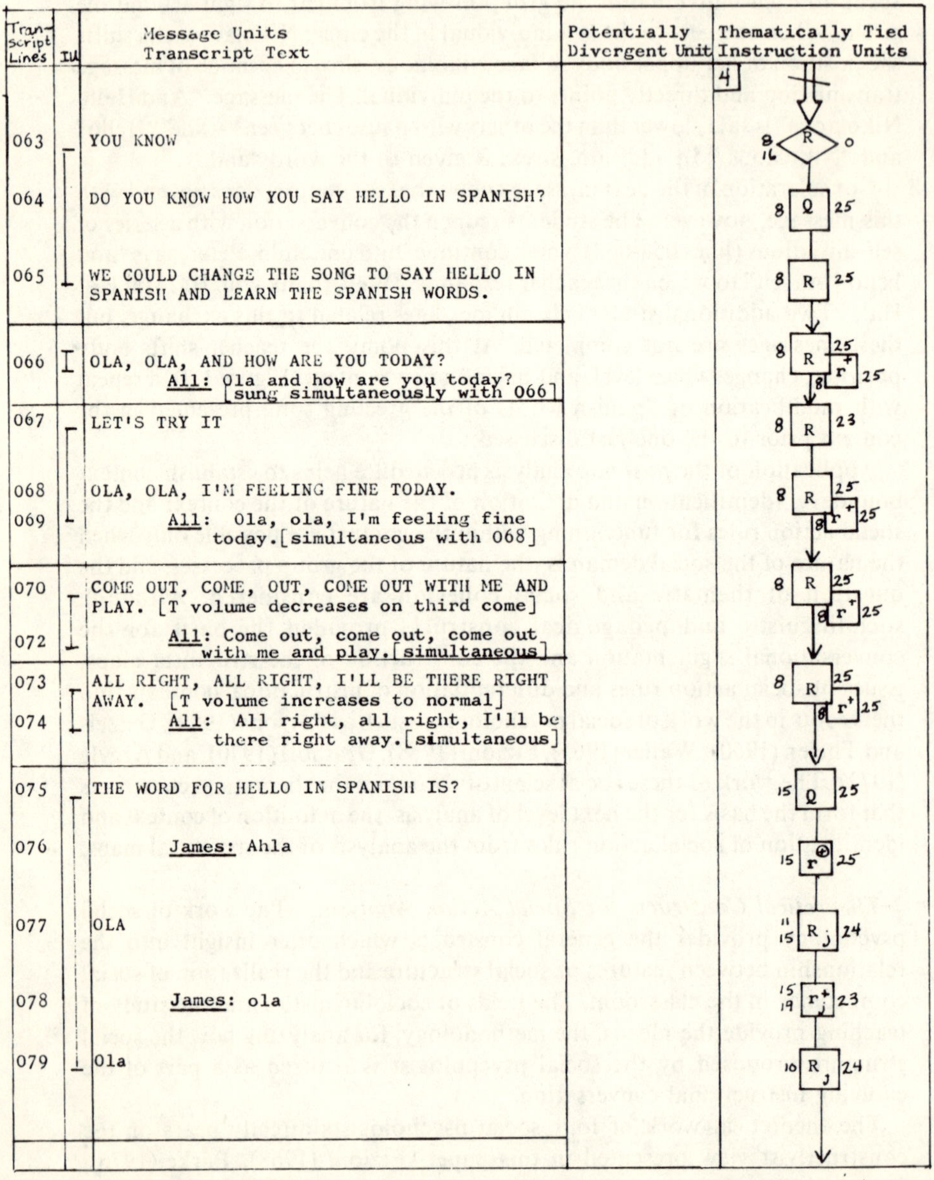

Transcript Lines	IU	Message Units Transcript Text	Potentially Divergent Unit	Thematically Tied Instruction Units
063		YOU KNOW		
064		DO YOU KNOW HOW YOU SAY HELLO IN SPANISH?		
065		WE COULD CHANGE THE SONG TO SAY HELLO IN SPANISH AND LEARN THE SPANISH WORDS.		
066	I	OLA, OLA, AND HOW ARE YOU TODAY? All: Ola and how are you today? [sung simultaneously with 066]		
067		LET'S TRY IT		
068 069		OLA, OLA, I'M FEELING FINE TODAY. All: Ola, ola, I'm feeling fine today.[simultaneous with 068]		
070 072		COME OUT, COME, OUT, COME OUT WITH ME AND PLAY. [T volume decreases on third come] All: Come out, come out, come out with me and play.[simultaneous]		
073 074		ALL RIGHT, ALL RIGHT, I'LL BE THERE RIGHT AWAY. [T volume increases to normal] All: All right, all right, I'll be there right away.[simultaneous]		
075		THE WORD FOR HELLO IN SPANISH IS?		
076		James: Ahla		
077		OLA		
078		James: ola		
079		Ola		

FIG. 1.3. Map of Instructional Conversation: Teacher M Phase III of the *Welcome Lesson* (Spanish Song).

178

Transcript Lines	IU	Message Units Transcript Text	Potentially Divergent Unit	Thematically Tied Instruction Units
				4
080	I	OR BUENOS DIAZ. THAT'S ANOTHER WAY OF SAYING GOOD DAY.		13 R$_J$ 23
081	I	BUENOS DIAZ. [looks at James and Stephanie]		13 R$_{J/S}$ 24
082		Stephanie: You know what? I want to be—	8 q$^o_{st}$ 24	
083 nv		[Teacher looks at Stephanie and waits for Stephanie to complete message]	10 R$_{st}$ 24	
084		Stephanie: [voice trails off. No further message]	o 23	
			END OF	PHASE III
			END OF	LESSON

FIG. 1.3. *(continued)*

of how people through their interactions with, and actions on, the behaviors of others form the social constructs of the classroom and enact their view of the world.

Etzioni succinctly captures how researchers must view the problem of studying how individuals make sense of what is going on around them when he states that . . . while individual action is possible, it cannot be understood except against the . . . social action of which it is a part, on which it builds, or against which it reacts (1968, p. 2). Actions viewed this way are context-dependent but observable when the ties between behaviors in context are considered. According to Etzioni, the core problem for researchers interested in social action research in the classroom is an "explication of the capacity of act" (p. 52). This explication must attend to how individual group members process concrete and specific "bits of knowledge," e.g., the structural and functional cues available during interaction, and then how these bits become synthesized into "a hierarchical structure or action role which provides a contextuating orientation for bits or items of knowledge" (p. 157). *Contextuating orientation* refers to the orientation or view of the world held by individuals; i.e., what cues individuals attend to and how they enact their view of the world. Observation of cues available for the individual to attend to and how that individual acts within the context in relationship to others in the context permits description of the hierarchical structure or contextuating orientation being used. For example, a teacher who expects children to respond only to, or interact only with, him/her, as seen in instructional chains, is projecting a view of teaching that differs from one who expects children to ask questions, take part in decision making, or guide their own actions. Both these teachers, through their actions, indicate that the teacher's role is guiding learning; their view of what this means, however, differs when their implementation of instruction is viewed. The teacher's actions in relationship to the students build the social norms of the classroom.

Etzioni suggests that the norms about method of task-completion, patterns of acceptable interaction based on individual group members' roles in various situations, and acceptable types of solutions to problems are created over time. He defines norms as the "super-unit relation" between bits within the "hierarchical structure." These "super-unit relations" or the norms of behavior are strong enough that individuals do not have to constantly restate behavior expectations:

A typical contextuating orientation does not depend on any specific bit or group of bits. Some bits can be removed with little effect on the orienation. . . . If all bits are removed . . . and no new ones supplied, the orientation may still be maintained on normative grounds alone. But, we expect, this would strain the contextuating orientation and leave it potentially open to rapid transformation (1968, p. 158).

According to Etzioni, teachers and students during their interactions in various contexts are creating norms for functioning as a group and as an individual within a group. Consideration of the individual's actions within the group can help define the nature of contextuating orientation of the group as well as that of the individual. Contextuating orientation defined in this way, is akin to a social rule. These rules, unlike those of grammer, are not static, rigid rules for structuring, but rather are context-dependent and must be negotiated for each context. The social action rule is a general orientation for action, the specific aspects of which are negotiated and determined for each situation.

Etzioni's construct of contextuating orientation is related to Gumperz's (1976) definition of *tying*. Gumperz suggests that tying is a measure of the extent to which a person works with the message or messages of others. Conversation units and structures can be identified by observing the cues that show how the individual is working with his/her own messages or the messages of others. These cues Gumperz labels *contextualization cues*. Message determination is dependent on observation of these cues (Green, 1977; Green & Wallat, 1979). This brief discussion of the overlap between the constructs of sociolinguistics and social psychology demonstrates the validity of the method of analysis for the study of social action as projected in this study.

The work of Parke (1976), Dweck (1976), and Yarrow, Rubenstein, and Pederson (1975) supports the view of Etzioni and Gumperz. Each of these researchers has shown the reciprocal nature of social processes between children and adult. These researchers have shown that from infancy onward, the control of responses in social contexts is not limited to adults (Parke, 1976); the child attends to and actively manipulates a variety of social cues from adults (Yarrow, Rubenstein, & Pederson, 1975); and the child's role as an active social problem solver is based on recognition of verbal and nonverbal contextuating cues (Dweck, 1976).

These social psychologists pose a constructivist view of the nature of interactions. With this brief discussion, we have brought the reader full cycle. The methodology presented is a constructivist methodology. That is, it permits identification of conversational structure as it is constructed by the participants as they interact with and act on the messages of others. The methodology is based on a theoretical view of people as active creators of their environments; no attempt is made to prejudge actions. The methodology can be defined as a sociolinguistic ethnography in that it combines both the social and the linguistic dimensions of the situation being studied.

Identification of the nature of context. Earlier in this section, we demonstrated how context boundary could be identified by using contextualization cues as well as by considering the onset of the next context. The question now is, "What is the nature of the context?" Two factors contribute to such a definition: the nature of group and the nature of the thematic cohesion. Asking the question, "When is group?" permits the identification of the nature of context. In the map segments presented earlier (Figures 1.1, 1.2, and 1.3) three separate contexts have been identified using this question.

In Figure 1.3 (page 178) the context is group singing. This definition was arrived at by considering: (a) teacher statements, e.g., line 067 "Let's try it." (b) teacher's actions, e.g., shift from facing Nikolaous to facing group as a whole, and shift from "talking" voice to "singing" voice and (c) children's actions (e.g., children and teacher sing simultaneously). Consideration of these cues to contextualization showed that the context was group and the task, singing.

The validity of this definition was checked by exploring the teacher's taped statement of goals and by discussing the findings with the teacher who is a member of the action research team. This step of the procedure was possible since the teachers in the study record their goals, objectives, and reactions for us at the end of each day's taping. This recorded statement by the teacher is analyzed after the videotape analysis is completed. The observed goals on the videotape are then checked against the stated goals from the audiotape. The process of checking perspectives is completed when the observed goals are confirmed by the teacher. This validation procedure is but another step in obtaining an ethnographically adequate description.

A second type of validation of what was required, the contextuating orientation needed, occurred spontaneously in two separate settings.[2] The first was a parent meeting. Two children were present at this meeting. One child was perceived by both the teacher and researcher as quiet; the other was perceived as highly verbal. When the song segment came on the playback unit both children began to sing with the group. This action suprised all present, but it was not an isolated incident. When the videotape was shown to the entire class, the same thing occurred; the entire class began to sing spontaneously with the tape.

The contexts identified in Figures 1.1 and 1.2 were arrived at by similar methods. In Figure 1.2, context shifts from group as a whole to the individual within the group, as indicated by the teacher's actions and the students' responses. That the teacher was viewed as part of the group is reflected in

---

Peter's comments on line 060, "and hello yourself." The orientation for this situation is that each member of the group must have an opportunity to be greeted individually within the group. When the teacher stops with the children, Peter flags that she too is part of the group and should have an opportunity to be greeted and respond to the greeting. The context, therefore, is individual within the group and the topic is individual greeting. In Figure 1.3, the context returns to group with context content as singing.

In the present study five contexts were identified for Teacher M, six contexts for Teacher H. The fact that there was one more context for Teacher H is misleading. Teacher H had only five full contexts. One context was begun and stopped quickly. The teacher was observed changing her mind about what was to be presented. This break in context is presented in Figure 1.4. The teacher's actions, replacing Duso on a storage table, and her comment, lines 138–139, "Oh," "You know what I forgot?" lead to this determination.

Context, as just presented, is, as Erickson and Shultz (1977) and Cook-Gumperz and Gumperz (1976) suggest, a socially active notion, negotiated as a part of the evolving conversation. Observation of context boundary is possible by *post hoc* analysis of contextualization cues. The structural maps described in this presentation permit the researcher to retrace the steps of the teacher and students as they work together to construct the instructional conversation. *Post hoc* analysis of these maps permitted identification of instructional contexts. The boundary of a context was identified by observing both contextualization cues and the onset of a new physical orientation, theme, or instructional content. The nature of the context, its purpose, was identified by considering when is group, who is group, and the type of thematic and social cohesion required.

Once the contexts of the classroom instructional situation have been identified, the researcher can begin to ask questions about the nature of the classroom as a social system. In addition, the identification of context through sociolinguistic ethnographic analysis overcomes past researcher problems in data reduction. The contextual maps include the data needed for examination of social processes and social rules that were constructed within each of the differentiated forms of social organization, the contexts, in the classroom. In the last section of this paper, we present several initial rules we observed being formed on the third day of school as well as information about the validity of these rules from the viewpoint of the teacher participant.

THE IDENTIFICATION OF SOCIAL RULES:
A BEGINNING

The two 13-minute videotape segments that are the data for this paper were obtained on the third day of the school year. In these segments, five contexts

Transcript Lines	I U	Message Units Transcript Text	Potentially Divergent Unit	Thematically Tied Instruction Units
				1
136		WELL WE HAVE OUR FRIEND DUSO VISITING AGAIN [Teacher takes Duso puppet out]		8 R 23
137		Children: Hello Duso ...[unclear message to puppet Duso]		10 r+ 25
			Teacher changes lesson-aborts lesson	
			E N D O F L E S S O N	
				1
138		OH		8 R 23
139		YOU KNOW WHAT I FORGOT?		8/10 Q 23
140		St. X: [shakes hand that's raised]		8 r+x
141		YEAH, YEAH		10/16 R 24
142		NO		11 R 24
143		I FORGOT TO CALL YOUR NAMES [Teacher replaces Duso puppet]		8 R 23
144		St. X: And stand up		13 r°x 24/25
145		RIGHT, UH HUH		10 Rx 24/25
				2
146		OK		8 R 23
147		I THINK WE'LL START THE OTHER WAY. [indicates end of the alphabet]		8 R 25

FIG. 1.4. Map of Instructional Conversations: Teacher H Transition to Phase I and Phase I of *Greeting Lesson*.

were identified for Teacher M and six for Teacher H.[3] The contexts were found to differentiate lesson theme as well as expectations about the appropriate social skills to be used. This latter aspect of instructional conversations was shown to be accomplished concurrently with the enactment of the teachers' instructional goals.

The purpose of this section is the discussion of the conversational units that exemplify the social techniques that were used by teachers and children to support the accomplishment of the task and/or instructional topic of each context. Specifically, we will share the analysis of segments from maps which illustrate the situational appropriateness and/or the meaning of social behaviors being developed concurrently with the instructional transmissions. Whether these social actions identified in the 11 contexts develop into contextuating orientation norms as defined earlier by Etzioni can be determined only by longitudinal study of similar instructional situations. Such a longitudinal study was undertaken and is forthcoming. For the present discussion, however, only the initial rules identified from the instructional maps of the 13-minute segment of the third day of school will be presented.

Before turning to this discussion, one last analysis procedure must be dealt with, the verification of the rules identified. As described, the teachers were active members of the research team. Each teacher audiotaped her goals, lesson plans, and observations at the end of each day. Once these were taped, they were transcribed to permit analysis of the teacher's goals. This analysis was undertaken after the rules and goals were identified from the structural maps. The first step in verification of the rules was the determination of the congruence of the goals identified from contextual maps with those obtained from a content analysis of the teacher interviews. The second step in verification of rules was in-person interview with the teacher in which the tape was reviewed, the interview tape transcript discussed, and the rules clarified, and finally, the findings presented.

Theoretical Constructs and Research Findings on Rule Definition. Etzioni and the other psychologists presented previously provide the background constructs for the analysis of social action in the classroom, however, research on interpersonal behavior in small-group organization and membership provides the basis for the identification of the special social rules in this study. Past research on interpersonal behavior in small-group organization and membership supports the rules identified in this paper (Argyle, 1972). One of the assumptions of this research is that group cohesiveness is built during the active phases of forming and norming.

---

[3]Each teacher in this study had five completed contexts. Teacher H, however, began a sixth context which she aborted. The teacher began a lesson out of order and stopped before establishing lesson with the children.

Forming includes contexts in which members find out about the task rules and the nature of group. *Norming* refers to the development of shared perceptions and meaning of modes of verbal and nonverbal communication and the modes of characteristic interaction sequences in relation to the method, rate, standard of work, distribution of rewards, and rights and responsibilities.

The small-group organization research constructs of forming and norming strengthen our research goal of identifying the structural and functional cues available for discerning the contextuating orientation of the classroom. Formation of cohesion and social actions is not only observable through the cohesive dimensions of group interaction. As Mehan *et al.* suggest, breaches in cohesion act to highlight the actions. In this study, potential divergences of thematic cohesion were also explored to help determine social rules being constructed by the teacher and students.

Six rules were identified in the initial analysis. Three of these rules will be explored in detail:

> Rule Type I: Being a member of a group requires attending to cues that flag differentiated expectations for physical orientation and proximity.
>
> Rule Type II: Being a member of the group includes responsibility for enacting different patterns of responses.
>
> Rule Type III: Becoming a member of the group involves attending to differentiated social meanings of cooperative effort.

Emphasis on the different expectations for physical orientation and proximity depending on the contexts was found in both classrooms. Figure 1.5 illustrates one way in which this differentiation was achieved. In this instructional sequence, Teacher H signals the beginning of new context goals by focusing the children on the task of defining individual space for a new lesson that will take place.

In the context immediately preceding the one presented in Figure 1.5, the children were seated on the edge of a rug, equally distributed around three sides of the rug with the teacher at the front edge alone. In this segment, the teacher moves the children from the sides of the rug to rows in front of her. She accomplishes this by focusing the children on the task of defining individual space in a new way for the new lesson context. She forms the rows by calling on children according to the color of their clothing. This enables her to help the children establish individual space in the new context as well as create the new group structure, rows. In addition to the structuring, this procedure also permits the teacher to diagnose student direction-following and knowledge of color.

Transcript Lines	IU	Message Units Transcript Text	Potentially Divergent Unit	Thematically Tied Instruction Unit
				I
253		IF YOU HAVE MOSTLY GREEN ON		8 R 25
254		Michele: Not mostly but I have it		8 r^+_{md} 25
255		BUT MOSTLY GREEN		8 15 R 24
256		LIKE ANGIE HAS A LOT OF GREEN		8 15 R 25
257		YOU MAY COME AND SIT DOWN RIGHT HERE IN FRONT OF ME		8 17 R 25
258		BILLY HAS QUITE A BIT OF GREEN ON		8 17 R_{bw} 24 25
259 nv		Billy: [goes to front and sits down]		17 $^+_{md}$ 23 25
260		TURN AROUND AND FACE ME [to Angie F]		17 R_{af} 24
261 nv		Angie: [turns around]		17 r^+_{af} 23
262		CISSY HAS GREEN PANTS ON		8 17 R_{cc} 24 25
263		AND GINNY		8 R_{gr} 24
264		WHAT ABOUT YOUR CLOTHES?		8 15 Q_{gr} 24 25
265		TURN AROUND, HONEY [Puts hand on Billy]		17 R_{bw} 23
266 nv		Billy: [turns around]		17 r^+_{bw} 23

FIG. 1.5. Map of Instructional Conversation: Teacher H Phase I of the *Visual Discrimination Lesson.*

187

That group and individual space were defined as being in a specific row was cued by the teacher in several ways. When a child moved, breached the desired behavior, the teacher recentered the child on where s/he was to sit. The teacher also pointed to a place if the child did not readily find one. In one assistance she indicated that space was available between two other children. Observation of the children's behaviors in interaction with those of the teacher permits the identification of the space rules and the differentiation of group orientation for this teacher. Whether the children understand the rule is still an open question. Future observation of the children's behaviors in similar context will permit the researcher to make statements about the processes of reinstatement of norms or rules for action. At this time, Teacher H's rule as indicated by her behaviors is the only rule that can be identified. Whether this is in fact a rule for all such contexts, that is, contexts with similar goals, is dependent on observation of similar actions on the part of the teacher and students in future contexts. (cf. definition of reinstatement, Campbell & Jaynes, 1966).

Data analysis showed that Teacher M, also had rules for different expectations for physical orientation and physical proximity. She is concerned with forming group and defining individual space. In the context preceding the *Review* context presented in Figure 1.2, the teacher asked the children to come and sit around the edge of the rug in a circle and to find their own space. In this context one child enters the circle just as the teacher begins a song and sits in front of the teacher rather than in the circle with everyone else as requested. A second child also enters the circle and stands in an open space in the circle. He is included in the greeting song, "Rogan welcome, welcome, welcome everyone." As he is greeted, he sits in the circle. Child 1 participated in the song from the beginning but did not sit in the appropriate place. At the end of the first verse, the teacher moves her to an open spot in the circle; with this action, the teacher completed the structuring of group.

Verification of the norms. The evolution of differentiated norms within and across the contexts was validated by comparing observable contextualizations cues. For example, both teachers signaled their expectations verbally and nonverbally. As shown in Figures 1.6 and 1.7, each teacher mirrored their verbal expectations with nonverbal actions.

In Figure 1.6, Teacher M used nonverbal actions to indicate that children in different places in the group were welcome and that children were to join her in song while remaining in place. In Figure 1.7, Teacher H used nonverbal and verbal behaviors to signal specific expectations for physical positioning. In this segment, she took time to help each child find their own physical space. Observation of the complete sequence of the event, defining individual space, indicated that Teacher H has specific expectations for physical space. She expects children to sit along the sides of a rectangular rug, while she stands at

Transcript Lines	T.U.	Message Units / Transcript Text	Potentially Divergent Unit	Thematically Tied Instruction Units
				2 ↓
014		HELLO		8 R 25
015		THANK YOU [addressed to Stephanie simultaneously with new unit beginning to complete previous unit on lines 012-013]	10 R st 25 ↓	8 R 25
016		HELLO, AND HOW ARE YOU TODAY?		
017		HELLO [points to left side of circle]		8 R 25
018		HELLO [points to right side of circle]		8 R 25
019		All: hello [sung simultaneously with teacher]		8 r+ 25
020		I'M FEELING FINE TODAY.		8 R 25
021		COME OUT, COME OUT [waves hand toward self]		8 R 25
022		COME OUT WITH ME AND PLAY [waves hand toward self]		8 R 25
023		ALL RIGHT, ALL RIGHT, I'LL BE THERE RIGHT AWAY		8 R 25
024		All: I'll be there right away [sung simultaneously with T]		8 r+ 25
			END OF PHASE I	

FIG. 1.6. Map of Instructional Conversation: Teacher M Segment from Welcome Song (Phase I: Greeting Lesson).

Tran-script Lines	IU	Message Units Transcript Text	Potentially Divergent Unit	Thematically Tied Instruction Units
				2
012		GINNY I WOULD LIKE YOU AND CATHY TO GO OVER THERE PLEASE [Teacher moves· to students as she says this and touches them and points to place they are to stand]		8 17 R ⅗ 23
013 nv		Ginny and Cathy: [move to place indicated by teacher]		8 19 r + ⅗ 23

FIG. 1.7. Map of Instructional Conversation: Teacher M Segment from Welcome Lesson (Defining Individual Space).

the head of the rug. In this segment, when the children first came to the rug area, 11 children were seated on the right side of the rug, 8 on the left, and 5 opposite the teacher. After the first phase of this lesson, the teacher had moved the children so that they were equally distributed along each side of the rug.

Observation of contextualization cues is only one method of verifying these social norms. Verification of norms also occurs during face-to-face interviews with the teachers. During one such meeting of the research team, called to share the contextual maps and to verify the teacher's objectives, Teacher H elaborated on the accomplishment of her objectives. She verified the social rules identified through the sociolinguistic ethnographic system of analysis presented in this paper. She also stated that she spends a great deal of time creating norms for signaling group. Singing the good day song together, she stated, is an example of her definition of group. The purpose of activities such as singing, the day's calendar, and the daily greeting, that comprise the contexts identified in this study, centers around building group stability. Stability for Teacher H is obtained through structuring group activities that provide continuity across daily activities.

In the analysis of conversational segments, we found that both teachers desired individual space for children; however, the two differed in the way in which they realized this goal. In addition, both teachers desired group cohesiveness. This goal was realized in a similar manner, through song, for both teachers. The two teachers were also similar in the number of contexts that they constructed with their children. Teacher H explained this phenomenon: "With five-year-olds, it is important to change context often or you would lose them." Teacher M concurred with this statement.

The foregoing discussion was provided to show the process by which the researchers determined the social action rules and verified these rules with the participants. The section that follows presents a summary of each of the six rules identified to date:

Rule 1: Being a Member of the Group Involves Responsibility for Signaling Cues for Attentiveness.   Specific behavior cues of attentiveness include physical orientation and physical proximity. The appropriateness of the distance and proximity between teacher and student and between all group members may change as the topic and/or task of the group changes. Change in norms for physical behavior are related to characteristics of the group's formation and organization, i.e., when individuals come together in different ways for different activities.

The rules outlined here were based on the analysis of the contextual maps and the teacher's audiotaped instructional goals and not on an a priori basis. Rule 1, as well as the rules which follow, were verified by the teachers during sessions in which the contextual maps were shared.

The forming of rules for signaling attentiveness is exemplified in the 13-minute segments for both classrooms. Both classroom "circle" times were physically structured into a visible shape; i.e., a circular shape was maintained throughout the 13-minute segment in classroom 1, whereas classroom 2 changed its physical orientation from a square shape in context 1–5 to rows in context 6. The reader can see in the example presented in Figure 1.7, that time is spent on constructing the rule regarding attentiveness and physical orientation and proximity at those times when the group comes together for different activities. Although the videotapes for the remaining time samples during the school year have not been analyzed via maps, the authors were the video camera technicians throughout the study. Our observations suggest that the rule for signaling attentiveness and physical orientation and proximity has moved through the forming stage and has become a norm. The future task is, of course, to analyze the cues that both the teacher and children are reading among the group interactions that signal this rule.

Rule 2: Being a Member of the Group Includes Responsibility for Enacting Different Patterns of Responses.   Keying one's behavior to the behavior patterns expected in different contexts ranges from synchronizing all group members' responses together (e.g., singing in Figure 1.3 to synchronizing individual turn-taking within the group (e.g., individual greeting of each student in Figure 1.2).

The rule for shifts in synchronizing interaction is signalled through definite statements of expected behavior (e.g., "We're going to sing it's a rainy cloudy day") or through context shift cues, such as topic or instructional assignment change (e.g., shifts from singing to news and views for Teacher M and shift from singing to the calendar for Teacher H).

Rule 3: Becoming a Member of a New Group Structure in the Classroom Requires Coming Together in Different Ways.   The norms for coordination of the group with selected classroom physical space and instructional materials may change for different activities. The criteria for membership in the new group structure may change as the teacher's instructional goals change.

An example of specific criteria being available to group members as cues for coming together in a different way can be seen in the transcripts from classroom 2 when the children move from a square shape to rows in the front of the room in Figure 1.5.

Rule 4: Being a Member of a Group Involves Cooperative Effort.   This rule can be seen in the responses of students from both classrooms, e.g., spontaneous singing with Teacher M and all children singing with Teacher H. The rule of cooperative effort can also be seen in the absence of interruption while another student was sharing during news and views in classroom 1 and the lack of interruption when individual children were being greeted in classroom 2.

Rule 5: Becoming a Member of the Group Involves Clear Avenues of Access.   The right access may depend upon a child's position in the circle (e.g., clockwise) or upon personal charcteristics (e.g., color of clothes and order in which name appears in the pile of name cards) or on individual contribution of additional information to the theme of the lesson or subject or group rule. The latter aspect of the rule for gaining access can be seen in classroom 1 when a child gains by stating the rule that we talk "one at a time," and in classroom 2 when a child gains access by pointing out an example of a child who should be in a particular physical orientation position.

Rule 6: Being a Member of a Group Includes Speaking Rights and Responsibilities.   Although each individual has the right to speak in free conversation, the right to speak during instructional contexts is flagged by different cues. For example, if a person has been designated as the one who is to share, it is not then appropriate to interrupt to share a different idea. Eleven interruptions of this type across all contexts in classroom 1 resulted in refocusing statements, e.g., "We're listening to ——— now." Coincidentally, three interruptions of this type in classroom 2 resulted in refocusing statements which included "Oh, wait a minute, I asked Eric"; "Your name is not Brooks" or direct restatements of the instructional goals.

These rules indicate that the children in both classrooms have begun to create a contextuating orientation for multiple contexts in the classroom. The contextuating orientation in the first weeks of school is concerned with attending to verbal and nonverbal cues in order to answer the questions when is a group and what should my actions be in a group. How these rules evolve over time in connection with characteristic interaction sequences that these two groups create is one of the directions that will be addressed in the longitudinal study.

CONCLUSION

The basic goal of the project of which this paper is a part is to try to clarify how members of two classrooms construct "a system of standards for perceiving, believing, evaluating, and acting" (Goodenough, 1971, p. 41) in differentiated instructional contexts. The analytic system presented permits the researcher to isolate the situationally specific aspects and features of behavioral expectations. The maps serve to supply the contextual data needed for examining how social processes are being constructed, modified, selected, checked, suspended, terminated and recommended. The strength of this analytic system is its ability to visually display that "the manner in which individuals conceive of a task leads them to create a form of social organization which is adapted to it" (Moscovici, 1972, p. 26). The problem with the system is that the accomplished fact of constructing maps of instruction conversation lends itself to misrepresenting the actual state of complexity as something clear-cut, "static, regular, and harmonious (with) its elements held poised in some perfect pattern of functional relationships" (Halliday, 1973, p. 37) and easily available for participants to read.

The effect of reading a printed text of the classroom might be that the audience begins to think that the problem facing those interested in the study of what is the nature of teaching and what is the culture of the classroom is one of how human life submits to rules. Actually, this initial analysis of two kindergartens has demonstrated to us that the problem for those interested in the nature of teaching and the nature of the classroom culture is not how human life submits to rules but rather how the rules become adapted to life (Malinowski, 1976, p. 46).

Nevertheless, if we are to understand the nature of teaching, socialization, and the classroom culture, we need a means of systematically describing the actively constructed social action processes of the classroom. In this paper we have attempted to show how the sociolinguistic ethnography system that we use provides a means to answering these questions.

REFERENCES

Adams, R. Observational studies of teacher role. *International Review of Education*, 1972, *18*, 440–458.
Argyle, M. *The psychology of interpersonal behavior*. Baltimore, Md.: Penguin, 1972.

Blumer, H. The methodological position of symbolic interactionism. In Hammersley, M., & Woods, P. (Eds.), *The process of schooling: a sociological reader*. London: Routledge & Kegan Paul, 1976.

Bossert, S. T. Book review: Explorations in classroom observation, *American Educational Research Journal,* 1977, *14*(2), 180–181.

Campbell, B. A., & Jaynes, J. Reinstatement. *Psychological Review,* 1966, *73,* 478–480.

Cook-Gumperz, J., & Gumperz, J. J. Context in children's speech. In Cook-Gumperz, J., & Gumperz, J., *Papers on language and context*. University of California, Berkeley: Language Behavior Research Laboratory, 1976.

Dweck, C. S. Children's interpretation of evaluation feedback: the effect of social cues on learned helplessness. *Merrill-Palmer Quarterly,* 1976, *22,* 105–109.

Dunkin, M. J., & Biddle, B. J. *The study of teaching*. New York: Holt, Rinehart and Winston, 1974.

Erickson, R., & Shultz, J. When is a context? Some issues and methods in the analysis of social competence. *Quarterly Newsletter of the Institute for Comparative Human Development,* 1977, *1*(2), 5–9.

Etzioni, A. *The active society*. New York: Free Press, 1968.

Forsyth, L. *Patterns in the discourse of teachers and pupils*. Paper presented at the National Institue of Education Conference on Language in the Classroom, 1974.

Getzels, J. W., & Thelan, H. A. The classroom group as a unique social system. In Henry, N. B. (Ed.), *The dynamics of instructional groups*. 59th Yearbook of the National Society for the Study of Education, Part 2, 53–82. Bloomington, Del.: Public School Publishing Co., 1960.

Goodenough, W. *Culture, language, and society*. Reading, Mass.: Addison-Wesley, 1971.

Grathoff, R. H. *The structure of social inconsistencies*. The Hague: Martinus Nijhoff, 1970.

Green, J. L. *Pedagogical style differences as related to comprehension performance: Grade one through three*. Unpublished doctoral dissertation, University of California, Berkeley, 1977.

Green, J., & Wallat, C. What is an instructional context? An exploratory analysis of conversational shifts over time. In O. Garnica & M. King, (Eds.) *Language, children and society*. New York: Pergamon, 1979.

Gumperz, J. J. *Teaching as a linguistic process*. Unpublished paper for the National Institute of Education Conference on Language in the Classroom, 1975.

Gumperz, J. J. Language, communication and public negotiation. In P. R. Sanday, (Ed.), *Anthropology and the Public Interest*. New York: Academic Press, 1976.

Gumperz, J. J., & Herasimchuk, E. The conversational analysis of social meaning: a study of classroom interaction. In R. Shuy (Ed.), *Sociolinguistics: Current Trends and Prospects,* Monograph Series on Language and Linguistics, 23rd Annual Round Table Vol. 25. Georgetown, Va.: Georgetown University Press, 1973.

Halliday, M. A. K. Language as social semiotic: towards a general sociolinguistic theory. In A. Makkai, V. B. Makkai, & L. Heilmann (Eds.), *Linguistics at the crossroads*. The Hague & Paris: Mouton, 1973.

Halliday, M. A. K., & Hasan, R. *Cohesion in English*. London: Longman, 1976.

Handelman, D. Domains of definition in interaction: postscript to expressive interaction and social structure. In A. Kendon, R. M. Harris, & M. Key, *Organization of behavior for face-to-face interaction*. Chicago: Aldine, 1975.

Harris, R., & Rubenstein, D. Paralanguage, communication and cognition. In A. Kendon, R. M. Harris, & M. Key (Eds.), *Organization of behavior for face-to-face interaction*. The Hague, Netherlands: Mouton, 1975.

Lieberman, P. Linguistic and paralinguistic interchange. In A. Kendon, R. M., Harris, & M. Key (Eds.), *Organization of behavior in face-to-face interaction*. The Hague, Netherlands: Mouton, 1975.

Malinowski, B. *The dynamics of cultural change*. Westport, Conn.: Greenwood Press, 1976.

Markel, N. Coverbal behavior associated with conversational turns. In A. Kendon, R. M. Harris, & M. Key, (Eds.), *Organization of behavior for face-to-face interaction.* The Hague, Netherlands: Mouton, 1975.

McClellan, J. Classroom teaching research: a philosophic critique. In I. Westbury, & A. Bellack, (Eds.), *Research into classroom processes: Recent developments and next steps.* New York: Teachers College Press, 1971.

Mehan, H., Cazden, C., Coles, L., Fisher, S., & Maroules, N. *The social organization of classroom lessons.* Center for Human Information Processing, University of San Diego, La Jolla, California, December 1976.

Moscovici, S. Society and theory in social psychology. In J. Isreal, & H. Tajfel, (Eds.), *The context of social psychology.* New York: Academic Press, 1972.

Parke, R. D. *Social cues, social control and ecological validity. Merrill-Palmer Quarterly,* 1976, *22,* 111–123.

Parsons, T. The school class as a social system: some of its functions in American society. *Harvard Educational Review,* 1959, *29,* 297–318.

Phillips, S. *The invisible culture: communication on the Warm Springs Reservation.* Unpublished doctoral dissertation, University of Pennsylvania, 1974.

Sacks, H. On the analyzability of children's stories. In R. Turner, (Ed.), *Ethnomethodology.* Middlesex, England: Penguin, 1974.

Stenhouse, L. *An introduction to curriculum research and development.* London: Heinemann, 1975.

Wallat, C., & Green, J. L. Social rules and communicative contexts in kindergarten. *Theory into Practice,* 1979, *18,* (4), 275–284.

Waller, W. *The sociology of teaching.* New York: Wiley, 1965.

Yarrow, L. J., Rubenstein, J. L., & Pedersen, F. A. *Infant and environment: early cognitive and motivational development.* New York: Wiley, 1975.

APPENDIX A
A DESCRIPTIVE SYSTEM
FOR SOCIOLINGUISTIC ETHNOGRAPHY

DEFINITION OF FEATURES

Message units. A message unit (MU) is the minimum unit coded in this system. An MU is a minimal unit of conversational meaning on the part of the speaker. Each MU is defined in terms of its source, form, purpose, level of comprehension, and its tie. A message unit is comparable to a free morpheme in structural linguistic terms. The boundary of an MU is linguistically marked by contextualization cues. A message unit can be determined only in retrospect by considering the verbal aspects of the message and cues to contextualization.

The source. The source identifies the speaker—the teacher, the student, or other person (e.g., parent, visitor). In analysis, the source of a message unit is symbolized by recording a number code selected to represent the speaker. This convention is recorded in the appropriate column of the coding form for the MU under consideration (e.g., 2 for teacher, 3 for student, 4 for parent, etc.).

The person to whom the message is directed is also recorded whenever possible. The recipient of the message is assigned a number or letter, and this is then used as a subscript to that of the source. For example, if the teacher (2) spoke to Martin (7 or m), or Martin and Jane, this would be recorded as 2_7 or $2_{m,j}$. If the identity of the student to whom the source is speaking is not possible, then an "0" is used to indicate that the message was addressed to a specific person but that that recipient's identity is unknown (e.g., 2_0). The omission of a subscript indicates the message was addressed to the group as a whole.

The form. Two general forms are identified: the question and the response. Each is linguistically marked. The manner of describing message units is based on the assumption that all messages in an instructional conversation which are not questions are responses to either the question, another participant, or internal purpose of the speaker. Not all responses are the same type; therefore, three categories of response types have been identified:

    Type A Response +: This category encompasses all responses that could be expected and/or are predictable given the previous contiguous behavior. An expected or predictable response refers to those responses that meet the social, cultural, psychological, and semantic aspects of the situation. For example, if a teacher asks the question, "How much is one plus three?" a predictable or expected response would be a number. In contrast, an unpredictable response to this question would be "boys," or "bananas." The accuracy of the response is not a consideration. An incorrect response is noted by assigning the number 1 as a subscript to the response (+) code number (e.g., 5_1). This convention permits retrieval of errors in later levels of analysis (See Table 2, p. 205).

Type B Response 0: This category encompasses responses that are not predictable given the immediately preceding message unit (MU) Two types of responses are recorded as unpredicted responses:

1. *a spontaneous message* by a student,
2. *a response by the student other than the one designated* in the previous contiguous behavior.

Type C Response –: This category encompasses student nonresponse and comments, such as "I don't know," and "um."

NOTE: Questions about the accuracy of responses and about nature of responses (e.g., elaboration, divergence) can be answered after descriptive coding is obtained. These are issues in analysis and not necessarily issues in description of message unit and conversational evolution.

The Strategies

This feature refers to the purpose of the message unit. The categories that compose this aspect of message structure were designed to be identified from sociolinguistic and pedagogical cues rather than from inference. Given that a message unit may serve multiple functions, more than one strategy can be recorded for each message unit.

Focusing: A message is defined as focusing if used to initiate the discussion or an aspect of the discussion. Focusing is marked by a shift in content of what is being discussed. It can be a question or response strategy. Although focusing behavior may be coded as confirming, raising, etc., it is also coded as focusing because of the overriding function it performs, the shift of focus.

Focusing Marker: This feature refers to a limited class of items (e.g., OK, now) that are used to hold the speaker's place or turn in the conversation. This feature is identifiable primarily through consideration of the prosodic aspects of the conversational segment in which it occurs. The word will generally occur alone, have pauses on either side of it, and/or be spoken in an extended manner. This feature usually marks the boundary or closure of one aspect of a conversation. This feature is indicated by Ⓢ. This feature can be glossed as meaning, "stay with me" or "it's still my turn."

Focusing Frame: This feature refers to a limited class of items (e.g., OK, now, next, do you know what, and then) that precede a focusing statement and that indicate that a new focus will follow. The prosodic feature that accompany the transmission of the word(s) helps define this strategy as a frame for what follows. This feature is indicated by a ⑧. This feature can be glossed as meaning, "Get ready. Something is coming."

Ignoring: This strategy is solely a response strategy. If a participant asks a question or makes a response that requires a conversational action by the recipient and does not receive one, ignoring is occurring. This message type is marked nonverbally. This category is not used to "infer" a person meant to ignore a conversational message of the speaker. It is used only when no response occurs and one is required.

Confirming +: This feature refers to verbal and nonverbal acceptance of a preceding response. Confirming + may take the form of a question or a response. It is also used to code the answer to a yes-no question since a yes-no question is viewed as a request for confirmation regardless of observers' inference as to the speaker's intent. For example, the question: "Are you finished with your work?" may get a yes-no response. This response is appropriate in some situations, but in others it may be seen as inappropriate, since the message was intended as a directive. That the message was meant as a directive can be determined by its place in the flow of the conversation. By coding of form only, subjective interpretation is avoided.

Confirming-: This strategy refers to nonacceptance of the previous contiguous response or to "no" in response to a request for confirmation. Confirming – may take the form of a question or a response.

Continuance: A nonverbal or verbal message which can provide a cue to the speaker that the listener is following the speaker's message and the listener may continue his turn. This is referred to as *back channeling* in the sociolinguistic literature.

Extending: This strategy refers to messages aimed at providing additional or new information about a topic. This information can be spontaneously added, or it may be elicited, therefore extending may take the form of a question or a response.

Raising: This strategy refers to a message that is aimed at raising the level of the discussion. This message is required to be tied to preceding ones. This strategy can take the form of a question or a response.

Clarifying: This strategy refers to messages meant to bring about explanations or redefinitions of a preceding behavior. This strategy may take the form of a question or a response.

Editing: This strategy encompasses shifts or changes in content, form, or strategy after the original message began. This strategy encompasses false starts and words such as "um," "uh," that act to hold place within a message. This strategy indicates internal monitoring and/or mediating of the message is occurring.

Controlling: This strategy refers to messages concerned with the control of the interaction and/or the behavior of the participants. This strategy may take the form of a question or a response.

Refocusing: This strategy reestablishes a previous question or response.

Restating: This strategy refers to repeating all or part of the previous message of the original speaker either by the original speaker or by another individual in the group. It also refers to paraphrases of previous questions or response.

The Levels

Factual: Factual level comprehension is the lowest level of comprehension. It refers to information that was stated in the discussion or instructional conversation. Factual comprehension requires recall of facts from memory.

Interpretive: Interpretive level comprehension requires that information be inferred. This level requires that the participant provide information not specifically stated in the discussion or instructional conversation.

Applicative: Applicative level comprehension requires that the information obtained during the discussion or instructional conversation be used in new ways or in new situations. This is the highest level of comprehension used in this type of micro description.

The Ties

This feature of message unit structure recognizes that a message which occurs in discussion or instructional conversation is related to or builds on behaviors and/or messages of others. Messages may be tied across conversational units and across contexts. Four sources of ties have been identified for instructional conversations: the teacher, the student, instructional media aide, and the instructional situation.

Teacher: A message is said to be tied to a teacher if the message is (a) to build on the teacher's own purpose or goal (this purpose may be internal or external in nature); (b) to feed back, or respond to, the teacher's message.

Student: A message is said to be tied to a student if its purpose is (a) to provide feedback to the student; (b) to extend the student's response; (c) to use the response as basis of the next response; (d) to permit the student to build on his/her own message.

Instructional Media Aide: A message is said to be tied to the text, material, or media aide if it is observed to be the direct trigger for a message unit.

Context: A message is said to be tied to the context (e.g., lesson being constructed or classroom structure being created) if the contextualization cues observed indicate that an iconographic or social structure has been created; that is, all participants have a shared definition of the situation (e.g., lesson or transition). Contextualization cues that indicate construction of, and adherence to, instructional and social norms provide the basis for determining ties at this level of description.

Frequently, ties for this feature exist across time (e.g., across conversational units and/or across lessons).

INTERACTION UNITS

Resolved Interaction Units: Multiple Units

A *resolved interaction unit* is defined as a series of conversationally tied message units. Which message units tie to form an interaction unit depends on consideration of verbal aspects of the message and cues to contextualization. If the delivery of a message indicates that more is to follow (e.g., the rhythm, pitch, intonation contour), then that message and the one that follows are described as *tied.* Conversational "pull" rather than syntax and/or semantic tie is the key. Consideration of contextualization cues is critical to the identification of which message units tie to form interaction units and which do not. Interaction units are illustrated in the following example from a transcript of a classroom discussion. Lines 003 and 004 are tied as indicated by message delivery, as are lines 005, 006, and 007. Although the other message units are related thematically, their manner of delivery indicated that they were complete alone. Conversational ties must not be confused with thematic ties. Thematic ties are another level in the hierarchical structure of conversations and will be defined in the sections on instructional sequence units, phase units, and lesson units.

Resolved Interaction Unit: Single Unit

An interaction unit may be composed of a single message unit if the message unit is a completed message as indicated by contextualization cues. On the transcript sample, lines 001, 002, and 008 are examples of message units that are also resolved interaction units.

Unresolved Interaction Unit: Single Unit

Four types of unresolved interaction units can occur in an instructional conversation.

Type I: Noncompleted or interrupted units. If a behavior is begun and is not completed, it is coded as a message unit and the structure of the unit is coded for as many features as possible. For example, the teacher begins to ask, "Who can..." and a student interrupts with a question. This unit has been interrupted, but the source and the form can be coded. The identification of the other features is not possible from this fragment; therefore, the message unit and the interaction unit are unresolved. If all features of a message unit cannot be determined, then the message unit is said to be unresolved.

Type II: No response given. If a participant initiates a message that requires a response but receives none, the interaction unit is unresolved or open. For example, a teacher asks, "Who is this?" and receives silence. The teacher then asks the question in another way. "What animal do you think this is?" The interaction unit begun by the first question is unresolved since the teacher does not receive the expected response or closure.

Type III: Expected response not achieved. The teacher or student in this type of unresolved interaction unit asks a question which is postponed. The question receives no response. The questioner then indicates that the question will be considered at a later point. For example, a student asks, "Why did the tiger do that?" and the teacher responds with, "We'll come back to that later."

Type IV: Overt ignoring. An unresolved unit can occur if the teacher or student who is to respond to an initiation overtly, as indicated by a direct nonverbal gesture, indicates lack of cooperation. For example, if the teacher asks a question of Student B and Student B turns away from the teacher, this unit is said to be unresolved from a pedagogical point of view.

NOTE: As with message units, boundary for interaction units is determined only in retrospect.

Instructional Sequence Unit

An *instructional sequence unit* (ISU) is composed of a series of tied interaction units (IU). An instructional sequence is defined in terms of content. All interaction units which focus on the same aspect of the total conversation belong to a single instructional sequence unit. The ties for the instructional sequence unit are ties that exist across units thematically. The end of an instructional sequence unit is marked by a shift in the general content within the lesson. Contextualization cues do not play a central role in the identification of instructional sequence units. This unit corresponds to a step the teacher takes in building the pedagogical structure of a lesson. An ISU is composed of interaction units, which focus on a single subcontent of the lesson. Like message units and interaction units, the instructional sequence unit is determined only in retrospect. One cannot determine in advance whether or not an interaction unit will be part of the preceding instructional sequence unit or will begin a new instructional sequence unit. Instructional sequence units are generally composed of more than one interaction unit, but there are times in which an instructional sequence unit will be composed of a single interaction unit.

Phase Unit

A *phase unit* (PU) consists of a series of thematically tied instructional sequence units. Pedagogically a lesson is composed of parts or phases each with a distinct purpose (e.g., introduction, content presentation, evaluation period, or summary). Consideration of the pedagogical and social structure being constructed will determine which instructional sequence units belong to a phase unit and which do not. Consideration of who is group, when is group, and the expectations of behavior

Appendix Chapter 8

Transcript Line	Source	Interaction Length	Message Unit	Contextualization Cues
001	T	Single MU	THIS IS THE COVER PICTURE.	1. Points to picture. 2. Looks at students at beginning of statement and back to picture by end of message. 3. Voice drops on picture. 4. Pause 2 seconds.
002	T	Single MU	THE WAY THE TIGER WALKED.	1. Points to book title. 2. Hand moves across title as she delivers each word slowly and emphatically. 3. Head scans students and returns to look at book cover. 4. Pause 2 seconds.
003	T	Two MU's i.e. 003 and 004	AND IT'S WRITTEN BY SOME-BODY I DONT KNOW.	1. Looks at title then at students. 2. Says it rapidly. 3. Intonation falls off slightly on "KNOW". 4. Intonation rises and "AND" with "AND" stressed.

004	T		HER NAME IS DORIS CHACONES.	1. Teacher's focal point remains on students. 2. No pause between messages. 3. Intonation rises on "HER." 4. Kinesic shift of head with onset of message "HER." 5. Said rapidly. 6. Pause 1 second at end of message.
005	T	3 MU's	HAVE YOU HEARD OF THIS STORY BY HER?	1. Teacher's focal point remains on student. 2. Body moves in toward group. 3. Rising tone to indicate question.
006	STS		all; no	1. Some students say "no." 2. Others indicate "no" by shaking head from left to right several times.
007	T		I DIDN'T THINK SO.	1. Teacher's focal point remains on students. 2. Voice level drops to whisper. 3. Looks at book and back at students. 4. Pause 3 seconds.
008	T	Single MU	I'VE ALREADY READ IT.	1. Focal point on students. 2. Body leans in. 3. Pause 2 seconds.

provide the structural cues that can be used to determine phase units for a given period of time. Phase units are generally composed of more than one instructional sequence units, but there will be instances when a phase unit will consist of a single instructional sequence unit. Like all previously described units, the phase unit is determined in retrospect.

Lesson Unit

A *lesson unit* (LU) consists of a series of instructionally tied phase units aimed at accomplishing all lesson goals. Although lesson units are generally composed of a series of instructionally tied phase units, there are instances when a lesson unit will consist of a single phase unit. As is true of all the units previously described, the lesson unit is determined via *pos hoc* analysis.

TABLE 2

Descriptive Analysis of Instructional Conversations

Transcript line (1)	Source Teacher (2)	Source Student (3)	Form Question (4)	Form Response + (5)	Form Response 0 (6)	Form Response - (7)	Strat. Focusing (8)	Strat. Ignoring (9)	Strat. Confirming+ (10)	Strat. Confirming- (11)	Strat. Continuance (12)	Strat. Extending (13)	Strat. Raising (14)	Strat. Clarifying (15)	Strat. Editing (16)	Strat. Controlling (17)	Strat. Refocusing (18)	Strat. Restating (19)	Level Factual (20)	Level Interpret (21)	Level Applicative (22)	Tie Teacher (23)	Tie Student (24)	Tie Lesson (25)	Tie (26)	Unit Res. Resolved Interaction (30)	Unit Res. Unresolved Interaction (31)	Unit Res. Instruction Sequence (50)	Unit Res. Phase (60)	Unit Res. Lesson (70)
025	2			5			8												20			23				0				
026	2			5			8												20			23				0				
027	2			5															20			23				0				
028	2j			5			8								15					20					25		0				
029		3j		5			8								15					20					25		30				
030	2st			5			8													20					25		0				
031		3st		5			8													20					25		30				
032	2nv			5			8													20					25		0				
033		3nv		5			8													20					25		30				
034	2sn			5			8													20					25		0				
035		3sh		5			8													20					25		30				
036	2jo			5			8													20					25		0				
037		3jo		5			8													20					25		30				
038	2er			5			8													20					25		0				
039		3er		5			8													20					25		30				

Column groupings: **Source** = Teacher (2), Student (3); **Form** = Question (4), Response + (5), Response 0 (6), Response − (7); **Strategies** = Focusing (8), Ignoring (9), Confirming+ (10), Confirming− (11), Continuance (12), Extending (13), Raising (14), Clarifying (15), Editing (16), Controlling (17), Refocusing (18), Restating (19); **Level** = Factual (20), Interpret (21), Applicative (22); **Tie** = Teacher (23), Student (24), Lesson (25), (26); **Unit Resolution** = Resolved Interaction (30), Unresolved Interaction (31), Instruction Sequence (50), Phase (60), Lesson (70).

III COMBINING ETHNOGRAPHIC AND EXPERIMENTAL METHODS—A BEGINNING

9

Cultural and Situational Variation in Language Function and Use— Methods and Procedures for Research

William S. Hall and Larry F. Guthrie
University of Illinois, Urbana-Champaign

INTRODUCTION

It is widely believed that there are cultural differences in the functions and uses of language among various ethnic and cultural groups in the USA (Labov, 1970; Lein, 1975; Cazden, John, & Hymes, 1972; Hall & Freedle, 1975). In fact, the idea of a mismatch between speakers in language functioning and use is often given as one explanation of the educational difficulties some children have in school (Bernstein, 1964, 1972). Empirical support for this however, is, very thin. An examination of previous research shows at least three reasons for the lack of evidence: (a) The situations used to evaluate language have been quite restricted; they have concentrated primarily on language as used in schools or in strictly experimental situations. (b) There is ambiguity about the terms *function* and *use*—it is not clear whether they should be approached from the perspective of communication, cognition, or social parameters only. (c) The primary emphasis in recent work has been on content (vocabulary) and structure (grammar).

In order to overcome these weaknesses a different approach is required. Specifically, the approach should

(1) combine psycholinguistic and ethnographic methods;
(2) emphasize situational variation within as well as across settings;
(3) sample from Blacks and whites, lower- and middle-class subjects (groups never sampled before in a single study);

The research described in this chapter was supported by a grant from the Carnegie Corporation of New York. The preparation of this manuscript was supported by the National Institue of Education under contract No. US-NIE-C-400-76-0116.

(4) have a sample is large enough to permit supportable inferences;

(5) focus on the combined aspects of structure, content, and function in language;

(6) evaluate change in language use and function in the transition from home to preschool.

This chapter describes a major research project which uses the combination of methods just stated. The chapter also focuses on illustrative examples of how data analysis might proceed when such methods are employed.

STATEMENT OF ISSUES

The general hypothesis underlying the work to be discussed is that minority groups and the poor use language in ways that systematically put their children at a disadvantage at school. By sampling children from different cultural and socioeconomic groups, the research focuses on the consequences which different patterns of language function and use may have for the child.

The single most important issue in this regard is the consequences for the speaker—particularly with respect to his or her educational performance. Broadly speaking, these consequences may be social, cognitive, or educational—three areas which are certainly part of any theory of cultural variations in school performance. We shall now treat these in turn.

Social.   The social consequences of nonstandard speech for children can affect teacher-pupil as well as peer relationships. The consequences of a teacher's attitude toward a given dialect can be profound. For example, a teacher's attitude can affect his/her initial judgment about the intelligence of a child, how the child will fare as a learner, how he is grouped for instruction, and how his contributions in class are treated. This in turn affects the child's attitude about himself as a learner, his willingness to participate, and his expectations about results of his participation.

The consequences of nonstandard speech with respect to one's standing with peers may also be profound. It is often suggested that high status in peer and school settings requires opposing rules for using or not using language in various ways.

Cognitive.   A long tradition in the cognitive social sciences links language and thought. What is not clear is whether different patterns of language socialization in the home have directly discernable cognitive consequences.

We are particularly concerned in the current research with the evaluation of the cognitive consequences of patterns of language usage identified by Bernstein (1964, 1972). In his work, a basic question remains unanswered: Do cultural/class differences in language usage affect people in other than social ways (e.g., cognitively)?

Of concern are cognitive consequences which might result from differences in various aspects of language, such as vocabulary. Vocabulary differences clearly reflect differences in public access to one's ideas. These differences lead to different opportunities to talk about a given meaning or aspect of meaning as a consequence of which different speech communities would have different access to its members' and others' ideas. At a deeper level, different types of speech involve different opportunities to engage in certain basic cognitive processes. For example, the process of modification in the case of adjectives or adverbs, or the process of subordination in the case of conjunctions, could easily be affected by differentially elaborated vocabularies. There is also evidence suggesting that unrecognized differences in vocabulary result in misestimates of memory capacity and "general intelligence."

Educational. The possible educational consequences of speaking a nonstandard variety of speech can be illustrated for three areas: reading, ability to engage in "instructional dialogue," ability to deal with a kind of "metabehavioral" information. With reference to reading, a phonological mismatch can affect children's acquisition of phonic skills. Phonological mismatches are likely to lead teachers to misinterpret children's own reading of a sentence. (For example, if a child says "John pin" when he sees the phrase "John's pen," the teacher could misinterpret this as a mistake instead of a different pronunciation.)

In addition, semantic mismatches may affect children's expectations about the gist of the language that they are reading. Syntactic mismatches may also affect children's expectations about gist (see, e.g., Piestrup, 1973). Moreover, different cultures may promote different levels of metalinguistic awareness, and some cultures may provide more practice than others in those skills which are reasonably isomorphic to the kinds of processes that children must use in learning to read—for example, counting out rhymes and jump-rope chants which are based on alliterations or rhyming.

Certain patterns of early language socialization perhaps also hamper children's ability to engage in "instructional dialogue" when they enter school, i.e., the kind of communication situation in which a teacher and pupil engage in a question-and-answer routine: where the questioner has a specific answer in mind and the answerer's job is to guess what that answer is. The big difference between this type of interaction and the "normal" question-and-answer exchange is that the correctness of the answer is not necessarily judged on the truth value, but rather on its conformity to a strategy or plan for answering which the teacher has already constructed. The question is: Does the communication environment provide an opportunity to engage in interactions which are similar to that of instructional dialogue? Here, *similar* is used in the sense that the requirements of a correct answer are based on some ability to intuit the kind of answering strategy that the questioner has in mind, rather than on truth value or some kind of aesthetic organization of the speech act.

Patterns of language socialization that characterize some cultures/ classes are often said to interfere with a child's ability to deal with analytical or metabehavioral information, that is, the ability to analyze and make analytical statements about certain kinds of behavior not always reflected upon in everyday life. These include perceptual awareness (the ability to analyze a perceptual array into a set of geometrical or mathematical relationships) and behavior awareness (the ability to analyze the emotions of a person or those of a fictional character). To understand how being a member of a given speech community might affect the ability to make this type of analysis, it is necessary to consider whether different cultures provide differential opportunities to engage in the kind of metabehavioral analysis just mentioned. Since such analysis is a hallmark of schooling, it is a prime area for studying home/school mismatches (Scribner & Cole, 1973).

To see how these and other issues are dealt with in the research project, we now turn to a more detailed description of that work.

The Research

As a preliminary to the research, we undertook an exhaustive review of the literature in relevant areas and discovered several substantive limitations: the use of limited situations,: (a) the use of limited situations, (b) the ambiguity of the meaning of the terms *function* and *use* in language, (c) an emphasis on content and structure. In addition, we found that (d) the nature of the analysis used (e.g., correlational, experimental, survey) obscured pertinent information (cf. Mehan, 1978, 1979); (e) sample size was usually too small to justify inferences; (f) failure to study middle-class as well as lower-class subjects from all groups being compared restricted conclusions; (g) the important transition from preschool to the first grade was neglected.

Given the present state of knowledge, a number of pressing questions about the educational performance of urban poor people still remain unanswered. Certainly, the relation of language usage and school performance among different ethnic groups and groups defined by socioeconomic status (SES) is one of them. We believe that the research program described here and other studies like it will ultimately discover the path leading to a solution of these problems. As a first step in that direction, the research is aimed at three general questions about young children and the significant adults in their lives:

1. What are the important dimensions of language differences among cultural groups in the USA as defined by SES and ethnic group identity?

Specifically, these differences should lie in language structure and content, i.e., vocabulary, grammar, and phonology.

2. Do patterns of language usage distribute across social setting and speech situations in the same way for different cultural groups?

3. What are the cognitive consequences of variations in language function, especially the functions into which young children are socialized?

In conceptualizing the research, it was reasoned that a naturalistic study of language as used by young children (age 4½–5 years) would be required. Before this research, naturalistic studies of language usage of parents and young children were rare (cf. Ward, 1971; Horner & Gussow, 1974). Existing studies employed primarily interview-based and school-based data. Without evidence of more naturalistic language, the question raised in this chapter cannot be answered adequately.

To do a naturalistic study of language, an ethnographic method is the most pertinent. This method allows for fairly accurate descriptions of behavior as it emerges in context; thus both the talk itself and the context in which it occurs can be described. The behavior we wish to study has little descriptive value without the careful charting of its antecedents and consequences in context. This careful charting is what we mean by *ethnographic method*. For this research, then, extensive samples of language usage in natural contexts were obtained. These consisted of recordings of conversations between target children and their parents, siblings, teachers, and peers, representing a variety of physical and temporal contexts.

Further, it was decided to focus on the intellectual consequences of differences in language structure, content, and function as these interact with social class, ethnic group membership, and setting. In this regard, the work drew upon and extended two disciplines in the behavioral sciences: sociolinguistics and developmental psychology. With respect to sociolinguistics, it built upon and extended the work of Labov (1970) on the elaborations of structure, of Houstin (1969) on specific registers and shifts in same, of Ward (1971), Horner (1968), and Hall, Cole, Reder, and Dowley (1977), on the communication network as portrayed in the home and immediate surrounds. Regarding developmental psychology, it built upon and extended the work of Hess (1969) on cognitive environments, and White and Watts (1973) on the environment of the child in general.

Methods. The methodology employed here was what Hymes calls the *ethnography of communication* (Hymes, 1974). In a general ethnography, the goal of the ethnographer is a verbal recreation of the world of the target culture. It should be a descriptive account which members of the target culture recognize as their own experience of reality. In contrast, the ethnographic component of the research described here was more focused in that it concentrated on naturally occurring speech. By recording language in the everyday lives of the target children, actual language experiences of subjects were sampled. Data on other aspects of the subjects' lives were included only as they related to the functions and uses of language.

Language samples were collected through the use of audiotapes. There are several reasons for this. First, the complexities of language are too great to be captured by a participant observer's field notes. They could not capture, for example, the multiple functions of language in context. For the same reasons, checklist data would be inadequate. The limited perspective of checklists would also require that a more sophisticated data-collection method be employed. Audiotapes satisfy this requirement.

Second, the audiotape equipment (portable tape records with wire less microphones) was manageable enough to enable data collection in a number of different settings. Data were collected, for example, in homes, shops, moving cars, and on sidewalks. The mobility achieved in this way would not have been possible with, say, videotape machines. Even though videotape provides more complete data, in a study such as this its use would clearly have been problematic.

Finally, the tape equipment did not seem to cause any significant disruption in the normal behavior of the target children. The wireless microphones were, for example, sewn into colorful vests which target children wore without protest; in fact, they seemed quickly to forget about having them on.

Subjects.   Subjects were 40 preschool age children (4.5–5.0 years) divided equally according to race and SES as follows: lower-class Black (10), lower-class white (10), middle-class Black (10), middle-class white (10). SES was determined through the use of income and education indices from the scale developed by Warner, Meeker, and Ells (1949).

Procedures.   Language samples were collected over two consecutive days. Taping was done through the use of stereo tape recorders and wireless microphones worn by both the target children and the field worker. Target children wore vests with microphones sewn in; field workers clipped microphones on their ties. Although adults and nontarget children in the study did not wear microphones, the two mikes used were, in general, sensitive enough to pick up all significant verbal interaction with the children in the study.

In order to sample situational variations in language, each child was recorded in a series of ten temporal situations: (a) before school in the morning, (b) on the way to school, (c) during the transition to the classroom, (d) during free play, (e) during teacher-directed activity, (f) during snacks and toileting, (g) on the way home from school, (h) before dinner, (i) during dinner, (j) before bed. The setting for these temporal situations consisted of not just home and classroom, but playground and community as well as home and community. Additional recording was done of parents in a formal interview situation (see Appendix A) which investigated questions relating to the child and his home and school environments.

In the collection of data, the field worker tried to be as unobtrusive as possible. He rarely initiated conversations, but if spoken to, attempted to respond naturally. One of the field worker's responsibilities was to provide a verbal description to the *context*. For this research, the context included where the recording took place, where the subject was, who the interactants were, and what they were doing—both their verbal and nonverbal behavior. Furthermore, the descriptions of context often included what happened before and after, as well as simultaneous to, verbal interaction.

The length of the recordings in each of the temporal situations varied from 15 to 60 minutes. When summed, this amounts to a total of 420–500 minutes of talk for each child and about 300 hours overall. Handwritten transcripts were made of the recordings and coding on the computer punch cards and then computer tape. Each turn of talk was transcribed on a separate punch card (or two cards if necessary because of turn length), producing a total of 10,000 cards per child or 40,000 overall. On each punch card, in addition to the transcription of a turn, the following information was coded: subject number, SES, race, speaker, and situation.

RESEARCH QUESTIONS

In assembling the corpus, a series of 9 questions was formulated. In each, the interest was in group differences as they are related to the particular contexts and to the social, cognitive, and educational consequences for the child. The questions focus on three aspects of language: (a) differences in language structure and content; (b) patterns of language usage across groups; (c) differences in language usage across natural and formal settings. In the pages that follow we will present the questions, grouped according to the aspect of language upon which they focus.

Structure and Content

Question 1: Are there differences in the way Black and white speakers structure portions of the lexicon? There might be certain differences in the way in which speakers of Black dialect and Standard English structure prepositions. For example, Black Harlem adults have been observed to say the following to children: "John, sit *to* the table." In this instance, a standard English speaker would probably say: "John, sit *at* the table." The question is whether the rendering, "sit *to* the table" does not give the child a different relationship between himself and the object *table* than that interpretable from "John, *sit* at the table." Essentially, the first instance is more factive than locative. Such potential differences in structuring the lexicon are of special interest because of their implications for cognitive functioning as it is exemplified in standardized test performance.

On a broader scale, the reasons for asking this question are due to its centrality in human experience. Space and time, both of which can be readily revealed through prepositions, are basic coordinates of experience. Since only one object can be in a given place at a given time, spatial locatives provided an indispensible device for identifying referents. "Hand me the spoon on the table" identifies the spoon that the speaker is referring to. The place adverbial, "on the table," indicates a search field, and the head noun, "spoon," provides the target description. As Miller and Johnson-Laird (1976) indicate, how a search is to be executed depends on the particular preposition relating the target to the landmark: *on, in, at, by, under,* etc. How children learn to delimit the search field and the cultural variations in the way they do so is of extreme interest.

Brown (1973) has observed that "in" and "on" are among the first words children learn to use. This suggests that understanding the relation of a target to a search field comes early in the life of the child, as does the child's understanding of the topology of spatial relations in general. According to Brown, these understandings seem to grow naturally out of the child's mastery of sensorimotor coordinations in space and time.

Question 2: Are There Differences Between Vocabulary Used in the Home and in the School Situation?   Answers to this question might be found first in raw counts and frequencies of lexical items. In addition, little is known about social class differences in the way in which certain parts of the lexicon are structured. Miller and Johnson-Laird (1976) have provided a theory on how spatial relationships and verbs of motion might be structured, but no empirical evidence is available.

In the research program we are discussing, evidence on this question is being sought in two ways: (a) a search is being conducted of the naturally occurring data with respect to lexicon. An alphabetical list of all words in the *corpus* is being produced and coded for subject, speaker, and situation. Alphabetical lists for each subject are already available. In addition, Hall and Tirre (1979) have searched the *corpus* for the use of words from four standardized intelligence tests: the Stanford-Binet, the WISC-R, the WPPSI, and the Peabody. They found that overall, speakers produced more of the target words at home than at school; and that middle-class children produced more of the words at home than lower-class ones. No overall differences were found for race or social class. (b) A series of assessment interviews (Appendix A) adopted from previous work is being conducted with the children and their parents. These interviews are designed to assess the degree to which children's actual comprehension of certain terms incorporates the "rules" or relationships hypothesized in Miller's theory of lexical structure. The concern is with both raw counts and frequencies and the different contexts that any given vocabulary item enters in the communication network, on the assumption that frequency and variability of context are both important for completely developed word meaning.

Question 3: Admitting that Phonology and Grammar are Equally Important Determinants of Dialect Assessment, Does Phonology Play a Greater Role in Producing Misunderstanding Between Teacher and Student? This question can be seen to relate directly to the role of dialect in learning to read. Simons (1973), for example, has noted that, for learning to read, one major behavioral consequence of the differences between the Black dialect and Standard English phonological systems is that certain written words are pronounced differently by Black dialect than by Standard English speakers. The results of these differences are words that have a pronunciation unique to Black dialect, e.g., "nest"—"ness," "rest"—"ress," "hand"—"han." Moreover, there are words whose Black dialect pronunciation results in a different word, e.g., "test"—"Tess," "mend"—"men," "walked"—"walk," "cold"—"coal," "find"—"fine," etc. The latter result is an extra set of homophones for Black dialect speakers. These differences in pronunciation, for example, could interfere with the Black dialect speaker's acquisition of word recognition skills.

Questions 1–3 provide a view of vocabulary differences for children at different age levels, as well as for adults (e.g., mothers and teachers). The role of lexicon vis-à-vis basic readers, code-switching by context, and the role of parent-child interaction in vocabulary is being investigated, as is the relative importance of grammar and phonology in teacher-pupil misunderstanding. Further, a central issue in "bidalecticalism," namely, do grammar and phonology vary within, as well as across, settings, can be addressed through collecting data on these questions.

Patterns of Usage

Question 4: To What Extent Do Children Rely on Nonverbal as Opposed to Verbal Cues in Obtaining Information from the Environment and Communicating Information about the Environment to Others? This question is being asked for the target child in each setting where sampling of language was done. In the more structured situations, the work on referential communication guided the data collection. Among the questions being asked are (a) how does the target child acquire information from others (adults, older children, peers, etc.); (b) how does his information acquisition here differ, and/or how is it similar to that in the naturally occurring events of his everyday life?

Question 5: To What Extent are Children Likely or Able to Adopt a Hypothetical Stance Toward Linguistic Information? Verbs and conjunctions are important pieces of data needed to answer this question. It is important to analyze the use of verbs, for example, because they are essential for ascertaining meaning in sentences. Verbs are necessary for predication in English, and predication makes sentences something more than a string of word associations. The verbs of particular interest are those of motion (e.g., move, come, go, walk, jump, run, reach, arrive), primarily because they can be studied with young children. These verbs can occur in relatively simple sentences; they have a fairly obvious perceptual basis for reference; they combine spatial and temporal aspects; and children use them frequently. A detailed analysis of verbs of motion has been presented by Miller (personal communication) and Miller and Johnson-Laird (1976). Suffice it to say that the motion verbs—"come" and "go," "bring" and "take"—occur frequently in child language although they involve some rather complicated relations of the direction of motion to the region of the speaker and his addressee. An analysis of these verbs has been done for adult speech by Fillmore (1971). The data can be searched for spontaneous occurrences of these verbs to see whether they are ever misapplied or confused. The question is: Does the young child who uses motion verbs really understand them?

Miller (personal communication) has noted that analysis of verbs like "jump," for example, into their semantic components leads to several possibilities. The paraphrase, "She jumped the fence," would translate into something like "She did something with her legs that cause her to begin traveling over the fence," which includes such semantic components as motion, path, action, causation, etc. If young children use such verbs correctly, they probably do so on the basis of representations other than those revealed by semantic analysis. That this is probably the case has been suggested by Nelson (1973) in her hypothesis that concepts develop from intrareferent variations, not from interreferent variations. The semantic analysis represents a summary of differences between related words, whereas children may develop a concept of jumping without considering differences between jumping, launching, throwing, bouncing, and other related concepts. The verbs of motion provide useful materials with which to test these notions.

Question 6. Do Children Adjust Their Speech to Reflect the Contextual Needs of a Situation? For example, do children adjust their speech to accommodate the needs of others? Evidence from referential communication literature indicates they do, at least in experimental situations (Shatz & Gelman, 1973; Asher, 1978). Much less is known, however, about children's use of speech in natural settings or the effect of situational variables. The study by Hall, Cole, Reder, and Dowley (1977) is noteworthy in that it does measure the effects of situation on children's speech.

One approach with the present *corpus* might be to search for instances when subjects communicated information. These could then be coded for situation, listener, etc., and measured for accuracy or completeness.

Question 7: Concerning the Metabehavioral Activities of the Children: (a) Can They Describe Their Own Behavior and Inner States? (b) What is the Nature of the Lexicon that Children have Developed to Describe Their Own Behavior and Inner States? (c) What Kind of Metalinguistic Awareness have Children Developed?   Following a set of procedures developed by Gearhart and Hall (1979), and Hall and Nagy (1979), the *corpus* might be examined for evidence concerning the use of *internal state words* (e.g., know, sight, hopeful). Consideration, for example, would be given to (a) the percentage of internal state words used by different speakers in different contexts; (b) the semantic or pragmatic use of the words; (c) the relation of particular lexical items to mental activities. The hypothesis here is that the use of internal state words can facilitate the acquisition of metacognitive processes and help the child to become an active seeker, interpreter, and user of knowledge.

Investigations which follow from Questions 4-7 will, when finished, provide a check on the validity and situational variability in the language patterns formulated by Bernstein as *elaborated* and *restricted,* as well as Horner's use of *simple* vs. *elaborate tacts* in interpersonal communication. The structured setting data will be compared with that from the unstructured setting as a means for disentangling dominant modes of speaking from possible ones. Perhaps most importantly, answers to questions 4-7 will provide some much needed data on the implications of language socialization modes for cognitive skills—a point on which there is much controversy.

Comparison Across Settings

Question 8: Are There Situational Differences in the Use of Language Among Adults in "Structured" Situations?   An example of a structured situation which might be useful here would be the interview, both individual and group. Here it may be predicted that both middle- and lower-class adults will produce more language, and a more complex language, in group than in individual interviews, and that the difference in language between the two situations will be greater for the lower than for the middle class. The subject of such interviews could be videotaped situations like the following: child-parent interactions or child-teacher interaction. These interactions should be open-ended; the following are examples: (a) the child breaks (or is about to break something); (b) the child hurts (or is about to hurt someone, e.g., a younger sibling); (c) the child asks for help with a task in a situation where the mother appears to have just finished a burdensome chore; (d) the child asks for help with a task in a situation where the mother appears to be very busy; (e) the child does something inappropriate during an interaction with a strange member of the establishment (e.g., while the mother talks to a shopkeeper or to a doctor or nurse at a clinic or to a secretary or other office worker at school); (g) the child indicates an ability to do something independently in a home setting. Teacher-child interactions could be investigated along similar lines.

Question 9: What is the Proportion of Different Uses of Questions Across Different Cultural Groups? Efficient accumulation of information is critical to school performance, and questions are cues to provide information and elicit information-seeking behavior in the child. Moreover, they are a verbal means by which a child seeks information. The data on questions in adult-child and child-child interaction in natural settings are lacking; it is believed that the *corpus* will provide these data.

ANALYSIS OF THE DATA

Having amassed a tremendous amount of data from largely naturalistic sources, the problem becomes one of analysis. Obviously, any analysis should be planned in terms of some set of problems. In our case, we have articulated problems regarding the functional use of language in terms of a series of questions. Clearly, all these questions cannot be approached at once; some decision must be made about how to proceed. For example, one who wishes to focus on lexical analysis, might proceed as follows:

The first part of such an analysis could focus on the individual lexical item, i.e., vocabulary. Vocabulary variations might be looked at in a variety of ways, all of which could be treated against a grid formed by the combinations of four basic population groups (Black/white by middle class/lower class). This analysis should also include situational variation, (e.g., home vs. school, dinnertime vs. bedtime, lessons vs. free play, etc.). A simple word count would uncover, among other things, whether there is a reason to tailor initial reading vocabularies to special groups. Another aspect of this analysis involves matching the obtained vocabulary with vocabularies used in psychological tests, e.g., the Stanford-Binet; the WISC, etc. (Hall & Tirre, 1979). These two analyses are essentially frequency distributions. They are fairly easy to do, given the state of the data, and should yield two products: a "dictionary" of spoken words and a report detailing the relationship between obtained and expected vocabularies.

A third line of lexical analysis might involve searching the obtained vocabularies for lexical domains of special theoretical interest because they relate directly to established theories of cultural differences in language usage (e.g., function words, verbs, prepositions, etc.).

Another analysis of the lexicon might focus on mother-child interaction. This analysis might focus on the question of whether the mother's language in a formal, schoollike situation constitutes a context for the child's performance. Specifically, what might be looked at is how mothers talk to their children to ensure a high level of performance on schoollike tasks. The context here is taken as being constituted by what people are doing and where and when they are doing it (Erickson and Shultz, 1977). People in interaction become environments for each other's behavior (McDermott, 1976).

A different approach to analysis might concern investigation of constraints on conversation. When participating in conversations, children must continuously produce language which achieves communicative goals and is appropriate to the communicative situation at each point in the conversation. Thus, children are constrained both by the "local" circumstances of the conversation and by the need to achieve the personal goal which they bring to the conversation and which explains their decision to participate. Children are thus constrained from the bottom up by the grammatical form, illocutionary functions, and content of utterances which occur in the conversation; and from the top down by their own communicative goals. The analysis of talk in conversations must centrally involve the analysis of how children produce language which satisfies different kinds of constraints and of how they use their cognitive, linguistic, social, and cultural resources in producing appropriate talk. The goal of this analysis would be understanding the constraints on children's decisions in speaking and the manner in which they use the resources at their disposal when doing so.

If some turn made by a speaker is labeled i, and the turn that immediately follows it $i + 1$, then what is of interest is the unit consisting of the pair $i, i + 1$. How does i constrain $i + 1$ and how do children use the resources available to them in producing an appropriate response? These questions constitute the basic level of analysis. Other levels might consider, for example, how $i + 1$ relates to turns prior to i and $i + 1$. In this way, how higher-level discourse units in a conversation provide a link to the child's developing ability to produce and understand coherent discourse could also be considered.

The ability to produce and understand coherent discourse is one of the major accomplishments and requirements in becoming "schooled" in our culture. It is probable that cultural differences in the functions and uses of language will be apparent in the structure of conversations and that because of them an educational mismatch is effected, putting some children at a disadvantage in acquiring the ability to produce and comprehend coherent discourse. Given the current state of knowledge, one can list some classes of constraints and resources which operate in conversations: (a) illocutionary, i.e., the intentions motivating utterance type, such as questions, statements, etc.; (b) inferential content, i.e., relations in, among, and beyond the propositions to be interpreted; (c) grammatical form; (d) social relationships among speakers, both the status they bring to the interaction and the role they create; (e) shared meanings and prior knowledge; (f) settings; (g) the task in which one is engaged and one's conception of it; (h) the prior discourse in the same setting; and (i) cognitive demands of the task.

CONCLUSION

This chapter has described one attempt at a solution to a difficult educational problem—the failure of minority children to succeed in school. Although it is certainly not the only cause, we have suggested that a mismatch between the functions and uses of language at home and at school might have an important influence on the academic success of such children. It is believed that ethnic minority groups use language in ways that systematically put their children at a disadvantage in school. Language differences can have tragic consequences for children as they move from the home community into the middle-class world of the school. Socially, the child may experience both teacher and peer prejudice because of the dialect he speaks. The child may find that his speech patterns limit him cognitively as well. Language differences may place academic success out of reach.

We have described a research program designed to investigate these possible consequences in minority children. In the research, language samples were collected from an equal number of Black and white, lower- and middle-SES children. The children were recorded in a variety of physical and temporal situations and in interaction with parents, siblings, teachers, other adults, and peers. After a massive data-collection effort, a *corpus* of more than 300 hours of natural language had been obtained.

A series of nine questions guided the research; these questions focused on three aspects of language: (a) differences in language structure and content; (b) patterns of language usage; (c) differences in language usage across groups. Finally, in this chapter we presented three examples of possible approaches to data anlaysis which relate to these questions.

The plight of ethnic minorities in the American educational system should be the subject of a concerted research effort. But before any further steps are taken one caveat must be emphatically entered: answers will not lie in experimental, survey, or interview data alone. One must attend to the reality which minority children experience, and this can be achieved only through the inclusion of ethnographic methods in research methodologies. The research design reported on here is only one form that such studies might take, but all will at least have an ethnographic component in common.

REFERENCES

Asher, S. *Referential communication*. Urbana, Ill.: University of Illinois Center for the Study of Reading, Technical Report No. 90, 1978.

Bernstein B. B. Elaborated and restricted codes: their social origins and some consequences. In J. J. Gumperz & D. Hymes (Eds.), *Ethnography of communication*. Washington, D.C.: American Anthropological Association, 1964.

Bernstein, B. B. *Class, codes, and control*. London: Routledge & Kegan Paul, 1972.

Brown, R. *A first language*. Cambridge, Mass.: Harvard University Press, 1973.

Cazden, C., John, V., & Hymes, D. *Functions of language in the classroom*. New York: Teachers College Press, 1972.

Donaldson, M., & McGarrigle, J. Some clues to the nature of semantic development. *Journal of Child Language*, 1974, *1*, 185–194.

Dore, J. Oh them Sherriff: a pragmatic analysis of children's responses to question. In S. Ervin-Tripp & C. Mitchell-Kernan (Eds.), *Child discourse*. New York: Academic Press, 1977.

Erickson, F., & Shultz, J. When is a context? Some issues and methods in the analysis of social competence. *Quarterly Newsletter of the Institute for Comparative Human Development* 1977, *1*(2), 5–10.

Fillmore, Charles, J. Santa Cruz Lectures on Deixus 1971. Bloomington, Indiana: Indiana University Linguistics Club, 1975.

Frederiksen, C. H. Representing logical and semantic structure of knowledge acquired from discourse. *Cognitive Psychology*, 1975, *7*, 371–458.

Gearhart, M., & Hall, W. S. *Internal State Words: Cultural and Situational Variation in Vocabulary Usage*. Urbana, Ill.: University of Illinois Center for the Study of Reading, 1979. Technical Report No. 115.

Glucksberg, S., Krauss, R. M., Higgins, F., & Tory, E. The development of referential communication skills. In F. D. Horowitz (Ed.), *Review of Child Development Research* (Vol. 4). Chicago: The University of Chicago Press, 1975.

Hall, W. S., & Freedle, R. O. *Culture and language*. New York: Halstead Press, 1975.

Hall, W. S., & Nagy, W. *Theoretical Issues in the Investigation of Words of Internal Report* (Technical Report No. 146 Urbana, Ill.: Univ. of Illinois, Center for the Study of Reading, 1979.

Hall, W. S., & Tirre, W. C. *The communicative environment of young children: social class, ethnic, and situational differences*. Urbana, Ill.: University of Illinois Center for the Study of Reading, Technical Report No. 125, 1979.

Hall, W. S., Cole, M., Reder, S., & Dowley, J. Variations in young children's use of language: some effects of setting and dialect. In R. O. Freedle (Ed.), *Discourse production and comprehension*. Hillsdale, N.J.: Ablex Publishing Company, 1977.

Hess, R. D. Parental behavior and children's school achievement: implications for Head Start. In E. Grotberg, (Ed.), *Critical issues in research related to disadvantaged children* (Seminar #5). Princeton, N.J.: Educational Testing Service, 1969.

Horner, V. M. *The verbal world of a lower-class three-year-old: a pilot study in linguistic ecology*. Unpublished doctoral dissertation, University of Rochester, 1968.

Horner, V. M., & Gussow, J. D. John and Mary: a pilot study in linguistic ecology. In C. B. Cazden, V. P. John, & D. Hymes (Eds.), *Functions of language in the classroom*. New York: Teachers College Press, 1972.

Houstin, S. A sociolinguistic consideration of the Black English of children in northern Florida. *Language*, 1969, *45*, 599–607.

Huttenlocher, J., & Presson, C. C. Mental rotation and the perspective problem. *Cognitive Psychology*, 1973, *4*, 277–299.

Hymes, D. *Foundations in sociolinguistics*. Philadelphia: University of Pennsylvania Press, 1974.

Labov, W. The logic of non-standard English. In F. Williams (Ed.), *Language and poverty*. Chicago: Markham, 1970.

Lein, L. You were talking through O. H. yes you was. *Council on Anthropology and Education Quarterly*, 1975, *6*(4), 1–11.

McDermott, R. P. Criteria for an ethnographically adequate description of activities and their contexts. Paper delivered at the annual meeting of the American Anthropological Association, Washington, D.C., Nov. 19, 1976.

Mehan, H. Structuring school structure. *Harvard Educational Review*, 1978, *48*(1), 32–64.

Mehan, H. *Learning lessons*. Cambridge, Mass.: Harvard University Press, 1979.

Miller, G. H., & Johnson-Laird, P. N. *Language and perception*. Cambridge, Mass.: Harvard University Press, 1976.

Nelson, K. Structure and strategy in learning to talk. *Monographs of the Society for Research in Child Development*, 1973, *38*, (1–2 Serial No. 149).

Piestrup, A. McC. Black dialect inference and accommodation of reading instruction in first grade. *Monographs of the Language Behavior Research Laboratory*, 1973, *6*.

Scribner, S., & Cole. M. The cognitive consequence of formal and informal education. *Science*, 1973, *182*, 553–559.

Shatz, M., & Gelman, R. The development of communication skills: modifications in the speech of young children as a function of listener. *Monographs of the Society for Research in Child Development*, 1973, *38*, (Serial No. 152).

Simons, H. D. *Black dialect and reading interference: a review and analysis of the research evidence*. Berkeley, Calif.: University of California, School of Education. Mimeographed, 1973.

Ward, M. C. *Them children: a study in language learning*. New York: Holt, Rinehart & Winston, 1971.

Warner, W. L., Meeker, M., & Ells, K. *Social class in America*. Chicago: Science Research Associates, 1949.

White, B., & Watts, J. *Experience and environment: major influences on the development of the young child*. Englewood Cliffs, N.J.: Prentice-Hall, 1973.

APPENDIX

Statement of purpose: Today's interview is a second part of the language study that we are doing at _____ in conjunction with _____
_____ . You will recall that we recorded _____'s talk last school year. We have transcribed about 60 percent of this sample of talk. To make any interpretation of this talk meaningful, we need to get an estimate of the variety of home situations represented by the children in our sample. Of course, your responses will remain anonymous.

1. How many children do you have? What are their ages? Sexes? In what grades are they? In what schools? (NOTE: If not in school, determine whether employed and/or separated from the family.) Is any child in your family adopted?
2. What is your morning routine for getting the family out of the house?
3. What age children are most interesting? Why are the Xs more interesting? What does your husband think and why?
4. Let us return to _____ and school.
   a. How does he generally do in school?
   b. In what area has he improved in the past year? The least?
   c. How do you feel about his school progress? What do you expect him to achieve? What would satisfy you?
5. How do your other children generally do in school?
6. What organizations or clubs, if any, do you belong to (PTA, church, political, etc.)? Does your child know what you do in these organizations? ____ yes ____ no. How?
7. What are your favorite recreation pastimes? Your husband's? What recreational activities do you and your family engage in on weekends together? What places have you visited on weekends during the past six months? Why?
8. Do you usually plan your weekends and vacations ahead of time? How often? Who makes the plans?
9. Where have you, as a family, traveled during the past two years? Why were these places chosen? What specific activities take up most of your time at these places?
10. What newspapers and/or magazines do you subscribe to? Do you encourage your child to read them? If so, how? Do you discuss the article or stories in them in his presence? (Give examples) Does your child ever participate in these discussions—vs. listening?
11. Does your child take any lessons—musical, dance, academic subject? If so, what? How long has he taken these? How did you get started in this area?
12. What hobbies, if any, does your child have? How long has he been interested in this? What seemed to get him started in this area? (Note parent initiation.)
13. What kinds of toys, games, books, books, pamphlets, etc., have you bought for your child in the past two years? (Include birthdays and holidays) Give example. Preschool period? List.

14. Does your child have a library card? If so, how long has he had it? How did he come to get this card? (Note parent initiation) Do you remember the first few times he went to the library? Did anyone accompany him? Who? What kind of books have you encouraged him to read? Where else does he obtain reading material? Do you still read to him? Does he read to you? How often?

15. What appliances do you permit him to operate? How long have you allowed this?

16. Do you ask your child problems related to school activities that he is required to answer or solve on his own? Give examples.

17. Does your child have a desk of his own? If not, where does he work? What kinds of supplies are available for him to work with? (Observe) _____ paste, _____ ruler, _____ paper, _____ crayons, _____ paints, _____ others (Specify)

18. Do you have a dictionary in your home? If so, what kind? Does your child have a dictionary of his own? If so, what kind? Where are they kept? How often does your child use the dictionary? How often do you? When the child uses the dictionary, at whose initiation—his or yours? What other ways does your child have of learning new words? School, relatives, etc. Home dictionary: _____ yes _____ no. Child's dictionary: _____ yes _____ no.

19. Do you have an encyclopedia in your home? _____ yes _____ no If so, when did you get it? Why? Do you buy yearbooks to accompany the encyclopedia? Where is it usually kept? How often do you use it? How often does your child use it?

20. Do you have an almanac or fact book? _____ yes _____ no If so, when was it purchased? Who uses it? When? What other sources of reading materials does your child have available to locate answers to his questions—library, friends, etc.?

21. Do you have any workbooks or other kinds of learning materials which you use to help your child in his learning? What other steps, if any, do you take to insure that your child's learning environment is what you want it to be?

22. Does your child receive homework? Do you help him with these assignments? How much time do you find to work with him on these assignments per week? How much time do you and your husband spend providing direct help to your child in his school learning on weekdays? On weekends? (Also ask for preschool and primary grades)

23. How often do you and your husband discuss your child's progress in school? What generally results from such discussions?

24. Have you had any experience in teaching? What? Your husband?

25. When does your child usually eat dinner on weekdays? Who eats with him? Who does most of the talking at the dinner table? About what?

26. At what other times are you together as a family on weekdays? What are some of the things you do together at these times?

27. What are some of the activities your husband engages in with the child on weekdays? On weekends?

28. Are there any adults outside of you and your husband that your child is particularly friendly with? If so, what does he seem to like about them? What do you see as this person's special qualities? How often does your child see them? What does he do when he's with them?

29. Did any other adults live with you when your child was first born? If so, who? (not name) How long did they live with you? What was the age of the child when they left? (Note: If the child was close to them, ask the following questions). How much schooling did they have? How would you rate their use of language?

30. Did you have a job outside the home when your child was younger? If so, who took care of the child?

31. Did you read books to him when he was younger? If so, when did you start? When did you stop? How *regularly* did you read to him?

32. About how many hours a week does he usually watch TV? What are his favorite programs? Do you approve of them? If not, what do you do about them?

33. What are your favorite TV programs? Did you recommend that your child watch any particular programs in the past week? If so, which ones? Did you discuss any programs with him after watching them?

34. How would you describe your child's language usage? Do you help him to increase his vocabulary? If so, how? How have your helped him to acquire appropriate *use* of words and sentences? Are you still helping him in these respects? If so, how?

35. How much would you estimate you correct him in his speech? (example use of "ain't") How particular are you about your child's speech? Are there particular speech habits of his that you are working on to improve? Give examples, if so. Earlier?

36. Are there any languages other than English spoken in the house? If so, which ones? Who speaks them? Does the child also speak this language?

37. How much schooling do you *wish* your child to receive?

38. How much schooling do you *expect* your child to receive?

39. What is the minimum level of education that you think your child must receive?

40. Do you have any ideas about the kind of work you would like to see your child do when he grows up? Do you have any ideas about the kind of work you would *not* like your child to do?

41. How does your husband feel about the kind of work he's doing? Is this the kind of work he always wanted to do?

42. How do you feel, in general, about the accomplishments of your family? How far have you been able to accomplish the aspirations or plans with which both of you started your family life?

43. How important has education been in achieving these goals? How much importance is education going to have in the life of your child? Would his future status be radically affected if he does not attain the level of education you wish him to attain?

44. What is the education level of some of your close friends and relatives?

45. Do any of their children go to college or have they? Does this include all of the children? Are there any who did not complete high school?

45a. Have you met with your child's present teacher? What is her (his) name? If so, when? Why? Does the teacher usually initiate parent-teacher conferences? If you ask for a meeting, for what purpose? What other ways, if any, are you in contact with the school? Do you like X's teacher? What makes you like her? Dislike her?

46. Do you know your child's best friends in the neighborhood and school? Do you approve of them? How would you rate these children in their studies? Do you help your child in choosing his friends? If so, how?

47. Do you read biographies of greate people to X? If so, whose? Which ones have you read in the past two months? If so, whose?

48. Did you hug, kiss, or speak approvingly to your child in the past few days? If so, for what reasons?

49. What are some of the activities and accomplishments of your child that you praise and approve of? How do you do this? What things do you find you have to scold him for?

50. Have you thought about what kind of high school program you want your child to enroll in? If so, which one? Why?

51. How often does the school give out student reports? Who usually signs it. Do both parents see it? In what ways do you use the report?

52. Do you discuss his school progresses with him? What particular things do you discuss with him?

53. Do you have college plans for him? If so, what have you done to financially prepare for this? In what other ways, if any, do you prepare him for the attainment of educational goals? (e.g., acquaint him with colleges, telling him about what people learn in college, etc.)

54. About how often do you ask your child how well he is doing in school? What particular things do you ask him?

55. Do you know what materials he uses in different areas covered in school? Do you know at the beginning of the school year what things he will be studying during the year in each subject? If so, how do you find this out? (Note: get specific topics, not subjects, e.g., reading)
56. How much time do you think a child X's age should devote to school-type work?
57. Does he help you in the housework? If so, what responsibilities doe she have? How quickly does he carry them out?
58. Is the housework distributed among the members of the family? If so, who did the planning for such assignments? How regularly are these assignments followed? What factors, if any, come in the way of carrying out such plans?
59. How would you rate your child's habit of completing his work on time, not leaving a problem undone, correcting his mistaken, etc? How did he acquire these habits?
60. Do you ever have to change your own plans for the sake of your child's school work? If so, what kinds of plans have you had to change?
61. Have you had to sacrifice any of your major needs or desires, such as buying a new car, giving up a job, etc., for the present and/or future education of your child? If so, what did you give up? What were the immediate consequences?
62. Are you taking any courses or involved in a hobby? If so, what? How did you get involved in this? How are you doing it—formally or informally? Did you study any subjects or have a hobby during the past two years? If so, what?
63. When guests come to visit do you like X to hang around or go play?
64. Do you take X out with you when you run errands?

Turning to the final few questions, let me ask you about the neighborhood and the apartment in which you are living.

65. How is this as a neighborhood for children?
66. Where else have you lived? How did you choose it (them)?
67. How did you like it? Could you describe the layout of that apartment?
68. How long have you lived here?
69. How did you choose it?
70. Could you describe how this apartment is laid out?
    (NOTE: after entire interview, ask: Could you draw me those apartments?)

10 Social Dominance and Conversational Interaction— The Omega Child in the Classroom

Olga K. Garnica
The Ohio State University

INTRODUCTION

Even casual observation of classroom interactions involving teachers and pupils in the context of the formal educational setting tells us that these activities are social occasions requiring a complex and collaborative effort by the participants to make things function properly. The creation of successful and meaningful interactions during such social occasions requires that the participants share tacit rules to identify situational contexts, impute appropriate social meanings to the behaviors of others, and exhibit appropriate behaviors themselves (Gumperz, 1972; Hymes, 1974; Spradley, 1972). Thus, the smooth and orderly accomplishment of these social occasions necessitates that all the participants involved be perpetually and simultaneously engaged in doing the "interactional work" required on such occasions (Cicourel, 1974). As we know all too well, however, social interaction does not always proceed smoothly. As Bremme and Erickson (1977) state,

> To the extent that participants do not know or follow the rules the social group is employing in making sense, "trouble" results. If (according to the rules) they mis-identify the situation now, misinterpret others' behaviors, behave inappropriately themselves, the ongoing flow of interaction is interrupted, delayed. The accomplishment of the social occasion, at least momentarily, is jeopardized. And those individuals who repeatedly err in their social performance may be judged by others to be socially—and perhaps intellectually—incompetent (p. 154).

The last sentence is of greatest interest in this paper. I shall focus on the child participants in kindergarten classroom interactions who have very low standing in the social dominance hierarchy of the group. I refer to these children as *omega children.*[1]

The present study is the first in a series of papers presenting both quantitative and qualitative analyses of the verbal and nonverbal communication interactions of omega children with other participants in the social life of the classroom—the teacher and the other children. The purpose of these studies is to document in detail the interactional behavior patterns exhibited by these children and the reactions of the other members of the group to such behavior patterns. This information can be useful in several ways. First, knowledge about what types of behaviors result in "trouble" in the orderly flow of interactions can give us important insights into the structure of those tacit rules of social interaction that group members draw upon to carry out meaningful and successful interactions. Just as the study of ungrammatical sentences gives the syntactician information concerning the form of syntactic rules and constraints on their application, so the study of communicative behavior patterns which disrupt the ongoing flow of social interactions can provide information on the appropriate rules for such interactions. Since the rules that group members know and use to make sense of behaviors and situations are tacit and often quite subtle, the technique of studying violations of such rules can potentially contribute information as to the nature of these rules, information that may be difficult to ascertain through other means. Secondly, studying the communicative interactions of omega children can provide a basis for remediation strategies to establish interactional behavior patterns in these children which will help rid them of their omega status and make them more socially competent members of the group. As I shall attempt to demonstrate in this paper, the omega status of these children quite clearly has negative impact on the quantity and quality of child-child social interactions. The experience may well have an impact on the individual's social interaction for life. Furthermore, there is good reason to believe that the omega child's communicative behavior patterns may have a more immediate and drastic consequence for that child in terms of direct educational implications, because of the role such behaviors play in teachers' judgments of such individuals. Recent research suggests that teachers and other educators make informal judgments about students based on their individual behavior patterns and that these judgments play a role in the important decisions that they make about students quite early in the child's

[1]To the children and school personnel who made this study possible, particularly Lynn Cohen, I offer my sincerest gratitude. My thanks also to Leesa Cohen and Rachel Schaffer for their invaluable assistance during various stages of the project. This work was supported in part by a grant from The Ohio State University Graduate School.

school years. This has amply been demonstrated in studies by Cicourel and Kitsuse (1963), Erickson (1976), Leiter (1974), Rist (1970), and others. Consequently the following situation arises:

> ... students who perform in ways deemed effective in interaction situations may be deemed socially *and intellectually* more competent than those who do not. They may be tracked higher, advised toward higher ranked curricula, post-secondary programs, and jobs. If what studies indicate is broadly applicable, it is extremely important for students—*especially in the early grades* (emphasis mine) to be able to identify relevant situational contexts and rules for making sense within them (Bremme & Erickson, 1977, p. 159).

Given the potential immediate and later consequences of being socially competent early in life, there are relatively few studies of omega children, especially studies concerned with the detailed microanalysis of verbal (and nonverbal) communicative performance of such individuals in the classroom.

I shall present a brief survey of much of the information available on humans (and several other species which organized themselves into social hierarchy). This is followed by two sections labeled (a) *quantitative* analysis, (b) *qualitative* analysis. In the quantitative analysis section, I present and discuss several parameters of verbal conversational interactions of omega children as compared with a matched group of nonomega children. This analysis provides some broad insights into the nature of the omega children's verbal interactions with other children in the classroom setting. In the qualitative analysis section, I discuss two excerpts of child-child verbal interactions which occurred during the everyday social life of two children— an omega child and a nonomega child. The two speech events share many common features in terms of the purpose of the verbal exchange and the nature of the broader social context, but the process and result of these two verbal interactions differ dramatically and serve to highlight some additional points not readily determinable from the quantitative analysis of the children's verbal conversational behavior.

PREVIOUS RESEARCH

It is well known that humans, as well as certain other species, e.g., chickens, wolves, and apes, organize themselves into social hierarchies. In the case of human beings, an entire subfield of social psychology-sociometrics has developed around the study of this phenomenon. From the work of Moreno (1953) to that of numerous present-day researchers, sociometrics has made a steady contribution to our understanding of personal and social relations. Much effort in sociometry has been expended on the construction and evaluation of sociometric tests and on the development of methods for analyzing and presenting sociometric results. Some attention has also been given to the study of numerous personal and social variables related to sociometric results. On the other hand, comparatively few studies have dealt with the observed interactional behavior exhibited by members of a group as this relates to the social hierarchy status of the individuals in that group. I shall not review all these studies here, but shall concentrate on the information currently available about behaviors directed toward, and exhibited by, the lowest-ranking member(s) of a group.

Although in folk thought it is commonly believed that the lowest-ranking members of a social group are the victims of negative actions directed toward them by other members of the group, i.e., intimidation and abuse, this stereotypic expectation concerning the treatment afforded the lowest-ranking members has been questioned by several existing studies of actual social interaction in groups organized into social hierarchies. The empirical evidence currently available is consistent for both human and nonhuman groups alike.

In his study of the pecking hierarchy of chickens, Scjelderup-Ebbe (1922) observed that the hen ranking lowest in the pecking order was usually left alone by the higher-ranked members of the group. Similar behavior has been noted for groups of apes as well. For example, Imanishi (1959), who studied troops of Japanese monkeys (*macaea fuscata*) observed that the lowest-ranking members were most frequently positioned on the periphery of the group and only rarely engaged in what may be classified as social interaction with other members of the group.

Studies of interaction behavior patterns in groups of children where the rank order of the members is considered indicate similar results. Strayer and Strayer (1975) report that in their study of play groups composed of three-to-five-year-olds, the lowest-ranking members in the social hierarchy are the most infrequent targets of physical attacks by the other members of the group. Similar results were also obtained by Ginsburg, Wauson, and Easley (1977) in a study of school-aged children (third to sixth grade) engaged in the playground activity, football. Ginsburg *et al.* observed only one incident involving a low-ranking member of a group in which an antagonistic physical action occurred (hitting, kicking, pushing, etc.) as opposed to the occurrence of 15 such actions involving higher-ranking members of the group. In addition, they found that the lowest-ranking members of the team were at a further distance from the child in nearest proximity to them than were higher-ranking children and were involved in fewer physical interactions of a nonantagonistic sort as well. They were also most often located farthest away from the center point of group aggregation during play. Finally, Williams (1975) in a study of the social dominance hierarchy of the summer camp for adolescent boys observed that the lowest-ranked members were least likely to be involved in dominance interactions and rarely acted in antagonistic ways toward others.

Thus, these studies seem to refute stereotypic expectations that the lowest-ranking members of a social group are most likely to be involved in negative social interactions and indicate that rather than being the frequent target of physical aggression of higher-ranking members, these individuals are generally simply left to themselves. Their physical presence is ignored by the other members. The question of the nature of verbal interactions experienced by the lowest-ranking members has not heretofore been examined systematically.

DATA COLLECTION

The data analyzed in this paper were extracted from a larger body of material. This material consists of both video- and audiotaped recordings of the interactions occurring in two kindergarten classrooms. The data-collection procedure for the entire *corpus* of material is briefly outlined below.

Initial Observation Periods

The morning and afternoon kindergarten classes of one teacher were observed by two individuals on two separate days before beginning the data-collection period. During these observation periods, the observers familiarized themselves with the physical environment, the general activities of the class period, and the children in each class. One observer kept a running record of the flow of events in each classroom. The purpose of the observations was to arrive at some idea of the range and type of activities that occurred during the class period. The observation showed that the class period was divided into several subperiods that occurred on a regular basis (see Appendix A). The second observer kept a record of the activities of individual children in the class. A child was selected at random and observed for 15–20 minutes. A running account of the child's gross motor and verbal activities was developed from these observation notes.

Apparatus and Recording Procedures

The activities of the chldren in the morning and afternoon class were recorded on three consecutive days in the latter portion of the school year (mid-March) subsequent to two observation periods. The purpose of this observation period was to acclimatize the children to the presence of observers and recording equipment in the classroom and to pretest data-collection techniques as to their suitability for use in this particular context. Four types of records were kept.

1. Video Taping of Classroom Activities. A Sony Video-portapack equipped with a wide-angle lens was positioned in one corner of the classroom on a high tripod. The videorecorder was kept stationary in that position. Most of the classroom area was visible although the resolution of the recording was poor for the portion of the room farthest from the videorecorder, the rug area. As a result, videorecording of the first circle and last circle were not of sufficiently high quality to allow for detailed analysis. Other class activities, however, took place primarily within the confines of the middle portion of the room and were not affected by the difficulties associated with the resolution quality of the videotape. The videorecorder microphone was hung from the ceiling above the center of the classroom. The audio track of the videorecorder was useful for recording some of the conversations— those conducted directly underneath the microphone and particularly loud verbal exchanges taking place in other portions of the room. Most importantly, these recordings were of sufficient quality that most of what the teacher said during class time was retrievable from the audiotrack of the videorecorder. The depth tone, and loudness of the teacher's voice differed so much from that of the children's voices that it stood out above the other voices being recorded. So few of the teacher's utterances were inaudible that no separate audiorecording of the teacher's speech was deemed necessary for transcription.

2. Audiorecordings of Individual Children. The audiotrack of the videotape recorder was found to be inadequate for recording many of the conversations that occurred between individual children in the classroom. An alternate means of gathering such data was employed. An apparatus similar to that used by Mishler (1975) was devised which allowed for maximum freedom of movement for the child being recorded, while simultaneously producing high-quality recordings of conversational material. The apparatus consisted of a backpack containing a Sony TC55 cassette tape recorder equipped with a Sony electret condenser microphone. The child being audiorecorded wore the backpack across his/her shoulder and the microphone was clipped to a strap across the front of the child's chest. This arrangement allowed the child to move about the classroom freely and even engage in active physical play. The recording equipment provided high-quality audiorecordings of most of the child's utterances as well as most of the utterances produced by the children within 5–10 feet of the child. Two children in the class wore the backpacks during work time, play time, snack time for 30-minute periods. The recorders were in operation during these periods. Some children were given the opportunity to wear the backpacks at other times for shorter time durations. Thus virtually all the children who were willing to wear the apparatus had an opportunity to do so at least once during the three days of data collection.

3. Written Records of Classroom Activities. A written record of the general classroom activities was kept for both the morning and afternoon class on data-collection days. This record contained information on the nature of the activities occurring at a particular time, e.g., free play time, show and tell, teacher reading children story, etc., and a listing of the children who were being individually audiorecorded during the activity. Although this information was also available from the vidoetape, the written record facilitated locating specific sequences and served as a record of class activities during periods when the videotape was being charged. In addition, seating plans were made of the three tables in the classroom at different points in time during the class day. This facilitated identification of the children in the immediate vicinity of the children being audiorecorded. The charts were fairly accurate for seating arrangements during extended periods of work time and snack time. The records for free play time were less accurate, since during the period children often moved about the room more frequently. Thus, during the free play period more localized records of seating arrangements were also kept. Records of activities were kept by noting real time on the classroom clock. The time was also noted on all seating arrangement charts.

4. Written Records of Individual Children's Activities. A written record was also kept of the activities (verbal and nonverbal) of each child when that child was being audiorecorded (i.e., carrying the backpack). One of the observers was assigned to each child when the child put on the audiorecorder backpack. The observer was unobtrusively positioned on the periphery of the room as close to the child as possible and took notes on various aspects of the target child's activities. To avoid attracting attention, the observer shifted visual attention to other areas of the classroom at regular intervals. If approached by a child or addressed by a child (target or nontarget child), the observer simply said, "I'm doing some work right now and need to be alone. Could you please go back to what you were doing?" Requests for assistance were handled by referring the child to the teacher. Questions on the nature of the observer's activity were responded to briefly and directly with the following statement: "I am interested in what goes on in school. I'm busy now and need to be by myself. I can talk to you when I'm not working, okay?" The records kept by the observers included, but were not limited to the following notations: (a) nature of activity engaged in by the target child, (b) conversational partners of target child, (c) change in focus of the target child's attention, (d) incidents of physical contact between target child and others. In addition, as many audible utterances produced by the target child as possible were noted. Some activities of children in the immediate environment of the child were also noted. The time of the activity was noted. As mentioned in (c) shifts in seating assignments were noted. Obviously this written record was only a rough guide to the verbal and gross nonverbal activities of the child.

Nonetheless this record provided highly useful information for the transcription and interpretation of the target child's interactional exchanges.

Ratings of Social Dominance

The social dominance status of each child was determined by standardized sociometric procedures (Gronlund, 1959). The classroom teacher administered a sociometric test to each child in both the morning and afternoon classes following detailed instructions provided by the research investigator. The test was administered during a three-day period two weeks before the collection of any recorded material. The test was conducted informally and incorporated into the daily schedule of the classroom. Each child was interviewed individually. Each child was asked to help the teacher in planning future activities for the class by telling her the names of the children in the class that she/he would like to have "sit near you," "to have work with you," "to have play with you." Each child was asked to provide three choices in response to each of these three questions. The teacher told each child that his/her responses would be kept confidential and asked them not to discuss their responses with others in the class.

Since the sociometric procedure was meant to evaluate interpersonal relationships and to determine the group acceptance of individual pupils, multiple criteria were used. The criteria chosen covered the main aspects of the group's interpersonal and social relationships. The children's positive choices were tabulated into a matrix table in accordance with standard sociometric procedure. A separate matrix table was constructed for each of the two classes. The children were classified into the following sociometric categories based on the total number of choices received: star, above average, below average, neglectee, and isolate. This classification was based on Bronfenbrenner's (1945) fixed frame of reference, a table indicating the critical sociometric status scores for varying numbers of choice. The advantage of using a fixed frame of reference is that the number of individuals placed in the extreme categories (star, neglectee, isolate) can be compared across different groups of children even if the sizes of the groups differ, as was true of the two classes observed in the present study. In this system, a *star* is any child that receives more choices on the sociometric measure than could be expected by chance alone; a *neglectee* is a child who receives fewer sociometric choices than could be expected by chance. An *isolate* is an individual who receives no choices.

For this study, the children rated lowest in social dominance (neglectees and isolates) are grouped together under the label *omega children*. Six children, two boys and four girls, made up this group. Note that the sociometric procedure also called for the children to make negative choices on the three criteria discussed above (sit near, work with, play with). Negative choices result from sociometric questions that ask individuals to indicate those whom they least prefer to be with in group activity. Responses to negative sociometric questions allow for the identification of individual children that fall into another category—rejectee. *Rejectees* are individuals who receive more negative choices on a sociometric test than is expected by chance. The elicitation of negative choices allows us to distinguish those individuals who receive neither positive nor negative choices, i.e., "true isolates," from individuals who may receive no positive choices from the group but do receive negative choices, i.e., rejectees. It was judged desirable to request negative choices, despite the potential of some undesirable effects on the group, since it appeared possible that rejectees may actually be treated differently conversationally than children in the other categories (isolates, neglectees) subsumed under the omega child rubric. Great care was taken in the elicitation of these negative choices. The children were asked to indicate if there were any individuals whom they would choose *last* for each of the group activities rather than asking for a set number of individuals whom they did not want as associates. The number of negative choices for a given activity ranged from zero to four. Since these data are not considered in the study reported here, I will not discuss them further.

Quantititative Data Analysis

Subjects of Comparison.   All six children classified as omega children were included in this study. For purposes of comparing the verbal behavior directed to, and exhibited by, these children, a comparison group of children was necessary. Thus measurements were obtained for the verbal behavior of the omega children and a comparison group of six children selected at random from the class. The nonomega children were matched for sex with the omega children. Three 20-minute speech sequences were analyzed for each child in the study. Three children who ranked as stars were excluded as possible candidates for this comparison group—a boy from the morning class and two girls from the afternoon group. They represented the other extreme on the social dominance hierarchy.

Comparison Measures.   The comparison of the omega children with higher-ranking members focused on selected aspects of the conversational behavior exhibited by these two groups of children. Three 20-minute samples were analyzed for each of the omega children ($N = 6$) and for six nonomega children randomly selected from the other members of the class. The following measures were used in the comparison:

1. Number of conversational turns in all child-child conversations
2. Number of different child conversational partners in all child-child conversations

3. Number of attempts to initiate a conversation *by* the target child (to another child)
4. Number of attempts to initiate a conversation *to* the target child (by another child)
5. Number of times the target child's name is used by other children
6. Number of insults or taunts received by the target child
7. Amount of private speech produced by the target child.

These measures represent a range of conversational activities that were carried out during the periods of free play in the classroom.

Measures 1 and 2 are intended to capture the degree of participation in the conversational life of the classroom displayed by the target child. It was hypothesized that the omega children would have fewer conversational partners and that their exchanges with others would be brief and therefore reflected in a smaller number of conversational turns produced in these exchanges over all. Measures 3, 4, and 5 were examined to determine the degree to which the two groups of children (omega/nonomega) differed as to how often they sought out others for conversational interaction and, alternatively, how often they were sought out by other children for similar activity. It was expected that omega children would both seek out other children less and be less in demand as conversational partners by the other children. Measure 5 overlaps to a certain extent with measure 4, since the children in the study often used a child's name as a means to initiate conversational exchanges. This measure, however, also includes instances of nonvocative uses of a child's name. Even nonvocative use of a child's name carries with it, however, at least the implication that the child's existence is being recognized. Measure 6 was included in an attempt to capture the degree of isolation that a child was experiencing. It was predicted that children who were not often actively involved in conversation with other children in the classroom would produce vocalizations during the performance of various play activities which did not involve being an active participant with a conversational partner or that these children would create imaginary conversational partners. Finally, measure 7 attempts to capture the degree of overtly expressed rejection that the children experienced in conversational exchanges.

There are two ways to view the meaning of receiving insults or taunts. On the one hand, such activities are expressions of negative feelings directed toward another person and, therefore, serve to isolate the recipient of such verbalizations. On the other hand, to direct insults or taunts at another person is still to recognize the existence of that individual as someone worthy of receiving a communication (no matter how negative). Thus even such negative communications represent at some level a willingness to carry on exchange with that individual. The existing literature on individuals with low social dominance ratings leads to the hypothesis that the omega children would not have any more of the latter behaviors directed toward them than would nonomega children and perhaps even less.

Ratings on Comparison Measures.   A rater who did not know the social dominance status of children (omega/nonomega) rated the recorded material of these speech measures. The ratings were based on 20 minutes of activity for each child during one of the classroom free play periods. In previous pilot work a second rater was also used to code a subsample of the recorded material. Since there was good reliability between the two raters (the range was .79 for number of attempts to initiate a conversation by the target child to .90 for number of times the target child's name was used by other children), only one rater was used for the study. The unit of analysis used in rating the amount of private speech was the number of seconds that the activity occurred for each child in the study. The number of responses during each data period was used as the unit of analysis for the remainder of the measures. The rater had the videotaped and audiotaped data available as well as the written transcripts of the recorded material.

Results

The results for all the speech measures in the omega children/nonomega children comparison are presented in Table 1. The two groups of children differed on a number of measures. The following pattern was observed. There were marked differences on all measures except for measure 6 (frequency of insults and taunts received by the target child), when comparing the two groups of children. A Mann-Whitney U-test was performed for each of the measures. The results were statistically significant at $p \leq .01$ or better for all the measures except measure 6. As Table 1 shows, very few antagonistic verbal exchanges occurred in the data sample on measure 6. Six instances of such behavior were exhibited toward the omega children as opposed to four instances in the case of the nonomega children. Thus, as expected from studies of nonverbal behavior and social dominance, the number of antagonistic incidents involving individuals low in social rank was no different from the frequency of such incidences involving others in the group. Thus low-ranked members are not the targets of a high degree of verbal abuse as is commonly believed, at least in the context in which the children were observed.

As for the other measures, the omega children were observed to engage in fewer child-child conversations with different partners and to produce fewer conversational turns (measures 1 and 2). The differences were so marked for the omega/nonomega groups that the distributions for the two groups did not even overlap in these comparisons. The same lack of overlap in group

TABLE 1

A Comparison between Omega and Nonomega Children on Conversational Interaction Measures

Child	#1 Number of conversations initiated by another child to target child	#2 Number of Conversational partners	#3 Number of conversations to another child initiated	#4 Number of conversations initiated by another child to target child	#5 Frequency of use of target child's name	#6 Frequency of insults and taunts directed to target child	Amount of private speech produced by target child (total secs)
1	12	2	2	0	2	0	651
2	10	3	4	1	3	1	429
3	25	4	4	2	5	2	182
4	36	6	5	2	4	2	146
5	18	5	11	1	4	1	91
6	21	4	12	1	5	0	153
	$\bar{x} = 20.3$	$\bar{x} = 4.0$	$\bar{x} = 6.3$	$\bar{x} = 1.2$	$\bar{x} = 3.8$	$\bar{x} = 1.0$	$\bar{x} = 275.3$
1	87	12	12	11	13	0	67
2	92	11	9	10	11	1	39
3	79	8	14	15	14	1	96
4	84	10	11	12	15	0	79
5	88	11	11	9	8	0	56
6	91	10	10	13	9	2	84
	$\bar{x} = 86.8$	$\bar{x} = 10.3$	$\bar{x} = 11.2$	$\bar{x} = 11.8$	$\bar{x} = 11.7$	$\bar{x} = 0.7$	$\bar{x} = 70.2$

comparisons held for measures of the number of conversation initiations that were directed to the target child (measure 3) and the frequency with which the child's name was used by the other children (measure 5) during the play periods observed. Thus, the omega child does not seem to participate in verbal interactions with many other children in the group and even those exchanges that do occur are of short duration.

Furthermore, the omega children are hardly ever addressed by other children (measure 4). The range is 0–2 times for omega children as opposed to 9–16 times of nonomegas, which may partly explain why the omega child's name is heard considerably less frequently in the course of the verbal chatter in child-child conversations. The amount of private speech exhibited by the omega children is much greater than that exhibited by the nonomega children (measure 7). As indicated earlier, these differences are all highly significant.

The results for measure 3 indicate that two omega children exhibit a frequency of conversation initiation that is similar to that observed by the nonomega children. This deviation, however, is not great enough to reject the hypothesis of no difference between the two groups. Thus, on this measure also the omega children exhibit a lower frequency of conversation initiation in comparison with other children.

Discussion

The conversational variables are only a partial indicator of how the low-rank status of certain individuals in the classroom (the omega children) is exhibited in this everyday talk of the kindergarten children in this study. The emerging picture of the omega child seems to be one of a verbally neglected individual. Hardly any of the other children appear intentionally to engage the omega child in conversations and the omega child only frequently initiates verbal exchanges with other children. The conversational partner network of the omega child is drastically limited and thus the amount of speech that the child produces in productive, interactive social exchanges with other children is highly attenuated.

Interestingly, the omega child is not often silent. S/he produces a variety of verbalizations but these verbalizations consist of long self-directed narratives or conversations with pretend conversational partners and are ignored by the other children. Furthermore, the omega child's name is hardly ever heard in the context of child-child conversational interactions.

All these features present the omega child as a verbally neglected and isolated member of the group, a member of the group to whom the attention of even antagonistic verbalizations (insults/taunts) is denied. In light of these circumstances the omega child appears totally unrepresented in the verbal activity. This child produces vocalizations that are clearly not intended for anyone other than self. (Through this means the omega child might give a false impression to the casual observer of being verbally active.)

Admittedly, the sample used in this study is fairly small and the results are based on behaviors exhibited during a limited time period. Yet, the differences between omega and nonomega children's conversation patterns are very clear.

Qualitative Analysis

Although the quantitative analysis has given us some indication of the type of verbal behaviors exhibited by, and directed toward, the omega child, it has its limitations and does not fully represent the degree and quality of differences that exist in child-child conversational exchanges involving omega children and those involving nonomega children. It does not nearly approach an in-depth characterization of the plight of the omega child in the context of social verbal exchanges. Although the quantitative analysis has given us some information on what happens to the omega child in terms of verbal interaction with peers, it says little about how these patterns are actually carried out. Even less information is provided about how the joint verbal (and nonverbal) activities of the children in the classroom function to maintain the social dominance hierarchy at status quo.

Since this paper is only an initial attempt to delve into the issues concerning the nature and function of the verbal interaction status of omega and nonomega children, the material in this section will necessarily be preliminary. I present and analyze two multiparty conversations involving some of the children in the classrooms in which data were collected. In these two conversational segments, the context of the interaction is quite similar and the expressed goals and desires of one of the children (an omega child in one segment; a nonomega child in another) are similar. The differences between these segments are in the process and end results of the conversational interaction.

Context of Communicative Exchanges

In both interactional sequences the target child—an omega child in sequence 1 and a nonomega child in sequence 2—is engaged in the task of coloring a picture using different colored magic markers during a work time period in the class day. The sequences took place on different days and different children were involved as participants. In both sequences the target child is sitting at one of the three tables in the classroom and there are from four to six other children sitting at the same table who are engaged in the same activity. Since there is only one set of coloring markers at each table, the children are obliged to share the markers provided and the competition for the coloring markers is keen, especially for the more popular colors. From the observation and viewing of numerous instances of this activity, the rules for obtaining desired coloring markers seem to be the following: (a) if no other child is currently using the desired marker, the marker is free for use and available for the taking; (b) any marker being used by another is that individual's property until that individual gives up the object; (c) there is a time limit on possession of the individual markers and extended use of a particular colored marker desired by one or more others is considered a violation of the rule and noted verbally (and in some cases even nonverbally); (d) if a desired colored marker is in someone's possession, a child desiring that marker may put a "save" on the marker as next user; (e) when an individual has finished using a marker s/he may "auction" it with a phrase like "who wants the (*color or*) *marker?*" or some similar utterance; (f) the child receiving the marker from the "auctioneer" as the result of a "bid" is the new possessor of the marker. Other rules also apply but these are the ones most important for the sequences to be discussed. The entire procedure for obtaining, retaining, and relinquishing the markers will be clarified in the discussion of the sequences.

In both sequence 1 and sequence 2 the target child needs a marker being used by another and the target child puts a "save" on the marker verbally, directing the "save" utterances to the current possessor of the desired marker. Both sequences involve subsequent "auctions" of the desired marker.

Sequence 1—"How are you doin' with that pink?"

This sequence involves an omega child (child Al) in the transcript presented. Child Al and the other children present at the table are females. All the children are engaged in the same activity—coloring pictures of an Easter egg with colored magic markers. Child Al is the only omega child in the group. The seating arrangement is presented in Diagram 1.

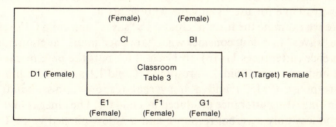

Diagram 1: Seating arrangement at table during sequence 1.

At the beginning of the sequence, child Cl is current possessor of the pink marker. The sequence is as follows:

1. Child Al: "How'r ya doing' with that pink? (Child Al—omega child— lifts up paper and points to two areas of her picture.)
2. Child Al: "For here and here."

3. Child C1: "There's no more room for it."
4. Child A1: "I wanted some of your pink. I *did.*" (61-second pause.)
(All children continue to color with their markers.)
5. Child A1: "Could I use some pink?"
6. Child C1: "Why? I'm usin' it an' it stinks."
7. Child A1: "Could I use some pink?"
8. Child E1: "Give me the green."
(to F1—Child E1 gives Child F1 a blue marker.)
9. Child E1: "The *green.* I said. The green's mine."
10. Child A1: "Could I—do pink after you're finished?"
11. Child C1: "Who needs the pink?" (C1 hold up pink marker.)
12. Child A1: "Me::::::" /Low pitch and very prolonged/ (Spoken
13. Child E1: "Me! Me:::! (Raises hand.) simultaneously)
14. Child F1: "Me" (Raises hand.)
15. Child F1: "I raised my hand first! (C1 gives pink marker to E1)
16. Child E1: "I didn't—I didn't want it."
17. Child A1: "What's in here"/very softly/(Looks at markers
remaining in container.)
18. Child A1: "Here's some blue"/very softly/
(Starts to color with blue marker)

Child A initiated four "saves" on the pink marker (utterances 1, 5, 7, 10). When Child C1 puts that marker up for "auction" (utterance 11), Child A1 affirms that she still wants the marker by responding verbally. The pink marker becomes the possession of Child F1 who had not put any previous "saves" on the marker. Child A1's "saves" are ignored by Child C1 at "auction" time but A1 does not protest but rather settles for some other color which is available for use by anyone who wants it.

Before we examine the form of child A1's "saves" and child C1's responses to those "saves" in detail, consider what happened in the "auction portion of the sequence (utterances 11–16). In 11 child C1 puts the pink marker up for auction and gets three "bids" in response. Child E1 and F1 both provide a verbal response ("Me!") and a nonverbal response (raise hand) to the "auction" initiating utterance produced by child C1. The omega child—Child A1—produces only a verbal response and in a low-pitched voice. Child F1 follows up with a verbal response, 15, emphasizing that her nonverbal response preceded that of the others making this gesture and gets the object being auctioned off by child C1. Neither of the other two respondents protests this action but their responses differ dramatically. Child E1 maintains that she didn't really want the auctioned object. Child A1, on the other hand, makes no such explanation or attenuation of her interest in the pink marker. She has, after all, already put "saves" on it four times. She offers no protest and selects another color.

It is instructive to consider the form of the child A1's "saves" on the pink marker and the responses of its possessor—child C1. Save 1 ("How'r ya doin' with that pink") is an indirect statement and does not overtly assert that she (child A1) needs the pink marker. What we have here is rather an implied save. The form of the next two "saves" (utterances 5 and 7) is that of a question and also a weak form of a save on the desired object. Child C1's response to these "saves" is interesting.

In response to the first save, child C1 says "There's no room for it," essentially implying that child A1 couldn't really use the pink marker. The response to the second "save," i.e., "Why? I'm, usin' it an' it stinks." follows along similar lines, suggesting that the pink marker is not a highly desirable item anyway because it smells bad, which is *not* the case as both these children and the others sitting at the table know also. The fact is that all the markers have a slightly unpleasant odor no matter what the color. Save 3 is ignored completely. Save 4 is followed immediately by an auction-initiation utterance—11.

Thus we see a situation where the omega child's saves for the pink marker are either rejected or ignored. In any case they are not taken seriously by the possessor of the desired object—child C1—possibly in part because these "saves" are not appropriate in form. The omega child's four previous "saves" are not considered at "auction" time, even though child A1 does produce a response to the "auction" initiation with utterance 12. This utterance, however, is missing the nonverbal component, i.e., the raising of the hand, which is present in the response of the other two children (E1 and F1).

This example further illustrates and may well serve to explain some of the results from the quantitative study. The omega child is generally ignored and isolated from the rest of the participants in the social situation. Verbal attempts on the part of the omega child to enter into the everyday flow of the of interactional life of the classroom are infelicitous in terms of the type of responses that the other child provides in response to such attempts—witness utterances 3, 6, and the ultimate outcome of the auction. These reponses may, of course, be due in some part to the inadequate form of the omega child's attempts to act as a member in good standing in the social group.

Viewing many similar sequences where the omega child attempts to participate in the group and be recognized as a legitimate and active group member reveals the following pattern: The omega child goes through the motions of being a member of the group, such as placing "saves" and making "bids," responding to auction-initiations, but these communications are not taken seriously by the other participants, i.e., they are rejected or ignored. If the omega child insisted on being taken seriously, s/he could have delivered an utterance like "I asked for it first" or "It's mine." When such an occurrence was in the data, the most frequent response to the omega child was an insult or a taunt. Illustrations of this type of reaction abound in the data but a thorough discussion of these sequences would entail a digression from our present task of comparing two sequences.

Sequence 2—"I need green"

Let us compare sequence 1 with a similar sequence involving a nonomega child of above average standing in the social dominance hierarchy of the group. In sequence 2 the target child—child A2—is coloring a picture of a turtle which was given to him as a special project by the teacher because it required connecting numbered dots prior to coloring the picture. All the other children are coloring a picture of an Easter egg (same picture as in sequence 1). All the other children at the table are also nonomega children. The seating arrangement at the time of the sequence is presented in Diagram 2. Children

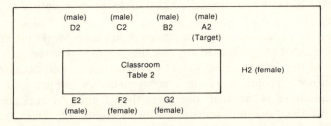

Diagram 2:   Seating arrangement at table during sequence 2.

A2, B2, C2, and D2 are males; children F2, G2, and H2 are females. At the beginning of the sequence, child H2 is current possessor of the green magic marker. The sequence is as follows:

1. Child A2:   "I need green."
2. Child A2:   When you're done can I have it?" (to H2) (H2 nods affirmatively.)
   (B2, E2, F2 conversation about yellow) (Child X comes over from other part of classroom and stands behind A2. He clutches A2's head with both hands.)
3. Child A2:   "Let *go* of it."
4. Child A2:   "Move."
   (A2 hits child X and child X leaves.)
   (Child Y comes over and grabs A2's paper.)
5. Child A2:   "It's *mine.*"
6. Child A2:   "Y (Child's name), you wan' me to write on your face? Gimme dis." (A2 pulls on paper.)
7. Child Y :   "Not it's mine. / mocking tone/
   (A2 and Y both pulling on paper)
8. Child A2:   "Give it"
9. Child Y :   "Mine knuckles" (A2 succeeds in retrieving his paper.)

10. Child Y : "Wha's that?" (Points to picture.)
11. Child Y : "It's a turtle." (Y grabs paper away again.)
12. Child A2: "Quit it!" (A2 and Y pulling on paper. A2 hits Y.)
13. Child Y : "Mine bus-"
14. Child A2: "*Mine* buster" (A2 retrieves paper. Y leaves.)
15. Child E2: "I need greenie. I need greenie."
16. Child E2: "How long you usin' it?" (to H2)
17. Child A2: "I'm using' it after *her*."
18. Child E2: "No you aren't."
19. Child A2: "Yes I am"
20. Child E2: "?m ?mm"
21. Child A2: "Yes I am."
22. Child E2: "?m ?mm"
23. Child A2: "Yes I am"
24. Child G2: "A2 (*child's name*) said it first. Right?"
    (A2 nods head)
25. Child H2: "Who wants gre:::n?" (H2 holds up green marker.)
26. Child A2: "Me:::" (H2 gives green marker to A2.)
27. Child E2: "Aw::::"

This sequence begins with two utterances by A2 in which the target child puts a "save" on the green magic marker ("I need green." "When you're done can I have it?") In response to the second utterance—the question—the child H2, the current possessor of the green marker, responds with a nonverbal affirmative action. After an ensuing number of events, i.e., B2, E2, and F2 conversing about the yellow marker and A2's interaction with child X and child Y, child E2 also initiates a save on the green marker (utterances 15 and 16). In the immediately following utterances child A2 refers to his previously declared "save" (utterances 1 and 2) with "I'm usin' it after *her*." Child E2 denies the legitimacy of child A2's previous "save" but child A2 repeatedly insists that his "save" has priority over those of child E2 (utterances 19, 21, 23) despite repeated protests to the contrary by child E2. Child A2's position is supported by a neutral member of the group, child G2, and child A2 nods his head in agreement. Child E2 does not make any response to the reminder offered by child G2 that indeed the first "save" on the green marker was A2's. In the next utterance H2 initiates an "auction" of the green marker (utterance 25). The only "bid" is produced by A2, the first child to put a "save" on the marker. Child A2 receives the green marker and child E2 utters a remark of disappointment ("aw:::").

Comparison of Sequence 1 and Sequence 2

In comparing this sequence with sequence 1, let us first consider the form of the original "save" put on the green marker by child A2 and the response of the current possessor of the marker. Child A2 initiates his "save" by a direct and precise statement of what he needs and follows up this need statement with a direct request for the green marker in the form of a question addressed to the current possessor of the marker. Thus A2 firmly establishes what he wants in the first utterance and forms a request in the second utterance that would be difficult to answer negatively without good reason, assuming there has been no previous "save" on the green marker (which is the case). In contrast, child A1 in sequence 1 initiates her "save" with a question which implies only that she wants the pink marker when child C1 is finished with it. In fact, the question "How'r ya doin' with that pink?" can be rightly interpreted in several other ways rather than as a request for the pink marker. For example, the question could easily be answered with utterances such as "I'm doing fine," "It's making my picture look pretty," etc. Furthermore, in utterance 2 child A1 again merely implies, rather than explicitly states, that she needs the pink marker. Only in utterance 10 does she finally ask, make a direct request for the marker, including the element of "when you'r finished" within the question. This latter element corresponds to the "when you're done..." part of child A2's question posed to the current possessor of the marker in sequence 2. In the case of child A2, this element is introduced early in the "save" initiation, whereas, in the case of child A1, it is missing from a number of prior utterances, e.g., 5 and 6.

At this point, it seems appropriate to pose the question, would child A1 have been successful in obtaining the pink marker, had she formed her "save" in a different way, e.g., in a direct manner similar to that of child A2 in sequence 2. Although there is no unequivocal answer to this question, I would suggest that the answer is probably "no," and the reason for this is that child A1 has omega-child status in this social group. From observations and from data gathered on other interactional sequences, too lengthy to present here, it is clear that as long as the omega child does not challenge his/her status as a member of the group who is neglected/ignored and excluded from the verbal mainstream of conversational interactions in the classroom, the omega child does not receive negative verbal responses. On the other hand, should the omega child step out of this role and refuse to accept the role of the excluded one, this behavior receives verbal retaliation in the form of teasing, name calling, etc. It seems that perhaps the reason that omega children do not receive more negative verbal responses than nonomega children is that they rarely step beyond the bounds of their role, i.e., being excluded. Attempts to break out of this role are met with negative verbal responses on the part of the other child(ren). If this analysis is ultimately shown to be correct, what we end with is that the omega child is faced with a dilemma—s/he must either put up with being verbally ignored, neglected, and isolated and settle for an existence as an individual who is marginal, to interactions in the group or s/he can be verbally assertive and thereby guarantee that s/he will be the recipient of a verbal response carrying negative effect. Judging from the results obtained in the quantitative study, we can tentatively say that omega children opt, for the most part, for the first of these two alternatives, if indeed it can be called an "alternative."

In situations similar to that illustrated in conversational segment 2 the omega child will occasionally make appeals to the teacher either (a) requesting help in righting some unfair or discriminatory behavior directed against him/her or (b) lodging a complaint against another child for directing some verbal negative response toward him/her. If the teacher responds by acting on the omega child's request—either type (a) or (b)—the omega child subsequently receives further negative feedback from the other children involved after the teacher departs. If the teacher does not act on the child's request, for whatever reason, the omega child is *also* faced with negative verbal feedback (direct or indirect) for making an appeal to the teacher in the first place.

Although teacher-child communications have not yet been explicitly examined, a review of the transcripts reveals the following pattern of child responses to appeals for interaction and assistance from the teacher. Negative verbal feedback is directed toward most children who appeal to the teacher to settle child-child disputes. In exchanges involving nonomega children most such disputes are settled internally as, for example, is evidenced in conversational segment 1, or by exhibiting antagonistic behavior (e.g., fighting) which summons the teacher indirectly to settle the dispute. The latter type of action occurs rarely in the recorded material. Thus, since the omega child cannot accomplish or perhaps is not allowed to achieve the former type of resolution, s/he is faced with an additional difficulty. The "damned if you do, damned if you don't" syndrome pervades the existence of the omega child and well illustrates the social situation of these children.

To return to our comparison of sequence 1 and sequence 2, a few additional comments are in order. First, in sequence 2, child A2 insists on the legitimacy of his earlier "save" on the green marker and this is upheld by another child of the group (G2). No on upholds child A1's attempt to place a "save" on the pink marker and child A1 herself makes no attempt to legitimize her claim to the pink marker after it has been auctioned away to someone else. She does not protest, but simply settles for another marker.

A second thing to note is that, although there is an "auction" in both sequences, child A2 is the only one to "bid" verbally on the object in sequence 2. In contrast in segment 1 two children other than child A1 make "bids" on the pink marker, yet they bid even though child A1 had repeatedly placed "saves" on it. An interesting final note: several times later on in the coloring activity of which sequence 1 is a part, child A1 places "saves" on the pink marker, but she never succeeds in obtaining it. The teacher finally calls an end to the work time and all the color activity is stopped. These sequences are clearly rich in material and could be analysed further for additional information if needed to support the present major points.

SUMMARY AND CONCLUSIONS

In this paper, I have reported on a preliminary investigation into the nature of child-child conversations involving *omega* children—children who rank low in the social dominace scale—in a kindergarten classroom situation using both quantitative and qualitative analysis techniques. These analyses indicate that, contrary to commonly held stereotypic expectations, the omega child is not a primary target of direct verbal abuse, i.e., insults, taunts, put-offs, etc. Rather these children are more frequently verbally neglected and ignored. Verbal taunts and abuse do occur when the child attempts to gain access to the group or when the child makes other attempts to move out of the omega role. These initial findings present a picture of an omega child as one ineffective in interaction situations.

If it is true, as numerous studies suggest, that socially ineffective children are deemed less competent not only socially but intellectually, and that such an evaluation of individuals has an impact on the course of the child's future in the school setting, then these findings are of significance for educators. This situation merits further serious investigation. Aspects of such further investigation have in fact been completed and other parts are still in progress. This work can be divided at the moment into three areas. First, it is necessary to examine the nonverbal communicative performance of the omega children in interactions with other children, especially as this nonverbal behavior relates to, and interacts with, the verbal behavior patterns observed. Some attention is given to aspects of the nonverbal behavior patterns of interaction sequences involving an omega child in the qualitative analysis portion of this paper. A more detailed and systematic study of this problem seems desirable, however, especially further examination of the teacher-child communications in the classroom.

The limited sample size of the data collected to date—two kindergarten classrooms—requires that this aspect of further research await additional data collections. The intuitive judgment of the two observers involved in the data-collection phase of the study reported in this paper suggests that differences between the subtypes do exist, at least in some respects, and that the negative impact of the omega child's communicative behavior on the evolution of that child's social competence may be attenuated or increased depending on the more specific social status with its accompanying behavior manifestations. Finally, it is not too early for teachers, parents, administrators, and other interested members of the school community to begin to consider potential strategies for dealing with the existing situation. The strategies must, however, be firmly based on a thorough understanding of the situation stemming from a systematic and well-founded analysis, such as can be derived from research findings. Clearly, the present study does not qualify as such and should be considered as simply a first step in that direction. It may be useful, for example, to complete an investigation of the communicative behavior of children classified as "stars," the highest-ranking members on the social hierarchy and presumably most effective individuals in the classroom, before we achieve a more complete understanding of the omega child's predicament. Whatever further action is necessary, either in terms of research or developing coping strategies, I have little doubt, after analyzing hours of classroom interaction transcripts, that it is well worth making the effort. Furthermore, I do not see this as a concern that is the sole property of teachers or educators, but rather a problem belonging to a larger community—a problem which need to be admitted and acted on by all individuals concerned with the development and future of young children.

REFERENCES

Bremme, D. W., & Erickson, F. Relationships among verbal and nonverbal classroom behaviors. *Theory into Practice,* 1977,*16* (3), 152–161.

Bronfenbrenner, V. The measurement of sociometric status, structure and development. *Sociometry Monographs,* No. 6, 1945.

Cicourel, A. B. *Cognitive sociology.* New York: Free Press, 1974.

Cicourel, A. V., & Kitsuse, J. J. *The educational decision-makers.* Indianapolis, Ind.: Bobbs-Merrill, 1963.

Erickson, F. Gatekeeping encounters: a social selection process. In P. R. Sanday (Ed.), *Anthropology and the public interest.* New York: Academic Press, 1976.

Ginsburg, H. J., Wauson, M. S., & Easley, M. Omega children: a study of lowest-ranking members of the children's play group hierarchy. Paper presented at the Annual Meeting of the Society for Research in Child Development, New Orleans, 1977.

Gronlund, N. E. *Sociometry in the classroom.* New York: Harper, 1959.

Gumperz, J. The speech community. In P. P. Giglioli (Ed.), *Language and social context.* Harmondsworth, England: Penguin Education, 1972.

Hymes, D. *Foundations in sociolinguistics: an ethnographic approach.* Philadelphia: University of Pennsylvania, 1974.

Imanishi, K. Social behavior in Japanese monkey *ma ca ca fuscata.* In *Psychologia,* 1957, *1,* 47–54.

Leiter, K. C. W. Ad hocing in the schools: a study of placement practices in the kindergarten of two schools. In A. V. Cicourel *et al.* (Eds.), *Langauge use and school performance.* New York: Academic Press, 1974.

Mishler, E. G. Studies in dialogue and discourse I: an exponential law of successive questioning. *Language in Society,* 1975, *4,* 31–52.

Moreno, J. L. *Who shall survive?* New York: Beacon House, 1953.

Rist, R. C. Student social class and teacher self-fulfilling prophecy in ghetto education. *Harvard Educational Review,* 1970, *40*(3), 411–450.

Scjelderup-Ebbe, T. Soziale Verhaltinisse bei Vogeln. *Z. Psychol.,* 1922, *90,* 106–107.

Spradley, J. P. Foundations of cultural knowledge. In J. P. Spradley, (Ed.), *Culture and cognition: rules, maps, and plans.* San Francisco: Chandler, 1972.

Strayer, F. F., & Strayer, J. An ethological analysis of dominance relations among young children. Paper presented at the Annual Meeting of the Society for Research in Child Development, Denver, Colorado, 1975.

Williams, R. C. Lord of the flies: an ethological study of dominance ordering in a group of human adolescents. Paper presented at the Annual Meeting of the Society for Research in Child Development, Denver, Colorado, 1975.

APPENDIX A

Description
of Classroom Activities

Class began after the bell rang with all the children sitting on a rug in front of a piano and the teacher sitting on the piano bench. During this initial period the teacher engaged in social conversation with the children (called roll, etc.). This period corresponds well to the occurrence that has been referred to by some in education interaction research as *first circle*.

The rest of the time was divided into periods of *work time, free play time, snack time,* and *last circle.* Transition periods for clean up and putting on clothes to depart also occurred. During *work time* the teacher assigned a particular project that was to be completed by every member of the class. The task was usually highly structured, e.g., the construction of Easter baskets from milk cartons, and included many, often involved, detailed sets of instructions from the teacher. The children were expected to stay at their seats during this period except to make trips to get materials at the request of the teacher. The children were free to choose the table and seats at whch they would be working during the work time.

During *play time* the children were at liberty to engage in any play activity as long as they remained within the confines of the classroom. Materials including blocks, a playhouse, wooden toys, drawing and painting materials, audio-visual equipment were available to the children. During this period the teacher walked from play area to play area and conversed with children individually and in groups. During cold weather, free play time was conducted totally indoors. At other times the children spent free play time in the school playground. Since data collection for the project was during cold weather, all the recorded free play time periods occurred inside the confines of the classroom. Both work time and free play time were terminated by a class for clean up by the teacher.

During *snack time* each child received milk in a carton and was permitted to eat any food that was brought from home. As during work time no special seats were assigned to the children; they were free to choose their seatmates. Snack time also ended with the teacher's call for clean up and a request to return to the rug area. The last period of the day can be called *last circle* since it in many ways paralleled the first circle in physical circumstances. Last circle sometimes included a period of "show and tell," at other times it consisted in the teacher reading a story. This is a general outline of the activity periods that occurred during each day in both the morning and afternoon classes.

11

Analysis of Teacher–Student Interaction— Expectations Communicated by Conversational Structure

Louise Cherry Wilkinson
Department of Educational Psychology
University of Wisconsin-Madison

INTRODUCTION

This chapter will report and discuss the results of a sociolinguistic analysis of the relationship between teachers' expectations of students' communicative competence in the classroom and certain aspects of teachers' language during interaction with students. The teacher expectation model, first introduced by Rosenthal and Jacobsen (1968), held that teachers form expectations of students' abilities; teachers interact differentially with students depending upon those expectations; and the expectations are directly related to students' achievement. This model stimulated a great deal of research for a decade; overall, the data lend some support to the model (Brophy & Good, 1974). The consistency of differential treatment as predicted by the model—across different abilities, across different grades—has not been investigated in previous research. The study reported here consists of a sociolinguistic

The data analyzed in this study were collected as part of a project at the Center for Applied Linguistics, "Children's Functional Language and Education in the Early Years (1975–1976)." The project was funded by the Carnegie Corporation of New York and codirected by Peg Griffin and Roger Shuy. The author of this report was a Senior Research Associate on the project. Additional funds for the analysis of data reported in the chapter were provided by the Wisconsin Research and Development Center for Individualized Schooling. Preliminary aspects of the data analysis have been reported in Cherry (1978) and L. J. Cherry and L. Berman *Teacher-student interaction and teachers' perceptions of students' communicative competence.* (Final report to the Center Royalty Fund Commitee, The Wisconsin Research and Development Center for Individualized Schooling, 1978).

The author gratefully acknowledges Penny Peterson's comments on an earlier draft of this paper.

analysis of samples of teacher-student interaction during classroom lessons taken from two preschool and three elementary grades. The study was conducted to determine whether the teacher expectation model adequately predicts the language production of these teachers and their expectations of the communicative competence of their students. The hypothesis of the teacher expectation model is as follows: Teachers perceive differential competencies among students in their classes; these perceptions result in differential expectations for achievement among the students, and these expectations, in turn, influence teachers' interactions with those students to produce differential performance among them, thus fulfilling the prophecy. (Brophy & Good, 1970; Rosenthal & Jacobsen, 1968; Cherry, 1978). Brophy and Good (1974) characterize the pattern of the self-fulfilling prophecy as the following:

> Teachers took more appropriate action to elicit a good performance from the highs, and that they tended to reinforce it appropriately when it was elicited. In contrast, they tended to accept poor performance from the lows, and they failed to reinforce good performance properly even when it did occur (p. 99).

Cherry (1978) has argued that there are at least two versions of the teacher expectation model. One version holds that teachers will consistently differentiate the behavior they direct toward students of different perceived competencies. Teachers' behavior during interaction is not seen to be highly affected by students' behavior during interaction. In addition, all teachers are expected to interact in a style which "fulfills their prophecy" about students' competencies. Another version of the teacher expectation model holds that teachers' behavior directed toward students of different perceived competencies is influenced by students' behavior during interaction. One implication of this second "interactive" model is that teachers' behavior will not be consistent across situations; in particular, if a large quantity of data is gathered on the same group of teachers and students. Another implication of the model is that there may be differences among teachers in their pattern of differential interactive behavior with students of different perceived competencies. The self-fulfilling pattern may describe only one pattern of interaction; some teachers may interact in a "remedial" pattern, in which the teacher attempts to assist the student who is perceived as less competent.

The consistency across grade levels of differential patterns of teacher-student interaction has not been addressed in previous research on teacher expectations. Grade level may affect both the patterns of teacher-student interaction and the manner in which teachers communicate their expectations. Several studies investigated whether teachers' expectations affected teacher-student interaction at various grade levels (Brophy & Good, 1974; Conn, Edwards, & Rosenthal, 1968; Dusek & O'Connell, 1973; Entwistle, Cornell, & Epstein, 1972; Jose & Cody, 1971; Rist, 1970; Saunders

& Ditullio, 1972; Lockheed, 1976). Whether the phenomenon of the self-fulfilling prophecy changes with grade level, however, has not been addressed by previous research, with the exception of a few preliminary studies (Baum,1976; Coulter,1978; Darnell & Goodwin, 1975) and a recently published study by Crano and Mellon (1978).

Crano and Mellon (1978) examined the relationship between teachers' expectations and students' achievement across grade levels in a longitudinal design employing a cross-lag analysis. They studied 4300 elementary school students to determine whether teachers' expectations affected students' academic achievement or vice versa. The results of their study showed that teachers' expectations of students' competence affected students' achievement; this finding corroborated the original teacher expectation model. Crano and Mellon's (1978) study did not directly address the central focus of the present study, even though their study examined teacher expectation effects at several elementary grades. Crano and Mellon did not include a separate discussion of variation in students' achievement as a function of both teachers' expectations and grade level. Their study suffers from the same drawback characterizing most previous research on teachers' expectations: The process by which teachers communicate their expectations to students has not been examined. One result of studies designed in this way is that individual variation in teachers' interactive style cannot be observed, nor can the relationship between the variation of individual teachers and grade level be examined.

The present study was conducted to assess the availability of language data in elementary school lessons and the adequacy of the teacher expectation model in predicting teachers' language behavior with students. Specifically, the following three questions were addressed in the study:

1. How much language data is available for analysis during classroom lessons in nursery, kindergarten, first, second, and third grades?
2. Do teachers differ in the amount of language data they produce while interacting with students during lessons?
3. Does the teacher expectation model adequately predict certain aspects of these teachers' language production with students for whom the teachers hold differential expectations of communicative competence?

METHOD

Subjects

The subjects for the study were 76 students in nursery (11), kindergarten (21), first (20), second (7), and third (17) grades, in 9 classes and their 9 female teachers. All subjects were middle- or upper-middle–class, native English speakers. They all were present at the site school for the full academic year. In addition, all provided informed consent to participate in the study. Table 1 shows the distribution of subjects by class and teachers' ranking of the students as above average or below-average on communicative competence in the classroom.

TABLE 1
Distribution of Subjects by Class and Teacher's Ranking

Class	Ranking	
	Above-average	Below-average
Nursery A	2	3
Nursery B	4	2
Kindergarten A	8	4
Kindergarten B	5	4
First A	5	5
First B	6	4
Second A	5	2
Third A	3	3
Third B	4	7
Total	42	34

Procedures

Ranking. Teachers were asked to rank the students in their classes according to how well they used language to communicate effectively in the classroom at the beginning of the school year. The teachers were then asked to divide their rank orders into the following groups: above-average, average, and below-average.

Data Collection. The present study required a sampling unit that would be comparable for all classrooms across grade levels. The unit of sample that was chosen was the *lesson,* an instructional activity which focuses on a particular topic and consists of a sequence of exchanges between teacher and students (Cherry, 1978). This definition allowed the sampling of units of teacher-student interaction from the video-audio-recordings made in the seven classrooms (see Cherry, 1978 for details). In the present study teachers formulated lessons by stating requirements for students during lessons, as in the following example: "I'm gonna write a word on the board, and if you know what the word says, put up your hand." During the lessons, both teachers and students remained in one area of the classroom and focused their attention on the teaching materials, such as the blackboard. Teachers expected students not to "call out" or reply simultaneously. If these behaviors occurred, the teacher responded with statements such as "I can only hear one of you at a time." Students were expected not to be disruptive during lessons, and teachers often responded to disruptions with replies such as "Excuse me, Sandy, may I have your attention."

The data for this study consisted of 15 lessons; 2 nursery, 8 kindergarten, 2 first-grade, 1 second-grade, and 2 third-grade. Each lesson was both video- and audiotaped. All lessons met the following criteria (after Cherry, 1978): (a) high technical standard in both audio and video; (b) both "panning" and stationary" cameras; (c) all subjects (both teachers and students) present; (d) recorded from the beginning to the end of the lesson. A description of each of the lessons is now given.

Nursery (N-A; 22 minutes). Teacher and children were carving a Halloween pumpkin. The children took turns drawing features on the pumpkin; the teacher then cut these features out. The children tasted the pumpkin, talked about the smell and feel of the pulp, and discussed what could be done with the seeds. The lesson ended when the children left the room in order to prepare for snack time.

Nursery (N-B; 41 minutes). The teacher and students were seated in a circle disucssing what should be done with the class pet, a bird, which recently died and was decomposing. The class then dicussed the funeral arrangements for the bird. The lesson ended after the teacher and students decided which part of the funeral arrangement each student would participate in.

Kindergarten (K-A; 11 minutes). The class is gathered in a circle around the teacher, who has a box of blocks which vary in shape, color, and size. During the lesson, the teacher attempts to have each student describe a block using these three attributes, so that the teacher can select one block from the box. After introducing the lesson, the teacher calls on each student to describe a block and then finds the block in the box and places it on the floor. The lesson ends when the students line up to go outside.

Kindergarten (K-A; 13 minutes). The class is seated at tables in front of the blackboard. The teacher writes "d" on the board and asks for words beginning with this sound by calling on individual students and then writes the appropriate answers on the board. After many words have been given, the teacher reads the words to the class. In the next segment of the lesson the teacher asks for words that begin with "b" and writes the appropriate answers on the board. The lesson ends when the teacher tells the class to look through magazines and cut out words that begin with "b" and "d."

Kindergarten (K-A; 20 minutes). The class is seated at desks in front of the blackboard. The teacher hands each student a bag full of *cuisenaire* rods (colored rods of different lengths used to teach elementary math) and asks him/her to find the longest one. After that the students are asked to find the next longest one and so on, until they have a "staircase" design (||||||ıı,.). The teacher walks around the classroom helping individual students to make sure they are doing it correctly. The end of the lesson occurs when the teacher says she will continue with the work another day.

Kindergarten (K-A; 4 minutes). The class is gathered in a circle in front of the teacher. The teacher writes the word "tree" on the board and asks if someone can read it. The teacher then asks the students to provide the names of things they think of when they think of "tree." The teacher writes the appropriate answers on the board. The lesson ends when the teacher reads the students a story about trees.

Kindergarten (K-B; 11 minutes). The class is seated in a semicircle in front of a flannelboard which has four objects on it. The teacher removes one object when the class is not looking, and then asks the students to guess which one she has removed. The teacher then puts up four rows of four objects, removes one object and asks the students which one she removed. Finally, the teacher removes one entire row, and asks a student to put the objects back in the correct order. The lesson ends when the teacher reads the students a story.

Kindergarten (K-B; 9 minutes). The class is seated in a circle around the teacher, who asks the students to name sets of objects in the room. The lesson ends when the teacher reads the students a story.

Kindergarten (K-B; 16 minutes). The class is seated at tables in front of the blackboard, and the teacher gives them mimeographed copies of a crossword puzzle which the teacher has written. The clues and answers all involve names of herbs and spices. The teacher reads the clues, and the students must guess the answers. The teacher shows the sutdents how and where to write the answers and provides some individual help for students. The lesson ends when the students hand in their papers.

Kindergarten (K-B; 6 minutes). The class is gathered in front of the teacher on the rug. The teacher has a series of pictures showing a woman in different body positions (e.g., touching her toes). The teacher shows the picture to one half the class, and calls on one student to verbally describe the picture to another student who cannot see the picture. This second student is later shown the picture so that s/he may determine whether the description was correct. The lesson ends when the teacher reads the class a story.

First grade (1-A; 23 minutes). At the outset of the lesson, the teacher asked the students to write their names on a piece of paper. She then dictated eight words to the class. After each word was written down, one student was called upon to spell the word out loud. The teacher then told the class to write down the sentence that she was going to dictate to them. The class discussed the format of a sentence, and the lesson ended when the teacher told the class to turn their papers over and to begin another lesson.

First grade (1-B; 8 minutes). The teacher started the lesson by telling the students that they were going to have visitors for a "hot cross bun" party. The class discussed the origin of the custom of eating hot cross buns on Good Friday. Copies of the recipe for hot cross buns were distributed in class and the teacher chose students to read portions of the recipe. The lesson ended after the pupils wrote their names on their copies of the recipe and then put them away.

Second grade (2-A; 16 minutes). The class was seated on the floor in a circle. The teacher distributed papers that asked questions about the Navaho Indians. These questions were read out loud by the teacher and then were discussed by the class. Afterwards, the teacher read the class a story about the Navaho's breakfast. The class talked about Navaho life and how it differs from their own. The lesson ended when the teacher told the class to put their papers away.

Third grade (3-A; 33 minutes). Various ways of forming plurals were discussed (adding, s, es, or ies). The children gave examples of words that used different types of plural endings. The class then examined the rules required when forming plurals. The lesson ended when the teacher asked the class to stand up and stretch.

Third (3-B; 35 minutes). The class and the teacher were seated in a circle on the floor. The teacher began the lesson by telling the students that she was going to turn on a light and leave it on forever. The class discussed how the teacher's behavior affected the environment—specifically its effect on energy conservation. The lesson ended when the teacher initiated a new topic of discussion.

Data Analysis: Transcription.   The lessons were transcribed from the audio- and videorecordings from the beginning to the end of the lesson. Transcribers used the audio- and videorecordings during the transcription process as well as the ethnographic reports which contained detailed information about the lesson recorded during the activity, and the tape indexes, which contained specific information about the activities of the teachers and students derived from the recordings of the lessons. All transcriptions were checked at least once by another member of the research team before being typed. After the transcriptions were typed and rechecked, the transcriber added contextual information. These included gestures, for example, whether a child complied with a teacher's request for action, or whether a child provided a nonverbal response to a teacher's request for information, among others.

Data Analysis: Coding.   The coding system used in the present study was developed by Cherry (1978). The lesson transcripts were coded by two researchers. After transcription, all the data in the lessons were coded. Data were eliminated from analysis only when a student's name was unknown or some part of an interaction was inaudible, or the student or teacher was not "on camera," or could not be identified. After the two researchers independently coded all the elicitation exchanges in all the lessons, the codings were compared. For analysis, discrepancies were resolved by discussion. The researchers independently coded all categories and reliabilities were calculated by dividing the number of agreements by the number of agreements and disagreements. The average reliability for these categories exceeded 91 percent. After reliability was computed, disagreements were discussed, solved, and then included in the analyses. The coding system used in this study consists of three levels: exchanges (teacher-elicit, teacher-list, teacher-reinitiate); elicitations (explicit, overexplicit, inexplicit); and feedback (positive, negative, neutral, no feedback).

1. *A teacher-elicit exchange* is a sequence of actions between the teacher and a student in which the teacher requests information from the student: it is assumed that the teacher expects a particular complete and correct response from the student. For example:

Teacher:	Any more words that are real words that go with tree?	(1)
	Jane?	(2)
Jane:	Leaf.	(3)
Teacher:	Leaf (writes on board).	(4)

2. *A teacher-list exchange* is a sequence of actions between the teacher and a student in which the teacher requests information; and (a) it is assumed that the teacher expects a particular complete and correct response from the student; (b) the student involved in the previous teacher-elicit exchange has provided a response to that request, which may or may not have been followed by teacher feedback; (c) any student may be involved in a teacher-list exchange. Example: This segment of the lesson involved providing words that "go with tree." (1), (2), and (3) comprise the teacher-elicit exchange; (4), (5), and (6) comprise the teacher-list exchange.

Teacher:	All right, Mary had her hand up.	(1)
Mary:	Tree.	(2)
Teacher:	Tree, we have.	(3)
	Arthur.	(4)
Arthur:	Cherry tree.	(5)
Teacher:	Cherry, all right.	(6)

3. *A teacher-reinitiate exchange* is a sequence of actions between the teacher and a student in which (a) the teacher requests information from a student, and it is assumed that the teacher expects a particular complete and correct response; (b) the student involved in the earlier teacher-elicit exchange has not previously provided a response to that request; (c) any student may be involved in a teacher-reinitiate exchange. In the following example, (1) and (2) compare the teacher-elicit exchange, and (3), (4), and (5) comprise the teacher-reinitiate exchange:

Teacher:	OK, Ann what is the second thing in the fourth row.	(1)
Ann:	(no reply)	(2)
Teacher:	John.	(3)
John:	The heart.	(4)
Teacher:	Good.	(5)

4. *An explicit elicitation* is a request for information which contains one of the following Wh- words, when that word is not a conjunction: what, which, why, how, who, where. These utterances are explicit because they are interrogative forms which focus upon the kinds of information requested, as in: "What's the first thing in the second row?" In the following example, from a third-grade lesson on ecology, the teacher provides an elicitation which contains a Wh- question and focuses upon the kinds of information requested.

Teacher:	What does the ozone layer do for us, Andrew?	(1)
Andrew:	That's something that keeps all the air from rushing out, and going into space and dissolving into no into nothing.	(2)
Teacher:	Not exactly.	(3)

5. *An inexplicit elicitation* is a request for information containing a vocative standing alone, the child's name. Inexplicit elicitation provides students with less information about the topic and does not help students to focus on the elicitation. An example of inexplicit elicitation is provided in the following excerpt, in which a class was discussing how the Navaho form their pottery.

Teacher:	Mary	(1)
Mary:	Um, it takes out the vapor and besides, the clay, um gets you know, heated, and um, even without some moisture, it's it's...	(2)
Teacher:	Something else happens	(3)

6. *An overexplicit elicitation* is a declarative, imperative, or interrogative request for information which focuses upon the acts involved in responding and is therefore very explicit. These utterances include declaratives, such as "Bonnie hasn't had a turn yet," imperatives, such as "Give me one word, one word that you think of when you think of 'tree'," and interrogatives, such as "Can you tell me another one?" The overexplicit elicitation focuses upon the acts involved in responding. The following example is taken from a third-grade class discussing plural formation:

| Teacher: | Give me an example, Lori, of a plural. | (1) |

| Lori: | Mouse and mice. | (2) |
| Teacher: | All right. | (3) |

7. *Positive feedback* contains an explicit positive evaluation word or phrase such as "yet," "right," "gorgeous," or a comparative word or phrase such as "that's better;" an utterance which specifies how the response will be used in the lesson, such as the teacher writes the response on the blackboard or comments on the response; an utterance may imply a positive evaluation, such as "That's one way of saying it."

8. *Negative feedback* contains an explicit, negative evaluation word such as "no," "not an answer," or a "function word" which indicates a negative evaluation, such as "but" or "though," as in "That's a pattern, but I was talking about sets"; an utterance which provides the reason for the inappropriateness of the response in a particular context, such as "We have 'dog'" in a lesson on words which begin with the letters "b" and "d":

Teacher:	Ron.	(1)
Ron:	I got two. "Puff" and "bear."	(2)
Teacher:	All right, "puff" begins the way "pig" begins.	(3)

In this instance, the student's word "bear" receives an implied negative evaluation in the teacher's feedback.

9. *Neutral feedback* allows the student more time to respond, such as "I'll come back to you", "Well, you think about it a minute;" also included are conversational, not evaluative utterances, such as "May I interrupt you?"

10. *No feedback* is the absence of a positive, neutral, or negative form.

Data Analysis: Measures. The following measures were calculated so that the research questions could be addressed:

1. How frequent are teachers' elicitations of information from students rated "above average" and "below average" during lessons? *The combined number of teacher-elicit, teacher-list, teacher-reinitiate exchanges divided by the number of minutes per lesson; and the total number of teacher-elicit, teacher-list, teacher-reinitiate exchanges divided by the total number of students.*

2. Do teachers differ in the frequency of their elicitations of information from students rated as "above average" and "below average" during lessons? *The combined number of teacher-elicit teacher-list, teacher-reinitiate exchanges for each teacher divided by the number of minutes in the lesson for each teacher.*

3. Do teachers of different grade levels differ in the frequency of their elicitations of information from students rated as "above average" and "below-average" during lessons? *The combined number of teacher-elicit,*

teacher-list, teacher-reinitiate exchanges for each grade divided by the number of minutes in the lesson(s) for each grade.

4. Do teachers differentiate between students rated as "above average" and "below average" by providing one group with:

    (a) more opportunities to participate in elicitation exchanges, *the total number of teacher-elicit, teacher-list, teacher-reinitiate exchanges;*

    (b) more explicit and overexplicit elicitations, *the total number of explicit and overexplicit elicitations divided by the total number of elicitations;*

    (c) more elicitations for which a student previously has been unable to provide a positively evaluated response, *the number of teacher-list and the number of teacher-reinitiate exchanges;*

    (d) more explicit positive evaluation of responses, *the total number of positive feedbacks divided by the total number of feedbacks.*

RESULTS AND DISCUSSION

The data are presented in Tables 2 and 3, and the results which are relevant to each research question will be discussed separately.

1. How frequent are teachers' elicitations of information from students during lessons? As can be seen in Table 2, there were 232 combined elicitation exchanges (teacher-elicit, teacher-list, teacher-reinitiate) over all; the total time for the lessons was 278 minutes and the total number of students was 76. The teachers showed an average of .83 elicitation exchanges per minute for these students, and an average of 3.05 elicitation exchanges per student. The

TABLE 2

Raw Frequencies and Adjusted Scores for Combined Teacher-elicit, Teacher-list, and Teacher-reinitiate Exchanges

| | Rank | | | Total adjusted for N |
	Above-average	Below-average	Total	
Nursery A	2	0	2	0.40
Nursery B	5	2	7	1.17
Kindergarten A	39	16	55	4.58
Kindergarten B	32	13	45	5.00
First A	16	5	21	1.91
First B	11	21	32	3.20
Second	0	3	3	0.43
Third A	6	13	19	3.17
Third B	27	21	48	4.36

data available for further analysis are very small, since the teachers' production of elicitation exchanges was infrequent.

2. Do teachers differ in the frequency of their elicitation of information from students rated as above average and below average during lessons? A one-way analysis of variance was computed for the combined number of elicitation exchanges for each of the nine teachers, which adjusted for the duration in minutes of the lesson; the results of this analysis yielded a significant effect for teacher, $F(8,67) = 5.207$, $p < .01$. Teachers show considerable variation in their production of elicitation exchanges.

3. Do teachers of various grade levels differ in the frequency of their elicitation of information from students rated "above average" and "below average" during lessons? A correlation coefficient was calculated for the combined number of elicitation exchanges (adjusted for duration of lessons) for each teacher in each grade; $r = .21$, which is not statistically significant with 7 degrees of freedom. There was a slight tendency for teachers of the upper grades to produce more elicitations in contrast to teachers in the lower grades.

4. Do teachers differentiate between students rated above average and below average by providing one group with more
   (a) opportunities to participate in elicitation exchanges;
   (b) explicit and overexplicit elicitations;
   (c) elicitations for which no student has previously been unable to provide a positively evaluated response;
   (d) explicit positive evaluation of responses?

Of the 54 possible comparisons for the 9 teachers across 6 measures, 5 did not show any difference; 26 showed a difference favoring the above-average students ("self-fulfilling" pattern); 23 showed a difference favoring the below-average students ("remedial" pattern). Forty-nine t tests were calculated for the comparisons which showed a difference; 4 of the tests were significant at the $p \leq .05$ for the self-fulfilling pattern, and 5 of the tests were significant at the $p \leq .05$ for the remedial pattern (2-tail). These results do not provide strong overall support for the teacher-expectation model, which predicts that teachers will interact with above-average students in a self-fulfilling pattern. As can be seen in Tables 3 and 4, teachers are not consistent in their pattern of interaction (self-fulfilling vs. remedial) across measures. The data show however, that some measures show greater consistency across teachers than other measures. It appears that explicit and overexplicit elicitations consistently show a self-fulfilling pattern (6 out of 9 teachers), positive feedback tends consistently to show a remedial pattern (6 out of 8 teachers).

Overall, the data from the present study suggest that the original version of the teacher expectation model is neither powerful nor consistent in its predictions. Any interpretation of the results of the present study must be

TABLE 3
Measure of Teacher's Speech

Measures

Class	Teacher elicit[a]		Teacher list[a]		Teacher reinitiate[a]		Combined TE, TL, TR[a]		Overexplicit and explicit elicitations[b]		Positive feedback[b]	
	Above	Below	Above	Below	Above	Below	Above	Below	Above	Below	Above	Below
Nursery A	0.50	0	0.50	0	0	0	1.00	0[c]	1.00	0	0	0
Nursery B	0.50	0	0.25	1.00	0.25	0	1.25	1.00	0.50	0.50	0.75	1.00
Kindergarten A	3.00	3.00	1.38	1.00	0.50	0.00	4.89	4.00	0.41	0.14	0.66	0.42
Kindergarten B	2.80	1.25	3.60	1.75	0.00	0.25	6.40	3.25	0.58	0.81	0.41	0.50
First A	2.20	0.80[c]	0.40	0.20	0.40	0	3.00	1.00[c]	0.88	0.80	0.25	0.60
First B	0.83	0	1.00	0.50	0.20	0.75	2.00	0.25	0.36	0.90[c]	0.33	0.75[c]
Second A	0	1.00	0	0.50	0	0	0	1.50[d]	0	0.50	0	0.25
Third A	1.33	1.67	0.67	2.67[c]	0	0	2.00	4.33	0.50	0	0.67	0.77
Third B	3.00	0.85	1.25	1.86	0	0.29	4.25	2.71	0.85	0.49	0.26	0.67

[a]These categories are means.
[b]These categories are proportions.
[c]$p < .05$
[d]$p < .01$

TABLE 4
Summary of Data[a]

Measure	Class								
	N-A	N-B	K-A	K-B	First A	First B	Second A	Third A	Third B
Teacher elicit exchanges	X	X		X	X				X
Teacher list exchanges	X		X	X	X	X			
Teacher reinitiate exchanges		X	X		X				
Combined teacher elicit, list, reinitiate exchanges	X	X	X	X	X				X
Proportion of explicit and overexplicit elicitations	X	X	X		X			X	X
Proportion of positive feedbacks			X					X	

[a] An "X" designates when the prediction from the teacher expectation model was confirmed; that is, the difference between the score for the above-average students and the below-average students is positive.

qualified, since the data available for analysis were so limited. These data suggest, however, that the relationship between teachers' expectations of students' abilities and communication during lessons is a complex interaction among teachers' expectations, the individual teacher, and the particular measure of behavior.

The results of the present study suggest that further research on the relationship between teachers' expectations of students' communicative competence is needed. The original version of the teacher expectation model, the self-fulfilling prophecy, may not predict teacher behavior when specific abilities are involved (such as communicative competence) or when the process of interaction between teachers and students is examined in detail. In addition, the present study suggests that individual differences among teachers are an important variable in the way teachers communicate their expectations of their students to them. This finding corroborates previous research (Cherry, 1978) and suggests that further research should be designed to focus upon teachers. Researchers need a large enough sample of teachers in order to estimate the variation among them in their interactive behavior with students. The data also suggest that grade may affect the quantity of teacher-student interaction; hence further research should include a separate analysis for variation due to grade level. In conclusion, the results of the study provide support for the interactive version of the teacher expectation model. Teachers' behavior toward students is not necessarily consistent across situations, and individual teachers may differ in the way they communicate their expectations of students' competence to them. Further research is needed to develop and test a complex model of the relationship between teachers' expectations and their interactions with students.

REFERENCES

Baum, M. *Sex and grade level of student context variables in elementary school teaching* University of Texas, Austin Research and Development Center for Teacher education, Report No. 76-12, December 1976.

Brophy, J., & Good, R. Teachers' communication of differential expectations for children's classroom performance: Some behavioral data. *Journal of Educational Psychology,* 1970, *61,* 365-374.

Brophy, J. E., & Good, T. L. *Teacher-student relationships: Causes and consequences.* New York: Holt, Rinehart & Winston, 1974.

Cherry, L. J. A sociolinguistic approach to the study of teachers' expectations. *Discourse Processes,* 1978, *4,* 374-393.

Conn, L. K., Edwards, C., & Rosenthal, R. Perception of emotion and response to teachers' expectancy by elementary school children. *Psychological Reports,* 1968, *22,* 27-34.

Coulter, C. L. *Sex and grade level differences in ratings of students by teachers and classroom observers.* University of Texas, Austin Research and Development Center for Teacher Education, Report No. 75-20, March 1978.

Crano, W. D., & Mellon, P. M. Causan influence of teachers' expectation on children's academic performance: A cross-lagged panel analysis. *Journal of Educational Psychology,* 1978, *70*(1), 39–49.

Darnell, C., & Goodwin, W. The kindergarten child 1971 or the class of 1984. Paper presented at the annual meetings of the American Psychological Association, Chicago, September 1975.

Dusek, J. B., & O'Connell, E. J. Teacher expectancy effects on the achievement test performance of elementary school children. *Journal of Educational Psychology* 1973, *65,* 371–377.

Entwistle, D., Cornell, E., & Epstein, J. Effect of a principal S expectation on test performance of elementary school children. *Psychological Reports,* 1972, *31,* 551–556.

Hymes, D. On communicative competence. In J. B. Pride & J. Holmes (Eds.), *Sociolinguistics.* Baltimore, Md.: Penguin, 1972.

Jose, J., & Cody, J. Teacher-pupil interaction as it relates to attempted changes in teacher expectancy of academic ability and achievement. *American Educational Research Journal,* 1971, *8,* 39–49.

Kist, R. Student social class and teacher expectations: The self-fulfilling prophecy in ghetto education. *Harvard Educational Review,* 1970, *40,* 411–451.

Lockhead, M. Beginning teacher evaluation study: Phase II, 1973–74. Final Report. Sacramento, Calif.: California State Commission for Teacher Preparation and Licensing, July 1976.

Rosenthal, R., & Jacobson, L. *Pygmalion in the classroom: Teacher expectation and pupils' intellectual development.* New York: Holt, 1968.

Saunders, B., & DiTullio, W. The failure of biased information to affect teacher behavior ratings and peer sociometric status of disturbing children in the classroom. *Psychology in the Schools,* 1974, *9,* 440–445.

IV POSTSCRIPTS

12

Discussion—
Needed Directions
in Face-to-Face Interaction
in Educational Settings

Barbara Hutson
(Roundtable Editor)
*Virginia Polytechnic Institute
and State University*

The roundtable discussion from the conference, Face-to-Face: Analysis of Social Interaction, presented here, was a fluid exchange of ideas, with its share of the simultaneous utterances and verbal tangles that often mark the spontaneous expression of ideas. Editing, where needed, was primarily for making the discussion clearer to readers, who would not have access to the full set of paralinguistic and nonverbal cues available to the roundtable participants and their audience.

In a few cases, the implicit coherence of the discussion was brought out by making more explicit a speaker's reference to earlier themes or speakers. At times, speakers referred to the keynote speech John Gumperz delivered earlier that day, and some of the themes introduced here were developed further the next day in research reports and discussion sessions. There was an attempt to preserve the logic of argument and the structure of the discourse.

The panel included both researchers who had considerable experience in analysis of social interaction and others who, though well grounded in their own disciplines, were less familiar with the field of ethnography in educational settings. Participants contributed questions from different viewpoints and drew out one another on basic issues in a way that might not have been possible in a more homogeneous group. Among the themes brought out were the need for considering the historical and institutional contexts within which ethnographic research is conducted; the replicability, control, and generalizability of this body of research; emergent methodologies that allow one to take into account the different viewpoints of various participants; and implications of this field of research for educating children and teachers.

Discussion often cycled back to an earlier theme, blending new ideas with those developed earlier. There was no unanimity of opinion, but enough common ground to allow open discussion of divergent viewpoints.

Roundtable Participants:

Carl Auria, Chairperson, Department of Educational Foundations, Kent State University

Louise Cherry Wilkinson, Department of Educational Psychology, University of Wisconsin, Madison

Ambrose Clegg, Chairperson, Department of Elementary Education, Kent State University

Carl Frederiksen, McGill University

Olga Garnica, Department of Linguistics, The Ohio State University

John Gumperz, Department of Anthropology, University of California

Martha King, Professor, Early and Middle Childhood, The Ohio State University

Arch Phillips, Chairperson, Department of Curriculum and Instruction, Kent State University

Tom Popkewitz, Department of Curriculum and Instruction, University of Wisconsin, Madison

Richard Prawat, Institute for Research on Teaching, Michigan State University

Maurice Sevigny, Director, School of Art, Bowling Green University

Moderator:

Normand Bernier, Department of Educational Foundations, Kent State University

Olga Garnica: When I first heard the words "educational setting" in the title of this roundtable, it occurred to me that we might ask what criteria, if any, might be developed to delineate what it is we call an *educational setting.* In some very broad sense, couldn't we say that practically every minute of everyday life is an educational experience of some sort? In a very narrow sense, couldn't we say that a formal classroom or teaching situation is what we'd want to call an educational setting? Where, between these two extremes, would we want to start drawing lines, or what criteria would we want to use to develop some notion of what an educational setting is?

John Gumperz: Although I think a lot of what interaction does depends on assumptions about the setting, I wonder whether we should worry about what an educational setting, as such, is or whether we shouldn't really be more interested in what an educational or learning process is.

One of the problems is really what our basic categories in studying interaction are. People say that context determines interaction. Do we mean that we need classification in a limited set of context categories? That's been the tradition, at least in the studies of language use. People have usually started defining "In a certain setting, such and such a thing occurs." If you take a cyclical view of saying that the nature of a setting is communicated, then you can't start with an a priori definition of setting, but you need to have something to hang your hat on, as you suggest. I just wonder whether we shouldn't really look at what is a learning *process* or what is a productive educational learning process and what assumptions do we make about environments and about contexts to recognize such a process.

Olga Garnica: I don't know whether I was so much concerned about the particular word "setting" or more concerned about where we might *begin* or how we might delimit what it is that we're studying.

Maurice Sevigny: I can't help thinking that we might end up ruling out teaching settings as educational settings. I get your point that we may want to extend beyond the classroom to perhaps parent-child relationships, but again this idea of instructional settings vs. educational settings vs. teaching settings may be an interesting notion to fool around with, because they may not all be the same thing.

Carl Frederiksen: Earlier today John Gumperz was describing his focus on what happens in a classroom; specifically, how children acquire an ability to understand the codes that enable them to get into the activities that will enable them to learn. I kept thinking of the need to look at a *range* of situations, and I guess I like the term *situation* better than the term *setting*. At least as I use the term, it relates more directly to the manner in which the situation is influencing the use of language. Setting is such a broad term; it could be a variety of things. I don't know if that is the general use of the term.

I think that it probably would be undesirable if the rationale we gave for research on social interaction was that we needed to understand what happens in a classroom solely. Social interaction occurs in a variety of situations, including those outside the classroom. I don't want to change the question, but I have a personal reason for having that interest. I don't think a lot of what we're studying when we're studying social interaction, and especially change in that interaction, is a kind of shift or an adaptation to the kinds of social situations children encounter in school.

If we want to understand the process of literacy development, we need to start from social situations that preschool children encounter, both in school situations and outside. So I guess that's a good question because it leads you to say we have to look at interactions in a variety of situations.

Maurice Sevigny: I see another question in what you're saying. It may be very important to know the situations that precede school in terms of social interaction, so that first grade teachers know what kinds of interaction skills children coming to them have. The teachers can then go from this point, rather than just assuming the skills.

Martha King: I think we need to do this if we're going to make the context of the school compatible with the context of the home. I'm thinking particularly of kindergartens and first grades, where the setting is so important. Children need a setting that allows them to link home experiences with school, to engage in some activities which they determine for themselves—perhaps in the home corner, in block play, or in water play, which we have found to be valuable in terms of youngsters' being able to bring their experience into the classroom. It generates a lot of talk, both referential and expressive.

The classroom context, in terms of what is there and how it's organized, is exceedingly important in determining the amount of language and the functions for which language is used. Unless we have certain conditions in classrooms, we find that children's use of language is limited, particularly in respect to imaginative language or heuristic function, speaking in Halliday's terms. We find primarily regulatory and interactional language, and surprisingly, very little personal language in some classrooms.

Tom Popkewitz: I have a question related to the discussion this afternoon. I'm not a linguist; I'm not a cultural anthropologist; my concern is the sociology of knowledge. One of the things that disturbed me (and maybe I didn't understand) was that the analysis of conversation seemed to be almost asocial and almost acultural. It was definitely apolitical. Most of the comments here assume that, for example, language in school develops in some sort of interchange between two people that is unrelated to the history of the institution, unrelated to the social context in which that institution is embedded, unrelated to the cultural world in which that institution exists, as though we could understand the interchange of two participants as independent variables, without trying to situate it in a historical context. This is a long way of asking if you want to respond to that, because I don't know if it's what you meant, or if there's more to what you've said.

John Gumperz: Well, actually, what you're talking about is a criticism that has been made of a lot of the work in symbolic interaction and the work in sociology usually labeled *ethnomethodology.* Some of the things I was talking about were specifically designed to avoid this. By, for example, taking into account the conventions that are created in the course of time in the classroom, symbolically you take in the history of what happened in that classroom. What happens in one month in the beginning of the year, in terms of what the teacher and children do, can feed into interpretations that are made six or seven months later in that classroom. In other words, one can look at symbolic aspects of communication as they reflect past history.

In studying aspects of ethnic differences in speech, for example, one can trace back stylistic features of Black English historically to certain kinds of conditions in the Caribbean and West Africa. There have been some studies of this kind.

One can also conduct conversational analyses of this kind by studying outcome, studying other people's reactions to various kinds of miscommunication. In fact, one can look at situations of conversational miscommunication in terms of the real status of the people who evaluate what goes on. If you have a relationship between minority and majority groups, and the minority and majority members miscommunicate, we can predict that each side will evaluate what goes on in pejorative terms about the other side. But one side's pejorative interpretations carry more force, because majority group members have the political power to argue with other majority groups to enforce their beliefs.

In other words, one can look at the interrelationship between what goes on and the power relationships or the examination process that determines mobility, by looking at outcomes. For those who look only at structure, I think what you said is right, but when we look at outcomes, we can see how these outcomes are evaluated. We can also look at ways of changing the basis for evaluation or changing strategies in relation to them.

Tom Popkewitz: It seems to me that there is an institution which these language games form. To talk about these language games without understanding the institution is to argue in a vacuum.

John Gumperz: One can look at the way these language games are *evaluated* by the institution and if one looks at this evaluation process one can see then, that over time, in fact, the evaluation process will favor certain kinds of strategies rather than others. We can study that in terms of how functional it is, and how well justified it is. If certain kinds of children's strategies may be perfectly functional within one setting but are pejoratively evaluated, then one can study ways in which this evaluation feeds back into teacher expectations and into children's performance.

Maurice Sevigny: I get very confused when you use the word "outcomes." From whose perspective are you talking: outcomes from your perspective as an observer, outcomes from the perspective of the teacher, or outcomes from the perspective of the learner?

John Gumperz: You, in fact, start with outcomes from the observer's perspective and then you ask how are these outcomes evaluated; what is the data on which to evaluate these outcomes? You take back your theory of what happens and take it to the teacher and take it to the child and then you compare these. There is no ultimate truth; all we can do is to try to arrive at *several* legitimate interpretations of the truth and look at the processes by which they were derived. By using a form of triangulation we may possibly come closer to some kind of neutrality or a more inclusive truth.

Carl Auria: Well, I wonder if you would pursue that idea about asking the youngster or the student his impressions; for example, you talked about a questionnaire as a way to verify your analysis of an episode or a situation. That raises all kinds of intriguing questions; that is, what kind of cues do you present to a child that might lead him to respond to you in a certain way, and how are you, as the analyzer observed by others, sure that you are not leading the child to a certain direction in answering your questions?

John Gumperz: I wasn't talking about a questionnaire actually. I was talking about questioning strategies. Two of our students at Berkeley have been experimenting with this for about three or four months each, trying to find ways of asking questions. Their suggestion at this moment is that children are able to answer by mimicking. In other words, you can't ask a child to evaluate. Usually a questionnaire asks the respondent to evaluate something in verbal terms. Children don't do that, but children reproduce various ways of talking, then you can use their responses to deduce indirectly what the child's system is, using methods quite similar to what a linguist uses when he tries to get phonemic distinctions in a language other than his own. In fact, I'm trying to suggest, as a methodology in questioning, that we use linguistic inquiry methodology at the *discourse* level rather than at the level of linguistic structure.

Carl Frederiksen: A criticism sometimes made is that we look at the language of speakers of nonstandard dialects or nonmajority culture in a standardized school culture—that is, not their own culture. Now I think that the way to get around that is to look at variation both in the settings and in the situations in which language is observed. By *setting* I mean root facts about who the participants are, what the physical situation is, social relationships among the speakers, and by *situation* I refer more to the activity that people are engaged in.

An example of this would be a set data set (a *corpus*) that was collected specifically for the purpose of studying dialect differences, and I mean by dialect differences more than looking at differences in phonology and syntax. I mean looking at differences in the discourse structures and uses of language by different groups.

I'm referring to the *corpus* that we're studying, which was collected by Bill Hall and Michael Cole at Rockefeller University. It's a *corpus* in which there are samples of lower and middle SES Blacks and whites in the New York City area. Each preschooler in these groups was observed on ten different occasions in a variety of situations across several settings, ranging from a home dinner table conversation to a nursery school setting. The nursery school setting included several different situations or activities. The home dinner table setting was a less structured situation than the school setting. We have only begun to look at the *corpus* and are dealing now primarily with the methodological issues.

If the argument Dr. Popkewitz raises is that you are not able to see the working of a group of nonstandard speakers in this standard environment, what you can do is to look at how this language is working in a *variety* of environments. This enables you to make a kind of comparison that just hasn't been possible before. If the criticism is on the basis of levels of analysis, that's an aspect of any science. There are various levels or perspectives, and clearly one level that we can look at is in terms of an analysis of the interaction that's taking place in particular situations. If you're willing to make that kind of argument, then the issue is what kinds of varying situations should you look at.

Richard Prawat: How useful is this approach as a tool for intervening? I'd like to see us get into that issue, which is the more applied kind of issue. Once you have begun to detect these participant structures in discourse, how are you able to use that information with teachers or with students to enable them to bridge the gap that's separating them in communication?

John Gumperz: Some ethnographic researchers (such as Susan Florio) provide feedback as a condition of their doing research. Once they have gathered naturalistic data, they may feed back to the teachers from the research record, giving them insight into their own strategies through analysis. In other words, they have developed a form of self-analysis that does not deal with matters of content or psychology, but with matters of strategy. The teacher learns in this way to analyze style, though not in terms of psychological issues that are usually properly dealt with by a psychiatrist. So I think that's one immediate thing that can happen.

Another advantage of looking at language as such is that once we identify certain kinds of linguistic strategies or patterns, I think we can devise more appropriate linguistic teaching strategies; we can stage more effective role-playing situations for helping students learn about roles.

We are also beginning to see certain cognitive and linguistic differences between speaking and writing. In other words, we know more about what's involved. For example, we know that learning to write is more than learning to put a sequence of words or even sentences on paper. There are certain cognitive demands. Writing requires different kinds of contextualization strategies because you can't rely on intonation.

So we're getting a new insight into the cognitive demands that a child faces in the process of learning to write. We may then be able to improve our strategies for teaching literacy. That's still ahead, though; a lot of research remains to be done. Carl probably knows more about that than I do.

Carl Frederiksen: I think there are two main reasons why the study of social or linguistic interaction is absolutely crucial to education. One is in order to describe more precisely what is happening in the classroom, as John Gumperz showed this afternoon. The other reason is to describe what is involved in becoming literate. Both of these purposes are as profound to education as anything I can conceivably think of; we could expound on just those two topics all evening.

Ambrose Clegg: I'd like to raise a methodological question and then, from there, a broader theoretical question. I realize that ethnography and the application of anthropology to education is relatively young, but one of the important claims is that ethnography tends to *generate* hypotheses rather than seeking to confirm them. But I wonder if many of the studies that you've talked about have gone that next step and have sought to verify those hypotheses that have been generated? And have they been verified under the experimental conditions that are often talked about in the literature?

John Gumperz: That's a good question!

Tom Popkewitz: I'll respond that there are some strands of sociology and anthropology that talk about the use of ethnography as a way of generating hypotheses. There are others that talk about it as an interpretive mode, which is talking about a different notion of science. This last group is not interested in generating hypotheses but in unraveling the texts of social living.

Someone raised earlier the question of how do you deal with reliability. Well, you can't. The event happened, and if you can understand it and give it some kind of logical coherence through the creation of appropriate metaphors (because that's what you're working with), then you've done your science. So I think we need to be aware of these two different notions of science. I know that I'm interested in the so-called hermeneutic or interpretive mode. I guess you would each have to respond in terms of your own work.

John Gumperz: I'm interested in exactly the same thing. It is essentially a hermeneutical operation, a cyclical process which constantly generates new hypotheses. That's really what linguistic field work is, as an alternative to conventional social science methods. But you can make certain predictions, which you can then test. If the predictions turn out to be true, well, you've done some kind of testing, though it's not necessarily statistical confirmation.

Ambrose Clegg: Well, I agree, but one of the claims often made in the literature for this approach is that the value of this method is generative rather than confirmatory. I'm asking whether we're at a point now where many of the conclusions from microcosmic analyses of classroom interaction can now be confirmed or rejected. And if confirmed, are we at a point where we begin to generate a larger systematic development of theory that will have applicability or implications for teacher education?

Maurice Sevigny: What do you mean by confirmation? Do you mean putting it into an experimental design?

Ambrose Clegg: Yes, precisely. That's the claim that's often made for this mode of research—that it will generate hypotheses that can later be tested experimentally.

Carl Frederiksen: At the risk of standing up for experimental design, and speaking as a psychologist who has done experiments in the past and will probably do experiments in the future, I think that this really deserves some serious thought. First of all, experiments are not the only way to acquire knowledge about a phenomenon, and naturalistic observation is not the only way to do it. Our general goal is to arrive at an understanding of the phenomenon of social interaction or of literacy development, for example. This is a problem that I've been wrestling with, and so have some of my colleagues.

All of those I work with believe that the issue is not so much one of an experiment vs. observation, but one of *degrees* of control or knowledge about the situation that you're studying. The issue isn't whether or not you actually controlled or manipulated it (because by that definition astronomy wouldn't be a science). The issue is how much you know in advance or are able to decipher about the structure of the situation. So I think there are various ways, as John described this afternoon, that you can inject some degree of control into the situation.

I think we need an interplay between naturalistic observation and experimentation. This hasn't taken place in the past because the experimental psychologists who did one kind of thing weren't interested in the other and the people who did the naturalistic observation weren't interested in doing experiments. I can't think of any better objective of a graduate training program than to produce people who can participate in such professional interplay.

John Gumperz: I would agree with that. We need the interplay, but we also need to be more informed about the *constraints* on experimental verification. There's also the argument that things can be true without being particularly useful for education.

One advantage of some of the insights that are gained through ethnography is that they can be used directly. By teaching a teacher to be an ethnographer, you give the teacher more control at that level. I tend to agree with Carl; I think we're just broadening the scope of research by freeing it from some of these constraints.

Carl Frederiksen: I would go one step further and say that experimental research should be derivative. This sounds incredible to some of my experimental colleagues, but really, the way to guarantee that experimental research will be relevant to education is to insist that the experiments be grounded in tasks that are representative of those that actually occur in educational settings. Now that is a heavy constraint and that constraint in and of itself would have a big effect. I don't argue that you shouldn't do other laboratory research, but it is overwhelmingly the case that experimental research is unrelated to the natural conditions under which learning takes place.

Louise Cherry Wilkinson: If we look at a field like referential communication research, we find tasks that are very strange in terms of any kind of use of referential language that I've ever seen in the classroom. It doesn't have to be that way; we could certainly study the functional aspect of speech in terms of tasks that are really part of the classroom. In that case we'd be dealing with phenomena that have greater generalizability or are more ecologically valid. I don't think that the experimental design necessarily restricts us to studying things that are very unusual even though that's become the practice.

Carl Frederiksen: Experimental designs can even be longitudinal or training studies. It's just that we have this restricted idea of what an experiment is or what measurement is.

Arch Phillips: It has to do with the length of the graph, Carl!

Ambrose Clegg: And how we've been structured to perceive this environment or the orthodoxy that it carries. But, to return to John's comments, I'm not sure that I want to agree entirely. I think it's important to recognize that the ethnomethodological approach is a very useful methodology. It has feedback and can be instructive in some ways. But it seems also that if it's going to be productive for people in education, somewhere along the line we ought to be able to generate more than just methodological concerns and some insights in terms of an approach or an attitude about teaching or training for teaching. Maybe you're saying it's primarily methodological.

John Gumperz: I don't think I'm saying that it is primarily methodological. It does involve attitudes about teaching. One popular attitude is that teaching is largely a craft, and that teacher training programs have to describe that craft. I'm not sure it's as much of a craft.

But just to change the subject slightly, to get back to Olga's question, I am concerned about comparability. One of the problems with some of the ethnographic work on comparing, for example, classroom environment and home environment is that these environments may not be directly comparable. I think that's what Olga's question implied. There are many things that happen in the home that are not educational in nature, so how do we focus on comparable situations?

Carl Frederiksen: What do you mean by *comparable?*

John Gumperz: Exactly, that the point. So how do we get comparability? I think we can take some kind of notion like activity or situation and define, perhaps in semantic terms, what that situation involves. For example, a teaching situation involves elements of informing, testing, and controlling. With such a definition, we can look for situations both in the home and in the school that have evidence of these elements. We would then have a theoretically sound basis for comparing situations more informatively, rather than grossly comparing home and classroom. So we are looking at some kind of experimental control.

Normand Bernier: Where does the culture of the school come in, in this kind of analysis? Isn't there a culture of the school as an institution that would define in many ways some of the prescribed behavior in that kind of interaction? You're getting at the perceptions of the individual which you can study through their behavior, but there are ways of studying an institution which could help one understand perceptions as well. Don't you come from this point as well, or shouldn't you?

John Gumperz: The culture of the school—I don't know how to interpret that term.

Normand Bernier: I'm not sure I know either!

Tom Popkewitz: I can give a concrete example of a study of symbolic interaction. Nell Ketty did a study of the different forms of interaction between teachers and students in three forms of a high school, the A, B, and C forms. She found that teachers interacted with the students very differently. The C student was thought stupid and was therefore treated as stupid. The A student was thought bright, but *bright* meant acquiescent to the teacher's definition of what knowledge is. So that if you accepted the teacher's answers without question, and the definitions of knowledge (in this case they were studying sociology), then you were the A student. The C students were not expected to have the right answers, the teacher disregarded them.

Now, you can interpret that in terms of *the culture of the school;* that is, there were certain definitions of what students should be doing and shouldn't be doing that resided in the context of that high school. We can also go to other literature to support that.

John Gumperz: That's like *Pygmalion in the Classroom.*

Tom Popkewitz: In a way, there's also the hidden curriculum. In part, it gives attention to how social conflict is treated in school contexts. The argument concerns whether children learn dispositions to social affairs which are concerned with consensus (and social passivity) or with conflict. These dispositions are related to a more general "climate of opinion" of the times. Because the dispositions underlie the social events of schooling and other institutions in society, they are psychologically compelling. There are a whole range of things, ideas, and ideologies embedded in the context of school that cannot be understood without reference to larger contexts.

Carl Frederiksen: How do you demonstrate something like that?

Tom Popkewitz: Well, I just gave you two research projects that did.

Carl Frederiksen: Yes, but how did they actually *demonstrate* it?

Tom Popkewitz: Nell Ketty went into a school and spent time in it. The questions were different from the questions here, and I think that needs understanding. That is, there are perspectives that people deal with as they interpret the world. Their perspective is the one of sociology of knowledge, so the questions are different and the findings are going to be different. They are interested in the culture of the school and how it influences definitions of reality, and so that's, in a sense, what they find. It's almost tautological, but most research is.

Maurice Sevigny: Well, you're talking about something that's already been learned— about a situation in which people have already learned culture. Now take the same instance with the first-grader who doesn't know the school culture. How can you deal with that issue when it's something yet to be learned?

Tom Popkewitz: We had a student who studied the socialization of kindergarten children. She wanted to understand how meaning is assigned to various objects in the classroom. She found that *work* was only what the teacher said you do. It it was an object of work, the child could touch it; if it wasn't an object of work, he could touch it only at recess. It had nothing to do with the quality of what they were doing, nothing to do with curriculum; it was the teacher's definition that mattered.

Arch Phillips: The teacher's assumptions about learning, whether or not they are examined, are always a key to the way the curriculum is actualized.

John Gumperz: One problem with such studies is that teachers always come out as enforcing their norms on others but, in a way, I think education really means forcing your norms on others. We want children to become literate. There are substantive matters to be learned but we need empirical studies of the effect of the evaluation process in general, not only of teaching, but of examination systems. What do examinations test? Do they test conformity to norms or do they test knowledge of substantive things?

In the elementary school, before we can answer this, we have to find out what's involved cognitively in certain kinds of tasks. This is why I seem to stress methodology—we need to refine concepts much, much more than we have in order to be able to distinguish these things. Some kind of control, for example, is necessary, but how do we distinguish between various kinds of control and their effects?

I know there are studies of the kind you mention but they are somewhat difficult to interpret because you don't know what the evaluations are based on in many of these ethnographic studies. Ethnography needs to be made accountable. Analyzing videotapes, including nonverbal behavior, is really a way of making these studies accountable and then really refining concepts. That makes it possible to verify or falsify certain kinds of propositions in replicable ways.

Normand Bernier: It seems to me that the context of the formality and the evaluation of examination that's built into the concept of learning in a school would automatically alter the nature of the interaction. If a parent and a child were in a learning situation, that would be different. It seems to me the interaction would reflect the different characteristics of institutions, would it not?

Maurice Sevigny: Yes, but what's important is not so much knowing about these facts but learning how the participants learn to deal with these facts.

Normand Bernier: Well, then wouldn't that have to be comparative? Wouldn't you then have to say, "Let's take a look at that interaction in this formal school setting and in this other setting and see what the difference is?" Wouldn't it have to be dealt with comparatively in order to gain the kind of knowledge that would have some value for looking at learning?

John Gumperz: This is how school ethnography got started, by comparing home interaction and school interaction. In home interaction evaluation builds on shared knowledge whereas in school interaction you can't assume shared knowledge. Although they build on shared knowledge, school personnel often assume shared knowledge that doesn't exist. In other words, everyone assumes that certain norms exist and these norms are the ones in terms of which behavior is evaluated; but it turns out that some people know what those norms are and operate in terms of them and others don't. That's one of the problems. We're still very much at the beginning of even being able to formulate all these questions.

Normand Bernier: I guess there is still a sense of its being ahistorical—in the sense of suddenly looking at a videotape and making a lot of studies on that analysis, then there is a historical reality for the institution as well as for the individuals coming to it.

John Gumperz: I think that just about anybody who does these studies would insist that a single videotape or a single set of videotapes of any one setting is never enough. That's only a starting point. You compare a variety of situations, as Carl Frederiksen suggested; you have a number of different kinds of settings in the home and in the school and you also study not only the text iself but the way the text is evaluated by various kinds of people.

Carl Auria: Would you pursue that—you say "evaluated by various kinds of people." What kinds?

John Gumperz: By children, by teachers, by judges of different backgrounds, by people with different kinds of social status.

Carl Auria: Now what kind of correlation (and that's a bad word to use perhaps in this context) do you find among the observers? For example, do teachers, children, and outside observers observe the situation equivalently or are there differences?

John Gumperz: If you are interested in process, then you are not disturbed if you find a difference. You find out what perceptions that difference is built on and you learn from the difference. Whereas, if you're looking at any kind of statistical evaluation, then differences are troublesome because they may invalidate your statistics.

Carl Auria: I'm not proposing looking at it in terms of level of significance but the ability to predict does imply some stability of perception. We recognize that the canons of reliability may not apply to ethnography in a typical way but you are assuming that personality perceptions are relatively stable over at least a short period of time.

John Gumperz: If, for example, you hypothesize that such-and-such a strategy is ethnically specific, you then have to test that hypothesis statistically. I predict that people of such-and-such a background will interpret this in a certain way and if they don't, I have to be able to explain on the basis of the theory why they don't or stand ready to revise the theory.

Carl Auria: So it is experimental.

John Gumperz: It is experimental in that sense, yes.

Maurice Sevigny: Because it's an experimental question, but some of the questions that ethnographers are asking are not experimental questions.

Ambrose Clegg: As Tom pointed out earlier, there is an important role for description and explanatory work and conceptualization and that's a whole respectable tradition in the field of ethnomethodology. I think we sometimes tend to ignore that notion of conceputalizing and finding reasoned explanation for things, supported by interpretable data.

Maurice Sevigny: I think we should take your original question further and ask whether there are ways we can make ethnographic data generalizable, besides experimentation, because that's not the only way to do it. Do you have an answer?

Carl Frederiksen: I can't say that we have the answer but I can say that we're not ethnographers. We're trying to study samples of children's conversations under natural situations and we're trying painstakingly to set up some sort of coding systems and methods of interpreting those coding systems. We separate coding from interpretation. We insist that our coding be replicable in the sense that we get good interscorer agreement. Now there's a lot of work involved in doing that and it's pedestrian compared to some of the things you get into in interpretation but I think it has to be done. That points out the problem in saying that kind of research either has to be ethnographic or it has to be experimental. There are all kinds of degrees between the two that have to be considered. They're all legitimate modes of research and they'll all contribute to a given research theme.

Ambrose Clegg: There's another aspect, though, that really bothers me and I haven't heard it explained very well—maybe I have missed it. You can get awfully involved in coding systems (and goodness knows, I've Flandered along a lot) but the problem with a lot of that is that it's been translated into very practical kinds of things and all sorts of implications have been drawn from it. We've been able to train a teacher to "Flander" a videotape in about four hours and get a high degree of reliability.

Tom Popkewitz: And lousy teaching!

Ambrose Clegg: Right! What's not said, though, is the body of research out of which Flanders developed his work. And I guess I am bothered when I hear about this coding system and that coding system and don't hear the antecedent which says "The coding system flows from small-group research" or whatever it is, and the data is fed back or expanded to develop or elaborate the theoretical constructs from which it came.

Carl Frederiksen: In a word of self-defense, I hope we're not guilty of that one. We're doing our damnedest to justify on theoretical grounds anything that we do. You're absolutely right—any kind of coding system that tries to buy reliability out of a lot of ————; I'd rather have unreliability and a certain amount of validity. You have to relieve yourself of all of these kinds of restraints, at least at the outset, or you don't know how to go about trying to do the next stage.

There's one other issue that underlies some of this earlier discussion and I'd like to return to it. We were talking about a teacher's standards or assumptions about what is right or what the curriculum should be. I thought the point that John made was that it is not inappropriate that there be standards, that education involves objectives and standards, so it really becomes more of a question of what those standards should be.

Tom Popkewitz: That's right.

Carl Frederiksen: And then how they get realized in terms of what an individual teacher does. That's another area toward which this whole research effort should be directed; for example, literacy objectives. I've been working with a group of teachers and reading specialists in Montgomery County, Maryland, developing new language arts objectives. They were starting with some Bloom-type taxonomies that were just outrageous, and there were some ways that you could apply even what we know right now to improve upon them. It seems to me that that's an important thing right there—how you define your standards.

Tom Popkewitz: That's a very good example. When you accept Bloom's taxonomy as a way of talking about curriculum, you are also accepting a whole range of assumptions about what school is about, what children are about, what knowledge is about. So you can't just talk about the dialogue of the people without understanding the notion of objectives. And that's where I think the notion of history goes beyond what you were saying. That is, the notion doesn't reside only in that classroom.

There's sort of an objective reality to those schools that seems to permeate different places. And so you need to understand, for example, that it's Bloom's taxonomy they're talking about because that clues you into a whole intellectual range of thought.

Normand Bernier: Or that it's compulsory or that there's a principal out there, and counselors, and people flunk. That's important to know, I would imagine.

John Gumperz: Exactly. This is what I mean by studying the evaluation process as such and seeing what it focuses on—how it leads certain people to flunk and not others.

Normand Bernier: But flunking itself is an important social reality of that institution and it is assumed...

John Gumperz: That some people must flunk and others will not.

Normand Bernier: And that influences the interaction.

John Gumperz: That's true.

Olga Garnica: There's a bigger structure, as I think you were trying to say, that really very much influences the school situation. The educational process, to take over your term, begins at birth, but at some point somebody steps in and says this child has to be part of this objective reality of chalkboard and desks and the like. Of course, the state does that; if you want to educate your own child, you're going to have trouble doing that because you are required to have certain kinds of...

Tom Popkewitz: Fire escapes.

Olga Garnica: Yes! It's next to impossible to do that any more in any of the states. There's some larger body that says there is going to be another kind of environment in which this educational process goes on *at this point.* For example, age 4 years, 9 months is, I believe, the minimal age for entrance to public schooling in this state.

One thing that hasn't been brought out is the expressive aspect of language rather than the referential aspect of language that goes on at the same time in the educational process at home. It seems that there hasn't been much mention of this expressive function of language in terms of an emotional or evaluative sense that permeates the school situation. The teacher has feelings about each of the students and evaluates and reacts to them in a personal way, not just in a way of evaluating their work, but also evaluating them as individuals. And maybe that is related to ethnic group.

John Gumperz: The actual evaluation process is always a combination of these personal judgments and the actual work, and some of us are trying to study empirically how these thing relate. For example, another fact about classrooms is that if, for example, we take 10 or 20 people in a seminar, we will always favor some over others. You can't constantly distribute equal attention over the whole group. If you introduce race or social class or any kind of cultural differences as a factor you bias this favoring process. That's partly a matter of personal evaluation, but there are certain ecological facts that skew these personal weightings. If we all had exactly the same background, this favoring process would be random but if you introduce race or cultural differences, you are skewing the process in some way. Once we know what's involved in evaluation and what evaluation is based on, we can then study these things empirically.

Olga Garnica: There's one variable that you can never erase and that is the sex of a child. I think maybe Louise could talk more than I can about that as a variable we could never eliminate no matter how homogeneous our classrooms become.

Louise Cherry Wilkinson: I have become impressed with the importance of the expectations that teachers form about students' competence. These expectations are related to the sex of the student. Most of these effects can be examine in the same ways John has outlined fcr studying ethnic differences.

Martha King: I'd like to follow up on Olga's comment in regard to expressive vs. referential langauge, because it probably has a ˎ reat deal to do with writing as well as speaking and generally reveals a great deal about the speakers—how they feel about themselves and how they construe the world. Through their expressive talk, people make public their very personal thoughts about events, ideas, and people. But expressive talk tends to be context-bound, making very heavy demands on the listener's knowledge of the speaker's world, which may explain why schools so often fail to support expressive language: an absence of shared contexts between pupils or between pupils and teacher.

Also, there's the matter of who decides *what* is to be talked about. In certain educational settings, children have little opportunity to initiate discourse.

I have read recently a study by Marcia Applebee (1977) which investigated the language used in classrooms that were classified as formal, informal, or mixed, in both conventional and open-plan classrooms (in northern England). By using tape recordings, she collected samples of different kinds and amounts of language from nine-year-olds, as they talked among themselves or to their teachers. She found that pupils initiated more talk, both with the teachers and their peers, in the informal environments; whereas, teachers tended to initiate the language in formal settings. If we're concerned about youngsters bring their own sense of the world to their learning tasks, then settings that allow children to initiate talk become important.

In this respect language research has something very special to offer to classroom teachers and to people who educate classroom teachers. Research that helps us to the see the *nature* of the world in which we live and work is exceedingly useful.

Louise Cherry Wilkinson: I'd like to follow up the point you mentioned. In studying a number of different contexts, we may find that things may be initiated more by students in one context and more by teachers in another. Walter Mischel has made a similar point in his discussion about individual differences in development; in unstructured situations these differences have a greater chance of emerging.

John Gumperz was talking this afternoon about the standard work in ethnography by Sinclair and Coulthard and the early work by Bellack, which addressed formal classroom lessons. Some of my own work and that of my colleagues at the Center for Applied Linguistics, as well as Mehan's and Cazden's work, also analyzes formal lessons. All of this work demonstrates that in a formal situation there are a number of formal strategies for initiation.

These initiations are necessary, I think, for certain kinds of learning, but we will never get a sense of other ways that things are learned in other contexts unless we move into those other contexts. There's an interesting paradox here: we might also miss an important part if we ignore the more formal contexts. Children may be initiating in formal contexts but not initiating in informal contexts where teachers are not allocating turns or setting things up. I believe we need to investigate patterns of initiation, for example, in both informal and formal contexts to fully understand the instructional process.

John Gumperz: It's also possible to take the hypotheses we have formed about the formal or informal situation and test them out pragmatically. In the situation I described this afternoon, where a child in a reading group refused to read, an adult from the same ethnic group interpreted the behavior as meaning "I want you to coax me." It would certainly be possible to test this hypothesis the next time such an incident occurred, by actually coaxing the child. We have the data to look at this, and I would predict that this interpretation would hold up. In fact, in these cases I am so sure we would find this that I am not even looking! (That's a linguist's sense of what's true.) We don't at this time have formal verification of this particular hypothesis but I think it can be found.

Arch Phillips: But there are so many variations in all of that, even within a Black or white or whatever group we happen to be talking about.

John Gumperz: That's right.

Arch Phillips: I guess that's always one of the confounding issues.

John Gumperz: That's why one has to look first for general principles, and generalizations have to be at the level that applies broadly between children and adults. That is, we are beginning to see from Cazden and Mehan's data and from some other data that children have different ways of contextualizing or formulating than do adults and we are beginning to see that children's speech is more context-bound. Now that's a beginning of a generalization; it has to be clarified a great deal. Once we do that, then we can use this kind of generalization to explain a whole number of specific phenomena.

Olga Garnica: What John is talking about is building what Dell Hymes has labeled as *human linguistics.* I would like to warn all of you who are going to run out to your nearest linguist that John Gumperz and Dell Hymes and a few people in this country are the people who are interested in building human linguistics, and the linguist that you happen to catch may not be so interested.

John Gumperz: The number is growing.

Olga Garnica: The number is growing slowly, but that's the kind of linguistics that needs to be developed, not the kind that currently exists.

I'd like to pick up on what Martha said about the expressive part of language, and relate a story that was told to me. The woman who told the story asked, "What do you think of this as a linguist?" A friend of hers, a middle-aged woman, had spent the war in a concentration camp in Germany. All of her family had been in concentration camps and none, except her, had survived. Later, she went back to college, and in her English 101 course the teaching assistant said, "Write a thousand-word theme on something you feel strongly about." So for the first time in this woman's history, she wrote about her experiences in the concentration camp, something she had not really opened up to many people about.

What she got back a week later was a corrected, red-penciled theme with an F on it, saying, "There are so many misspellings and *x* many dangling participles." There was no reaction to the other aspect she was obviously trying to express.

I didn't know what to say as a linguist; I thought maybe someone who was an educator could make some sane reaction to that.

Normand Bernier: That's called the culture of the school!

Olga Garnica: But there seemed to be something missing, some aspect that was not considered, but that could have specified what the T.A.'s role should be in this context. I imagine there are many children who get F papers back in grade schools after they have done their darnest to express some part of themselves.

Martha King: Undoubtedly, and because many very well-intentioned teachers are more concerned with the language than the message. We recognize that expressive oral language and sustained speech are important to writing, but in practice, we fall short in knowing how to make such things possible in the classroom. It isn't easy for teachers to work with children to create a context in which they can initiate and carry on sustained talk. The teacher must know and care for the children; but beyond that, the teacher must have the communicative skills necessary to keep the conversation going sometimes. Joan Tough's work in England, though criticized by some, is helpful in this respect.

John Gumperz: One of the problems with expressive language is really evaluating what's expressive in the first place. Expressive language is also the kind of language that creates havoc in the classroom sometimes, and teachers get worried about that. So how do you distinguish between the kind of expressiveness that's needed for creativity and the kind of expressiveness that tends to destroy the teaching process? In fact, there is a need for formulating some basic research strategies and ethnographic procedures for doing that.

Now one of the things that happens in the kind of situations that I've been studying recently—I haven't really been doing too much classroom observation recently; I've been trying to use some of the contextualization approaches for the study of interethnic communications among adults—and what I find is that in interethnic situations, participants cannot recognize—cannot distinguish between what's expressive and what isn't expressive; they can't distinguish between normal ways of indicating conversational involvement vs. lack of involvement and the ways of indicating excitement, extreme excitement. That is, they cannot distinguish degrees of expressiveness. The judgment of degrees of expressiveness is very culture-bound and one of the things we have to learn is how do we look at this in replicable ways and how do we teach ourselves to judge expressive behavior in the way that the people who are doing it judge it.

Richard Prawat: We seem to assume that there is such a data-rich environment out there that if we could get teachers to attend to more of that meaning, they would be better teachers. It seems to me that the teacher's problems is to *filter* out a lot of what's going on—they're dealing with a chaotic group environment; they've got to be selective.

Martha King: Fostering sustained coherent speech is critical to some learning in the classroom, yet oportunities to advance it are often overlooked or deliberately ruled out. I'm thinking particularly of storytelling and drama. We don't value these in our primary school today, even in many kindergartens and first grades. We have put in the workbooks instead. But we need to help teachers to see talk as a stream of discourse and to appreciate the logic of children's contributions. Teachers become excited when they discover the sense of story that children seem to have; but regrettably, many teachers haven't known how to interpret that language, whether oral or written.

Carl Frederiksen: Teachers can't be faulted, because they have had nothing else. In our discussion, we've been talking a lot about studying language as it occurs in different situations, with the emphasis on how the situation determines aspects of language use. That's terribly important, but there's also the problem of literacy and the ability to produce coherent and connected discourse, and our need to be able to specify what makes language coherent in that the utterances are related to one another.

I think that one can look at conversations as discourse and analyze them at the level of proposition or context. We can look at the relationship between the content of what a child says and the content of what was said in another utterance or in another turn.

We're trying to code the inferential relations that hold between utterances, to see what kind of inferences a child made in responding to what someone else said on a previous turn. If there was a request and the child responds to that request, you can show that the inference can be accounted for on the basis of relationship between these adjacent utterances. On the other hand, you might find that what a child says can also be related to what the same child said many turns before, a continuation of a theme. You can see evidence for two kinds of control: one is a reaction to what is said, to the immediate conversational frame; the other is an attempt to maintain a coherent theme. I'm talking about the structure of what a child is saying and I'm saying this is just as appropriate for asking how a child processes the visual world or other aspects of his experience. What we're really talking about is an ability to produce structured, coherent interpretations of language and other kinds of information.

Martha King: But when one is trying to look at this from the point of view of somebody in education and not a linguist, the problem is compounded. After searching through all of the work to see which of the systems of analysis one should use, one may decide to make his/her own.

John Gumperz: I think one of the things the linguists here are saying is that we have to work with you to learn how to do our linguistics more significantly and to be able to account for these things. I think that all of you are telling us as linguists that there are certain aspects of the message, especially the intersentential relations, that linguists haven't really looked at. The trouble is that, just as in experimental design, people have looked at certain kinds of methods; in talking about language, I think that people have looked at certain models of language that were not designed to account for the kinds of concerns that you have at all. So one has to learn to do linguistics differently at the discourse level and actually, that's, in part, why some of us linguists are in this business—because we want to learn to do linguistics better by applying our work to the real problems of education.

Carl Frederiksen: That's not strictly a linguistic problem; rhetoricians and psychologists have also had to deal with the problems of choosing models and methods that are relevant to problems in the real world.

Richard Prawat: Will these insights, when they are fed back to people, make their life simpler in some sense or more complex?

Martha King: Very much more complex.

Richard Prawat: That's a serious question. Are we coming back to teachers and saying, "Here are forty-seven more things you have to do, in addition to collecting lunch money and all these other tasks." That's what I'm worried about.

Martha King: It does help people to see how absolutely irrelevant much of what is happening in schools is.

Richard Prawat: Well, then, it could simplify the teacher's role by highlighting the really important things to attend to.

Tom Popkewitz: I know it's nearly time for us to end this part of the discussion and I wonder what you saw as the major issues of this panel.

Carl Frederiksen: I think there was a question of levels of analysis.... I mean there were those who were focusing on social interaction itself as a kind of social event. There were those who were interested in looking at the language that's used, and then there were those who were interested in looking at the consequences for the child of developing a particular kind of language use.

Tom Popkewitz: I guess the thing that suggests to me the vitality of the discussion is that there was a constant interchange about some methodological, some conceptual, some epistemological questions. The problem of science in education is that it's often just technology, and that the interrelationship between the way you think about a problem and the way you act on that problem sometimes gets lost. It seems to me that was constant throughout the discussion—we had to move at different levels to understand what the problem was or at least to deal with it. It also seems to me that it's this kind of conflict, at least in the history of science, that gives it its vitality and imagination and creativity. It would have been suspect to me to sit at this table and have everybody saying, "Yes, that's how we should do it."

13
Beyond Instructional Context Identification— Some Thoughts for Extending the Analysis of Deliberate Education

Normand R. Bernier
Kent State University

INTRODUCTION: THE RESEARCH FOCUS

Effective theorizing about education necessitates that knowledge and modes of inquiry be drawn from various academic disciplines. Indeed, inquiry in such fields as psychology and sociology has dominated research in education. Unfortunately, these academic disciplines with their unique structures, broad perspectives, and intellectual goals, often are identified as the foundations of education. This conception of the foundations of education is unfortunate for it is incorrect and distorts research in the field. The foundation of education is to be found in the *practice of education*. The teaching-learning process, wherever it occurs, is the basis and the substructure which should define our inquiry as educators. Unfortunately, the history of educational development reveals that research into educational theories drawn from the academic disciplines, and the studies of educational practice often do not coincide.

Educational ethnography arrives on the scene at a most opportune time, for it provides a perspective and a mode of inquiry which can function to establish the educational context as the focal point of discourse in education. Although the relating of grand educational theories to microanalysis of educational discourse may be a distant hope, it is only through such a linkage that educators will begin to unravel the Gordian knot we label *the educational process*. Until such a goal is achieved, the central focus of educational research should be precisely what this volume attempts to explore—the educational context. Such a focus provides a multitude of avenues of approach and encourages the cross-disciplinary study of the teaching-learning process.

The purpose of this essay is to identify some factors that future face-to-face interaction research on the process labeled *teaching-learning* might consider in order to move toward a more holistic view of the educational context. The approach suggested here is based on uncovering the transactional quality of the teaching-learning process. The transaction is viewed as incorporating both the inner processes of individuals in face-to-face interaction and their external activities. Both the inner processes and external activities reflect predispositions which individuals have brought to the face-to-face interaction. I refer to the identification of these predispositions or belief systems as *ideological mapping*.

Ideological systems are studied generally as characteristics which societies or communities exhibit and which can be analyzed as social and historical developments; the approach suggested in this article calls for focusing upon the face-to-face interaction which we label *teaching-learning*. Individuals are carriers of ideological systems which reflect their socialization within ideological groups. Through the observation of the sign systems which are exhibited during face-to-face interaction, one can obtain clues to the ideological systems which each of the participants utilizes to define "his/her reality." When such clues are codified according to an ideological matrix, and combined with the information given by the participants concerning their perceptions, meanings, and intentions, ideological maps can be developed.

Since individuals involved in human transactions carry with them predeveloped systems of meanings which may effect new meanings created in new contexts, it is imperative that these systems be analyzed as part of the transaction. Since the teaching-learning transaction exists in order to bring about some alteration in the perceptual world of the participants, it behooves researchers to analyze the nature of the dynamic transactional process in such a way that shifts in meaning, perceptions, and intentions can be detected and analyzed.

The foundations of this exploration should be clarified at the onset. Unlike some other contributions to this book, this anlaysis does not emerge from a rigorous naturalistic study of discourse nor from a detailed critique of literature in ethnography. Rather, it results from a sometimes painful attempt to reexamine and reconceptualize some of the theoretical constructs which have dominated pedagogical research. It also rests upon the intellectual conviction that the individual-environment are one. Dewey and Bentley (1960) stressed this fundamental ontological reality when they affirmed:

> The organism, of course, seems in everyday life and language to stand out strongly apart from the transactions in which it is engaged. This is a superficial observation. One reason for it is that the organism is engaged in so many transactions. The higher the organism is on the evolutionary scale, the more complicated are the transactions in which it is involved (p. 138).

Context, therefore, when referring to social realities identifies individuals-in-relationship. To emphasize this point, the term *transaction* will be utilized throughout this chapter to refer to the process called face-to-face interaction, for it conveys more precisely the point that I will argue: that the relationship among individuals in instructional contexts extends into their symbolic universes and their ideological maps. These internalized social constructions of reality form mind engrams which individuals bring to a social situation. These mind structures form a vital aspect of the human network which is created in face-to-face transactions.

IDEOLOGICAL MAPS: THEIR COMPOSITION

Individuals behave according to the manner in which they perceive reality. Perceptual frames of reference emerge from a complex mixture of factors and influences but central to the process of perceptual orientation are the ideological maps which individuals have internalized. These belief systems provide a foundation for the selection and sorting processes involved in perceiving, categorizing, excluding, judging, inferring, defining, and intending. In *Beyond Beliefs: Ideological Foundations of American Education*, Williams and I (1973) described ideologies as:

> an integrated pattern of ideas, system of beliefs, or a "group consciousness" which characterizes a social group. Such a pattern or system may include doctrines, ideals, slogans, symbols, and directions for social and political action. Ideologies also include objectives, demands, judgments, norms, and justifications, and in this sense they are value-impregnated systems of thought which may be perceived as sacred (p. 27).

Once these socially learned complex systems are internalized, they become referents for behavior. Such an affirmation does not deny spontaneity or creativity but rather asserts that spontaneity and creativity occur within a person's ideological frame of reference. Briefly states, human beings involved in transactions may be observed to be activating complex belief systems internalized in early childhood and developed throughout their lifetime.

Ideologies establish systematic ways of dealing with individuals, events, and settings by providing individuals with expectations and anticipated outcomes for certain behaviors. Although ideologies are tied to prior social learning, people may alter them according to their everyday experiences. The developmental nature of the construction of reality, of course, prevents the total reformulation of perspective. Berger and Luckman (1967) emphasized this important quality of human awareness when they wrote:

> I apprehend the reality of everyday life as an ordered reality. Its phenomena are prearranged in patterns that seem to be independent of my apprehension of them and that impose themselves upon the latter. The reality of everyday life appears already objectified, that is, constituted by an order of objects that have been designated *as* objects before my appearance on the scene (pp. 21–22).

Personal ideological systems, that is, belief systems reflecting perceived reality, are continuously reformulated and redesigned by everyday experiences. Since reformulation sometimes includes internalizing mutually exclusive beliefs camouflaged by various forms of self-deception, ideologies cannot be compared to neat philosophical constructs which can be logically dissected. Syncretism characterizes the process of ideological formation. The content of ideologies which have been internalized by an individual is situated throughout the entire range of the unconscious-conscious continuum of the human psyche. Since ideological maps define reality, they serve people as security blankets. Ideological maps assist individuals as they approach everyday life by offering them a point of view, a platform for analysis, a foundation for evaluation and judgment, and a rationale for behavior. When ideological maps are weak, people suffer the terror of anomie.

Ideological maps, as previously emphasized, are rooted to the past. An individual does not relate merely to his/her immediate physical or social environment, this "thinking reed" who can both remember and plan ahead inhabits a symbolic universe of meanings which are embedded in the history of his/her social group and which reflect his/her unique biography.

Ideological maps contain referents for conscious choice as well as expectations about other individuals' referents. Indeed, within our ideological maps we include typifications not only about other persons, but also about events and places. These typifications often provide us with a ready-made response to our environment. Herbert Blumer (1972) stressed the importance of symbols and meanings in human transactions:

> ... human beings interpret or "define" each other's actions instead of merely reacting to each other's actions. Their "response" is not made directly to the actions of one another but instead is based on the meaning which they attach to such actions. Thus, human interaction is mediated by the use of symbols, by interpretation, or by ascertaining the meaning of one another's actions (p. 238).

It is precisely during human transactions, especially face-to-face transactions, when meanings, assumptions, and typifications can be applied, modified, confirmed, and consequently, observed and analyzed. Fortunately, communication provides an access point to unearthing the meanings, assumptions, and typifications which are integral to ideological maps. Berger and Luckmann (1967) say:

> Human expressivity is capable of objectivation, that is, it manifests itself in products of human activity that are available both to their producers and to other men as elements of a common world. Such objectivations serve as more or less enduring indices of the subjective processes of their producers...These indices are continuously available in the face-to-face situation, which is precisely why it affords me the optimal situation for gaining access to another's subjectivity (p. 34).

The analysis of typifications about teachers and schooling, for example, which are expressed in face-to-face transactions during teaching-learning scenes provides a useful access to the subjective world of both teacher and learner. Study of this ideological perspective is of special importance to researchers concerned with optimizing the teaching-learning process.

The term *ideology* should be viewed as metaphor serving to identify that complex systematic perspective which each human carries. Such a perspective could be labled a *root metaphor,* a layman's paradigm, a cognitive structure or a symbol system. The term *ideology* was selected because it more directly asserts the transactional quality of the development of individual belief systems.

THE EDUCATIONAL CONTEXT—A TRANSACTIONAL PROCESS

The use of ideological systems to view individuals involved in transactional activities such as teaching-learning offers a foundation for analysis which when combined with other approaches may help to broaden our field of vision. The perceptual lenses and conceptual toys we utilize to study ourselves cannot be limited to just a few modes of observing or constructing reality. Efforts to bridge the gap which exists between the study of the histories of settings and the biographical development of individuals with the direct observation of face-to-face transactions are urgently needed. Ethnographers cannot luxuriate in the myth that the subjects they observe are amnesiacs, solely defined by present transactions. Thus, context as viewed from this approach is a sociopsychological reality embedded in ideological constructs. These constructs emerge from unique biographies of individuals, the histories of settings, and the activities of individuals within the settings. Transactions are dynamic processes which alter perspectives but which also are defined by preestablished orientations.

A study of contextualism implies focusing upon the transactional quality of the teaching-learning process in order to unravel ideological implications. Within such a scene, the participants serve as adjuvants rather than catalysts to one another. An adjuvant in a chemical process implies that the substance cooperates with the activities of another substance to produce results which neither substance can produce independently. Unlike a catalyst, which serves as a condition for a chemical process to occur, an adjuvant is itself an integral part of the process. Thus in utilizing the chemical metaphor in describing a teaching-learning scene, one is stressing that all participants willingly or unwillingly involved in a teaching-learning activity are in some degree transformed by the dynamic process. Unlike a catalyst, none of the participants can leave such a face-to-face transaction exactly the same as s/he was before. Inner processes have been involved. Norman K. Denzin (1977) observed this dimension when he wrote:

> The conversation has two sides: one spoken and one internalized in terms of thought. As conversationalists talk to one another, they also talk to themselves, and in this process each enters into the organization of the other's experience (p. 4).

It is important to emphasize that physical presence in a social setting need not imply participation or involvement in a transaction. Throughout this exploration, the teaching-learning scene implies that participants are, in fact, involved and that such participation extends further than mere ritualistic, habitual behavior characterized by psychic withdrawal. A transaction implies that individuals are not merely involved in mutual habituation but also experiencing the process of teaching-learning albeit in a unique way.

Ideologies as mapping systems which serve individuals with a perceptual gyroscope also function to detemrine language usage. Language is a social phenomenon and its uses, even in contemplation, must be related to social realities to be understood. Language usage, of course, is determined by a developmental process and although it is rooted to an ideological system it may or may not be tied to a self-aware language or speech community. When ideological systems are attached to a community of identification which possesses a unique speech character, their influence upon individuals are profoundly intensified. In pluralistic societies such as the United States, this form of speech community identification can intensify the problems confronted in teaching-learning scenes. Because signs in human discourse are attached to ideological and cultural systems—and often function as symbols of group affiliation—they often become attached to conceptions of self-identification and profoundly influence self-concept, motivation, sense of belonging, and capacity to participate meaningfully in teaching-learning scenes. Language communities have been observed to influence the teaching-learning process, but it should be emphasized that ideological speech communities also influence the nature of the teaching-learning process. In recent years, this latter issue was confronted as the hippies' speech community encountered the definitions of appropriate speech behavior within major social institutions, especially schools.

The phenomenological realities which give direction to the teaching-learning transaction and which are rooted in the subjective world of the participants must be analyzed as an integral part of the educational process. Although it is assumed that a meaningful analysis of the teaching-learning transaction must inevitably focus upon the social involvement of individuals in face-to-face transactions, it must be recognized that such a task is not as clear as is sometimes implied; indeed, such research is fraught with danger. Ethnographic research to this date has merely revealed the tip of the iceberg. Yet, how does one confront the nagging affirmation by Duncan in *Macbeth:* "There's no art to find the mind's construction in the face"? The proposed ideological rubric attempts to meet the challenge which Duncan's question reveals.

THE IDEOLOGICAL DEFINITION
OF EDUCATIONAL ROLES

Williams and I, in our analysis of the ideological foundations of American education, identified six major belief systems which give direction to education in the United States. In each case, a teacher model was suggested to illustrate the way in which these ideologies are activated in schools. The belief systems identified and their teacher models are: Scientism—behavior modifier; Romanticism—artist; Puritanism—moral exemplar; Progressivism—facilitator; Nationalism—patriot or ethnic exemplar; Educationism—professional. Our research focused upon the social and historical development of the aforesaid ideological systems, but our observations of teachers involved in the educational process alerted us to the sometimes uncanny consistency with which individuals behaved according to identified ideological systems. Behavioral expressions and language style served as important clues in discovering ideological assumptions. The definition of one's role, for example, relates to ideological assumptions and, in turn, influences the behavior of individuals within the role. It became readily apparent that a teacher who perceives himself or herself as a moral exemplar behaves in a way quite different from the educator who identifies as a facilitator. Similarly, they view appropriate student behavior in quite distinct ways.

Our analysis would have been significantly enriched had we combined our historical and social analysis with a detailed ethnographic study of the teaching-learning process in various settings involving individuals with differing ideological perspectives. The combination of such a macro approach to the analysis of ideology with comparative studies of educational scenes is promising. The reader may respond positively or negatively to one or more of the ideologies listed earlier, but the rubric utilized in the ideological analysis was based on the assumption that each ideology contained the potential for wisdom and ignorance, goodness and evil, and gentleness and harshness.

Ongoing study of ideological systems and educational practice reveals that even though individuals are not necessarily monistic ideologically, they tend to reflect certain fundamental assumptions about teaching and learning which can be traced to one of the aforementioned belief systems. Face-to-face transactions when viewed from such a perspective may reveal that effectiveness in a teaching-learning scene may be less rooted in the form which education takes than in the degree to which there is a complementarity of ideological orientation between and among teachers and learners.

In addition to potential contributions of ethnographic studies at the teacher-student level of analysis, future studies of ideological mapping can contribute to educational research and educational development at other levels. Since concepts such as validity and reliability are also based in ideological constructs, the judgment of effectiveness in teaching and the disagreement which it often generates reflects, in part, the ideological diversity within the educational community. The perceived role of the teacher is attached to belief systems about the function of education. Indeed, a major intent of schools of education is to cajole would-be teachers into an educationist attitude. Professional socialization implies the teaching of educationism. Within schools, however, a variety of ideological positions finds expression. Whether it is reflected in such current issues as the puritan back-to-basics movement or to the human relations programs of progressivists the ideological matrix is reflected in all school activities and throughout the social system.

Whereas ideologies influence the climate of the school, individual teachers in their classrooms will strongly influence the matrix of the teaching-learning transaction. Teachers often establish the ideological climate of the classroom, but how much it represents a meaningful reality to the learners may be a major determiner in predicting the weather in the classroom. This exploration does not intend to elaborate on each of the previously mentioned ideologies. Yet, the reader should be aware that ideologies carry with them expectations about behavior that may imply, for example, the well-documented process orientation of the progressivist teacher, or the laconic directness of puritan moral exemplar, the logical ordering of the learning system of behavior modifiers, or the spontaneous behavior of the romanticists.

It should be emphasized that deliberate education significantly alters the nature of perceiving learning. It imposes the considerations of the nature of *teaching* onto the learning process. The emphasis upon deliberate education—the teaching-learning transaction—rather than upon learning *per se,* creates some interesting questions and dilemmas which relate to the synergistic or dialectic relationship between and among varied ideological systems.

Learning and teaching follow the ideological orientations of the learners and teachers. Their socially developed phenomenological realities provide an orientation for growth and development. The cognitive structures, learning strategies, affective modes of expression, participation patterns, styles of processing information, and attachment of significance and relevance to certain knowledge emerge from an individual's subjective construction of reality. Other differences are significant as well. Postural-kinesics, proxemic shifts, voice tone, prosody, facial expression, participant structures, and ritualistic patterns also reflect ideological assumptions about human behavior.

THE IDEOLOGICAL DEFINITIONS OF SETTINGS

In addition to role models and behavioral styles which emerge from belief systems, individuals also carry as part of their psychic baggage definitions of settings which influence behavior within those settings. For example, visitors, except under unusual circumstances, are expected to whisper in St. Patrick's Cathedral but are encouraged to shout at sports events in Madison Square Garden. That environments influence behavior is obvious. The major concern of this article, however, is not the physical setting *per se* but rather the *perceived* environment, that is, the environment as ideologically and culturally defined. The educational scene rather than the educational setting is the focus of this exploration. The way individuals behave in educational settings will be directly influenced by the meanings they attribute to the environment as a setting for behavior. The nature of the setting as perceived in relationship to the educational task will significantly influence the nature of the communication patterns that are established. The term *school;* for example, is historically rooted; to say a place is a school is to make an ideological statement about purpose, expectations, and appropriate behaviors. *Schooling,* for example, invariably implies pedagogy rather than andragogy even when it is designed for an adult population. It implies sequentialism, formalism, institutionalism, evaluation, and specified codes of conduct. Indeed, the puritan antecedents in the history of schooling linger and although the unschooled may no longer be viewed as prime targets for Old Deluder Satan,[1] they are viewed as dropouts and targets for the new deluders—unemployment and crime.

Typifications about the educational setting labeled school is an important part of our psychic baggage. Consequently, these typifications influence

---

[1]*Old Deluder Satan* refers to a famous 1647 law which established a form of compulsory education in colonial America and from which district control of the American school system derives (Baum and Edwards, 1972).

speech systems, instructional styles, learning modes, and definitions of appropriate behavior.

A danger in focusing our research solely upon the nature of teaching-learning process within schools is that such a focus distorts our perspective. Learners experience a variety of concomitant teaching-learning scenes in a variety of settings in addition to schools throughout their lifetime. It becomes increasingly clear that the effectiveness of the teaching intended in any setting depends, in part, on the degree to which learners can negotiate the different strategies utilized in diverse settings. Indeed, a fundamental question which remains is to what degree does colinearity of ideological orienation between a teacher and a learner, and between concomitant teaching-learning scenes in various settings, influence communication effectiveness and learning capacity.

Deliberate education implies that a prescribed network of communication is to be established. The prescribed network of communication will reflect the ideological orientation of the individual(s) who dominate the teaching-learning transactions. The actual network of communication which characterizes the teaching-learning transaction, however, may differ significantly from the prescribed form. Unless the individuals involved in the transaction perceive through an ideological prism reflecting some degree of complementarity, the actual communication network will reveal dissonance. The breakdown of the teaching-learning transaction is inevitable unless the participants can bridge the differences among their ideological systems and unless they can arrive at some shared conception of the purpose and meaning of the educational process. Otherwise, what will be taught, or rather what will be learned, will reflect not rationally established goals or aims but rather accidental learnings. We cannot ignore the most romantic educators among us who argue that the only effective teaching is that which emerges from spontaneous authentic behavior, but we must recognize that when deliberate education is institutionally established it must be based on more than spontaneous behavior or serendipity. When behaviors contradict the ideological assumptions, disruptive events occur. Goffman's (1959) statement of such disruptive events applies readily to those classrooms where ideological dissonance occurs:

> ...we can assume that events may occur within the interaction which contradict, discredit or otherwise throw doubt upon the projection. When these disruptive events occur, the interaction itself may come to a confused and embarrassed halt (p. 12).

A variety of studies on intrainstiutitonal models of teaching-learning does exist, but what is urgently needed are studies based on a comparative analysis of the teaching-learning transaction as it occurs in different settings. Because of the inherent conceptual and behavioral limitations imposed upon schooling practices, debates about useful and appropriate forms of education usually revolve around a relatively narrow range of differences. The inherent limitations of such debates and research focuses become obvious when one compares these pedagogical issues to the teaching-learning transactions which occur in crisis centers, hospitals, recreational settings, and rock concerts. Indeed, the success of the music industry in challenging the basic ideological assumptions which dominate most schooling practices has created a cultural bifurcation that should not be ignored. The corrupting influence of ideological sedimentation around the concept "schooling" remains, and significant changes in the folkways of schooling do not appear to be forthcoming. The folkways of schooling need to be studied separately from the teaching-learning transaction in order to clarify their peculiarities and their relationship. The concept of "deliberate education" must be freed from its present definition which equates it with schooling. Observing children playing school should suffice as a warning to would-be researchers that perhaps the revitalization of research into teaching-learning may be achieved by focusing upon a comparative analysis of different educational settings and upon the complex educational configurations which incorporate all teaching-learning transactions.

The focus upon the educational configuration which includes, among others, the home, the youth community, the mass media, the church, should not be interpreted to mean that an ideal educational configuration exists when all parts are in a synergistic, mutually supportive relationship to one another. Indeed, a tragic consequence of ignoring educational configurations is the automatic reward given to those students in school whose life space is characterized by a narrow parallelism which just happens to coincide with the schooling folkways. The valuable studies of the effects of the "hidden curriculum" in the school must be extended to studies which analyze the concomitant teaching-learning scenes which occur in the "ignored curriculum" of the entire educational configuration.

CONCLUSION: RECONCEPTUALIZING EDUCATION

In modern, complex, and pluralistic social groupings such as many public school classrooms, shared meanings and common ideological structures are not easily identified. Indeed, shared meanings and co-linearity of ideological perspectives may be less than is generally assumed and social cohesion may rest upon external controls or poorly articulated phrases which reflect ambiguity rather than consensus. Under such conditions, life in the classroom can often be characterized by conflict, failure, and confusion.

The role of the public school must be reconceptualized to reflect ethnographic realities about the classroom and about the teaching-learning transactions which occur outside the school. The public school is a *contact point* where a variety of converging cultural and ideological patterns can be analyzed and deciphered by teachers and students. The evaluation of effective schooling must be determined according to the degree to which it serves as a significant multicultural and multi-ideological contact point. The manner in which school teachers and students negotiate cultural and ideological diversity should be a matter of intense study. How do teachers and students, for example, decipher the symbolic universes which each of the following cultures represent: the folk culture of the neighborhood, the cosmetic culture of the mass media, the varied alternative cultures whether ethnic, religious, or other intentional life patterns, and the high culture gleaned by the brahmins from tradition?

Schools historically have served as agencies which function to assist the home and the church to perpetuate the values of the social group. In modern societies such a task is no longer appropriate or possible. Folk cultures differ markedly from the popular culture presented through the mass media. Not only are modern metropolitan areas characterized by ethnic and religious pluralism, but also by other "taste" cultures based on emergent institutional patterns and alternative lifestyles. The role of the school, therefore, is to assist learners in monitoring these diverse cultural and ideological constellations which affect their lives so that they can function effectively in varied settings and be able to make rational choices among the increasing number of alternative ways of living their lives. When such a goal is achieved, students will become ethnographers and participate with their teachers in the on-going analysis and refinement of the teaching-learning transaction. When such a reality is achieved, education rather than training will characterize the teaching-learning transaction.

REFERENCES

Berger, P. L., & Luckmann, T. *The social construction of reality: A treatise in the sociology of knowledge.* Garden City, N.Y.: Doubleday Anchor Books, 1967.
Bernier, N. R., & Williams, J. E. *Beyond beliefs: Ideological foundations of American education.* Englewood Cliffs, N.J.: Prentice-Hall, 1973.
Blumer, H. Society and symbolic interaction, in J. F. Glass & J. Straude (Eds.), *Humanistic society: Today's challenge to sociology.* Pacific Palisades, Calif.: Goodyear Publishing, 1972.
Braum, S. J., & Edwards, E. P. *History and theory of early childhood education.* Belmont, Calif.: Wadsworth Publishing Co., 1972.
Denzin, N. K. *Childhood socialization.* San Francisco, Jossey-Bass, 1977.
Dewey, J., & Bentley, A. F. *Knowing and the known.* Boston: Beacon Press, 1960.
Goffman, E. *The presentation of self in everyday life.* Garden City, N.Y.: Doubleday Anchor Books, 1959.

14

Inference in Preschool Children's Conversations— A Cognitive Perspective

Carl H. Frederiksen
McGill University

Recently an interesting convergence has occurred involving two lines of research on children's discourse: linguistic and ethnographic research on the structure and organization of language and social interaction in children's conversational discourse on the one hand; and psychological research on the cognitive processes and knowledge structures that underlie discourse comprehension and production on the other. The convergence I have in mind involves a recognition and analysis of the centrality of *inference* in conversational interaction and discourse processing. This paper will examine some implications of conceptions of inference in ethnographic and linguistic analyses of children's conversations for cognitive theories of discourse comprehension and production.

An important problem for cognitive theories of discourse processing is to account for how inferencing processes are contextually constrained; that is, to explain how inferences are regulated by discourse features and structure, and framed by an individual's prior knowledge and contextual knowledge. While cognitive studies of discourse processing in comprehension have demonstrated a variety of effects of discourse and knowledge structures on comprehension, and identified a variety of kinds and contexts of inference,

I would like to acknowledge the assistance of John Dore who introduced me to the complexities of conversational discourse and to his approach to the analysis of children's conversations. Of course, any errors committed either in describing his work or in using his coding system are solely my responsibility. I would also like to thank William S. Hall for generously making his corpus of children's conversations available to me and for facilitating the analysis through a series of workshops he organized at Rockefeller University during 1977 and 1978.

they have only begun to develop an account of how inferencing processes reflect constraints imposed by a text and its context of use. The problem is to explain how children learn to make inferences that are *contextually appropriate* in interpreting other's language, whether that language consists of an extended written text or utterances in the context of a conversation.

Accounts of conversational inference developed in ethnographic studies of conversational interaction have focused directly on this problem of the contextualization and appropriateness of inferences. Two aspects of this work have particular significance for the development of a more adequate cognitive theory of discourse inference. First, conversational inference has been shown to involve the construction of contextual *frames* that make conversational language interpretable and communication possible. These contextual frames are not fixed language structures but, rather, are cognitive structures that are actively negotiated by participants in a conversation through their linguistic interaction. Second, processes of conversational inference have been explicitly linked to discourse features and structures that *regulate* conversational interaction and inference. Conversational inferences may be regulated through linguistic and paralinguistic "contextualization cues" that signal interpretive frames (Gumperz, 1977), and by means of illocutionary and propositional discourse structures that display their interpretive frames (Dore, 1979).

In contrast, many cognitive psychologists have tended to view frames as fixed slotted structures (called "schemas") that exist as a part of a comprehender's prior knowledge rather than as structures generated through interaction with text. Such *schema-based* theories of comprehension have viewed comprehension as a process of "schema instantiation" in which texts are interpreted by filling slots in expected prototype structures. These theories fail to explicitly link such inferences and frames to features of texts or text structures, or to account adequately for the comprehension of natural texts that have a high degree of structural variation. While alternative *text-based* approaches to inference in comprehension do link inferences directly to text propositions and structures and consequently can describe inferences in comprehension of highly variable text formats, they fail to provide an adequate account of how inferences are limited to those that are appropriate to a particular text and context. What appears to be required is an *interactive* theory of inference that describes how a comprehender interacts with text to *construct* an interpretive frame that reflects both text properties and prior or contextual knowledge. Ethnographic studies of conversations offer just such a theory of inference in which interpretive frames are linked directly to discourse features that signal them and structures that display them. Thus, ethnographic accounts of conversational inference have direct relevance to a central theoretical (and methodological) problem in research on discourse comprehension.

While I hope to demonstrate in this paper that conversational interactions exhibit processes of inference and their control that have implications for a general theory of discourse comprehension and production, I also hope to explore in a preliminary way how techniques developed by cognitive psychologists to study inference in comprehension may be applied fruitfully to the analysis of conversational inference. An example will be presented to illustrate the application to conversational discourse of the inference analysis procedures developed in our work on comprehension (Frederiksen, 1979, 1980; C. Frederiksen, J. D. Frederiksen, Humphreys, & Ottesen, 1978), and the results will be interpreted to illustrate how they pertain to the theoretical issues raised in the first part of the paper. However, before proceeding to empirical examples, we need to examine ethnographic perspectives on conversational inferences in greater detail to see more precisely how they can contribute to an interactive theory of conversational inference.

ETHNOGRAPHIC PERSPECTIVES ON CONVERSATIONAL INFERENCE

Ethnographic analyses of conversations view conversations as social interactions in which language functions as a primary means by which social activities are accomplished. Language may represent the principal product of or reason for social activity, or it may represent a means by which participants in a shared activity communicate in jointly accomplishing the activity. While different research approaches to conversational discourse emphasize different aspects of language and social interaction, they share interests in: (1) the nature and organization of conversational discourse units and rules for their use, (2) strategies and norms for regulating language and social interaction in conversations, and (3) the nature and role of contextual frames in the interpretation, production, and structure of conversational discourse. In much of this work, interest centers around describing communicative competency; that is, knowledge of language structures and principles for their use that underlie ability to communicate in conversational settings. This knowledge includes knowledge of means of speaking, norms for the regulation of conversational interaction, and pragmatic knowledge required for interpretation of speech acts.

Recent work in child language (Dore, 1979) and the ethnography of communication (Gumperz, 1977) has begun to focus on what a participant in a conversation does in interpreting others' talk. This work emphasizes processes of communication in settings of conversational interaction, rather than the knowledge required to participate in conversations. This concern with processes of conversational interaction has led directly to a focus on conversational inference. In one characterization of conversational inference,

Gumperz (1977) has focused on analyzing processes of interpreting others' language in context. He has described conversational inference as a process of "situated interpretation" in which a participant in a conversation interprets aspects of others' speech, called contextualization cues, that signal interpretive frames, together with information about the social context of an interaction, to infer an interpretive frame that makes others' language meaningful and communication possible. In another characterization of conversational inference, Dore (1979) has focused on the structure of the discourse children produce in conversations. In his analysis, Dore interprets the structure of children's speech acts and their relationships to others' speech acts as reflections of underlying cognitive plans and inferencing processes. These processes enable them to produce language that simultaneously satisfies the illocutionary demands of others' speech acts and the cognitive demands imposed by the framing task or social activity of which the conversation is a part. In this manner, the structure of children's conversations *displays* the task or activity that frames the conversation. In both of these characterizations, processes of conversational inference are treated as central to describing language structure and use. These processes of conversational inference involve an interaction of language codes with contexts in the interpretation of others' talk and the communication of intended meaning.

Before examining the topic of conversational inference in greater detail, it will be useful first to examine background research on the knowledge underlying communicative competency from the standpoint of its relevance to a cognitive theory of inference in conversations. For more extensive analyses of the ethnographic and linguistic literatures on conversational interaction, the reader is referred to the recent papers of Dore (1979) and Gumperz (1977).

Discourse Units

Any account of conversational discourse, whether it represents a conversation in terms of the structure of the discourse produced, in terms of processes of social interaction, or in terms of underlying cognitive structures and inferencing processes, must confront the problem of identifying and characterizing language units in conversations. In cognitive and psycholinguistic work, as well as in much of theoretical linguistics, the emphasis has been on grammatically encoded or presupposed propositional structures. However, as was observed by Austin (1962), utterances do more than grammatically and lexically convey propositional meanings; they also convey information concerning illocutionary relationships to other speakers' prior or subsequent speech acts. Thus, a question conveys both a propositional content and an illocutionary force, viz., that a question was asked that requires an answer. Furthermore, an intended illocutionary meaning may not always correspond to the conventional illocutionary value of an utterance type, but may have to be pragmatically inferred from context (as, for example, in the case of indirect requests). Thus, a basic conversational discourse unit is a speech act consisting of an utterance that grammatically encodes or presupposes an intended illocutionary force and one or more propositions.

Much effort has been directed at theoretically and empirically identifying different types of speech acts, and with analyzing the principles by which speakers interpret the illocutionary intent of others' speech acts in situations of indirect speech. Efforts to specify principles of cooperation that enable participants in conversations to interpret each others' speech acts including those that are indirect (Grice, 1975) may be viewed as pragmatic efforts to account for interpretations of meaning that go beyond grammatical or illocutionary theories (Dore, 1979).

Just as cognitive psychologists and discourse linguists have been attempting to characterize the structure of discourse units beyond individual propositions, students of conversational interaction have sought to identify principles by which speech acts group into more inclusive discourse units, and to characterize the nature of these units (e.g., Dore, 1979; Sinclair & Coultard, 1975). Units that have been identified include conversational sequences, that is, "canonically related" sequences of speech acts (Dore, 1979); speech events consisting of segments of thematically related language plus context (Gumperz, 1977); and still larger units that correspond to specific types of frames such as jokes (Bauman & Scherzer, 1975; Sacks, 1974) genres such as myths and narratives, and task contexts such as lessons (Hall & Cole, 1980; Cook–Gumperz, 1977; Green & Wallat, 1979, 1980.

In conversational discourse, as in other discourse, as the unit of analysis becomes larger the extent of variation within a unit increases. The issue of how to characterize knowledge of discourse units whose realization in a particular situation is variable has not yet been addressed satisfactorily by cognitive psychologists. Consequently, ethnographic and linguistic descriptions of highly variable discourse structures and of principles, maxims, or rules for their selection, interpretation and use are of particular significance to building a more adequate theory of how knowledge of discourse structures develops and is employed in comprehension and production.

Regulative Processes

Conversations involve a continual process of social interaction among participants' in which speech acts and their relationships enable the communication of knowledge and cooperation to occur. This communication occurs in a socially negotiated task environment in which the structure of participants talk reflects both a sequence of related speech acts and conversational turns, and the structure of the task or social activity in which the participants in a conversation are engaged. A major requirement, if such communication is to occur, is the smooth regulation of the flow of interaction through language as reflected in turn taking, tying, asides and side sequences, openings and closings, etc. (Sacks, 1972; Sacks, Schegloff & Jefferson, 1974). If this flow of talk is not smoothly regulated, then communication will break down and the conversation will lack coherence. These *regulative processes* are apparent in adult conversation and appear in preschool children's conversations as children learn principles for turn-taking and for producing speech that is topically and conversationally related to their own and others' speech acts (Garvey, 1975; Keenan, 1974; Dore, 1977; Ervin–Tripp, 1977; Bloom, Rocissano & Hood, 1976; Keller–Cohen, 1978).

Regulative processes have their counterpart in extended text production in the need to produce sentences that flow in a coherent and connected manner. As we consider the relationship of communicative processes in conversations to processes involved in "literate" communication through extended discourse (Cook–Gumperz, 1977), regulative strategies which may appear relatively explicitly in conversations must develop into strategies for regulating the production of literate texts in the absence of an explicit need to regulate interaction with other speakers. Children may have particular difficulty with the regulative aspects of extended text production in part because of the absence of an explicit interactive basis for these processes in written language. A major demand of mastery of ability to compose extended literate texts is to acquire new regulative strategies to govern the flow of language production. Thus the regulative strategies and devices apparent in conversations represent aspects of text generation and interpretation that are important to all discourse communication.

Contextual Frames

Perhaps most significant for cognitive theories of comprehension is the notion of a *frame* as a cognitive structure that imposes contextual constraints on the interpretation and production of speech acts in conversations. One notion of frame coming from structural linguistics is a fixed language structure having "slots" that are filled by other language structures if they satisfy contextual constraints associated with the frame. This notion of frame as fixed structure was extended by cognitive anthropologists to cover such sequences of conversational acts as question–response sequences (Frake, 1977). For example, question frames contain response slots that are to be filled by utterances that qualify as responses. Thus frames have been used to account for fixed types of discourse structures that are assumed to be known to speakers as an aspect of their communicative competency.

This notion of a frame as a knowledge structure corresponding to a fixed type of discourse structure corresponds to the idea of a fixed discourse "schema" in cognitive psychology, except that in cognitive psychology fixed schemas have been proposed for discourse structures which are much more extensive, e.g., entire stories. In these theories, a schema is considered to be a known structural representation containing variables (or slots) which, through a process of "instantiation" (i.e., slot filling), enables a person to interpret a discourse by matching it to an already known structure (the schema). Schema theories of comprehension view comprehension as a kind of pattern recognition in which inferences function to insert text propositions into slots in a schema or text prototype. For example, "story schemas" have been proposed to account for children's knowledge of story structures which they apply in comprehending story structures (Mandler & Johnson, 1977; Rumelhart, 1975; Thorndyke, 1977).

A major problem for this concept of frame as fixed structure is the high degree of variability present in conversations and extended discourse structures. For example, while examples of question–response sequences frequently occur in conversations, "noncanonical" sequences also occur (Dore, 1979). Even in canonical cases, a question frame accounts for only the illocutionary aspects of any given segment of conversation classifiable as such a sequence. Variation occurs in the form and content of the utterances that constitute the sequence, and in the relationship of the sequence to prior discourse and to the social and situational context in which it is embedded. The extent of this variability increases as the size of the discourse segment increases to include larger topically related stretches of conversation (such as scenes, Gumperz, 1977), events (Frake, 1977), or entire speech activities (Gumperz, 1977). To account for this variability and change in discourse structure over the course of a conversation, ethnographers and ethnomethodologists have modified the concept of frame to refer to structures that are actively constructed by participants in a conversation through their interaction to make communication of meaning possible (Frake, 1977). Thus the concept of frame has been extended in two important ways. First, the scope of the concept has been extended to include larger units of contextualized discourse; and second, the concept of frame as fixed structure has been related with a notion of frame as constructed by participants in a conversation through their linguistic interaction.

Collins, Brown and Larkin (1977) have recently addressed this problem from a cognitive perspective, distinguishing between a *nongenerative* target structure (or schema) which is fit to a text by a process of filling variables in the structure, and a *generative* structure which, like a grammar, "can produce a potentially infinite number of possible models" (p. 2). In the case of generative structures, "the control exercised by the target structure is more subtle, requiring the growing of the target structure hand in hand with filling in the variables of the model" (p. 3). The problem is to specify the characteristics of generative structures and the processes by which they are constructed.

These two extensions of the concept of frame are in fact closely related since the expansion of frames to encompass the wider social contexts of conversational interaction led to an interactive notion of frames as constructed contexts of interpretation that are negotiated by speakers and reflected directly and indirectly in their conversational exchanges. The connection stems from the observation that social contexts and the interpretive frames associated with them change during the course of a conversation. Thus, a participant must, at the opening of a conversation make a preliminary interpretation of the situation and other participants' talk, construct an appropriate contextual frame to represent the speech event as it has developed thus far, produce conversational acts that at the same time satisfy local conversational constraints and communicate an intended meaning within the frame, and reinterpret the frame as the interaction develops and the activity changes or becomes more completely negotiated. Thus, such a frame is closely associated with a process of conversational inference, and resembles more a plan than a fixed slotted structure (Bruce, 1979; Deutsch, 1975). Of course, to the extent that conversational interactions or other language structures become stereotyped, formulaic, or ritualized and consequently recurrent with relatively little variation in form, frames could become relatively fixed structures for generating or interpreting discourse.

Conversational Inference

A major consequence of this expanded conception of frame is that frames cannot be specified *a priori* as structures for interpretation without reference to processes of interaction between a language user and text. The problem in accounting for the structure of conversations becomes one of understanding how conversational discourse reflects participants' frames as they develop and are negotiated throughout a conversation, and how other participants' discourse leads them to modify their frames. These processes of conversational inference occur against a background of production of contextually appropriate speech acts and strategies for regulating the flow of the conversation. Since frames are not fixed structural entities that can be described without reference to specific situations of conversational interaction, they must be inferred by participants from other participants' talk. Thus, the concept of a constructed or generated frame which was found to be necessary to describe conversational discourse structures is closely connected to processes of inference that generate these structures. The focus of investigations of children's conversations thus shifts from a concern with describing the structure of conversational discourse, to describing processes of conversational inference which generate the frames that make conversational discourse structured units of language and regulate the sequential production of speech acts.

Gumperz (1977) has proposed a characterization of conversational inference which explicitly links inferencing processes to discourse frames: conversational inferences occur whenever participants in a conversation assess others' intentions and base their responses on "situated" interpretations of others' language. These interpretations reflect the context in which others' language is situated. Conversational inference is a semantic process in which participants assign propositional and illocutionary meaning to utterances in a manner which reflects this process of context-bound interpretation. Unlike rules of grammar, conversational inferences involve choices among possible interpretations of speaker meanings, choices that are constrained by "what the speaker intends to achieve in a particular interaction as well as by expectations about others' reactions and assumptions" (Gumperz, 1977, p. 9). These interpretations reflect consistent assumptions about the interaction, although changes in assumptions may occur as communicative strategies change during the course of an interaction. Thus, conversational inferences produce representations of participants assumptions about the interactive context of conversational acts, that is, contextual frames, which enable them to choose among possible interpretations of others' communicative intents.

If conversational inference is viewed in this way, a primary concern in describing these processes of inference is to identify sources of information—linguistic, contextual and cultural—that speakers use to construct interpretive frames. In this context, three questions may be asked: What linguistic features or structures form the basis for such inferences? How are contexts represented and used as a basis for interpreting utterances in conversations? and To what extent is use of linguistic and contextual information based on culturally specific knowledge and expectations?

Gumperz has centered his investigations of linguistic sources of conversational inferences on prosodic and paralinguistic features of language, demonstrating how prosody operates to signal interpretive frames, changes in frames (such as topic shifts), deviations from expected frames (contrastiveness), and relationships of utterances to discourse frames; and how paralinguistic cues distinguish degrees of formality or involvement, and signal topic changes and asides. By examining these co-occurrence relationships of language features to interpretations, evidence is obtained for a social system by which language devices are used to regulate conversational inferences. Other language features that signal inferences include cohesive features (Halliday & Hasan, 1976) and topicalization patterns (e.g., Grimes,

1975), both of which involve grammatical forms functioning at the discourse level to signal expectations concerning the structure and coherence of a conversation.

In addition to prosody, paralinguistic cues and grammatical features, the propositional content and illocutionary values of utterances constrain speakers' constructions of interpretive frames. "Grammatical forms signal both the propositional content and illocutionary force of an utterance" which are interpreted pragmatically in terms of conversational maxims (Dore, 1979, p. 45). The propositional content and pragmatic functions of utterances signal an interpretive frame which then "influences the interpretation of subsequent content and functions" (p. 46). In summary, inferences are linked to surface and semantic discourse features and structures which consequently may provide a basis for warranted descriptions of processes of conversational inference.

It is much more difficult to establish how speakers represent contexts and use them in interpreting utterances in conversations. Two strategic approaches appear to have been taken to this problem. The first emphasizes a general concept of the social context of an interaction as a type of "speech activity" such as lecturing, discussing, or chatting. These culturally specific speech activities are not precisely classifiable or describable since they vary in detail from one instance to another, but they constrain production, action and interpretation in conversations. Since a shared concept of speech activity is essential to communication, speakers must find means in language and social interaction to convey their sense of a speech activity. Analyses of these language devices, especially in situations in which there is a failure of communication (e.g., Gumperz's 1977 work on interethnic communication) provide one source of evidence for the functioning of contextual frames in conversational inference.

A second approach used in child discourse studies examines the functioning of contextual frames in task-oriented dialogues such as in school or instructional settings. This approach enables more specific descriptions of context-framed inferences by capitalizing on an ability to independently analyze aspects of the contextualizing task and then investigate how these aspects are reflected in the structure of children's exchanges. At one level, one can attempt to identify components or phases of tasks that can be used to segment and assign structure to dialogue. Dore (1979) has referred to this relationship of language to task components and phases as one in which a text *indexes* the phases and components of socially accomplished tasks. This indexing relationship stems from the fact that tasks determine the structure of texts produced during their enactment. At another level, task types or structures have been used to interpret differences in the language structures children produce in different situations. For example, Hall and Cole (1980) have argued that children's conceptions of task influence the extent and kind of language they produce, even when the content or topic of discussion is fixed. Thus, a conversational interaction with an adult not at the supermarket following a trip to a supermarket could be interpreted by children as either an "examination" task or as a "giving and getting" task, and these differences in interpretation of task were reflected quantitatively and qualitiatively in their talk.

In summary, ethnographic accounts of conversational inference have characterized these inferences as processes whereby participants in conversations generate contextual frames to enable them to interpret the communicative intent of others' speech and produce appropriate speech acts. These contextual frames may be generated from prior culturally specific knowledge, e.g., of specific speech activities, or from socially and situationally defined task contexts of conversational interaction. Inferencing processes that generate contextual frames are directly linked to discourse features (such as contextualization cues, cohesive features, and topicalization patterns) which signal interpretive frames (such as types of speech activities or changes in frames), and to grammatically encoded or presupposed propositions and illocutionary relations which reflect the structure and organization of tasks or social activities that frame the production of conversational discourse. Conversational inferences also occur in a "local" context of conversational exchanges in which speech acts and conversational turns are mutually constrained by their content and illocutionary effects, and principles of topical relevance and cooperation that regulate participants' production of sequences of speech acts.

Thus, to communicate effectively in conversations, participants must produce discourse which simultaneously satisfies *local* constraints associated with the propositional content and illocutionary demands of other's speech acts, and global constraints associated with contextual frames that structure larger stretches of conversational discourse. To accomplish both requires that a language user make inferences. Inferences are required to produce appropriate speech acts contingent on others' speech and to construct appropriate contextual frames using available linguistic and extralinguistic resources—contextualization cues, semantic discourse structure, and any contextualizing task or activity—to interpret or communicate the frame. A full account of the cognitive inferencing processes underlying conversational discourse therefore will have to describe these inferencing processes, their regulation by local text demands, and their relationship to global contextual frames as they are reflected in the structure of conversational discourse and task contexts.

COGNITIVE ANALYSIS OF INFERENCE
IN CHILDREN'S CONVERSATIONS

Approaches to the analysis of inferences in comprehension developed by cognitive psychologists can contribute directly to such an account of the inferencing processes language users employ in conversations. These approaches focus directly on the cognitive processes and propositional structures individuals employ in comprehending (or producing) language. They share with ethnographic studies an interest in how discourse structures interact with a language user's prior knowledge in controlling inferencing processes in comprehension. It is just such a cognitive account of the inferencing processes of individuals participating in conversations that ethnographic accounts of conversational inference appear to require.

Despite their different objectives, there is a certain parallelism between ethnographic studies of conversational inference and psychological studies of inference in comprehension. Like students of the ethnography of communication, cognitive psychologists studying discourse comprehension have had to face issues of: (1) the nature of texts as structured discourse units that are reflected in the knowledge structures readers or listeners acquire in comprehending them; (2) the manner in which texts require or invite inferences for their comprehension, thus regulating the inferencing processes readers or listeners employ in comprehending these texts; and (3) the nature of language users' knowledge, of discourse structures and world knowledge, and how such prior knowledge is used to frame comprehension of texts. The first of these issues is directly parallel to a concern with the units, structure and organization of conversational discourse and language users' knowledge of rules or maxims that underlie such structure. The second issue is parallel to the study of regulative processes in conversations in its focus of how text propositions and features regulate inferential discourse processing through the requirements for inference they impose on a comprehender. The third issue is parallel to the study of contextual frames in its focus on discourse frames (e.g., story schemas) and prior knowledge structures, and how such frames are employed by a reader or listener in comprehending text. The essential difference between the two approaches is that ethnographers ask "Where do frames come from?" while cognitive psychologists assume that frames are already given and ask "How are frames used in comprehending texts?"

There is one further parallel between the two approaches, that is, the initial emphasis on the knowledge underlying structure in discourse rather than on processes of discourse communication. Thus, parallel to the emphasis on communicative competency in ethnographic studies of conversations, cognitive studies of discourse comprehension have emphasized the discourse structures and propositional knowledge that underlie the ability to comprehend connected texts. Recent work on inference in comprehension, however, like work on conversational inference, has begun to shift the focus more directly to inferencing processes in comprehension. This work has capitalized on explicit models of the propositional structures encoded in discourse and knowledge acquired from texts (Frederiksen, 1975; Kintsch, 1974) to generate theoretical taxonomies of inferential operations enabling procedures for coding the inferences subjects make in comprehending and recalling the content of discourse (Frederiksen, 1979, 1980; C. Frederiksen, J. D. Frederiksen, F. Humphrey & J. Ottesen, 1978). Also emerging from this work on discourse inference is a framework for an interactive theory of inference in comprehension in which language users employ their prior knowledge and text-based information interactively in comprehending texts. Before attempting to apply the methods of propositional analysis and inference coding we have developed to conversations, it will be useful first to examine how cognitive psychologists have approached these three issues, and the theoretical framework and methods of analysis that have resulted from this work. For a more extensive review and analysis of these issues, the reader is referred to a recent paper of Frederiksen (1980).

Discourse Structure and Knowledge Structure

A primary reason why psychologists have come to view discourse comprehension as central to human cognition is that discourse is viewed as a reflection of connected thought processes and coherent knowledge structures. A language user must uncover this structure in understanding texts and be able to generate such structures in producing coherent discourse. Consequently, by studying individuals' developing ability to acquire knowledge from or produce discourse, one is investigating fundamental characteristics of how individuals acquire, represent and construct extended knowledge structures. As a consequence of this focus on the representation and acquisition of knowledge, cognitive psychologists' interest has centered around the propositional content and structure of discourse since these discourse structures ought to reflect most directly the propositional structures represented in semantic memory (e.g., Anderson & Bower, 1973; Frederiksen, 1975; Kintsch, 1974; Rumelhart & Norman, 1975). Thus, propositional analyses of discourse in cognitive psychology are intended to provide a means of specifying propositional information encoded in natural language texts as a basis for studying the propositional structures individuals acquire in comprehending them. The propositional structures proposed in different systems of analysis, while they vary in detail, are intended as theories of how semantic information is represented in memory, and to provide heuristic models that would permit analysis of acquired knowledge structures. Issues of how propositions are related to sentence structures are regarded pragmatically—to be resolved as computational models of how individuals assign propositional readings to sentences (see, e.g., Clark & Clark, 1977; Danks & Glucksberg, 1980; de Beaugrande, 1980; Wilks, 1976).

In general, psychologists attempting to specify propositional structures for texts have been confronted with two problems. The first is to specify propositional information that is explicitly encoded in the sentences that comprise a text (Frederiksen, 1975; Kintsch, 1974). While investigators differ in the detail or explicitness of their representations, the objective is to specify only that propositional information which is explicitly encoded in a text. The set of such propositions has been referred to as a "text base," to differentiate it from a larger propositional knowledge structure (the "message base") from which the text base is derived. Thus, a text encodes certain propositions explicitly (the text base) which a listener or reader must use to inferentially reconstruct a speaker's or writer's intended message base. Comprehension, thus, involves building an interpretive structure for a text using the available text base together with one's prior and contextual knowledge to build a model of the writer's or speaker's intended meaning.

When comprehension is viewed in this way, a second problem arises of how to specify this second aspect of discourse structure—the characteristics of the underlying structure which is only partially reflected in the text base and surface features of a text. The problem is, of course, that such text structures are not explicit and must be inferred. Two contrasting approaches have been taken to this problem: a "text-based" approach, and a "knowledge-based" (or text grammar) approach. In the text-based approach (Crothers, 1978; Frederiksen, 1980; Kintsch, & Van Dijk, 1975; Van Dijk, 1977), text base propositions are operated on by inferential operators or macrorules to generate new propositions which collectively define a discourse macrostructure. High level propositional structures are generated by applying sequences of such operations or rules until the structural representation is complete. An intriguing aspect of this approach is the extent to which high level representations can be generated in this manner. A major problem with the approach is specifying which inferences to make among all of the possibilities.

The contrasting knowledge-based approach begins with a prior text structure or class of structures for a particular type of discourse (e.g., a "story schema" or "story grammar," Rumelhart, 1975; Mandler & Johnson, 1977). The analysis of story structure is top down, beginning with a schema which contains slots (or variables) which are filled with appropriate text propositions. In most applications of the story grammar approach, a particular structural realization of the grammar is taken as given and stories are written to satisfy the required structure (Mandler & Johnson, 1977; Stein & Glenn, 1978; Thorndyke, 1977). It is not clear how a text grammar can be used to generate a structure for a story when a particular structural realization is not specified in advance (Collins, Brown, & Larkin, 1978), nor is it clear in light of the shift away from derivational grammars in studies of sentence comprehension, what psychological significance should be attached to the formulation of story frames in terms of derivational rewrite rules.

Experimental studies of discourse comprehension motivated by these two theoretical approaches have provided abundant evidence that during comprehension, readers or listeners acquire propositional knowledge structures that reflect both aspects of the surface features and propositional structure of discourse, and their prior knowledge. In text-based approaches, interest has centered on how the propositions subjects acquire from texts (as inferred from text recalls) are influenced by surface textual features (e.g., cohesion and topicalization) and the propositional structure of texts. This work has shown that acquired propositional knowledge reflects an interaction of the propositional structure of a text with aspects of its surface realization as discourse, particularly cohesive features and topicalization patterns. Both textual features and propositional structures exert powerful effects on the structure of propositions recalled from discourse. Text-based approaches generally do not assume a fixed *a priori* structure for a text, but rather study the propositional structures individuals assign to texts. These investigations typically reveal developmental and individual differences in the propositions language users incorporate into their discourse recalls, as well as large numbers of propositions that are inferentially related to text propositions.

In the knowledge-based approach, interest has centered on how subjects' interpretations of stories reflect their expectations concerning the conventional structure and organization of stories, and the extent to which stories being read (or listened to) conform to this expected "target" structure. Studies have focused on the effects of departures from such target structures on subjects' story comprehension (as reflected in story recall). Employing stories constructed to conform to a hypothetical story structure, evidence has been found that when stories depart from conventional structure, subjects have greater difficulty comprehending them. They also produce inferences which appear to reflect an attempt to make "ill-structured" stories conform better to expected conventional story frames (Stein & Glenn, 1978; Mandler & Johnson, 1977; Thorndyke, 1977).

In summary, studies of propositional knowledge structures acquired in comprehending discourse have demonstrated both text-based and knowledge-based discourse processing. Thus, comprehension appears to combine both text-based and knowledge-based processes acting interactively as listeners or readers build a propositional structure for a text. Inferences typically occur in text recalls that reflect text properties—both propositional structure and textual features—and discourse frames such as conventional or expected "genre structures", scripts (Schank & Abelson, 1977), and specific lexical and world knowledge. Thus comprehension appears to be an intrinsically inferential process in which inferences, regulated by text information and framed by prior knowledge, enable a language user to construct an appropriate interpretive structure for a text that goes beyond the propositions explicitly encoded in a text.

Inference in Discourse Comprehension

Once it is recognized that comprehension is an intrinsically inferential process, the focus of research shifts away from issues of text structure and knowledge representation as the central issue for a theory of comprehension, to issues of how inferential processes operate in discourse contexts to produce interpretations of texts that integrate text and inferred propositions into coherent knowledge structures. In this shift of emphasis to describing inferential processes, text and prior knowledge structures are viewed as important to describing processes of text and knowledge based inference. That is, a theory of discourse inference will have to answer the following questions, each of which centrally involves issues of text or knowledge structure:

What *types* of inferences do language users make in comprehending discourse?

When, that is, in what *contexts'* do they make inferences?

Why do langauge users make inferences? That is, what *functions* do their inferences accomplish?

How do language users know which inferences to make among all of the possibilities? That is, how do they limit their inferences to a restricted set that is *contextually appropriate?*

Investigations of both text and knowledge based inference in comprehension can be viewed in terms of how they attempt to answer these four fundamental questions.

The most extensive attempt to classify *types* of inferences is that developed in our own work on children's comprehension (C. Frederiksen et al., 1978; Frederiksen, 1979, 1980). In our classification different types of inferential operations are associated with different ways in which propositions can be related. Since our model of propositional structure enables us to specify different kinds of propositions, semantic information within propositions, and interpropositional relations (Frederiksen, 1975), we can specify exhaustively the possible ways in which propositions may be related or, equivalently, how one proposition may be derived from others by means of inferential transformations. Our approach to analyzing the types of inferences children make from a text involves coding inferential operations that connect the propositions children incorporate into their text recalls to contingent propositions in the text base. Inferences which connect propositions within a text can also be analyzed giving us a sophisticated means of characterizing the internal coherence of texts and of the texts children produce during recall. Thus the classification of types of inferential operations may be used to classify inferences that relate propositions from different samples of language (e.g., that connect text and recall), or to analyze structure within a language sample. Since inferences operate on propositions, relations of discourse propositions to extralinguistic contextual (e.g., task) information also may be coded when such contextual information is represented as propositions. These methods of propositional analysis and inference classification are potentially applicable to the analysis of conversational inferences. The last section of this paper explores such an application and includes a more detailed description of our propositional structures and classification of inference types. It should be noted that Crothers (1978), and Trabasso and Nichols (1978) also have developed approaches to classifying inferences, the former consisting of types of inferences that are required by specific cohesive features of texts, and the latter consisting of types of inferences associated with connecting event chains in narrative discourse.

Investigations of *contexts* in which inferences occur have emphasized both discourse contexts and language users' prior knowledge. Discourse contexts of inferences which have been studied include specific linguistic structures that require or "invite" inferences such as premises and presuppositions (Clark, 1977), anaphoric relations in text (Nash–Webber, 1978; Clark, 1977; Ortony and Anderson, 1977; Garrod & Sanford, 1977), and verb-related semantic case inferences (Paris & Lindauer, 1976). Crothers (1978, 1980) has recently attempted to systematize a variety of textual contexts for inference, emphasizing relationships of cohesive features, presuppositions and premises to the underlying propositional coherence of text. Other investigators have emphasized the propositional text base as a context for inference, either exploring theoretically types of rules that can be applied to text propositions to generate global macrostructures (Van Dijk, 1977), or classifying the inferences that children make in comprehending and recalling texts (Frederiksen, 1977, 1980; C. Frederiksen et al., 1978). Language users' prior knowledge structures or "schemas" also have been studied as contexts which frame inferences (Stein & Glenn, 1978). Knowledge structures studied vary from global structures for specific discourse formats such as stories, to scenarios for recurrent event sequences ("scripts," Schank & Abelson, 1977), and specific lexical and world knowledge. Altogether, research on contexts of inference has only begun to explore the great variety of contexts in which inferences occur and the manner in which these contexts interact as constraints on inference.

Three broad categories of *functions* of inference have been emphasized in research on inference in comprehension (C. Frederiksen et al., 1978). In the first, which we may describe as a "connective function," inferences are made to connect text propositions that are not explicitly related in a text. Connective inferences enable a language user to "bridge" text propositions to build an integrated propositional structure for a text, thus enabling a language user to comprehend the coherence that is present in discourse. Crothers (1978) has attached particularly central significance to text coherence in his emphasis on characterizing hòw inferences function to connect text propositions. A second function of inference is to generate a global macrostructure for a text. This "macrostructure function" of inference is emphasized by Van Dijk (1977) and in schema approaches which conceive of inference as a process of filling slots (or variables) in fixed discourse schemas. Both of these functions of inference, connective and macrostructure functions, operate internally on a text, treating discourse respectively as a coherent language unit, or as a realization of a conventional discourse format. Inferences, also, are required to relate the content of a text to one's prior knowledge or to knowledge of the content in which a discourse occurs. This "extensive function" involves extending a text's meaning by relating it to other knowledge and is particularly important in situations in which texts are used as sources of new knowledge or learning, and situations of use of language for communication in social settings.

While psychologists have been exploring a great variety of types, contexts, and functions of inferences, only a fragmented theory of discourse inference will result unless psychologists and other language researchers begin to address the central problem of how language users recognize what inferences are appropriate in specific contexts to accomplish specific functions. The question of *contextual appropriateness* is central to our approach to discourse inference and provides a rationale for our coding and analysis procedures. Briefly, our strategy is to classify all inferences children make in retelling different types of discourse (including stories and conversations) and then study the sepcific contexts in which inferences occur. Our objective is to characterize children's cognitive adaptations to the inferential requirements of different discourse contexts. These adaptations may involve the use of textual features and propositions to regulate inferences at a local level, and the construction of contextual frames to guide the construction of a global interpretive model for a text. Different genres or situations of language use present different contexts for inference and functions that inferences may serve. The problem we are studying is how the language user recognizes these varied contextual constraints on discourse inference and uses them to regulate and frame inferential processes in comprehension.

Inference in Children's Conversations

The segment of conversation I have selected for analysis comes from the extensive corpus assembled by Hall (described by Hall and Guthrie, Chapter 9 in this volume). The segment selected was recorded during a teacher-directed activity (Spelling Name—a task requiring that a child use rubber stamp letters to print his name) in a nursery school setting. The target child in this sample was selected for the following reasons. First, a directed activity was chosen because it facilitates the analysis of task frames as contexts for conversational inference. Second, the situations, conversational exchanges, and teacher language are fairly typical of conversational interaction in directed nursery school activities. Hence, the conclusions we might draw about conversational inferences might reasonably be taken as hypotheses appropriate to other similar situations of conversational inference. Finally, the segment of conversation contains inferences that reflect a variety of contextual constraints. The name of the child in this segment has been changed, but still reflects orthographic constraints present in the child's real name. The conversation was edited to reflect the spelling of the fictitious name.

Illocutionary Constraints on Inference. One way in which conversations can constrain inferences is through the illocutionary requirements of participants' speech acts. For example, requestive conversational acts (C-acts) impose a demand to respond appropriately, and regulative C-acts control sequences of turns, regulate conversational flow and signal changes of topic. When participants produce talk that satisfies the illocutionary requirements of others' speech acts, the result is sequences of related speech acts. Inferences that connect C-acts within such conversational sequences reflect these local illocutionary constraints.

To explore conversational acts and sequences as contexts for inference, the Directed Activity segment was coded using Dore's system for classifying speech acts. The coding categories used are summarized in Table 1 (reproduced from Hall & Dore, 1980). Figure 1 contains the transcript of the Directed Activity segment. Turns are numbered and identified by speaker; utterances within turns are lettered. The right hand column in the Figure lists the speech act codes assigned to each utterance. Two codes have been assigned to an utterance if the C-act appears to reflect two illocutionary functions in the conversation. For example, an assertion may also function as an indirect request.

Groupings of C-acts into conversational sequences are represented in the second column of Figure 2. In this figure, C-acts are identified by speaker and listed in the sequence in which they occurred in the conversation. Arrows connect related C-acts and conversational sequences are enclosed in boxes.

TABLE 1
Codes, Definitions, and Examples of Conversational Acts.[a]

Code *Definition and Example*

Requestives solicit information or actions.

RQCH   *Choice Questions* seek either/or judgments relative to propositions: "Is this an apple?"; "Is it red or green?"; "Okay?"; "Right?".

RQPR   *Product Questions* seek information relative to most "WH" interrogative pronouns: "Where's John?"; "What happened?"; "Who?"; "When?".

RQPC   *Process Questions* seek extended descriptions or explanations: "Why did he go?"; "How did it happen?"; "What about him?"

RQAC   *Action Requests* seek the performance of an action by hearer: "Give me it."; "Put the toy down."

RQPM   *Permission Requests* seek permission to perform an action: "May I go?"

RQSU   *Suggestions* recommend the performance of an action by hearer or speaker both: "Let's do it!"; "Why don't you do it?"; "You should do it."

Assertives report facts, state rules, convey attitudes, etc.

ASID   *Identifications* label objects, events, people, etc.: "That's a car."; "I'm Robin."; "We have a boat."

ASDC   *Descriptions* predicate events, properties, locations, etc. of objects or people: "The car is red."; "It fell on the floor."; "We did it."

ASIR   *Internal Reports* express emotions, sensations, intents, and other mental events: "I like it."; "It hurts."; "I'll do it."; "I know."

ASEV   *Evaluations* express personal judgments or attitudes: "That's good."

ASAT   *Attributions* report beliefs about another's internal state: "He does not know the answer."; "He wants to."; "He can't do it."

ASRU   *Rules* state procedures, definitions, "social rules," etc.: "It goes in here."; "We don't fight in school."; "That happens later."

ASEX   *Explanations* state reasons, causes, justifications, and predictions: "I did it because it's fun."; "It won't stay up there."

Performatives accomplish acts (and establish facts) by being said.

PFCL   *Claims* establish rights for speaker: "That's mine."; "I'm first."

PFJO   *Jokes* cause humorous effect by stating incongruous information, usually patently false: "We throwed the soup in the ceiling."

PFTE   *Teases* annoy, taunt, or playfully provoke a hearer: "You can't get me."

PFPR   *Protests* express objections to hearer's behavior: "Stop!"; "No!"

PFWA   *Warnings* alert hearer of impending harm: "Watch out!"; "Be careful!"

Responsives supply solicited information or acknowledge remarks.

RSCH   *Choice Answers* provide solicted judgments of propositions: "Yes."

RSPR   *Product Answers* provide Wh-information: "John's here."; "It fell."

RSPC   *Process Answers* provide solicited explanations, etc.: "I wanted to."

RSCO   *Compliances* express acceptance, denial, or acknowledgement of requests: "Okay."; "Yes."; "I'll do it."

RSCL   *Clarification Responses* provide solicited confirmations: "I said no."

RSQL   *Qualifications* provide unsolicited information to requestive: "But I didn't do it."; "This is not an apple."

RSAG   *Agreements* agree or disagree with prior non-requestive act: "No, it is not."; "I don't think you're right."

RSAK   *Acknowledgements* recognize prior non-requestives: "Oh."; "Yeah."

Regulatives control personal contact and conversational flow.

ODAG   *Attention Getters* solicit attention: "Hey!"; "John!"; "Look!"

ODSS   *Speaker Selections* label speaker of next turn: "John"; "You."
ODRQ   *Rhetorical Questions* seek acknowledgement to continue: "Know what?"
ODCQ   *Clarification Questions* seek clarification of prior remark: "What?"
ODBM   *Boundary Markers* indicate openings, closings and shifts in the conversation: "Hi!";
       "Bye!"; "Okay"; "All right"; "By the way."
ODPM   *Politeness Markers* indicate ostensible politeness: "Please"; "Thank you."
       Expressives non-propositionally convey attitudes or repeat others.
EXCL   *Exclamations* express surprise, delight, or other attitudes: "Oh!"; "Wo
EXAC   *Accompaniments* maintain contact by supplying information redundant with respect to
       some contextual feature: "Here you are"; "There you go."
EXRP   *Repetitions* repeat prior utterances.
       Miscellaneous Codes
UNTP   *Uninterpretables* for uncodable utterances.
NOAN   *No Answers* to questions, after 2 seconds of silence by addressee.
NVRS   *Non-verbal Responses* for silent compliances and other gestures.

1. Reproduced from Hall & Dore (1980).

Conversational sequences are numbered in the upper right hand corner. This segment of conversation contained twelve conversational sequences, ten of which were initiated by the teacher (Tch) and two by the target child (TC, sequences 9 and 10). Teacher-initiated sequences were all requestive sequences; child-initiated sequences occurred late in the conversation and consisted of one sequence initiated by an assertive (022, Figure 1) *(I did it upside down.)* and completed with the teacher's agreement (RSAG: *That's all right*), and one initiated by a requestive (024, Figure 1) *(What E?)*. All other utterances of the target child were responsives and all except (026 Figure 1) *(Oh)* were in response to teacher requests. All talk not contained within these twelve conversational sequences consisted of assertives produced by the teacher. To investigate how C-acts regulate conversational inferences, we will need to investigate inferences which connect related C-acts depicted in Figure 2. Any inferences which occur within conversational sequences and connect pairs of related C-acts will be interpreted as inferences regulated by illocutionary constraints.

Propositional Constraints on Inference. A second way in which conversational discourse can constrain the inferences of participants is through the propositional content of their talk. Propositional constraints can operate in conjunction with illocutionary constraints as, e.g., when a response to a request involves inferences based on the propositional content of the request, or independently of illocutionary constraints. Whenever an utterance involves inferences based on other prior utterances, these prior discourse propositions are acting as constraints on conversational inference. Such constraints will always operate if speakers are attempting to "be relevant," producing coherent discourse which is connected to one's own and others' talk. The analysis of propositionsal constraints on inference requires that propositions encoded in or presupposed by participants' talk be specified. Then given such a specification of propositional content, inferential relations among propositions can be analyzed.

Figure 3 presents the propositional analysis of the Directed Activity segment employing the propositional structures developed by Frederiksen (1975, 1977) as simplified by C. Frederiksen et al. (1978). In the present use of the system, propositions are represented in "predicate-argument" notation, each numbered proposition consisting of a "head element" (the predicate) and a list of labelled semantic relations (or arguments). These labeled relations represent categories of semantic information contained within propositions. Thus, a stative proposition (e.g., 19.2) has an object as its head element and identifying relations from those listed in Table 2 as arguments. An event proposition (e.g., 10.1, 11.2, 21.4) consists of an action as head element and two types of relations as arguments: case relations appropriate to the type of event frame (processive or resultive, see Table 3), and identifying relations which specify information about the time, location and manner of the action (Table 2). Stative or event propositions may also contain argument slots representing truth-value, modality, tense and aspect categories specified in Frederiksen (1975). In Figure 3, argument labels are in upper case followed by a ':' and either the lexical information that fills the argument slot in the proposition or a number referring to another proposition. For example, in 11.1, the THEME slot is filled by proposition 11.2.

TABLE 2
Identificational Semantic Systems

System Type	Concepts	Semantic Relations
Temporal	objects, actions	absolute (clock) time (TEM); elapsed time (duration) (DUR)
Locative	objects, actions	location at point, on path, or in region (LOC)
Stative	objects	attribution (ATT), classification (CAT), part-whole (PRT), symbolic content (if object is symbolic) (THEME), determination (GEN, DEF, TOK), quantification (UNIV, NUM, σ)
Manner	actions	attribution (ATT), classification (CAT), part-whole (PRT), symbolic content (if action is symbolic) (THEME)
Degree	attributes	extent (DEG)

TABLE 3
Semantic Case Systems

System Type	Semantic Case Relations	Action Type
Processive	patient (PAT) related object (OBJ),	processive
	action (ACT)	relative processive
	goal (animate patient) (GOAL)	processive
Resultive	agent (AGT)	resultive
	instrument (INST)	"
	affected object (OBJ)	"
	prior state (SOURCE)	"
	physical result (RESULT)	"-physical
	symbolic result (THEME)	"-cognitive
	goal (animate agent) (GOAL)	"
	recipient (REC)	

Propositions may also represent entities consisting of two or more propositions that are connected either relatively (as in comparatives, relative time or location) or by means of dependency relations (conditional, causal and logical relations, Frederiksen, 1975). In the present example, only one relative relation occurs: ORD (the order relation in proposition 8). No examples of dependency relations occurred in the participants' talk, but inferences involving dependency relations among propositions did occur. Therefore a list of dependency relations is given in Table 4. The notation for propositions representing order or dependency relations is: relation label in head element position and connected propositions as arguments. For example, in Proposition 8, the head element is ORD (after) and the arguments are *L* and *what?* (an interrogated slot. *What comes after the L?*).

In comparison to stories or other school texts that we have analyzed, the most striking feature of the propositions produced in this conversation is their incompleteness; very little semantic identifying or case information is expressed directly. When filled, case slots frequently contain pronouns indicating anaphoric references to prior text or exophoric reference to the framing task (Halliday & Hasan, 1976). Since events and states are specified in such a minimal way, participants in the conversation must be able to infer the missing semantic information to understand others' talk and produce appropriate utterances. This point becomes apparent when one tries to interpret individual utterances out of context and in the absence of information about the nature of the Spelling Name task.

TABLE 4
Dependency Systems

System Type	Dependency Relations	Properties
Causal	causative (CAU)	functional relation
Conditional	contrafactual conditional (COND)	contextually ambiguous
Logical	material conditional (IF) material bicondi- tional (IFF)	contrapose
Disjunctive	nonexclusive alternation (OR-ALT)	
Exclusive	exclusive alternation (OR-EXCL)	
Conjunctive	(AND)	

Other inferential demands are reflected in the content of what propositional information is expressed. For example, Proposition 8 interrogates an object connected to another object by an order relation; Proposition 9 specifies the interrogated information. Propositions also exert powerful constraints on inferences based on them since text-based inferences operate on these propositions to produce new related propositions. Such inferential relations among propositions produce the internal structure that makes talk coherent and connected. Table 5 describes the types of inferential relations that exist. Any propositions that are connected inferentially to other text propositions satisfy propositional constraints. Note that an inference may reflect both propositional and illocutionary constraints (e.g., 9), or it may reflect propositional constraints that are independent of illocutionary constraints.

Frame Constraints on Inference. While conversational inferences may be regulated by local constraints associated with the propositional content and illocutionary demands of speech acts, inferences also may reflect global constraints associated with the structure of the setting, situation and task content within which the conversational interaction occurs. Whenever participants produce utterances that refer to a task or other contextual frame, or involve inferences based on a contextual frame, then frame constraints may be operating to control conversational inference. Frame constraints may operate in conjunction with propositional or illocutionary constraints to control inferences, or they may operate independently. For example, when the teacher asks the target child, *What's your last name?* (010g, Figure 1) and the child replies, *I don't know how to do that* (011, Figure 1), both teacher and child are referring to the Spelling Name Task. The teacher's requestive is not

TABLE 5
Types of Inferential Relations

Inferential Relation	Definition and Codes
Identifying Operations	
Lexical Operations	Specify propositions that unpack give lexical concepts, or concepts that lexicalize given propositions: UNPK, LEX: -OBJ, -ACT, -ATT, -ABC (abstract concept)
Object Identification	Specify how an object or set of objects is related to or distinguished from other objects: OBJ: -ID, -ATT, -CAT, -SUB, -PRT, -THM, -TOK, -GEN, -DEF, -UNIV, -NUM
Action Identification	Specify how an action is related to or distinguished from other actions: ACT: -ID, -ATT, -CAT, -SUB, -PRT, -THM
Locative Identification	Specify a spatial location for an object, state, or action: LOC: -OBJ, -ACT
Temporal Identification	Specify temporal information about an action or state: TEM, DUR, TNS, ASPCT: -ACT, -OBJ
Degree Identification	Specify the degree of an attribute, location, or time: DEG: -ATT, -LOC, -TEM, -DUR
Event Specifying (Case) Operations	
Case Operations	Insert information into case slots in event frames: CASE: -ACT, -AGT, -PAT, -OBJ, -REC, -INST, -RSLT, -SRCE, -GOAL, -THM, -RLACT
Event Generation	Specify new event frames that incorporate given objects or propositions into their case slots: EVNT: -ACT, -AGT, -PAT, -OBJ, -REC, -INST, -RSLT, -SRCE, -GOAL, -THM, -RLACT
Relations among Propositions	
Superordinate/Subordinate Operations	Specify propositions superordinate/subordinate to give propositions: SUP, SUB: -OBJ, -ACT, -ATT, -LOC, -TEM, -(Case Relation)
Relative Operations	Specify metric/nonmetric relations connecting objects or events: REL: -DEG, -TEM, -DUR, -LOC, -NMET
Causal, Conditional and Logical Operations	Establish causal, conditional or logical dependencies among propositions by specify-causal, conditional or logical relations among given propositions, or generating causal, conditional or logical antecedents/consequents of given propositions: CAU, COND, LOG: -REL, -ANT, -CONSQ; OR: -EXCL, -ALT; AND
Truth-Value and Modal Operations	Modify the truth-value or modality of a proposition: MOD; NEG; INT: -YN, -CON, -PROP

connected to prior conversational acts and so reflects an inference from the task frame; and the child's response, while it satisfies the illocutionary demand to respond, does not involve a direct inference from the teacher's request but rather a reference to and inference from the task frame. Thus, to study the operation of frame constraints in conversational inference, we need to examine propositions that refer to or represent the structure of a framing task and incorporate inferences based on that task.

To explore task frames as contexts for inference, we need to be able to represent task structures. In addition, we must be able to identify aspects of task frames that are directly reflected in the talk of participants in the task. To provide a means for describing tasks, we have found it convenient to adopt the terminology of procedures from artificial intelligence (e.g., Winston, 1977) in which tasks are conceptualized as procedures (programs) that themselves may be composed of (possibly recursive) subprocedures. Descriptions of a procedure may vary in detail, ranging from a detailed description in which all subprocedures that comprise a procedure are fully implemented as working programs, to relatively gross descriptions in which only major subprocedures high in a procedural hierarchy are identified or described. Procedures also can be described declaratively in terms of propositions or natural language descriptions. Thus, declarative descriptions or references to procedures can and do occur in task-oriented conversations.

We have exploited these ideas in analyzing the Spelling Name Task by identifying only those procedures in the Task that were referred to by participants in the conversation. The procedural description for the Spelling Name Task is given in Figure 4. All procedures identified in the Figure were referred to in the conversation. For example, the PRESS STAMP subprocedure is referred to by the target child in 020, Figure 1, (*It's hard to press.*), and the teacher refers to the subprocedures USE FINGER and PUSH DOWN in 021c (*use your finger and push down*). To investigate frame constraints on inference, we will need to identify task procedures associated with particular propositions in the conversation, and examine any inferences that connect such propositions to the procedures they describe or refer to.

Figure 4 depicts the results of our task analysis. Procedures identified in the Figure correspond to procedures referred to in the participants' talk. Thus, the procedural analysis of the task necessarily is incomplete: task procedures *not* referred to do not appear. It can be seen from Figure 4 that participants in this directed activity referred to procedures at five different hierarchical levels. In Figure 2, procedures specified in Figure 4 are listed in the sequence in which the references to them occurred. Propositions referring to each procedure are listed to the left of each procedure. For example, the conversation began with the completion of the SPELL NEXT NAME procedure with references to the subprocedures IDENTIFY NEXT LETTER and FIND LETTER = L. Next there was a boundary marker, followed by a reference to the procedure SPELL NEXT NAME (with the NAME variable set equal to LAST). The next reference was to IDENTIFY LAST NAME, and so on. By examining these *procedural contexts* of propositions and inferences, one can investigate how conversational inferences reflect frame constraints associated with the task frame.

Analysis of Conversational Inference. To investigate inferential processes in conversations, we need to first code all inferential relations which connect propositions expressed in the conversation, and then to analyze interactions of illocutionary, propositional and frame constraints in controlling inferences. The method is essentially correlational—to analyze co-occurrence relationships of inferences to illocutionary, propositional and task contexts. If inferences are found to coincide with illocutionary relations among speech acts, then we would have correlational evidence for the operation of illocutionary constraints on inferences; if propositions occur which incorporate information derived from task procedures, then we would have evidence for frame constraints; and the occurrence of inferences connecting propositions is itself evidence for propositional constraints on inference. Furthermore, these different types of constraints may interact or they may operate independently in constraining inferences. Thus co-occurrences of contextual constraints on inferences provide information concerning how participants in conversations employ illocutionary and propositional constraints to regulate their inferences, and their knowledge of task structure to frame their inferences in discourse comprehension and production. While the evidence we are considering is correlational, observations are made repeatedly over time permitting investigations of how inferences and their contexts change over the course of a conversation.

Inferences are coded for each current proposition by first identifying any *contingent propositions* that occurred prior to the propositions such that the current proposition may be derived from the contingent proposition by applying one or more inferential operations. Table 5 summarizes the categories of inferential relations (or operations) used to code inferences that connect a current proposition to prior contingent propositions. The relations fall into four major classes: (1) operations that identify objects or actions— lexically, by expanding ("unpacking") lexical concepts, or specifying stative, locative or temporal information; (2) event specifying operations that either specify case information in event frames or generate new events that incorporate events or text propositions into case slots; (3) operations involving relations among propositions including operations that generate: superordinate or subordinate propositions; relative relations connecting propositions (e.g., order or equivalence of time and location); and causal, condition or logical antecedent or consequent propositions; and (4) operations that modify the modal information or truth-value of a proposition. Figure 1 lists contingent utterances and inference codes for each utterance in the segment of conversation. Examples of many of these types of inferential operations occurred in the segment of conversation analyzed.

Figure 2 depicts graphically the inferential relations coded in Figure 1. Each proposition listed in Figure 3 is represented in Figure 2 as a circle containing a proposition number. Propositions connected by inferential relations are connected by arcs (labelled arrows) pointing from a contingent proposition to a current one. Arcs are labelled by the inferential operation that relates a current to a contingent proposition. Figure 2 also depicts each proposition adjacent to the C-Act code that describes the speech act whose content it represents. Furthermore, each proposition is also adjacent to any task procedure it refers to, and inferential relations which connect propositions to task procedures are also represented as labelled arcs. Thus, figure 2 displays all information pertinent to an analysis of contextual constraints on conversational inference.

Examination of Figure 2 reveals examples of inferences reflecting all three types of constraints. An example of an inference regulated by illocutionary constraints and propositional content is found in the first conversational sequence. Here in proposition 9 the target child identifies an object interrogated in proposition 8 by the teacher; his response satisfies both illocutinary and propositional constraints. The teacher's initial request interrogates an object to be identified in the IDENTIFY NEXT LETTER procedure and so reflects a frame constraint; the child's response exhibits the result of "executing" this procedure and so it too reflects a frame constraint. Examples of requestive sequences in which the response reflects propositional or frame constraints that do not coincide with the illocutionary constraint are found in conversational sequences 3 and 4 (Figure 2-b). In conversational sequence 3, the teacher produce a requestive that introduces the SPELLING LAST NAME procedure to the child and interogates the child's last name (Proposition 10.3). (To answer the teacher's question, the child must execute the procedure.) The child responds not with the requested information but with a reference to a procedure. This conversational exchange thus illustrates inferences that reflect frame constraints. Sequence 4 contains another example in which the child's response (Proposition 13) also satisfies the illocutionary demand to respond, but involves an inference from the child's previous response (Proposition 11.2) and the task frame.

Close examination of Figure 2 appears to indicate that the participants in this task-oriented dialogue are making inferences that reflect an interplay of local illocutionary and propositional constraints and the task frame. The teacher in general controls the conversation with a series of requestives and assertives that are organized by the task frame. The child responds to the teacher's requests with inferred propositions which reflect an ability to respond appropriately to local illocutionary and propositional demands of the teacher's talk, to make inferences that connect his utterances to his own prior utterances (i.e., displaying a certain degree of internal coherence in his talk), and to base his inferences on his knowledge of the task frame and his ability (or inability) to execute task procedures.

Conversational inferences displayed in this conversation appear to be explicable only in terms of processes of contextualized inference that reflect both text-regulated constraints and global constraints associated with the task. The plausibility of this conclusion stems primarily from the plausibility, objectivity and detail of the analysis performed. To explore the generality of the conclusions reached across communicative settings and situations, and for different populations of language users will require extensive analysis of conversations, combining qualitative analyses of the kind reported here with quantitative analyses of frequency counts derived from the qualitative analyses. The corpus assembled by Hall (Hall & Gutherie, this volume) appears to be an ideal environment in which to conduct such studies. Such analyses would be of great interest both to ethnographic accounts of social interaction, and cognitive theories of discourse inference.

REFERENCES

Anderson, J. R., & Bower, G. H. *Human associative memory*. Washington, D.C.: Winston, 1973.

Austin, J. L. *How to do things with words*. Cambridge, MA.: Harvard University Press, 1962.

Bauman, R. & Scherzer, J. the ethnography of speaking. *Annual Review of Anthropology*, 1975, *4*,

Bloom, L., Rocissano, L., & Hood, L. Adult–child discourse: Developmental interactions between information processing and linguistic knowledge. *Cognitive Psychology*, 1976, *8*, 521–552.

Bruce, B. Plans and social actions. In R. Spiro, B. Bruce, and W. Brewer (Eds.), *Theoretical issues in reading comprehension*. Hillsdale, N.J.: Lawrence Erlbaum Associates, 1978.

Clark, H. H. Inferences in comprehension. In D. LaBerge and S. J. Samuels (Eds.), *Basic processes in reading: Perception and comprehension*. Hillsdale, N.J.: Lawrence Erlbaum, Associates, 1977.

Clark, H. H. & Clark, E. V. *Psychology and language*. New York: Harcourt, Brace, Jovanovich, 1977.

Collins, A., Brown, J. S. & Larkin, K. M. Inference in text understanding. In R. Spiro, B. Bruce and W. Brewer (Eds.), *Theoretical issues in reading comprehension*. Hillsdale, N.J.: Lawrence Erlbaum Associates, 1978.

Cook–Gumperz, J. Situated instructions: Language socialization of school-age children. In C. Mitchell–Kernan and S. Ervin–Tripp (Eds.), *Child discourse*. New York: Academic Press, 1977.

Cook–Gumperz, J. & Corsaro, W. Social–ecological constraints on children's communicative strategies. In J. Cook–Gumperz and J. Gumperz (Eds.), *Papers on language and context.* (Working Paper #46, Language Behavior Research Laboratory), Berkeley, CA.: University of California, 1976.

Crothers, E. J. Inference and coherence. *Discourse Processes,* 1978, *1,* 51–71.

Crothers, E. J. *Paragraph structure inference.* Norwood, N.J.: Ablex Publishing Corp., 1979.

Danks, J. H. & Glucksberg, S. Experimental psycholinguistics. *Annual Review of Psychology,* 1980, *31,* 391–417.

deBeaugrand, R. *Text, discourse, and process: Toward a multidisciplinary science of texts.* Norwood, N.J.: Ablex Publishing Corp. 1980.

Deutsch, B. G. Establishing context in task-oriented dialogues. (Stanford Artificial Intelligence Center. Technical Note 114), Stanford University, 1975.

Dore, J. Children's illocutionary acts. In R. Freedle (Ed.), *Discourse comprehension and production.* Norwood, N.J.: Ablex Publishing Corp., 1977.

Dore, J. The structure of nursery school conversations. (Unpublished manuscript). Rockefeller University, 1979.

Ervin-Tripp, S. Wait for me rollerskate. In C. Mitchell–Kernan and S. Ervin–Tripp (Eds.), *Child discourse.* New York: Academic Press, 1977.

Frake, C. O. Plying frames can be dangerous: Some reflections on methodology in cognitive anthropology. *Quarterly Newsletter of the Institute of Comparative Human Development,* Rockefeller University, 1977 *1,* 1–7.

Frederiksen, C. H. Representing logical and semantic structure of knowledge acquired from discourse. *Cognitive Psychology,* 1975, *7,* 371–485.

Frederiksen, C. H. Semantic processing units in understanding text. In R. Freedle (Ed.), *Discourse comprehension and production.* Norwood, N.J.: Ablex Publishing Corp., 1977. (a)

Frederiksen, C. H. Inference and the structure of children's discourse. Paper presented at the Society for Research in Child Development, New Orleans, LA., 1977. (b)

Frederiksen, C. H. Structure and process in discourse production and comprehension. In M. A. Just and P. A. Carpenter (Eds.), *Cognitive processes in comprehension.* Hillsdale, N.J.: Lawrence Erlbaum Associates, 1977. (c)

Frederiksen, C. H. Discourse comprehension and early reading. In L. B. Resnick and P. A. Weaver (Eds.), *Theory and practice of early reading.* Hillsdale, N.J.: Lawrence Erlbaum Associates, 1979.

Frederiksen, C. H. Perspectives on inference in comprehension of texts. *Text,* 1980, (in press).

Frederiksen, C. H., Frederiksen, J. D., Humphreys, F., & Ottesen, J. Discourse inference: Adapting to the inferential demands of school texts. Paper presented at the American Educational Research Association meeting, Toronto, 1978.

Garrod, S. & Sanford, A. Interpreting anaphoric relations: The integration of semantic information while reading. *Journal of Verbal Learning and Verbal Behavior,* 1977, *16,* 69–75.

Garvey, C. Requests and responses in children's speech. *Journal of Child Language,* 1975, *2,* 41–64.

Green, J. & Wallat, C. What is an instructional context? An exploratory analysis of conversational shifts across time. In O. Garnica and M. King (Eds.), *Children, Language, and Society.* London: Pergammon Press, 1979.

Green, J. L. & Wallat, C. Mapping instructional contexts. In J. Green and C. Wallat (Eds.), *Ethnography and Language in Educational Settings.* Norwood, N.J.: Ablex Publishing Corp., 1980.

Grice, H. P. Logic and conversation. In P. Cole and J. L. Morgan (Eds.), *Syntax and semantics, Vol. 3: Speech acts.* New York: Academic Press, 1975.

Grimes, J. *The thread of discourse.* The Hague: Mouton, 1975.

Gumperz, J. J. Sociocultural knowledge in conversational inference. In *28th annual roundtable: Monographs series on language and linguistics.* Washington, D.C.: Georgetown University Press, 1977.

Gumperz, J. J. The conversational analysis of interethnic communication. In E. L. Ross (Ed.), *Interethnic communication.* Proceedings of the Southern Anthropological Association, Athens, GA, University of Georgia Press, 1977.

Hall, W. S. & Cole, M. On participants' shaping of discourse through their understanding of the task. In K. Nelson (Ed.), *Children's language, Vol. 1.* New York: Wiley (Halstead Press), 1980.

Hall, W. S. & Dore, J. Lexical sharing in mother–child interaction. (Technical Report No. 161, Center for the Study of Reading) Urbana, IL.: University of Illinois, 1980.

Hall, W. S. & Gutherie, L. F. Culture and situational variation in language function and use. Methods and procedures for research. In J. Green and C. Wallat (Eds.), *Ethnography and Language in Educational Settings.* Norwood, N.J.: Ablex Publishing Corp., 1980.

Halliday, M. A. K. & Hasan, R. *Cohesion in English.* London: Longman, 1976.

Keenan, E. O. Conversational competence in children. *Journal of Child Langauge,* 1974, *1,* 163–183.

Keller-Cohen, D. Context in child language. *Annual Review of Anthropology,*1978, *7,* 453–482.

Kintsch, W. *The representation of meaning in memory.* Hillsdale, N.J.: Lawrence Erlbaum Associates, 1974.

Kintsch, W. & Van Dijk, T. A. Comment on se rapelle et on resume des histoires. *Languages,* 1975, *40,* 98–116.

Mandler, J. M. & Johnson, N. S. Remembrance of things parsed: Story structure and recall. *Cognitive Psychology,* 1977, *9,* 111–151.

Nash-Webber, B. Anaphora: A cross-disciplinary survey. (Technical Report, Center for the Study of Reading), Urbana, IL.: University of Illinois, 1978.

Ortony, A. & Anderson, R. C. Definite descriptions and semantic memory. *Cognitive Science,* 1977, *1,* 74–83.

Paris, S. G. & Lindauer, B. K. The role of inference in children's comprehension and memory for sentences. *Cognitive Psychology,* 1976, *8,* 217–227.

Rumelhart, D. E. Notes on a schema for stories. In D. G. Bobrow and A. Collins (Eds.), *Representation and understanding: Studies in cognitive science.* New York: Academic Press, 1975.

Rumelhart, D. E. & Norman, D. A. The active structural network. In D. A. Norman and D. E. Rumelhart (Eds.), *Explorations in cognition.* San Francisco, CA.: W. H. Freeman, 1975.

Sacks, H. An initial investigation of the usability of conversational data for doing sociology. In D. Sudnow (Ed.), *Studies in social interaction.* New York: The Free Press, 1972.

Sacks, H. An analysis of the course of a joke's telling in conversation. In R. Bauman and J. Sherzer (Eds.), *Explorations in the ethnography of speaking.* Cambridge, Cambridge University Press, 1974.

Sacks, H., Schegloff, E., & Jefferson, G. A simplest systematics for the organization of turn-taking for conversation. *Language,* 1974, *50,* 696–735.

Schank, R. & Abelson, R. P. *Scripts, plans, goals and understanding: An inquiry into human knowledge structures.* Hillsdale, N.J.: Lawrence Erlbaum Associates, 1977.

Sinclair, J. McH., & Coultard, R. *Towards an analysis of discourse: The English used by teachers and pupils.* London: Oxford University Press, 1975.

Stein, N. L., & Glenn, C. G. An analysis of story comprehension in elementary school children. In R. Freedle (Ed.), *Advances in discourse processing. Vol. 2.* Norwood, N.J.: Ablex Publishing Corp., 1978.

Thorndyke, P. W. Cognitive structures in comprehension and memory of narrative discourse. *Cognitive Psychology,* 1977, *9,* 77–110.

Trabasso, T. & Nichols, D. W. Memory and inference in the comprehension of narratives. In J. Becker and F. Wilkining (Eds.), *Information integration by children.* Hillsdale, N.J.: Lawrence Erlbaum Associates, 1978.

Van Dijk, T. A. Macro-structures and cognition. In M. A. Just and P. A. Carpenter (Eds.), *Cognitive processes in comprehension.* Hillsdale, N.J.: Lawrence Erlbaum Associates, 1977.

Wilks, Y. Processing case. *American Journal of Computational Linguistics,* 1976.

Winston, P. H. *Artificial intelligence.* Reading, MA.: Addison–Wesley, 1977.

FIG. 1. Coded Transcript: BF-Directed Activity

Protocol: *BF-Directed Activity*
Segment of Conversation: *Spelling Last Name (8-35)*

Speaker	Turn Number	Utterance Transcript	Contingent Utterance	Content Operation(s)	C-Act Type Function
Tch	008	What comes after the L, Bill?			RQPR
TC	009	Another L	008	OBJ–ID	RSPR
Tch	010a	OK,	009		RSAG
	b	find the L	009	EVNT-OBJ	RQAC
(TC)	c	(tacit compliance)			NVRS
Tch	d	OK.	010c		RSAG
	e	OK, now			ODBM
	f	Last name,			ASID
	g	what's your last name?	010f	EVNT-OBJ, INT-OBJ	RQPR
TC	011	I don't know how to do that.			RSQL
Tch	012	I'll tell you the letter, OK?	011	COND-ANT	RQCH-TAG
TC	013	I don't want to.	011	EVNT-GOAL	RSCO
Tch	014	Bill Fenner!	010g	OBJ-ID	RSPR
	015a	Fenner,	014	repeat	RSAK-REP
	b	do you want to try Fenner?	011	EVNT-GOAL, -ACT	RQCH
			014	EVNT-THM	
TC	016	No.	015b	NEG	RSCH
TC	017	OK?	015b	repeat	RQCH-TAG
TC	018	Too hard.	015b	ACT-ATT	RSQL, ASEX
			016	COND-ANT	
Tch	019a	Oh,			RSAK
	b	I could help you.	015b	COND-ANT	ASRU
	c	It starts with an F.	019b	COND-ANT, OBJ-PRT	ASRU
			015b	COND-ANT	

(continued)

FIG. 1. (continued)

| Speaker | Utterance | | Content | | Function |
	Turn Number	Transcript	Contingent Utterance	Operation(s)	C-Act Type
Tch	d	I'll hand you the letters	019b	ACT-PRT	ASRU
		and you do them, OK?	015b, 019d	COND-ANT, COND-CONSQ	RQCH-TAG
Tch	019e	How's that?	015b	CASE-OBJ	ODRQ
	f	I'll hand you all the letters.	019d	ACT-ATT	ASRU
	g	First comes an F.	019d, 019c	OBJ-NUM, repeat	ASRU
TC	020	It's hard to press.	019f, 019d	SUB-OBJ, ACT-PRT	RSQL, ASEV
Tch	021a	Just use your (false start)			
	b	That's it,	020	SUB-ACT	ASEV
	c	use your finger and push down	021c	COND-ANT, NEG, SUP—ACT, MOD, ACT-ATT	RQAC
	d	you don't have to push a lot,	021d	repeat	ASRU
	e	really, you don't have to push a lot.	021d	CASE-RSLT, ITER	ASRU
	f	Just, just one gentle push will do it		ACT-ATT	ASRU, RQAC?
	g	F (5″).	019g	OBJ-ID	ASID, RQAC?
	h	E.	015a	OBJ-PRT	ASID, RQAC?
	i	Here, I'll stamp it for you.	021c	LEX—ACT	ASRU
	j	(14″) F,	019g	repeat	ASID
	k	E (6″)	019h	repeat	ASID, RQAC?
	l	OK, good.			ASEV
TC	022	I, did it upside down.	021i	ACT-ATT	ASDC
Tch	023a	That's all right.	022	ACT-ATT	RSAG
	b	Here's an N.			ASID

336

Speaker	No.	Utterance	Ref	Category	Code
TC	024	What E?	021h	OBJ-IDENT, INT-CON	RQPR
Tch	025	Right there	024	LOC-OBJ	RSPR
TC	026	Oh	025		RSAK
Tch	027a	There's an N.	023b	repeat	ASID
	b	No, No,			PFPR
O	c	This hand, this hand.			ASID
	028	I'm a clown!			
Tch	029a	N	027a	OBJ-ID	ASID
	b	Now there are two N's in your last name	029a	OBJ-ID	ASRU
	c	so you have to do the N again.	010f	OBJ-PRT	ASRU
	d	And then comes another E.	029b	COND-CONSQ	ASRU
	e	Ah! Excuse me please,	029b	REL-OBJ	
	f	could you stop the running!			
		(side sequence)			
	g	Gotta do the E again.	029d	EVNT-OBJ	RQSU
	h	This one.	029g	OBJ-IDENT	ASID
TC	030	It's lost.	029h	OBJ-ATT	RSQL, RQPR?
Tch	031	Here it is.	030	LOC-OBJ	ASDC, RSPR?
TC	031a	And the last letter is, the last letter is the letter what?	029b	OBJ-PRT	RQPR
	b	Do you know what your last letter is?	031a	EVNT-THM	RQCH, RQPR
	032	N	031a	OBJ-IDENT	RSPR
Tch	033	What?	029a	repeat	ODCQ
TC	034	N, N.	032	INT-CON, repeat	RSCL

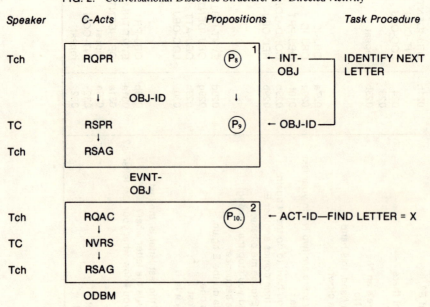

FIG. 2. Conversational Discourse Structure: BF-Directed Activity

Speaker	C-Acts	Propositions	Task Procedure
Tch	RQPR	P_8 ¹ ← INT-OBJ	IDENTIFY NEXT LETTER
	↓ OBJ-ID ↓		
TC	RSPR	P_9 ← OBJ-ID	
Tch	RSAG		
	EVNT-OBJ		
Tch	RQAC	$P_{10.}$ ² ← ACT-ID—FIND LETTER = X	
TC	NVRS		
Tch	RSAG		
	ODBM		

Speaker	C-Acts		Propositions		Task Procedure

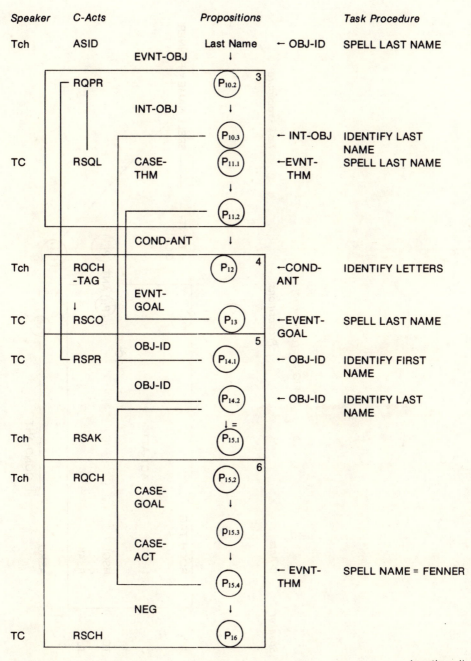

Speaker	C-Acts	Propositions	Task Procedure
Tch	ASID	Last Name ← OBJ-ID	SPELL LAST NAME
		EVNT-OBJ ↓	
	RQPR	$P_{10.2}$ 3	
		INT-OBJ ↓	
		$P_{10.3}$ ← INT-OBJ	IDENTIFY LAST NAME
TC	RSQL	CASE-THM $P_{11.1}$ ←EVNT-THM	SPELL LAST NAME
		↓	
		$P_{11.2}$	
		COND-ANT ↓	
Tch	RQCH-TAG	P_{12} 4 ←COND-ANT	IDENTIFY LETTERS
		EVNT-GOAL	
TC	RSCO	P_{13} ←EVENT-GOAL	SPELL LAST NAME
TC	RSPR	OBJ-ID $P_{14.1}$ 5 ← OBJ-ID	IDENTIFY FIRST NAME
		OBJ-ID $P_{14.2}$ ← OBJ-ID	IDENTIFY LAST NAME
Tch	RSAK	↓ = $P_{15.1}$	
Tch	RQCH	$P_{15.2}$ 6	
		CASE-GOAL ↓	
		$p_{15.3}$	
		CASE-ACT ↓	
		$P_{15.4}$ ← EVNT-THM	SPELL NAME = FENNER
		NEG ↓	
TC	RSCH	P_{16}	

(continued)

339

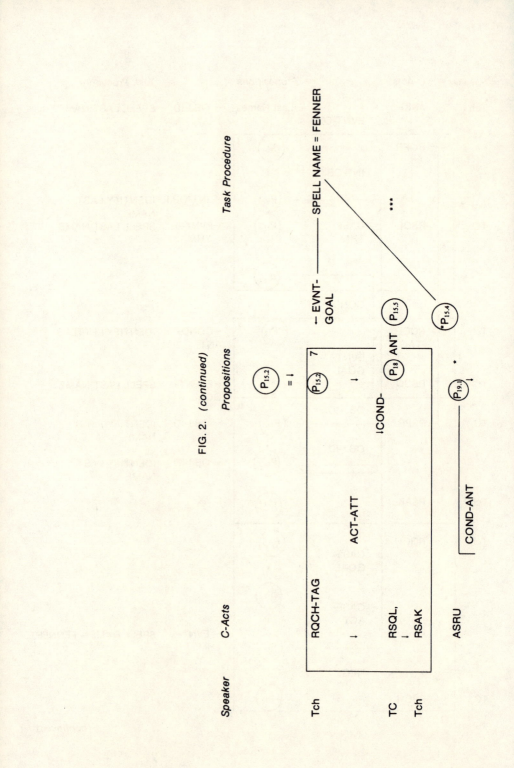

FIG. 2. (continued)

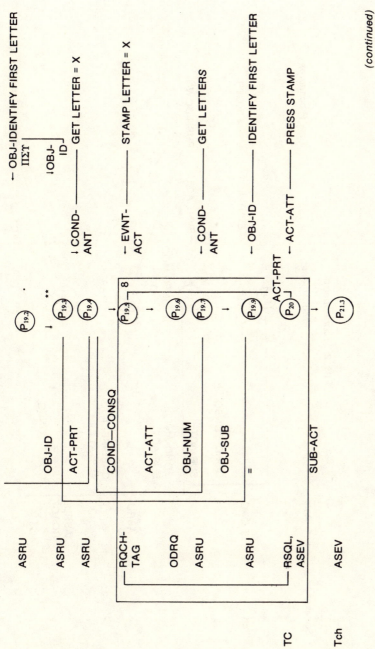

(continued)

341

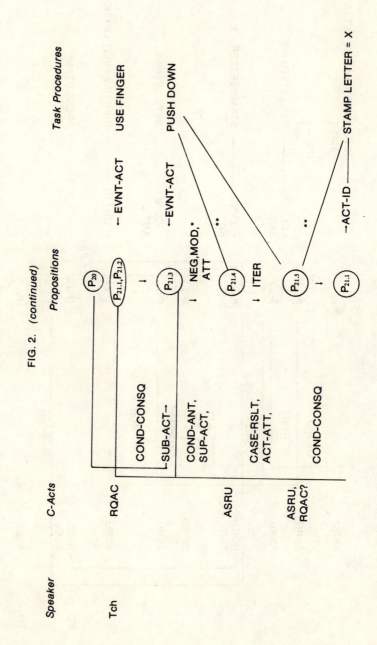

FIG. 2. (continued)

342

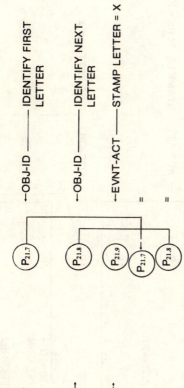
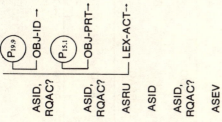

(continued)

* - COND-ANT
** - CASE-RSLT

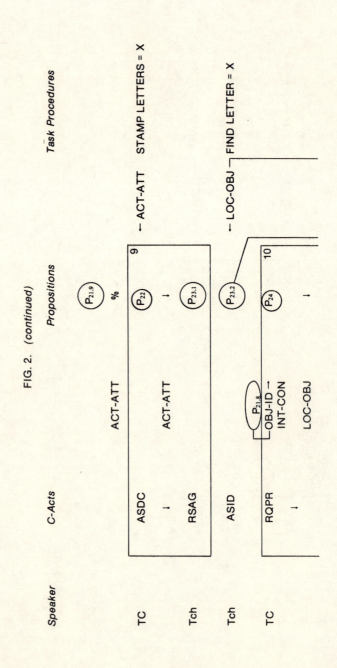

FIG. 2. (continued)

344

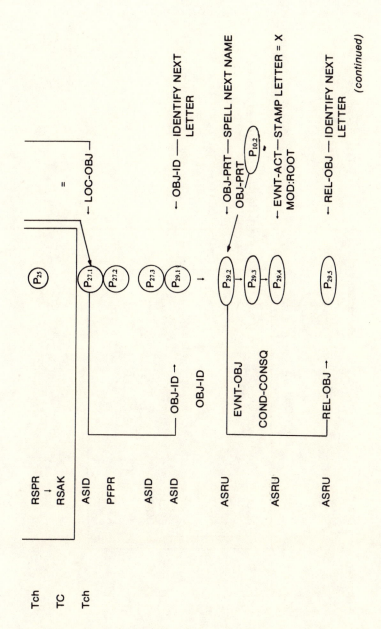

(continued)

FIG. 2. *(continued)*

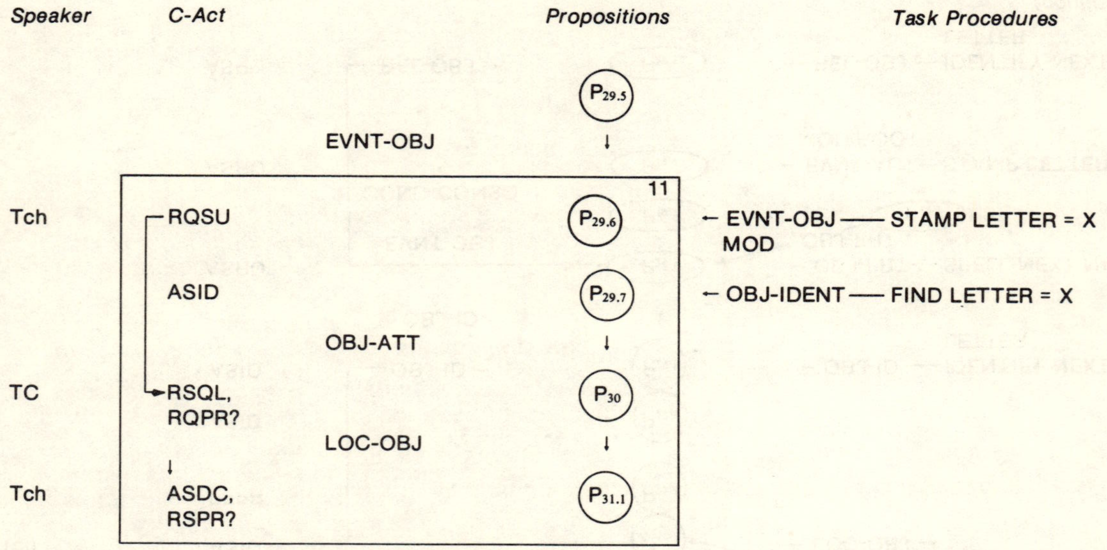

Speaker	C-Act		Propositions	Task Procedures

Task Procedures

← EVNT-OBJ —— STAMP LETTER = X
MOD

← OBJ-IDENT —— FIND LETTER = X

Propositions

$P_{29.5}$ →

11

$P_{29.6}$ $P_{29.7}$ → P_{30} → $P_{31.1}$

C-Act

EVNT-OBJ

OBJ-ATT

LOC-OBJ

RQSU

ASID

RSQL, RQPR?

ASDC, RSPR?

Speaker

Tch

TC

Tch

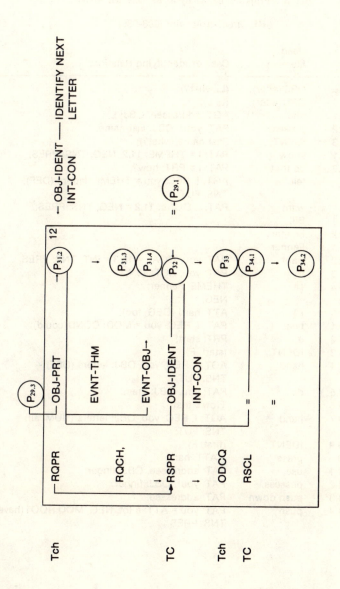

FIG. 3. Propositional Analysis: BF-Directed Activity

BF-Directed Activity (008–035)

Proposition Number		Head Element	Case or Identifying Relations
Tch	8	ORD(after):	(L, what?);
TC	9	ORD(after):	(L, L);
Tch	10.1	find	AGT: addressee, OBJ; L;
	10.2	possess	PAT: your, OBJ: last name;
	10.3	IDENT:	(last name, what?);
TC	11.1	know	PAT: I = THEME: 11.2, NEG, TNS: PRES;
	11.2	do that	PAT: I = PRT: how?;
Tch	12	tell	AGT: I, REC: you = THEME: letters (DEF), TNS: FUT;
TC	13	want	PAT: I, GOAL: 11.2 = NEG, TNS: PRES;
	14.1	Bill	
	14.2	Fenner	
Tch	15.1	Fenner	
	15.2	want	PAT: you, GOAL = 15.3 = INT, TNS: PRES;
	15.3	try	PAT: you, ACT: 15.4;
	15.4	( )	THEME: Fenner;
TC	16		NEG;
Tch	18	( )	ATT: hard (DEG: too);
Tch	19.1	help	PAT: I, REC: you = MOD: COND(could);
	19.2	it	PRT: start;
	19.3	IDENT:	(start, F);
	19.4	hand	AGT: I, REC, you, OBJ: letters (DEF) = TNS: FUT;
	19.5	do	PAT: you, OBJ: them;
	19.6		'How's that'
	19.7	hand	AGT: I, REC: you, OBJ: letters (NUM: all) = TNS: FUT;
	19.9	IDENT	(first, F);
TC	20	press	= ATT: hard;
Tch	21.1	use	PAT: addressee, OBJ: finger;
	21.2	possess	PAT: your, OBJ: finger;
	21.3	push down	PAT: addressee;
	21.4	push	PAT: you = ATT: a lot, NEG, MOD:ROOT(have to), TNS; PRES;

348

Proposition Number		Head Element	Case or Identifying Relations
	21.5	push	RESULT: 21.6 = ATT: gentle, ASPCT:ITER(just one);
	21.6	do it	
	21.7	F	
	21.8	E	
	21.9	stamp	PAT; I, OBJ: it, GOAL: (for) you = TNS:FUT;
	21.10	F	
	21.11	E	
TC	22	do it	AGT: I = ATT: upside down, TNS: PAST;
Tch	23.1	that	= ATT: all right;
Tch	23.3	N	LOC: here;
TC	24	IDENT:	(E, what?);
Tch	25	( )	LOC: there;
TC	26		'Oh'
Tch	27.1	N	LOC: there;
	27.2		'No, No'
	27.3	IDENT:	(hand, this);
O	28	clown	CAT: I, TNS: PRES;
Tch	29.1	N	
	29.2	last name	PRT: (N, N);
	29.3	possess	PAT: your, OBJ: last name;
	29.4	do	PAT: you, OBJ: N = ASPCT:ITER(again), MOD: ROOT(have to);
	29.5	run	PAT: you = ASPCT:CESS(stop), TNS:PRES, ASPCT:CONT;
	29.6	do	OBJ: E = ASPCT:ITER(again, MOD:ROOT(gotta);
	29.7	IDENT:	(, this one);
TC	30	it	ATT: lost, TNS:PRES;
Tch	31.1	it	LOC: here;
	31.2	IDENT:	(last letter, what?);
	31.3	know	PAT: you, THEME: 31.2 = INT, TNS:PRES;
	31.4	possess	PAT: your, OBJ: last letter;
TC	32	N	
Tch	33		what?
TC	34.1	N	
	34.2	N	

349

FIG. 4. Task Frame: Spelling Name Task

Task Frame: Spelling Name

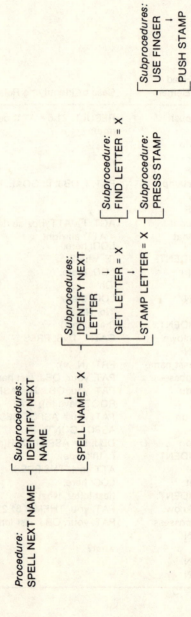

Procedure:
SPELL NEXT NAME
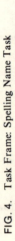

350

SUBJECT INDEX